LOVE

LIFE

WALK

Daily Stories & Thoughts From 43,000 Miles Walking Across America Eight Times with Steve Fugate, the Love Life Guy.

Printed in the United States of America

First Printing 2016

ISBN-13: 978-1537527796
ISBN-10: 1537527797

SPECIAL THANKS

Thanks for the gift of Life. Thanks to both my precious children, Michele (Shelly) Lynn Fugate Morgan, and Stephen (Stevie) Lee Fugate, for your support and for being with me every step of the way in my heart, I love you both so very much. Thank you Cora Lee Robertson for giving me two of the world's most wonderful and beautiful children. Thanks for the love from my sister Jeanne Boger. Thanks to Jeanne Brockway for helping me get through the loss of my son. Thanks to Larry Pesin for always being my friend and never failing to be there. Thanks to friends Carol and Jim Tabbert for all your help and support. Thanks to Coffee Regional Medical Center in Douglas, Georgia for being the finest hospital I've ever seen. Thanks to the wonderful talents and devoted friendship of Ray Karno. Thanks to Larry Massett of NPR's Hearing Voices, friend and critic. Thanks to Mark Baldwin, Borealis Press, friend and critic. Thanks to Sonya Fenney for giving me my van/house. Thanks to Thai & Diamond Dang for giving me my travel trailer/house. Thanks to friends Rocky and Barbara Ballas. Thanks to Jim and Patsy Cadenhead. Thanks to my wonderful late friend, Dave "Doc" Loomis, author of *Happiness-Use It Or Lose It.* Thanks to my friend, cowboy poet, David, "Buffalo Bill" Nelson, and his wife, Jean. Thanks to Eudora Struble for all your help. Thank you Carl Short for your time and generosity. Thanks to all my Facebook friends. Thanks to Ola Faye Johnson for being the prettiest girl in my third grade class in South Lebanon, Ohio.

Due to the personal intimacy shared with me in many of my stories and because of just being nigh impossible to contact such a high number of individuals for permission in so many different places, I have changed most names. Also, because of some locations of my encounters being of such low population, just the story alone could identify the individual, so I've changed some location names as well, or, not revealed the location. I have though, been to every location mentioned and every encounter is real. Be warned also, that in trying to be as accurate as possible in the retelling of my encounters, I have kept the language others used in relating their story to me and sometimes, to express my own personal emotions

April 2001 I went to California for the very first time in my life and started my walk from Point Reyes National Seashore at the Pacific Ocean. My daughter would orchestrate my trip and keep tabs on my whereabouts. On a Sunday in Sausalito, California with a "LOVE LIFE" sign over my head and getting ready to cross the Golden Gate Bridge, thinking I was ready to share love of life with the world and walk across America. Very first car, driver yells, "You fuckin' idiot!" while flipping me off. Without hesitation, I responded, "Up yours!" There I stood, "LOVE LIFE" over my head and my middle finger held high. I had a long way to go…

Table of Contents

The Appalachian Trail Part 1

About two years after the failure of my 28-year marriage, my 26-year-old son, Stevie, came back to Vero Beach, Florida, to live with me and help in my business until he found employment in his chosen field. I started realizing my son had a problem with alcohol. (I didn't realize how serious his drinking problem was because I drank so much myself.) In fact, he had an auto accident while under the influence of alcohol and was charged with DUI. And to add to the problems for this young man that had never been in trouble in his entire life, his car was totaled and he had a huge court ordered restitution to cover for damage to the other vehicle. At the same time, the company that had just agreed to hire him to work in his chosen field for the first time, cancelled all their newly recruited employees due to the loss of a large contract.

I told him the situation wasn't that bad and we could work through the problem. I had no idea how this was going to come about, but I had to put his mind at ease some way. Just a few weeks later, I saw a magazine article about the Appalachian Trail. I had no idea what the Appalachian Trail really was. I thought it to be some old trail that my ancestors in southeastern Kentucky used to reach their area of the Appalachians. Reading about the wilderness trail stirred an adventuresome spirit I had not felt since my youth. And then I had a brainstorm, why not leave my business in the capable hands of my son and embark upon this adventure of a lifetime?

My son had grown up in the business and was comfortable with every facet of it. My thought was that several birds could be brought down with one stone. The responsibility would be great for my son. I knew he always put his best foot forward when given a challenge. My plan was that he would be concentrating so much on his new responsibility that he would have to limit his drinking and meet the new challenge. As part of the plan, he would keep all profits from the business to help him speedily pay off the restitution payments. My son seemed excited about the plan and eagerly volunteered to help orchestrate my 2,175 mile thru-hike of the Appalachian Trail form Springer Mountain in Georgia to Mt. Katahdin in Maine.

March 28, 1999, my son and then girlfriend drove me to the southern terminus of the Appalachian Trail at Amicalola Falls State Park in Georgia. Stevie and I walked around the park and hiked a small section of the trail together. My son became very excited and stated that he would like to thru-hike the "AT" the following year. My original idea kept getting better, father would take out the old century with a thru-hike and son would bring in the new century with his thru-hike. I was delighted!

Figure 1. My son Stevie, and I, at Amicalola Falls, Georgia the day before I started my thru-hike of the Appalachian Trail on March 28, 1999.

My First Hike Ever!

Amicalola Falls Welcome Center is the official registration station for Appalachian Trail thru-hikers. While signing in, the lady, who brought out the official registration book told us of a lady who had registered the day before us. She started off with, "You just ain't gonna' believe the lady we had in here yesterday mornin'... I swear! She comes in to register for her thru-hike and asked which one of those roads out there is the Appalachian Trail," she laughingly related. "I told her, ma'am, the trail is not a road, the trail is a, well... it's a trail," shaking her head and rolling her eyes she continued, "And then she looks at me in total amazement and said, "you mean it is not paved?" And, she is looking at me as if I'm the one out in left field! I really thought at first she was surely just a kiddin'! And then after I explained the terrain of the trail and that it is an extremely narrow and rugged footpath she looked totally surprised and asked, how am I supposed to carry all my stuff?" She was shaking her head even more now and says, "I told her, you have to carry it on your back in a backpack like everyone else does. She just said, Oh and went out the door, she seemed pretty upset." She goes on with the story, "A ranger came in and said, whose grocery cart is that outside with all that stuff in it? I walked over, looked out the door, sure enough, there she was standing next to a grocery cart filled with all kinds of camping stuff!"

There's the story of a thru-hiker who emerged from the "AT" parking lot at Newfound Gap in the Tennessee - North Carolina Smokies. A pudgy sandaled tourist hailed him: "Hey buddy, where's that path lead to?" The hiker silenced him with one word: "Maine."

I started out the next day at 6:00 am, and by the way I had never hiked a day in my life. I started up the incline, which my son, the day before, had to convince me was not simply a dried up creek bed. It was cold, about 28 degrees. Much in contrast to the low 80's I had left behind in beautiful Vero Beach, Florida. I think I started to hyperventilate, probably from a combination of the cold weather and anxiety brought on by my new endeavor. Just a few steps into the steep climb and I was unable to get my breath. Being forty pounds overweight and carrying a backpack well over fifty pounds was also a factor I'm sure. I knew then this was a stupid idea, I needed to be back in sunny Florida. I turned to yell for my son and girlfriend to wait up and carry my fat ass back to Florida, but they were gone! My heart was pounding, my head spinning and I was having a real hard time getting my breath. I had been deceived into thinking this was going to be a breeze! I had watched several times a video of "Thru-Hikers" at various stages of their hikes and I never saw one thru-hiker hyperventilate. And not one of them bastards warned me against taking on such an insane quest. One young man did give warning to learn all the words to at least three songs, though. This obviously was not going to be a breeze and, I would come to regret not learning all the words to at least three songs. And then, pride and stubbornness took over and I began rationalizing that I would look like a complete ass for bragging to all I would hike the entire Appalachian Trail. One might quit with some dignity after a few hundred miles, but not five feet! I stood there a few moments allowing my breathing to become somewhat normal and my ego to kick in, and then continued in the direction of Maine. "Wow, this hiking stuff is hard!" I had to admit. And that damned backpack felt like a hundred pounds instead of fifty. "Wonder where that lady put that grocery cart?"

It was still early morning and, just sauntering along that first day of hiking, I looked up in front of me and to my utter astonishment and pleasure, walking toward me was one of the most beautiful young women I ever laid eyes on. She had long flowing dark brown hair, a face seen only in movies and magazines, and every other attribute you can think of to conjure up the image of a truly magnificent-looking woman! I really did momentarily think, "I must be dreaming." And before I could think, "What is a woman this beautiful doing out here by herself?" I saw at her side, the largest wolf-dog I'd ever seen. I think she sensed my shock and to let me know I was not sleepwalking, she filled her face with a most beautiful smile and said, "Hi, are you doing the whole trail?" I stuttered out, "Uh... yeah, I'm going all the way." The beautiful and intimidating wolf-dog surprised me by putting his monstrous head against my hand. "He likes you," spoke the dream. You can only imagine how relieved I was. Even so, I was still very careful of my movements in his presence. It was quite evident in that magnificent animal's eyes and the manner in which he postured at her side, this was not only her best friend; this was her body guard as well. Lord, have mercy on the person who ever makes him prove it. "He didn't like the guy who was just in front of you," she said. "He growled at him and watched him until he moved past me." I told her I hadn't cared for him either and told of some improper questions he had asked that made me uncomfortable to the point I made an excuse to stop and let him go on past me. He had actually asked how much money I carried on me at a time. (Nothing like that ever happened to me again during my entire hike of the Appalachian Trail.) She told me there had been many times her wolf-dog had shown a distinct discernment for not-so-nice people. She told me she and her wolf-dog had thru-hiked the whole trail the previous year. I was totally impressed, my first encounter with a real thru-hiker! I met many more after that, of course, but none any more beautiful and certainly none that well-protected.

Before I decided to do the Appalachian Trail, I had never hiked a day in my life. There is an eight-mile trail called the Approach Trail that takes you from Amicalola Falls State Park in Georgia to the southern terminus of the Appalachian Trail atop Springer Mountain. My son and I had agreed that, if I did the extra eight miles which really did not count at all in an official thru-hike of the AT, he would then do it as well when he hiked it the next year. After I reached Springer Mountain I had hiked a little over eight miles, the recommended distance for a beginner on their first day I had read. So, I was looking for a site to pitch my tent even though there was plenty of daylight left because I had started very early. Well, along comes a 19-year-old from Maine who had been hiking since he could walk, and he decides he would like to hike with me. Okay, I'll hike a little longer. I never thought to ask if he had done the Approach Trail, I just assumed he had. Well, he hadn't, he had only just started right there at Springer Mountain where all the other sane people start. He obviously made the mistake of assuming I too was sane and had just started. I was struggling to keep up with this muscular and well experienced 19-year-old; remember, I was 53 and at least thirty pounds overweight. I was too proud to be smart and simply tell him I was spent and was stopping for the night. So after a while I started saying things like, "I'm way too slow for you, why don't you just go on ahead of me." And being a fine young gentleman, he kept answering that it was okay he would just hike slower so that I might keep up with him. Thanks a lot! Finally, after it was nearly dark and my feet were ready to explode out of my boots, he decided to stop. I can still remember his exact words, "Well, I think we should stop now because it is recommended that you only do about eight miles on your first day." Thus, I did 16 miles on my first day.

My 19-year-old companion's trail name was "Red." Trail names are nicknames given to you by yourself or by other hikers for various reasons. I have no idea why they called him "Red" for he was not red headed. Now the trail name later attached to me was much more obvious: "No Clue." "Red" and I fell into a wonderful situation that first night of our thru-hike. We camped with a group of hikers who had hired a man with the trail name, "Pittsburgh" to lead them on a fully supported thru-hike of the AT. In other words, "Pittsburgh" and his van would carry all their gear and supply meals whenever possible. To the delight of "Red" and me, "Pittsburgh" invited us to share a meal of beef stew with them. As "Red" and I gorged ourselves, "Pittsburgh" explained to his clients why they should share food they had paid for and why they should always extend a helping hand to other hikers whenever possible. He further explained that they never knew when they too might need some kindness when out on the trail. He called this kindness "trail magic" and said this is the true spirit of the trail. "Red" and I both started eating faster just in case they didn't agree with "Pittsburgh's" trail philosophy.

One member of "Pittsburgh's" group was known as "Chance." "Chance" was maybe forty, and had once been pretty high up the corporate ladder. He told me he found he had a knack for gambling and, unlike so many others; he actually made money at it. And like actors move to Hollywood to pursue their careers, "Chance" moved to Las Vegas, and was not there long before he was given the name, "Chance." He only did sports betting, he told me. He said he decided he needed an extended break from the hustle of Vegas and felt it was the right time to pursue his dream of hiking the Appalachian Trail. He had a serious back problem though and knew he couldn't carry a heavy backpack for long periods of time. But he knew that where there was a will there was a way and he eventually found out about "Pittsburgh" and his service. While I'm listening, I'm questioning in my mind, "Wow is it really possible to possess a talent for gambling? Can one really be exceptional at luck?" I was admiring the state-of-the-art expensive hiking gear he had and mentioned how blessed he was to be able to buy the best of whatever he needed. He then explained that after he had decided to hike the Appalachian Trail, he walked into an outdoor outfitter store in Vegas to look around and make some decisions on what exactly he needed for his thru-hike. Upon entering the store there was notification of a contest that awarded the winner several hundred dollars in their choice of equipment from the store. He filled out the entry form, dropped it in the box, looked around the store taking note of available gear and prices and then went home. "Chance" took a chance and a week or so later he was notified that he had won the contest. He told me this very nonchalantly; I don't believe he was at all surprised.

I arose early the next morning with every muscle in my body aching. My feet were throbbing with pain. According to the books I had read in preparation for my quest, I was still six to eight weeks from getting my "trail legs." "Trail legs" mean your body has adjusted to the rigorous extremes you are subjecting it to. At this point the only thing keeping me from quitting was that I did not want to look bad.

Blood Mountain, Scary Name

A few days and blisters later I was getting better at pitching my tent and preparing meals on my little wood-burning camp stove, but I still wasn't worth a damn at hanging my food in a tree away from bears, so I just quit doing it. I nearly always had a bottle of bourbon with me and had I thought bears would get that I would have become expert at hanging it. Nearly every night I was horribly awakened by what sounded like at least two women being slowly murdered at the same time. Some more experienced hikers tried to convince me that the sound comes from a source only eight inches tall and has feathers. They said it was an owl, a barred owl, I think they said. I was not convinced. The bodies are still out there somewhere.

I had to climb Blood Mountain, Georgia's highest point on the AT, in a cold, miserable rain and dense fog. Again I am thinking, "What the hell have I gotten myself into?" But it did help to find out the name Blood Mountain, came from a fierce battle fought there between the Cherokee and the Creek and not the horrible deaths of past thru-hikers.

These words of advice from journalist and author John Kieran, who wrote on hiking in 1953: *"Take to the woods on windy days. It's quieter there. Keep your ears open. You can always hear more birds than you can see. Keep your eyes open. There are flowers in bloom through most months of summer. Take the sun over your shoulder for the best views. Avoid slippery footing as you would the plague, and don't sit on wet ground. Keep walking."*

That Damn Trail!

At Neel's Gap, Georgia, I visited the Walasi-Yi Center, a building made of stone and American chestnut by Roosevelt's Civilian Conservation Corps in the 1930's and is the only time in its entire length the Appalachian Trail passes through a building. It now operates as an "outfitter" store catering to hikers. I took advantage of their services, they helped me adjust my backpack and pointed out a few things I really didn't need and hence lightened up my load. They explained to me the advantage of 'trekking poles', two very light walking sticks. And they called a nice gentleman, Keith, who picked me up and took me to his place, Goose Creek Cabins, near Blairsville, Georgia, and I spent the night in a real bed. Ok! Next morning I'm good to go. Lighter pack, new trekking poles, and great night's sleep in a real bed. Nothing can stop me now. Wrong! By 5:00 pm I was back at Goose Creek cabins with a severely sprained ankle. I still don't know how I fell. Keith loaned me a pair of crutches to get around on. A physical therapist staying at the cabins looked at it and said it was a really serious sprain and I should stay off of it for at least fifteen days. Four days later I limped my butt back out on that damn trail. Once you start a thru-hike something takes over in you. You just have to make it to Maine. No matter how miserable you become out there and no matter how much you start missing the creature comforts at your feet, the trail calls to you after you leave it. Many were the times I would rush down a mountain, get off the trail, enter a restaurant for a highly anticipated hot meal and catch myself staring out the window at the mountains, longing to be back up there. That damn trail! I was on my way to loving it.

Trail Names

As I got miles and weeks further down the Appalachian Trail, I found that there was an endless chain of fascinating people on the trail if you took the time to stop and talk to them, which I almost always did. After the initial greeting, I would ask their trail name. Many were given by their fellow hikers but most seemed to have named themselves. One could write a book just on the "trail names" and how they were arrived at. There were names like "Rerun" who was 80 years old and on his third thru-hike of the "AT." He did his first when he was 60. I contributed a "trail name" myself to a gentleman in his early 70's who, instead of stopping his hike or even complaining each time he had a new pain in one of his joints, simply wrapped the sore area with Ace bandage and continued walking. At one point he had so much bandage wrapped around his body he looked like a mummy. So I thought it quite befitting to dub him, "King Tut." I don't know if "King Tut" finished his thru-hike. If he didn't, it damn sure wasn't from a lack of tenacity. There were many other interesting trail names like, "Ermo," "Little Dipper," "Downhill Hopeful," "B Plus," "Stone Monkey," "Sky," "Leaf Peeper," "Redneck Rye," and "Never Alone." And an older couple who took their name from the most popular staple eaten on the trail, "Mac & Cheese."

Then there was the young lady I encountered one morning literally beating the hell out of her backpack with her hands and then shaking it profusely. A young man whom I had met earlier, "Giggles," saw the bewildered look on my face. "That's "Whack-A-Pack," he explained, "Her first night on the trail she stayed in a shelter, [three sided structures along the "AT"] when she woke the next morning and was loading up her pack, she thought she felt something moving in her pack. She did in fact!" He continued, "A mouse from the shelter had made a nest in her backpack during the night and had given birth, she screamed for a real long time." he pointed out. Well, from what I saw, it damn sure wasn't going to happen to her again.

I started running into "Giggles" and "Whack-A-Pack" quite often on down the trail. "Giggles" was so infatuated with "Whack-A-Pack" he followed her everywhere and actually made quite a nuisance of himself. He was shamelessly in love with her. She acted as though he was the biggest pain-in-the-ass on the trail. It was totally obvious she did not feel the same way he did. He was always asking the other hikers if we had seen "Whack-A-Pack." If they knew where she was camping, had she gone into town, and so on? "Whack-A-Pack," on the other hand, was saying things like, "Don't tell Giggles you saw me" and "That guy is driving me nuts!"

"Giggles" made the mistake of thinking an older man might know more about what would turn a woman's heart, so he mistakenly confided in me. "No Clue," he says, "do you think 'Whack-A-Pack' is at all interested in me?" Hoping to put the young man out of his misery and back on track, I said, "No." I could not believe his answer, "Thanks No Clue, but I think you're wrong." And he kept right on chasing after her and she kept right on ignoring him. I was really feeling sorry for him watching him make an ass of himself. So I took him aside one day and shared what I felt might help him, "Look Giggles, I don't know if this will help you or not, but I read something once, I think it went like this: "If you want a woman to love you, fill her to the brim with love for herself, all that flows over will be yours." You would have thought I had wrapped her in a package and handed her to him! He just kept shaking my hand and saying, "Thank you No Clue, thank you, thank you!" over and over. He said he was going to find "Whack-A-Pack" and took off up the trail. I never saw "Giggles" or "Whack-A-Pack" again. But, a few years later, doing a section of the trail, I was told they both finished their thru-hikes and "Giggles" had pursued "Whack-A-Pack" all the way to her hometown. And evidently she had a change of heart; they had been happily married for a few years. What in the hell changed her mind? See, us older guys haven't a clue about them either??

I would soon discover I had found not only a new geographical region of the U.S. and a unique manner in which to see it, but a whole new subculture. For 28 years I had been consumed with running a business and helping my wife, Cora, raise a son and daughter, Stevie and Shelly. I had no idea that out there on that beckoning footpath was a whole different world. One made up of fascinating individuals who answer the trails soul finding call, individuals such as "So What".

"So What"

I was just a few days out of Goose Creek Cabins, still limping my way down the trail when I met a unique southern gentleman who looked a lot like Gene Hackman. He had a wonderful Mississippi drawl and a smile that put one at ease immediately. He started the conversation with, "How y'all doin? Y'all goin' all the way?" I told him yes and then sat down at his fire with him. After telling me his trail name was "So what," I of course had to find out how that came to be. He was an executive with a large grocery chain in Mississippi until he had a heart attack and had to have a triple by-pass. With the heart problems came early retirement, which he did not want, he was only 52. And the bad side of life wasn't done with him yet. Only a few months after the by-pass he was in a severe car wreck and had to have very serious back surgery. He told me that some months later he was reading an article about the Appalachian Trail and he got excited. He said he yelled for his wife to come out of the kitchen and said to her, "By God I'm gonna' do this damn trail!" as he was pointing excitingly to the article. His wife, naturally concerned for his health, started arguing with him. She began pointing out his physical handicaps that made it impossible for him to hike the Appalachian Trail. To which he answered, "So what!" Within months he was out on the trail. He visited his doctor after a few months of hiking and the doctor asked him what he had been doing differently because he looked wonderful and his heart was strong. I had made yet another new friend. With every new acquaintance, I became more excited about the prospect of my son Stevie hiking the trail and having those same wonderful experiences.

"The ultimate purpose of the Appalachian Trail... to walk to see. And to see what you see." Said Benton MacKaye, founder of the 2,174 mile trail from Maine to Georgia.

A Tent Leveler

Not only were the trail names clever and often humorous out on the trail, likewise were the names given to foods, procedures and places. People who give voluntary aid and food to thru-hikers are called "trail angels." That kind and generous act is called "trail magic." Trail mix is called "GORP," an acronym for "Good Old Raisins and Peanuts." And an "All You Can Eat Restaurant" is called an "AYCE." The act of getting food from hiking groups, Boy Scout troops, and tourist, is called "Yogi-ing" from the old Yogi Bear cartoon. One morning at a shelter, a thru-hiker, "Rockfish," asked if I would like to have a cup of coffee with him. It was a real cool morning and that sounded really good; I could certainly use a good hot cup of coffee. He then says to me, "All I have is 'tampon coffee,' I hope you don't mind?" And just as I started to tell him I just remembered the doctor telling me I would drop dead instantly if I ever drank coffee again, he proceeded to drop into two cups of hot water, little packets with strings on them, just like the little strings on uh, teabags, only they contained coffee. I had never seen them before. It wasn't as good as fresh brewed, but hey, it damn sure tasted better than it sounded.

I must take credit for the naming of a substance occasionally carried by some thru-hikers on the trail. It came about one evening at a shelter somewhere in North Carolina. I was sitting in the shelter eating my freshly prepared Ramen noodles with pieces of beef jerky added. In front of me was my tent pitched at quite an angle, but it was the most level spot available. I prefer the privacy of a tent over the restricting and often over-crowded shelters. And I can belch, fart, and scratch my ass without offending or bothering anyone else. Also at the shelter were three young ladies I had met earlier, from up north somewhere, New England area I believe. One of the young ladies, looking out at my tent said, "'No Clue,' it looks as you are going to be quite uncomfortable tonight with your tent being so unleveled." "Oh, that," I said. "That's not a problem; I have a 'tent leveler.' To which she responded, "Yeah right, there is no such thing as a 'tent leveler.' "Sure there is," I said. "Yeah, that's right, they're just three dumb broads and they will be gullible enough to believe there is actually such a thing as a 'tent leveler!'" Another part of the trio chimed in. "Yeah, let's joke around with the girls!" And, "Yeah, they'll never know the difference!" said the third one. "No, I'm really serious!" I assured them. And the first non-believer, who was now sitting next to me, said, "Well, let's see it work then. "Hey, just hold on, let me finish eating and I'll gladly demonstrate it for you."

I told them. "Yeah right!" the three of them answered nearly in unison and equally sarcastically.

A few minutes later I finished eating and retrieved from my backpack my bottle of Kentucky Bourbon, Wild Turkey 101, affectionately referred to as "the dirty bird," tilted up the bottle and took a healthy swig. The young lady next to me said, "What're you doing "No Clue," thought you were going to level your tent?" "I am leveling my tent!" I explained. "Well," She responded, "it certainly doesn't look level to me!" "Hey, these things take time." I countered. I then proceeded to take another good swig, looked toward my tent, stretched my arm out with my thumb sticking up, squinted my left eye, looked down my arm and moved my head from side to side as though I were focusing in and said, "Now it's getting there, yup, it's starting to level right up!" "Well, it certainly doesn't look level to me!" She said. And while the other two were nodding their heads in agreement, I turned to her with the bottle outstretched and said, "That's certainly understandable. Here, try this." A big smile came over her face as she accepted the bottle. She took a good size drink and to my amazement never even flinched. She sat there a few moments, took yet another good sized drink and announced, "By God he's right the damn thing is getting level!" Thus the term "tent leveler" was born.

Vitamin-I

Ibuprofen is a much-used treatment out on the trail. Everyone, young and old, uses it for its anti-inflammatory qualities to help ease the pain in muscles and joints resulting from scrambling over rocks with big heavy backpacks attached to one's torso. So much so, that thru-hikers called it "vitamin-I." At one post office somewhere early into Virginia, I was sitting outside and going through my "mail-drop" package (a package sent containing supplies,) along with several other hikers who had picked up their "mail-drops" as well. Some young hikers were sitting next to me and spotted the huge Ziploc bag nearly full of "vitamin-I" my girlfriend, Jeanne, had sent me. She knew they were hard for me to find in the little country stores along the trail and that they were very expensive if I did find them. So she had bought four bottles of 500 pills each somewhere at a budget price and then dumped them all in the plastic bag, wanting to make sure I had no pain all the way to Maine. The "tent leveler" helped with that as well. Upon spotting my stash, one young man exclaimed, "Holy shit, how'd ya get all that "vitamin-I?" I said, "I buy 'em by the pound." "No shit!" exclaimed one, and at least two were actually reaching for their wallets and saying, "How much a pound man?" and, "Here, get me a pound of those, will ya man?" I swear, it was so funny.

Even with the discomforts and the new challenges I had to face I really did feel happier than I had in the years since my divorce. I had actually grown accustomed to tent camping, eating Ramen noodles and candy bars for nearly every meal, and hiking virtually nonstop 10 to 12 hours a day. I also now had a peace of mind knowing my son was doing great and was apparently responding to my plan designed to take his mind off his woes with the responsibilities of operating our business. A little bonus for the extreme torture I was putting my body through, I lost 48 pounds in 60 days, and I did it eating Snickers bars.

"I have met with but one or two persons in the course of my life who understand the art of walking, that is, of taking walks ... who had a genius, so to speak, for sauntering" ~ *Henry David Thoreau*

Attacked!

Early into Virginia I saw my first bear. All I really saw was his rear-end, going as fast as possible to avoid an encounter with a human being. He looked like a black blur. I remember thinking how fortunate I was he was running away from me instead of toward me, because just the day before, I saw a poster warning about a bear. It warned there was a bear in the area that was showing no fear of humans and was being a nuisance. Others had been recounting their bear sightings to me, and now I had my own. I had started to worry I might hike the entire "AT" and not see a bear. I couldn't wait to relate my own bear story.

Later that evening I found the perfect tent site. The wind had been blowing hard for the last two days making it very hard for us to pitch our tents. So I was delighted to find a nice flat spot next to an outcropping of rock, slanted just right and large enough to help protect my tent from the wind. I pitched my small solo tent and made my huge backpack safe from wind and probable rain by lodging it under a ledge of the huge rock. When choosing a tent I chose lightweight over space, so there was no room for my backpack.

I was in for the night, the wind was howling loudly outside but I was snuggled in my sleeping bag studying my topography maps for the next day's hiking challenge. All of a sudden something lunged into the side of my tent with great force. My reaction was instantaneous. I arched my back, lifted my legs in the air directly level with the intruder and with a fear and adrenaline induced scream I kicked the beast with all my might. The force of my kick pushed it back from the tent. I don't think I had ever been more frightened in my life. Immediately the beast rammed the side of the tent again. I screamed even louder this time and kicked with everything I had, throwing my whole body into it. Again, I had kicked it back. Had I scared it off, had I killed it? My mind was racing. I thought of the bear I had seen just hours before, and even worse, the bear the poster warned about. I was so frightened, my heart felt as if it would pound itself right out of my chest. I just sat there in an upright position waiting. Waiting and praying that the bear or whatever it was would not attack again. I stayed in that position for hours staring at the spot where it had tried to come into my tent, praying to God I would still be alive come daylight. Sometime near dawn, I finally fell asleep.

When I awoke, delighted to be yet breathing, I cautiously stepped around the tent to check the tracks and see if there was damage to the tent. And there it was; I had killed it! My backpack was lying there dead. The force of the wind had dislodged it from its perch and the forty-pound backpack had fallen against my tent. When I kicked it the first time it merely hit against the rock and immediately fell back against the tent once more. And evidently, the second kick was so hard the backpack must have bounced off the rock and to the side just enough to hit the ground instead of the tent, and that's where it died.

Why I Was Called "No Clue"

Also in Virginia I declared war against the rules and regulations of Shenandoah National Park. Perhaps it is my southern heritage that inspires me to be a rebel when I feel that my "rights" are being infringed upon. We thru-hikers were greatly offended by the exorbitant fees being charged for not only lodge accommodations and food within the park, but tent sites as well. Most thru-hikers have to be very frugal to stretch their finances for six months. I and a few others had surmised that Park officials were deliberately eliminating suitable spots for tenting by piling debris on them. This tactic was designed to force the thru-hiker to pay the Parks unjustified high fees at their designated camp sites.

This pissed me off. It bothered me because of all the wonderful young people I had met on the trail who were struggling with finances as it were, and, my own son was going to be out there the next year. Why do they have to charge the thru-hiker for a simple tent site that should be free? The thru-hiker does not leave near the footprint in the park that the "weekend camper" does. I am convinced that this is not what Benton McKaye and the other pioneers of the Appalachian Trail intended. My dear sweet momma would have said, "Those sonsabitches!" My tactic in my little war against the park officials was taking the time to remove the debris from as many potential tent sites as was physically possible. And the ones I actually tented at, I left a message for the park rangers. I fastened a notice encased in a waterproof Ziploc bag and secured it to a tree easily seen from the trail. They read something like this, 'No Clue' (my trail name) pitched his tent and spent the night here ... KISS MY ASS!" I was so proud of my mischievous little self. And even more so when my fellow thru-hikers started noticing my rebellious tactics, finding my notes humorous, and talking of my antics up and down the trail. And of course, the park rangers had no way of knowing who in the hell "No Clue" was.

Near the end of my 100 mile trek through The Shenandoah National Park, I was approached by a fellow thru-hiker who came up to me and said, "Hey, are you 'No Clue,' the guy who is leaving the notes for the park rangers?" I proudly answered, "Yes I am!"

He introduced himself as "Sir Pees-A-Lot" (a no-brainer, right?) and told me how great he thought it was and how my little notes were giving him many chuckles. We were saying our goodbyes and I asked him how he knew I was the infamous "No Clue?" He informed me that he saw my name displayed on the back of my backpack. "What balls you have!" He said. The moment he was out of sight, I scrambled out of my backpack and sure enough, there it was for all behind me to see, "NO CLUE." I had put my name on my sleeping mat with a permanent marker so it would not be confused with the many like ones being used on the trail. It was on the backside of the mat and so when I rolled it up and fastened it to the bottom of my backpack... "Sir Pees-A-lot" had confused 'having balls' for having "No Clue."

What a Woman!

Quite surprising to me were the number of young ladies thru-hiking the Appalachian Trail alone. I met "Cassiopeia" in Virginia, a noticeably beautiful young woman in spite of her attempts to dress down and hide the obvious. That was general advice from the experts for ladies contemplating hiking the trail, "*Dress down, and try not to attract attention to you. Wear no makeup, (extra weight to carry anyway) no revealing clothing, etc.*" She was about thirty and was walking home; she was from Maine. I heard that there was a very upset boyfriend back home who had not wanted her to leave. Supposedly, she decided to hike the "AT" after the boyfriend made it clear he had no intentions of getting married. She was travelling with a very small Jack Russell Terrier that was a very large pain in the ass. He yapped at everything larger than him, which was everything. He was so much of a pain in the ass, a couple times I was thinking that maybe any kind of meat would be better than plain Ramen noodles. One morning I came upon "Cassiopeia's" tent pitched very near the trail. She was sitting in her tent which was completely open in the front, revealing her as she brushed her golden colored waist length hair. The sun's rays were just coming over the mountains behind her, through her tent and onto her hair; the picture was surreal. She looked like a goddess. I had to gulp hard and take a deep breath so I could say "good morning" without revealing I had discovered her secret: how very beautiful she was. The ball cap she wore constantly had been hiding her hair and helped to cover that angelic face. She returned the "good morning" and we talked briefly about how far we each intended to hike that day. And then I left as though I had not seen a thing. I almost felt as if I had happened upon her while undressing.

Another young lady thru-hiking alone was "Gypsy," a 23 year-old free spirit, one of the fastest hikers on the trail. She and I became friends and talked often. She had been pretty much on her own since her early teens. She was doing the trail with little or no money. She would pick up little jobs in the "trail towns" and she would work at the hostels for food, showers, and shelter. She would often hike at night and very fast, trying to make up time spent making money and bartering for her needs or just being young and goofing off. I worried about her getting hurt and cautioned her often and asked her to at least slow down on the more difficult sections. She didn't listen. One morning while climbing a particularly steep rocky incline, near Catawba, Virginia, I looked up, and there in front of me were four thru-hikers, each holding the corner of a hand-made stretcher. "Cassiopeia" was one of the hikers sharing the load. And to my utter dismay, on the stretcher was "Gypsy." She had fallen on the rocks the previous evening and sustained injuries to her hip preventing her from getting back up. She had been forced to stay there alone for a couple of hours. Eventually "Cassiopeia" and the other three came along. They surmised that it would be dark by the time they were prepared for moving her and too dangerous to attempt. They made her as comfortable as possible and the four of them slept there at her side on a steep incline, on a bed of rocks.

At daybreak they started on their plan to get "Gypsy" off the mountain and to safety. One of the hikers was a young Cherokee man who had the skills to make the more than adequate stretcher. The materials were provided by a thru-hiker called "The Wyoming Skateboarder," who had been the brunt of many jokes and laughter due to all the unnecessary and heavy gear he carried. Things like a hatchet, a very heavy tarpaulin, and heavy rope. All the things needed to build a stretcher. Bless "The Wyoming Skateboarder;" he was just another lesson in why we all should obey one of the thru-hiker mantras, "Hike your own hike." I relieved one of the heroes and we continued on down the mountain taking turns struggling over the rocky and steep terrain. "Gypsy" was in much pain and was terribly frightened that we might drop her on the rocks. At one point she became near hysterical. I could certainly understand, she was unintentionally being tossed from side to side, up and down, and she felt totally helpless over the very terrain that caused her injuries. So I bent down next to her ear and said, "Sweetheart, if this stretcher starts to drop, I will throw myself under it and break your fall." She looked up and said, "Can you do that?" "Absolutely," I said. She very sweetly said, "Okay," and never mentioned being dropped again.

We finally encountered two old farmers in a pick-up truck on an old dirt road that crossed the trail near the foot of the mountain. They stopped and offered to take Gypsy to get professional help. The old men helped us load her in the truck; they were both very kind and concerned. I figured "Gypsy" would have little or no money, so I took her hand and slipped some money into it. I then asked if she had enough money for a doctor or perhaps had insurance coverage. Before she could answer, "Cassiopeia" spoke up and said, "I have money, I'll take care of it." That's when I saw why she couldn't hide her beauty. Inner beauty will not be hidden. I heard later that "Gypsy" cracked her hip and had to get off the trail. "Cassiopeia," true to her word, took care of the medical expenses. I never saw "Gypsy" or "Cassiopeia" again. I heard later that "Cassiopeia's" boyfriend proposed to her over the phone in order to get her off the trail and back to him. She told him yes she would come home and marry him but she intended to go back and finish her thru-hike. He reluctantly agreed. I was told she did get married and did finish the Appalachian Trail. What a woman!

From the Bottom of my Heart

That long and beautiful, seemingly endless footpath was taking me not only to Maine, but to my soul, the inner core of my being. This trail was touching my heart and was changing my outlook on life. I still had no idea just how much I would change though. That much beauty, a continuous beauty, and beauty very few will ever experience in a silence away from the rest of the world to create the purest solitude imaginable. Add encounters with special and unique individuals who seek to fill their hearts with the joy and peace of the trail and in turn unintentionally aid others in their personal quest. How could one not change? The proper attitude for a thru-hike of the Appalachian Trail was put to me with these meaningful words from Melody Blaney, who wrote a book about her thru-hike , "There are two ways to hike the trail" she said, " you can hike it from the bottom of your feet, or from the bottom of your heart." She then added these wonderful words of assurance, "I can see you are doing the latter." I thought my heart would burst. She, in the true spirit of the trail, must have sensed I needed encouragement at that time.

"In wilderness is the preservation of the world"~ Henry David Thoreau

Salud!

On my 54th birthday, June 17th, 1999, I hiked into the city of Waynesboro, Virginia, and checked into a nice motel. I decided I would treat myself to one of my favorite dishes, white clam sauce over linguini. I searched the phone book and found an Italian restaurant within walking distance. All I had in the way of clothing were nylon hiking shorts with "cargo pockets" and nylon tee-shirts. Both sets were badly stained. This was a special occasion and I did want to look nice on my 54th birthday. Then I remembered, attached to my backpack was a very brightly colored dress tie!

Just before starting my hike, I was in a local bar, the Long Branch Saloon, in Vero Beach, Florida, telling a car salesman friend of mine my plans to thru-hike the Appalachian Trail in just a few days. My friend gets this really surprised look on his face and shaking his head in amazement, says, "I can't believe this!" and still shaking his head, he reaches down and takes hold of his beautiful tie and says, "See this tie man, one of the best friends I ever had gave me this tie." He then became very serious and told me this story. "My friend and I worked together for years selling cars, me and everyone else at that dealership knew he had put back money for years toward a thru-hike of the Appalachian Trail. He talked about it often." Then my friend looked down at the floor and said, "He got cancer before he could carry out his dream. Hell, he never made his fortieth birthday Steve! I really loved that guy man." Still holding onto the tie his good friend had given him, he explained to me, "This has become my lucky tie. Whenever we have slow sales, I wear this tie and it always works. I had a great day today!" He then undid the tie and with eyes welled up with tears, handed it to me and asked, "Steve would you carry this tie on your hike of that trail?" "Absolutely," I answered.

How touching, this man was giving up his "lucky tie" that meant so much to him to symbolically send his friend on the thru-hike he was unable to do. I felt honored. So, now that I had proper attire, I tied the best knot I could and headed to the Italian restaurant wearing this expensive, brightly colored tie with drab green cargo shorts and an even drabber green tee-shirt. The waiter never mentioned my attire or even seemed to notice my fine tie. I was appalled at such rudeness. At the table across from me, were two plain-clothes detectives. I saw their badges on their belts and overheard them discussing the training seminar they had attended that day. They were in conversation about the day's doings and their occupation in general, but I did catch both of them glancing over at me occasionally. That's a police officer's job, you know, noticing odd looking things, you know, the weird shit. Finally, the one nearest turned to me said, "That's a fine looking tie you have on." "Why thank you!" I said, "Today is my birthday and I just felt like dressin' up." I shared with them the significance of the tie. They bought me a beer and, wished me a happy birthday and proposed a toast. We raised our glasses and one of them toasted, "Here's to you, to your friend and to his friend!" They both said, "Salud!" nodding their heads in agreement and respect. I had a great birthday. I was having the time of my life.

Never Daydream…

At Duncannon, Pennsylvania, a little over 1,100 miles from my starting point of Springer Mountain, my then girlfriend, Jeanne, flew up for a visit. We had a great time. My son was reporting that all was well at home and business was going great. I was a little over half way to Mt. Katahdin in Maine and my conquest of the Appalachian Trail. But regardless of all the fun and the good news, within just a day or so of leaving Duncannon, I began worrying about my son, I just felt uneasy. I would call and tell him of my concerns and he would insist that all was well and I had no need to worry. The uneasy feeling still would not go away though.

There are two key rules out on the "AT" to follow, particularly when you travel at the pace of most thru-hikers, never take your eyes off the trail, being ever conscience of your next step. And never daydream to the point where you are not concentrating on what you are doing and what is around you. Due to the "gut" feeling concerning my son, I found myself breaking both those vital rules of the trail; I had already fallen three times.

Pennsylvania is called, "where your boots go to die" by thru-hikers, due to the extremely rocky terrain. Falling on those rocks can be quite serious. On my last fall I had received some deep cuts and nasty bruises. But the scariest incident was not a fall on the rocks but what came out of the rocks. I had seen two "rattlers" since I had been on the trail. Both sightings were in Virginia and uneventful. Because I had my mind somewhere other than the trail, I don't know how the hell that big fat "timber rattler" got in front of me. Maybe he was daydreaming as well. All I remember is that dreaded sound. There was no mistaking that sound. I should have been tuned in to a possible encounter, I had been stepping from rock to rock all day, and it was 100 degrees, the perfect setting for a rattlesnake.

There he was, fully coiled, head reared back and ready to strike! That terrible, intimidating rattling sound! I knew he was warning me, I knew that he knew I was too big for prey and he didn't want to waste his venom on me (I felt the same way.) Knowing these facts, it was still extremely unnerving. I'm not sure how long he was, but he was the largest I had seen. I was nearly on top of him from my point of view, less than six feet away. Also, I had been climbing and was on an incline, he was higher than me. The fear of being bitten in the upper body now gripped me as well. And I figured I was at least 30 to 40 miles from help. I needed to step back to gain a safer vantage point. I didn't dare take my eyes off him. I had to step backwards without looking. I would be descending over jagged rocks backwards! And as if the situation were not tense enough, due to a dry spell in the area, I was forced to carry extra water, putting my backpack weight at about 60 pounds. So, without any other real choice, I leaned forward to gain some leverage and then stepped backward and downward. When I did so, it sounded as though the rattle would come off his tail! I made it I did not fall to my death. I used the same precarious procedure again and was now two big steps further away from him, I now felt out of harm's way, sort of.

My camera was hung around my neck so I started snapping pictures of my foe. After having them developed weeks later, the first four pictures were no more than blurred rocks. I had been shaking so badly that only a couple pictures were clear enough to recognize the subject. After taking the pictures I picked up two throwing size rocks. I threw the first one and it landed right beside him. He rattled louder but he didn't move. I knew I could put the next rock right on his head, possibly killing him. I realized I was angry at this snake because he had made me look bad; he caused me to feel afraid and insecure. That damned snake had humiliated me and hurt my pride. How dare him! As I stood there and we both studied each other, I recalled a few years back, in Florida, while my two children were yet small. My wife and I had seen coral snakes in our backyard. Coral snakes are extremely venomous, so we were frightened for our children's safety. We made the decision to kill the coral snakes. With that memory came the realization, "He's not in my backyard I'm in his backyard." I gently dropped the rock at my side and that magnificent creature slithered away.

The Appalachian Trail Part 2

July 17, 1999, was a beautiful Sunday morning on Blue Mountain Summit in Pennsylvania. I was crossing the road headed for the north side of the "AT," an old pickup truck pulled up beside me. The driver stuck his head out and asked, "Are you the hiker from Florida; your trail name "No Clue?" The fear gripped me immediately, how in the hell did he know that? He told me I had an emergency at home and he would drive me to the nearest payphone. I could not remember ever having felt so frightened, the fear gripped me! I instantly became horrified that something had happened to my son, my little boy. "Dear God," I kept repeating to myself, "Please, oh God please let it be only an injury! He's been in a car wreck but he's going to be alright!" I climbed into the backseat of the truck. The driver, Todd Gladfelter, was ferrying two female hikers to one of the numerous trail-heads in the area. All three occupants were completely silent as we rode toward a payphone. I kept agonizing as to what the emergency could possibly be, no one offered to try to assure me that everything would be alright. They already knew what I was soon to find out. I remember hoping the news would be the serious illness of my eighty year old mother, even guiltily willing to hear of my mother's death, anything than either of my babies.

We pulled up to an old country store and Todd pointed to where the phone was. I remember now that he and the two hikers walked away a few feet and just stood there looking at the ground with an occasional nervous glance at one another. I was shaking so badly I could barely punch in the number of my home phone. My daughter answered, I blurted out, "Shelly what is wrong, what has happened?" Between sobs, she screams, "Just get home, just get on a plane and get home!" Now I am totally horrified. "Shelly, you have got to tell me what is wrong, has Stevie been in a car wreck or something?" She then screams out the most horrible words that had ever entered my ears, "He's gone dad, our Stevie is gone, he killed himself daddy!" My beautiful only son had gone down to the beach, placed a gun in his mouth and blown the back of his beautiful head off and ended both our lives!

I fell back away from the phone as though I had been physically shoved away from it, and I screamed. I could not stop screaming. In my mind was a line by Marlon Brando from an old very popular war movie, over and over, "The horror, the horror!" I was completely incapacitated. I could not think, I could not move. I could only scream. This could not be happening to me. My life was over. My charming, witty, intelligent, and handsome son, my pride and joy, my proud contribution to the universe was now gone.

Todd and the two ladies took hold of me and placed me in the back seat of the truck. One of the ladies stayed in the back with me while I screamed. They all tried to comfort me. Todd dropped the ladies off at their prearranged hiking spot and we drove on up to his home in the Blue Mountains. His wife was waiting when we pulled up, she came off the porch running and jumped immediately into the back of the truck and wrapped her arms around me. "What do you want to do, what can we do for you?" She asked. "I need a place to scream!" I said. "We have lots of room for that," she said, and pointed me toward the barn. Todd's wife is Cindy Ross, a successful author of adventure and travel books. Todd and Cindy both write about their adventures and raise Llama's on their Pennsylvania farm.

After practically bathing me, they gave me decent clothes for my flight home. Todd drove me to the airport at Allentown to board a puddle jumper to Washington's Dulles Airport where I would change planes for Orlando. I barely remember a very quiet, calm, and composed Todd Gladfelter taking my credit card and approaching the ticket counter. I was just standing there like a zombie waiting to be told what to do. Evidently there was a discrepancy about the address or something with my credit card and Todd was trying to work it out. And then I heard Todd say, "What the hell is wrong with you people? For God's sake give the man his damn ticket and let's get him home! Can't you see the condition he's in? For crying out loud, just do it!" The stunned agent just looked at him in disbelief; she then punched the right buttons and gave the man my ticket. It worked; I was taken immediately to my plane.

I could no longer control myself; I no longer cared about anything other than the horrible indescribable pain in my very being. I started screaming on the plane. There were about twenty five people onboard and nearly all tried to comfort me. There were both men and women holding my hands and patting my back with affection. When we landed at Dulles International, attendants were waiting for me with a wheelchair; I could not walk. I was no longer a functioning human being.

An employee of Delta Airlines was pushing me to my next flight when a tall attractive African American lady with a walkie-talkie in her hand approached me. She was obviously someone of authority; she was issuing commands to a small entourage accompanying her. She stood in front of me and asked very gently, "Mr. Fugate, do you think you can get out of that wheelchair just for a moment?" I replied that I wasn't sure. She patiently coaxed me to stand up. Upon standing, this beautiful woman wrapped her arms around my neck, put her lips to my ear and whispered, "Mr. Fugate, I Love you, we all love you and are here for you, and God loves you." She then asked if I thought I would be able to board the flight to Orlando. I told her I didn't know. I didn't know anything, my mind was not functioning. All I could do was cry and repeat over and over, "my little boy, my beautiful little boy."

I was sent via ambulance to a nearby Washington D.C. hospital emergency room. I was given mild sedatives that had no effect what so ever. A case-hardened emergency room doctor approximately my own age, with tears running down his face, pleaded my case to his superiors that I needed stronger drugs. The two EMT's from the ambulance stayed at my side during my emergency room visit. They informed me they had asked permission to be the ones to drive me back to the airport. They asked if that was okay with me, to which of course I agreed. It is still hard to believe how touched everyone was by my tragedy and how they all tried to comfort me.

On the flight headed for Florida, the steward was instructed to allow me to stand in the back with him as soon as the seat-belt light went out. He tried to comfort me as best he could between serving drinks not only with words but in handing me several of those "little bottles." They, like the emergency room medication, had no effect. Somewhere during the flight he looked at me and said, "It makes you wonder why God would do something like this?" I was totally surprised by my immediate answer, "Oh, God didn't do this, it was allowed to happen though, and I've got to go find out why."

Figure 2. Obituary picture for my handsome little boy.
September, 1972 - July, 1999. I Love you so very much!

I went home to bury my little boy. I was asked by most of his fine young friends, "Why?" I had no real answer. My son left twelve notes to his loved ones and friends, but there was no complete answer to, "Why?"

I am convinced there is no pain equal to that of losing a child. The grief is indescribable. I felt as though someone had taken an axe and chopped out my heart while I was yet breathing! My son, my beautiful son was gone. I can in no way fully describe the pain; I do not know how to scream on paper.

For weeks I just made the required movements to function as a normal human being and try to run my little business. The pain was unbearable, I cried almost constantly and at day's end I would go home and try to drink myself to death. There was no comfort. My caring girlfriend, Jeanne, tried as hard as anyone possibly could to give me comfort. I was a terrible companion for her. I believe, if one has lost a child and not taken their own life, and aren't in an institution, they are doing quite well. I really did not care if I lived or died.

I wrote this during that time:

Oh God I cried, my soul relieve,
The emptiness of my heart speaking
From that echo chamber where I grieve.
My life is over, my child is missing.
Restore to me if only my sanity,
To walk among the living, not the dead.
My soul is pacing, waiting, on me.
Oh God it's hard, its life I dread!
Where's it hidden, this life I miss?
In fields of cloud above the dew,
Or further still in a heavenly abyss?
Find him please, for he took mine too...

I decided I had to finish the Appalachian Trail in honor of my son who also had wanted to hike the trail the next year after I finished. I had to show my son that my life would go on and I had forgiven him. I also feared losing my mind if I didn't commit to something. I completely immersed myself in preparing for my completion of the "AT" and thus shortened some of my daily crying spells. The nights were still a frightening place to visit though.

I became totally involved with my hike. I was determined to have the lightest backpack on the trail by researching and buying the lightest gear I could find. I stayed as busy as possible, keeping my mind occupied and working to provide extra funds for my venture. Getting my backpack weight down from 50 pounds to 22 pounds, I discovered the formula for creating a much lighter backpack; the lighter the weight on your back equals lighter the weight of your wallet.

And so, I went back out there to finish that damn trail. That beautiful 2,178 mile foot-path turned into trail therapy for me.

"Never did I think so much, exist so vividly, and experience so much, never have I been so much myself... if I may use that expression... as in the journeys I have taken alone and on foot." ~ Jean-Jacques Rousseau

Just a Nice Guy!

April 1, 2000, I climbed off a Greyhound bus in the town of Tamaqua, Pennsylvania, the closest town with bus service, to Blue Mountain Summit, where I had stopped my hike after receiving word of my son's suicide. Before I left, I had called the Tamaqua Chamber of Commerce to get information about available motels, etc. I told my story to a Chamber employee and why I was coming to Tamaqua. She requested I send her a copy of the article on me from my local paper. I did so and she sent me a map of their little town and where I was to pitch my tent. Tamaqua had no motel accommodations. I was to pitch my tent at the firefighters training ground.

The bus had arrived very early and I walked down to check on my designated tent site. It was not a nice spot, there was no level ground and it was quite far from everything. So I did what I always did when in doubt, I found a bar and had a couple shots of Kentucky Bourbon.

After leaving the bar I started back toward the firefighters training ground. As I was passing the spot where the bus had dropped me off I heard someone yelling at me. I turned, and across the street there was a guy with bleached blonde hair standing next to a new Cadillac. He continued yelling, "Hey, yahoo, are you the hiker from Florida?" His mannerisms and the way he sounded, appeared to me, this guy was gay. I am not. Why the hell is a little gay guy with bleached blonde hair yelling at me? And he knows who I am! I slowly acknowledged him and nodded my head yes. He shouted across the street, "Where have you been? I came here to meet the bus and you were not here, I have been looking all over for you!" I am totally bewildered and just stand there looking at him. I don't know what the hell to say to him. Then he starts waving his hand frantically for me to cross the street to his car. I was not in a hurry to do so, but I did, very reluctantly. He begins explaining to me, using more gestures that in my mind, told me he was no doubt, gay, "I am the city manager for the city of Tamaqua, the director of tourism, and I am editor of our local paper. I took a look at where they want you to stay tonight and it is just not acceptable to me." We now have one thing in common anyway. He continued, "We have got to find you another place to spend the night!" I'm thinking, "It's not going be your place." "Come on," he says, gesturing toward his new Caddy, "We are going to find you a nicer place to stay and tomorrow I will pick you up and take you to the Appalachian Trail. I also want to do a story on you for our paper."

I climbed into the Caddy. He drove us to a convenience store with a nice level patch of ground next to it and behind it was the Schuylkill River. The spot was far enough from the road for safety, and quiet, and was near enough to the store for morning coffee or whatever. It was the perfect spot. He informed me he had been looking for a nicer place for me over the last two days. He says, "Now I'll just go in the store and inform the girl working that you will be here for the night." I am starting to trust this flamboyant little guy. He comes out of the store in a huff. "That dumb little bitch!" He says. "What a fuckin' idiot she is, she says she is afraid to let you stay here, she is not sure whether the land belongs to her boss or not, or if he would approve." And then he says, "When I asked her to simply call her boss and find out, she told me she was afraid to bother him!" He stands there for a moment, obviously thinking on how to solve the problem. "You know," he says, "There is a possibility this land belongs to the city of Tamaqua, and I represent the city damn it!" On that note, he marches back into the store. When he came back out I could see he was now in complete control of the situation. "Pitch your tent." He says. "Oh, the land does definitely belong to the city?" I asked. "Hell I don't know, I just told her it did, fuck her, she's too chicken shit to call and find out!" He goes on, "The police officer on duty now is Bob, he already knows you are here and will check on you. At 11:00 p.m. Frank comes on duty and he will be checking on you also." I could certainly see how he was able to handle all the positions of responsibility he held. This little guy got things done. He continued, "I know that you have the rest of your gear waiting at the post office for you. They normally do not open until 8:00, but I have talked to them and they will let you in at 7:00. Just knock on the door and they will let you in. And you can stay there and get your gear together. I will pick you up from the post office, interview you in the car and drop you off at the "AT" trail-head."

Just as he said, Bob came by, and then Frank. Both were extremely courteous and caring. Both men asked me to let their city manager know they had carried out his instructions to check on me. I sensed a deep respect from both, for their city manager. The kind of respect you have to earn. I knocked at the post office door at 7:00 a.m. and they led me to a table with my package sitting on it. I organized all my gear into my pack and looked out the window to see it pouring the rain... on a brand new Cadillac, waiting for me.

When he saw me running for the car he jumped out in the cold pouring rain to assist me. He questioned me about my son and why I felt I had to finish the Appalachian Trail, interviewing me for his newspaper article. He was very thorough, patient, and understanding. As we were stopping at the trail-head for the "AT", he turned to me and apparently struggling to get the words out, said, "My brother committed suicide, I still haven't been able to forgive him. I am still so damn mad at him for breaking my heart!" The tears were streaming down his face. "I understand." I said. He continued on, "I am embarrassed to confess this, I have lived here my whole life and I had no idea where this trail was." Then he looks me right in the eye and says, "I don't know anything about the trail, but I asked around and was told about this little trail here. Now this is not the actual "AT" trail-head, the official access point is just a couple hundred yards from here, over there on route 309. But I just thought it might be a little easier on you, not having to go to the exact spot where you first found out about your son." He helped me get my gear from the car, he reached out to shake my hand, and I surprised him and myself, and gave him a big hug instead. He wrote a great story on me.

"I am ever learning to follow only my own heart, and in the process of finding the heart of me, I find an enormous amount of Love there for my fellow human being. I am in pursuit of a heart-governed mind." Steve Fugate

I Love New Yorkers

I finished the mountains of Pennsylvania, mostly in a cold rain. That was my mood though, dismal. I cried almost constantly. I missed my beautiful son so very much! It had been nine months and the pain was sometimes as if he had died that very week. I was driven by something, I'm not sure what, I only knew I had to climb Mt Katahdin in Maine. As I look back, it was as if I would meet my son on top that mountain with some sort of decree, absolving him from all guilt and responsibility for his desperate last minute decision. And he would see how much I loved him. The journey became an obsession, and I was miserable.

I trudged on through New Jersey and into New York. I was on the Appalachian Trail at a time when there were hardly any other hikers out there. It was still a little cold for the weekend hiker. The south bound thru-hikers don't start until around the first of June and the north bound thru-hikers were still down south that time of year. So it was natural that the locals would be curious as to why I was out on the trail at that time. I would explain that I had to stop my hike the year before, they would ask me why, I would explain that I had to stop because I lost my son and I would start crying. I just couldn't control it, it had already happened several times.

I went into a little deli near Arden, New York, for breakfast one morning. It was operated by three Italian looking young ladies who were, no doubt, from the city. There was no way you could mistake that accent. As I was paying my bill, one of the young owners just had to know why a thru-hiker was out there that early in the year. In the strongest Bronx accent you could imagine, she asked, "Wadda' ya doin' out hee-ah dis toime ah da yee-ah?" I answered that, "I went a little over half way last year and now I'm out here to finish." And then I just wanted her to hand me my change and let me run for the door. But, she being the typical "have to know" New Yorker, she naturally said, "Well, how coime ya didn't finish last yee-ah? I mean, afta awl, ya wah already out dere?" And of course she was using her hands and shoulders to emphasize her point. I couldn't believe she was pursuing her curiosity, and I blurted out that I had to quit because I lost my son! I couldn't control it the tears started to pour. She immediately came out from behind the register with both arms up in the air with hands signaling for her partners to follow and she said loudly, "Hug toime!!" She wrapped her arms around me and the other two followed suit and did the same.

Thirty years of operating a business in Florida dealing with New Yorkers had caused me to think I didn't like New Yorkers much. But then, there I was, standing in a New

York deli, the center of a "group hug" from three New York Italian ladies, maybe from the Bronx. I simply, had a wrong attitude. I Love New Yorkers. I Love everybody!

"I went to the woods because I wished to live deliberately, to front only the essential facts of life, and see if I could not learn what it had to teach, and not when I came to die, discover that I had not lived" ~ Henry David Thoreau

Little Beverly

It seemed though, that no matter how hard I unknowingly tried to remain miserable, I kept having little encounters with people who, unknowingly, just were not going to let misery stand. In Bear Mountain, New York, the trail winds through Trailside Museum and Animal Exhibit, the site of America's first Nature Trail. I was walking through the tunnel-like nocturnal animal exhibit, with my head down when I was approached by a very pretty young lady in her twenties. "Are you a thru-hiker?" she asked. I looked up startled and told her I was indeed. She then said, "Children, children, come here quickly!" In an instant I was surrounded by little munchkins, kindergarten age, I think. There were two other young teachers there as well. She introduced me to the class, "This gentleman is a thru-hiker, and he has walked over a thousand miles to get here and he is walking on to Maine!" There was an instant chorus of "Wow!" from the sweetest voices on earth. She then said, "Let's ask him some questions, I'll go first!" And she asked, "Do you ever get lonely out there?" I answered, "Yes, as a matter of fact; I just got off the phone with my girlfriend in Florida." There was a pretty little blonde girl right in front, and with eye's opened wide as though totally astonished, asked, "You have a girlfriend!?" I, with a slight smirk, answered, "Yes I do." And with eyes still wide, she said, "Wow! You're too old to have a girlfriend!" The three young teachers, in unison, while trying to keep from bursting out in laughter, said, "Beverly!" Undaunted, little Beverly continued, "You're too old to have a girlfriend, you're supposed to be married to a grandma!" "Well, I do have a girlfriend," I said, sheepishly. "Is she pretty?" Beverly asked. "I think she is." I said. Then the precious little darling asked, "Is she as pretty as Miss Davis?" A crimson faced Miss Davis said, "Beverly!" Struggling for an answer to this one, I said, "To me she is." To which, with eyes even wider, she exclaimed, "Wow!" I looked at a blushing Miss Davis, being teased by her co-workers and said, "That sure beats getting an apple doesn't it?" She was speechless. Life and all its wonderful participants were not going to let me stay unhappy.

Graymoor Friary

That same evening, I was planning on getting out of the cold and misting rain by staying at the Graymoor Friary. My *Appalachian Trail Data Book* said that the monks at the friary offered a free nights lodging to thru-hikers. I was really looking forward to being inside for the night in a warm bed. I found the Friary and started looking for the building where my hot meal and warm bed were awaiting me. I approached a very old nun; I'm betting she was in her nineties. I mean, this woman was really old. And she was very short and round. She was very pleasant though, and when she smiled, only one tooth showed. I asked her where they let the thru-hikers stay. She told me they were no longer doing that. Some convent somewhere had burned down recently and the homeless nuns were offered shelter in the dormitory formerly provided for thru-hikers. But they did allow hikers to camp at the baseball field she said. The kind old nun continued, "The wonderful Brothers here at the friary have donated their building for such a wonderful cause!" All I could think was "Screw the Brothers and the homeless nuns too!" Now, I had to pitch my tarp and sleep in the friggin mud at the friary baseball field. And, I would have to eat those fuckin' Ramen noodles again, in the friggin' rain, in the cold friggin' rain. "Yes," The old nun informed me, "The Brothers have taken an oath of poverty you know." I said, "Well, I haven't! If they really want to experience poverty Sister, have one of 'em come down here and trade places with me. I'll go up there and eat a hot meal, sleep in a warm bed, and wake up to a hot breakfast. And the seeker of poverty can come down here in the cold drizzling rain and try to get that damn wood burning stove lit to heat up those damn Ramen noodles and then crawl under a tarp to sleep and then wake up in a cold rain without a hot breakfast. Now that Sister is poverty. They should be delighted to swap places!" That old woman bent over and slapped her knees in laughter! Every time she came up for air, I could see that one tooth; she looked so very sweet and seemed to be having a grand time. Hell, I started laughing too. The two of us must have been an odd sight; standing in the cold drizzling rain, doubled over in laughter in front of a big statue of some damn Saint (probably the one that started all that poverty oath crap). We said goodbye and I headed for the baseball field, in the rain. As I lay under my tarp, I could visualize the monks up there in warm beds with full tummies, experiencing all that terrible poverty. I could also visualize the round face of that sweet old nun laughing with her one tooth shining; I had made her laugh. Good.

"Love Life with all your heart and Life will not only make your own heart bigger with more understanding, Life will introduce you to other bigger hearts with more understanding." ~ Steve Fugate

Never Quit!

Somewhere near Wingdale, New York, I had hiked out to the road wanting to get a room and out of the rain. I came upon a gentleman, about my age, sitting in the drizzling rain fishing in a small stream or pond, not sure which, couldn't see past the trees. Though it seemed quite cold to me, he was wearing but a tee shirt and was barefooted. I greeted him; he smiled and asked was I hiking all the Appalachian Trail. I told him yes, but that I was heading for town to get a motel for the night. He said he was just giving up on fishing and would be delighted to give me a ride to a motel. I accepted and then he immediately asked, "You're not quitting the trail, right?" I told him I was not quitting and it was just for the night to get out of the rain.

As I was climbing into his old pickup I saw a very small sticker on my side of the windshield that said, "U. S. Navy SEAL Teams" and I immediately said, "You're a SEAL?" he didn't answer. As he was starting the truck he looked over at me and asked again, "Now you're not planning on quitting your hike, right?" "No, I am not quitting." I said. We rode a little way in silence but my curiosity just wouldn't let it go, and so I said, "I only live about thirteen miles from the U.S. Navy UDT/SEAL Museum in Ft. Pierce, Florida." His face lit up immediately and he excitedly said, "Really, I was just there in November!" I had found out what I wanted to know, November is when the SEAL's have their annual muster at the UDT/SEAL Museum and most former SEAL's try to attend. He never said another word about being a SEAL, but as soon as we pulled up in front of the motel he said, "You promise you're not quitting and you're going all the way, right?" "Oh yes sir, I am going to hike all the way to Mt. Katahdin in Maine!" I assured him. "Good, good! The best of luck to you sir!" the former U. S. Navy SEAL Team member said. The man, being about my age, and once a member of the SEAL teams, almost assuredly had to have been in serious combat during the Viet Nam war. The man just wanted no part of quitting. Fascinating.

From Henry David Thoreau's Walden: *"We need the tonic of wilderness, to wade sometimes in marshes where the bittern and the meadow-hen lurk, and hear the booming of the snipe; to smell the whispering sedge where only some wilder and more solitary fowl builds her nest, and the mink crawls with its belly close to the ground.... we never have enough of nature. We must be refreshed by the inexhaustible vigor, vast and titanic features, the sea-coast with its wrecks, the wilderness with its living and its decaying trees, the thunder-cloud and the rain that lasts three weeks and produces freshets. We need to witness our own limits transgressed, and some life pasturing freely where we never wander."*

Bullwinkle

I barely remember the hundred forty two miles of Connecticut and Massachusetts. I was way too busy dealing with the pain of my grief which constantly occupied my mind. I did manage a visit to the covered bridge at Cornwell Bridge, Connecticut for pictures though, only because it was a request by my very supportive girlfriend, Jeanne. I was still keeping a bottle of bourbon in my pack, to ensure my getting some sleep. My favorite tourist attractions in New England were its liquor stores.

I had just entered Vermont that day and was less than two miles from highway 9, which would take me the five miles into Bennington. I chose a small overgrown meadow just off the trail to pitch my tarp. I was using a very thin, light weight tarp for shelter instead of the much heavier tent. I had sacrificed comfort for a lighter load on my back. About 10:00 pm I awoke from a dream in which I was being charged by a bull moose! It had been so real like I could still hear his hooves hitting the ground! Then it dawned on me, "Shit, I'm awake and I still hear the sounds of hooves, and they're getting louder!" It became obvious that a large bull moose was charging toward me and would over run my tarp! I just knew I was about to die! I could hear him snorting and panting as he charged by within a few feet of my tarp. I never did see him. I wasn't about to look death in the face. I heard him galloping off into the woods. I was told later by some locals that it was mating season and I was probably in "Bullwinkle's" (trail name) territory and he was challenging a possible threat. I had not been in the woods that long.

After "Bullwinkle," I was awakened again at about 11:30 pm; this time it was a storm. Other than hurricanes, it was one the fiercest lightning storms I ever witnessed. The night was lit up as if I were under flood lights. I could actually see the lightning coming up from the ground. Or so it appeared. The rain was in torrents. The only thing keeping me safe was the fact my tarp was pitched in vegetation much higher than it was. I had smashed out a place to pitch it and so was protected from the wind, somewhat. The lightning was constant and never let up all through the night. My prayer was, "Lord, please let at least one bolt of lightning find and kill that fuckin' moose!"

The storm let up around 6:00 am and I scrambled to get my gear together and hightail it for the road and hitch a ride into Bennington. I barely made it to the road and the electrical storm started again. I truly do not remember ever actually being in a harder rain or seeing so much lightning! All I could do was stand there and be drenched. If a car did come by, I figured they couldn't see me anyway. I was just looking in the direction of where I thought the cars might be coming, hoping to see one. All of a sudden there was an incredibly bright flash of light accompanied by a terrible cracking sound. Lightning struck a tree, no more than a hundred feet in front of me. For a few seconds I could see nothing but bright light, I could see nothing at all. It probably didn't matter, I couldn't see for the rain anyway. But it still scared the hell out of me. Then I heard the sound of a vehicle right beside me and a male voice yelling, "Hurry up and get in!" I went toward the sound of the voice and got my wet ass inside. He asked, "Where do you want to go?" "Home, I wanna' go home!" I said. He started laughing because he knew by my backpack I was probably a thru-hiker and headed for Maine. Still chuckling, the fine young man said, "Where do you really want to go sir?" He dropped me off at a motel in Bennington, the only way to ride out a storm.

Coyote Comfort

The Green Mountains of Vermont were so lush and green, they are so very beautiful, and I enjoyed hiking in them. I was still grieving my little boy terribly, and still crying daily. In the solitude and privacy of those soothing mountains, I could scream as loud as I wanted and for long periods at a time. After most of these long screaming sessions I usually felt somewhat better. I never knew when the torturous pain of grief would attack me. Sometimes I would be in a grocery store buying supplies and I would just start crying. Often I would have to leave the store so others wouldn't think me nuts. I called these attacks, 'panic attacks.' I had to keep pushing on though. I was obsessed with showing my little boy that it was okay; I would still finish that trail. I was able also to get my mind somewhat off my pain by thinking about my little girl, Shelly, who was helping orchestrate my hike, sending my "mail drops."

As I crossed the bridge over the Connecticut River to enter New Hampshire and the town of Hanover, I looked down and saw the Dartmouth rowing team practicing. I stood there and watched them for a long time. Those fine young men, God keep them alive; do not let their parents suffer what I've had to suffer. The terrain was changing, getting a little more rugged than Vermont. It was still quite beautiful though. My Appalachian Trail Data Book described a new hexagon shaped shelter that had only been built the year before. They had named it Hexacuba, maybe because it was only a mile and a half from Mount Cube.

I reached it early one evening and it was beautiful. It was made completely of pine logs and they still looked and smelled fresh. I didn't usually like staying in the shelters but this one was different, I decided to spend the night. And I was completely alone, how wonderful! After I had cooked my meal and laid out my bed I sat up against the back wall and, wow, I could not believe the view. Nothing but mountains of green lay before me and there was not a sound, the quiet too was beautiful. I thought of how beautiful my son was and I started crying. And then I started screaming, screaming out the pain in my heart. I felt so detached from everyone and everything; I continued to scream louder and louder. Somewhere during my screaming, I realized I was not crying alone. There were others crying with me. There was a chorus of sorrowful voices blending with my own. I was not alone, I had understanding companions. Coyotes were howling along with my screaming, or so it seemed. When I cried out louder, they seemed to howl louder. I stopped so as to listen to their forlorn call. As they ceased their cries, I could hear the yelps of their young. It was a spiritual experience for me, it was soothing, and I felt comforted and not alone. As I heard the presence of their young, I felt the presence of mine, both of them. I soon fell asleep.

I had taken my mind off my own heartache because the coyotes had gotten my attention with their cries. I kept thinking about the sweet yelping sounds of their young. Within days I was thinking about the young of others, that I had to do something to prevent the young of others from doing what my little boy did, that parents would not have go through the horror. This would become a life changing experience for me.

"I have met with but one or two persons in the course of my life who understand the art of walking, that is, of taking walks ... who had a genius, so to speak, for sauntering" ~ *Henry David Thoreau*

Pissed off Fat Chicken

The trail in New Hampshire was getting tougher. And according to other hikers, the harder parts were yet to come, after Franconia Notch. In Gorham, New Hampshire, I stopped at a hostel called "Hikers Paradise" that offered all-you-can-eat pancakes made to look like the sole of a boot. I ate them until I thought they would come back up. That place was great! Back on the trail, I was somewhere between Dream Lake and Mt. Success in an area of large pines when suddenly, not more than twenty feet to my left I heard a very loud crashing noise, as though all the trees around me were falling down. I could barely make out what appeared to be the bodies of at least three moose bulls charging down the slope. What a noise they made! I now had two moose encounters but still had not seen a whole moose. Everyone had seen moose but me, it seemed. I heard of moose sightings all the time. I had only heard them and seen little bits of them through the trees. I wanted to see a moose!

What I did see a lot of though, were wood grouse. Wood grouse are birds that look like little fat chickens and act as though injured when they feel their nest is threatened. I encountered at least four of these performances. Some are much more dramatic than others. I witnessed one little fat mama chicken that should have been given an Oscar. She, the mother wood grouse, dives at the intruder, me, first and then acts like her wing is broken in an attempt to get the intruder to go after her, and not her babies. They will actually flop around on the ground and act as though they are hurt very badly and are indeed easier prey than their babies. I had one experience with a wood grouse I could never forget. I heard her coming; by now I was quite familiar with that high pitched shriek and the sound of those beating wings. I had my camera around my neck and as I raised it to get a shot, BAM, she hit me. She actually flew right into the side of my face! I couldn't believe it; I was being attacked by a fat chicken. The impact stunned her and knocked her to the ground. In my initial shock of being struck in the face, I became angry. Then I heard the babies crying; hey, I couldn't hurt their mommy. There I stood, my glasses were lopsided on my face making everything a blur cause I can't see a damn thing without my glasses in front of my eyes, blood was trickling from my nose, and the babies were chirping louder and louder. I interpreted the baby bird's cries as, "Hey, get 'im mom! Boy oh boy, you see mom hit 'im with that left!" and, "Hit 'im again mom you got 'im in trouble!" The whole scene became quite humorous. She was actually on the ground but a second or so and flew off. I shared my wood grouse story with some locals as soon as I had opportunity, none of them had ever heard of a mother grouse carrying her guise to such extreme. They all surmised she must have been a new mother and she miscalculated. No one had a definite answer.

"Half the walk is but retracing our steps. We should go forth on the shortest walk, perchance, in the spirit of undying adventure, never to return... prepared to send back our embalmed hearts only as relics to our desolate kingdoms." ~ Henry David Thoreau

Moose in the Mist

**Figure 3 Moose in the Mist picture taken by me atop
Saddleback Jr. Mountain on the Appalachian Trail in Maine, 2000**

Maine, beautiful Maine! I had never been in Maine before, the beauty of Maine, in my mind, is hard to equal. To be on a mountain top and look in any direction and behold nothing but tree covered mountains and abundant lakes; lakes so remote, you seldom even see boats on them. Northern Maine is serenity, beautiful serenity and beautiful solitude.

I was in Maine and still had not seen a moose. Everyone else had, just not me. It was probably about 9:30 am and I was just reaching the summit of Saddleback Jr. and the whole mountain top was totally encased in a cloud. I had to strain to see even a few feet in front of me. I thought I saw movement just in front of me; I could barely make out the outline of a moose rising up from where she had been lying. She was less than twenty feet from me, directly on the trail. It seemed like she would never quit getting up. Her shoulders were as high as my head. She never moved after she stood up, she just stood there and stared at me. It was so unexpected; I had been told moose never go up to the higher altitudes. I had nowhere to go, there were no trees to climb. I was screwed. I decided to photograph my killer. So I took about eight pictures, she just kept looking at me. She soon tired of modeling, turned very slowly and stepped a few feet off the trail, so as to let me by. I took advantage of the opportunity and walked on past her. I looked back a few times to make sure she wasn't charging me, she was still there. I was so excited; I saw a real live moose up close and in person! I was pretty excited about still being alive too. I called my moose encounter, "Moose in the Mist."

A couple hours later I met two young men hiking south. I excitedly started telling them of the moose I had encountered just ahead of them and the wonderful opportunity they may have to see a real live moose. Instead of being impressed with my sighting, they informed me they were from Maine and that they saw moose all the time. I thought they were quite flippant about it. One of them even questioned that I really saw a moose; he said that moose weren't known to go up to the higher altitudes. How dare they not show interest in a man's first real eye to eye moose sighting.

It had been raining so I decided I would bed down for the night in a shelter. I hiked another ten miles to the Spalding Mountain lean-to. I got settled in after my meal and couldn't wait to tell the other occupants my exciting "Moose in the Mist" story. There were only two other hikers and I wanted a bigger audience to tell my adventure of a lifetime to! So, I decided to wait at least 'til dark to let my audience grow. It only grew by one, another north bounder like me. I started my story, "Hey, I ran into a huge moose cow this morning." The late arrival interrupted me and said, "Speaking of moose, I ran into two south bounders coming off Saddleback Mountain who said a big female moose kept them at bay for nearly two hours up on Saddleback Jr. They said she would not let them down the trail at all and even did a couple false charges at them before stepping off the trail, allowing them to make a run for it." "Were the two guys from Maine?" I asked. "Yeah, they did say they were from Maine." He said. I started laughing, the moose obviously had good discernment, and she hadn't liked them either. Now the story was even better. After I told my part of the story the four of us had a great time laughing. The late thru-hiker, like me, and the moose, hadn't cared for the Maine hikers either. I found out later from locals that in black fly season as it was, the moose go to higher altitudes to avoid the flies.

Mt Katahdin

Monson, Maine was the last town before the "Hundred Mile Wilderness", a stretch of wilderness about 115 miles long that ended at Mt. Katahdin, the end of the trail. I stayed in town for two days because of shin splints. They were so painful, and I would like to know how you get shin splints in both shins at the same time? It's an injury, how the hell does one shin know the other one has it and needs to start hurting too... huh? I increased my 'vitamin-I' intake and pushed onward. Somewhere soon after leaving Monson, I suffered a groin pull as well, talk about being miserable.

After his ascent of Mt. Katahdin in 1846, Henry David Thoreau described it so - *"I entered within the skirts of the cloud which seemed forever drifting over the summit...."* It appeared to Thoreau, *"as if some time it had rained rocks, and they lay as they fell on the mountain sides... they were the raw material of a planet dropped from an unseen quarry..."*

I made it to Mt. Katahdin on July 15, 2000; exactly one year after my little boy killed himself. As bad as the physical pain was from the groin pull and shin splints, the mental pain was much greater. Climbing Katahdin was a bitch for me. My daughter had made up a collage from pictures of our beautiful Stevie and added lines from a Lennie Kravitz song they both liked. I was to hang the collage from the famous wooden sign at the top of Katahdin. I had not looked at a picture of my little boy since I lost him, I just couldn't. I was dreading having to look at his picture. I had kept it hid in an envelope at the bottom of my pack.

**Figure 4, me placing pictures of my beautiful little boy, Stevie, and words composed
by his loving sister, Shelly, atop Mt. Katahdin, Appalachian Trail, July 15, 2000.**

Climbing Mt. Katahdin was the hardest part of the entire trail for me, it was extremely difficult and I was in intense pain. When I finally reached the summit there were probably twenty people up there, it was the first clear day in several days, some had been camped out for three days waiting for the weather to clear so as to climb Katahdin. There is a sign on the way up, a reminder of how quickly extremely severe weather can happen, *"DO NOT GO PAST THIS POINT AFTER 12:00 NOON NO MATTER THE TIME OF YEAR."* I struggled over the rocks to the famous sign denoting the terminus of the Appalachian Trail. I pulled out my daughter's tribute to her little brother and I immediately burst out in tears. I used a piece of wire and tied it to the sign, and just stood there sobbing. All were looking at me and I cared not. After my crying had ceased some, a woman who had climbed Katahdin with her two sons approached me. She told me her sons were 13 and 15. She told me someone had told her the reason for my anguish, and asked if I would mind sharing my story with her sons. I'm not positive of her motives; she only said she felt it would help them. There were a few others there and they listened as well. There were a lot of tears. I guess that was the first time my tragedy was used to help others. I had hiked the 2,175 miles from Springer Mountain in Georgia to Mt. Katahdin in Maine. I was a certified 2000 miler. But my real journey was just beginning....

Appalachian Trail ~ *John Davis*
To know the cold morning he simply
shifts inside his mummy bag
to measure the marbled sky:
so soft the valley and the first owls
voice and the bronze mountain
of maple trees and a whistling,
Somewhere in the giant hush of the forest
a whistling - a stream - a bird - a music
so simple he can hum it past hickory
and oak, always back to the oak
those leaves like stubby footprints.
He's taken to shaking their hands on the trail
and talking, gently talking to rocks
calling the pitch and white pines
by name down the trail, down
down to Georgia in the slow cold
of November as the pine needle trail
switches back and back up.
Beside his tent he eyes the merciful
and moth-like frost, scrunches low,
sights down the miniscule glaciers,
the coming snow. Maybe death will be a learning:
to squeeze into the cold and keep warm.
Maybe the spirit remains a wild blueberry and ripe.
But that whistling. What is that whistling?

My "LOVE LIFE" Walk Across America

It dawned on me while I was out on the Appalachian Trail, the horrible tragedy that had befallen me, happens to others. I was finding out the key to a happy life, no matter the situation; get your eyes off yourself. The easiest way to do that, turn your eyes toward others. I had no idea how I was going to go about it; I just knew I had to help others.

My mother lost two children, a little boy at 18 months and my 14 year-old twin sister. In her grief she nearly destroyed her life and the lives of her three other children. I was determined not to make the same mistake my dear mother had made. Emotions have energy and I believe grief is the strongest emotion. And I am certainly not alone in my belief that the loss of a child is by far the worse grief. So, my personal analogy was, my mother had unwittingly allowed the energy generated through her grief to do harm instead of good. We forgive you mom, as none of us have the right to judge a parent in their reaction to, and method of, handling the loss of their child. The terrible pain in their hearts blinds them. I wanted to convert my energy and aim it in the right direction.

Two things had been running through my mind constantly, the fact that in one of my son's suicide notes he had said he hoped some good could come out of his death. And on the day of his funeral, my daughter and I were in my bedroom trying to comfort each other. Shelly, all of sudden started yelling at me, "Damn you, damn you, why couldn't you have given Stevie your love for life!" I was completely stunned. I stammered out, "Honey, I didn't know I had a love for life." And from her little broken heart, she yelled back, "Of course you do you idiot! Just ask your friends, damn it!" She had never spoken to me that way. I reached out and took her in my arms; this was my other baby, the only one I had left. A few weeks later I did what my daughter said, I individually asked three different friends if they thought I had a love for life. All three laughed and basically said, "Sure you do."

So, I came up with this creed, I wanted no other parent to suffer the horror I had suffered, and I wanted no other young person to miss out on loving life. I was not able to give my own child my love for life but by God I was going to do everything I could to give it to the children of others. And some way, somehow, I would heed my son's words and make some good come out of his death.

I decided I had to get started practicing my new creed. I began calling every organization that pertained to helping young people and particularly those organizations aimed at youth suicide prevention. I also tried various religious groups, to no avail. I just didn't seem to fit in anywhere. I think it was mostly me, I just didn't feel comfortable with any of the groups I approached. So... I started my own damn group. I decided to walk across America with my message. I knew I couldn't walk up to every person I saw and say, "Hey, don't take your own life!" And then it hit me, "LOVE LIFE!" Loving life is the exact opposite of the depression which creates disdain for life. I would walk across the U.S.A. with a big sign over my head encouraging others to "LOVE LIFE."

"Pain is an unseen and powerful hand that breaks the skin of the stone in order to extract the pulp. Your pain is the breaking of the shell that encloses your understanding."
~ Kahlil Gibran

April 2001 I went to California for the very first time in my life and started my walk from Point Reyes National Seashore at the Pacific Ocean. My daughter would orchestrate my trip and keep tabs on my where about. On a Sunday in Sausalito, California with "LOVE LIFE" over my head and getting ready to cross the Golden Gate Bridge, thinking I was ready to share love of life with the world and walk across America. Very first car, driver yells, "You fuckin' idiot!" while flipping me off. Without hesitation, I responded, "Up yours!" There I stood, "LOVE LIFE" over my head and my middle finger held high. I had a long way to go…

Bridge Dancing

I still have no idea why I told all my friends back home in Vero Beach, Florida that I would dance across the Golden Gate Bridge. But being as I did say I would, I had no choice but to dance. I strapped on my "LOVE LIFE" sign just before I stepped onto the bridge. It would be my first time wearing the sign facing that much traffic, and if that wasn't embarrassing enough, I was going to dance! As I stepped onto the bridge I looked up and saw hundreds of cyclist coming toward me, and they all cheered as they saw my "LOVE LIFE" sign. Lots of cars were blowing their horns also. I just stood there; there was no way I was going to dance. What would I tell my friends when they asked me if I danced across The Golden Gate Bridge like I said I would? I had to dance. I turned my headset on and I started dancing. I felt like a complete idiot, but I had to stand by my word! As I danced and the cyclist and motorist yelled and honked out their approval, I actually started getting into it!

Okay, I conquered my fear of the dancing; I was in the middle of the Golden Gate taking a break beside one of the huge girders, out of the ferocious wind, I looked up. Coming toward me was a police cruiser, with its lights flashing, directly behind that, a huge truck with large flashing arrows running from the top and down each side. When I first saw the truck, the lights were flashing yellow. The police cruiser stopped beside me and the lights on the truck were now flashing red. "I'm in serious trouble, right?"

The officer gets out of the car and approaches me, as he walked toward me, a barrage of profanity poured from the cyclist and autos aimed at the poor officer. He had a big smile on his face, was super courteous, as he explained, "Sir, I'm going to have to ask you to remove your sign." And I very courteously asked, "Why?" He told me it was a law, no signs what-so-ever were permitted to be displayed on the Golden Gate Bridge. I said, "Sir, you and I both know, with the number of suicides committed off this bridge, this sign should be paraded up and down the bridge constantly." "I know." He answered, "But I have to do my job sir." Many, on the bridge were still hurling obscenities at him. I told him I would certainly comply. It was such a hassle to unhook from my cart; I asked if he would mind unhooking the sign for me. I explained that it was merely fastened with four Velcro straps. He unfastened the sign, placed it flat and on top my cart under a couple bungee cords securing my load.

The officer was almost back in his car and I yelled over the roar of the wind and the obscenities, "Hey, can I still keep on dancin'?" "Absolutely, keep on dancin'!" The fine gentleman yelled back. Just as the officer was starting to pull out and the big arrows on the truck had changed to flashing green, I made my first step forward. As soon as I was out of the protection of the girder, the wind hit my sign just right, breaking the rigidity of the sign and caused the top part of the sign to be perfectly upright on top of the cart, and very readable. The people on the bridge erupted into cheers and yelled out what they saw, "LOVE LIFE!" I turned and saw the officer point to the sign. I shrugged and mouthed out, "you did it sir!" There was really nothing the poor guy could do. Traffic was starting to move and the crowd was yelling like crazy. He just shook his head, motioned with his hand for me to continue and mouthed, "Never mind, go on." I stuck the earbuds back in to the sounds of *The Rolling Stones* singing *Honkytonk Women* and continued dancing. I was cheered the rest of the way across the bridge.

Big Horse, Vintage BMW

On a Saturday, near Point Reyes, National Seashore, California, trying to follow the American Discovery Trail. I encountered a very beautiful young lady, late twenties perhaps. She was astride the highest horse I've ever seen. She was wisely wearing a helmet due to his immense size. She said he was a freak, both parents were average size. I forget how many hands she said the beautiful animal was. Anyway, her horse and my sign brought on conversation. She suffered from depression she revealed. We discussed it at length. When I mentioned the Appalachian Trail, she said her boyfriend aspired to do the Pacific Crest Trail. She said the three things he cared about most, her, his vintage BMW, and a desire to do the PCT. She pointed out that it was impossible though to hike the PCT because she just could not be left alone for six months.

I disagreed with her. I told her that it could very well be the best thing ever for both of them. That she should encourage him and help orchestrate his trip. That she could join him at some of the really great and beautiful places the PCT passes through. She could meet him at motels and hostels along the way. She could find great spots to stay, to eat, and pick him up off the trail and go enjoy them together. And that perhaps she may even want to hike a little with him and even tent with him some?? You should have seen that pretty girls face when I mentioned being in a tent! Hilarious. I talked right past it though. I told her it could be the most romantic thing they've ever done. I asked her if she loved him as much as he loved her. I asked her if she wanted to stay in depression or be healed. I told her I felt her present situation in Life was based around fear. She was hard, let me tell you. She nodded yes a couple times to some things I said. Then, the tears started coming, yup, she loved somebody as much as herself! She towered over me sitting on that magnificent animal, and I feel she at first felt that an advantage, looking down on someone suggesting she change her secure little world. Well, I'm one persistent little bastard, and, I had truth on my side. She pulled herself together. She said, while sniffling, and now avoiding eye contact with me, "Thank you." And maneuvered that fine steed around me and was gone.

Well, Monday morning after our encounter, I'm walking through the busy morning traffic of San Rafael, California, displaying my "LOVE LIFE" sign, and all of sudden, some nutcase starts blowing his horn again and again. I look up as he is passing me and he is going absolutely nuts in his car! He has both hands off the wheel at times. He is alternating pumping both fists in the air and he is screaming! He was actually jumping around his car as he passed me! I swear the guy was nuts! I'm standing there totally bewildered by this exhibition, as I'm certain were the other observers from their cars, when it finally dawned on me... he was driving a vintage BMW! Talk to people, care about them, and just love them.

"Love is the strongest and yet, gentlest power in the Universe. Loves power is manifested thorough gentleness and patience. Those we Love, we can more easily be gentle and patient with. Gentleness and patience are obviously, instruments of Love. Let's use them then on every fellow human being we have opportunity to display them to, and not only to our closest loved ones. We need not run up to every individual and shout, "I Love you!" We need only to practice gentleness and patience to display Love, to change, each, our little portion of the world. If we all were each gentle and patient with all, the condition of human kind would start to change immediately. The power of Love would take over and change the world. It all starts with a Love Life attitude. Let's Love Life and start watching our own little portion of the world begin to change." ~ Steve Fugate

Making Movies

Figure 5. Camera car for Nissan commercial.

Figure 6. With production crew Nissan commercial.

I had just entered U. S. highway 50 at Pollock Pines, California. Since entering California a little over two weeks before, I would be traversing my first major four lane highway. I decided to get off the trails due to rumors of several feet of snow still on some foot trails in the Sierra's.

I had been on the highway for ten minutes or so when it dawned on me that I had noticed no traffic. Just as this was dawning on me I look to my left, and just off the highway were a man and woman with walkie-talkies in their hands and they were staring at me with their mouths agape. With my biggest smile, I waved to them, they did nothing but stare, as if they were refusing to recognize my existence! I thought, "What stuck-up assholes." Just around the bend, I saw another couple to my right. They too had walkie-talkies and a look of disbelief with mouths opened wide. At least the woman waved back, half-heartedly, anyway. Then I look up in front of me and there is a California State Trooper pulling his cruiser right up to me, his lights flashing, and he is laughing. He gets out of the car and walks toward me shaking his head and laughing. Between the laughter, he says, "You have made my day! No, wait a minute; you probably have made my year!" And I said, "I am happy to provide such entertainment for you sir, would you be so kind as to explain how this came about?" Still laughing between sentences' he explained to me that they had just shut down 25 miles of this scenic stretch of winding highway 50 through the Sierra's to film a Nissan commercial. Doing the filming of the commercial was a production company out of L.A. with a 45 man crew plus two professional NASCAR drivers to do the driving at speeds up to 125 miles per hour. They had stopped all vehicular traffic at all entrances to the highway. Because of always walking toward traffic, I had entered via an exit instead of one of the entrance ramps. They had everything secured and ready to go. The driver of both the new prototype Nissan and the 1975 Ford Ranchero powered by a 428 big block and converted to a camera car, were staged and ready to go! And then... here comes this complete moron walking toward them with a big sign over his head, "LOVE LIFE." And he is waving at everyone, more proof, he is the complete moron. And I thought *they* were acting like idiots.

The trooper was equipped with a walkie-talkie to directly communicate with the production crew. They are asking him what the hell is going on and when can they begin filming. It has to be costing them lots of money every minute they are held up. The trooper calmly (between chuckles) tells them he has to ask me some questions; I think he was enjoying making them wait, I found out later how much locals in the Sierra's resent 'outsiders' from Southern California.

The trooper asked me (between more chuckles) for ID and if I were an American citizen. I answered yes and proudly handed him my "Sunshine State" driver's license. He hands my license back and then keys the walkie-talkie to make sure they hear too, he begins to explain, "Because this is a federal highway and you are an American citizen, I cannot legally stop you from continuing your forward progress. I can only ask you to." He then proceeded to very courteously ask me if I would please leave the highway momentarily and apologized for the inconvenience to me. You could hear the groaning coming from the walkie-talkie. I think the trooper was really enjoying it. I said, "Why don't they just leave me in the commercial, I think it would be a unique addition?" He said, "I already suggested that, I told them they should zoom in on you and your sign and say, 'If you want to love life like this guy does, buy a new Nissan!' He said they were not amused. Now we were both laughing.

Going along with the jovial mood I said, "These are my demands, I want a Gatorade every fifteen minutes and a chair to sit in while I drink it." Again, we laughed, but I did start walking toward the next spot where I could get completely off the highway. There was a nice young man there and he did have a soda and a chair for me. He explained everything to me as we waited for the two machines to come roaring down through the Sierra's. It was extremely exciting. And then we heard the roar of the big block 428 breaking the peace of the mountains. And I had a front row seat. Watching them film that car going through those Sierra curves at that high rate of speed was fantastic. I was at a live movie!

After that segment of filming, the production company waited before moving to the next "shoots" for me to walk where they were, allowing me to visit with the crew, meet the drivers, and take pictures of the camera car. I was not allowed to take pictures of the new Nissan though, so what, I wanted to see that big block 428 Ranchero. They were all very courteous to me; it was a tremendous adventure for me. I saw the trooper two days later and he was still laughing.

Eric Zimmerman

It was a very hot summer day and I was getting ready to cross some of the most arid and desolate lands in the United States. Knowing this, I was starting to question just what the hell was I thinking to take on such an enormous and challenging undertaking. I had just entered Fallon, Nevada, the home of the U.S. Navy Fighter Weapons School, also known as "TOPGUN," when I saw a very skinny little guy with nothing on but a pair of Levi's that appeared to have been put on brand new, at least a year before and then never washed. They were completely tattered at the bottoms from scraping the ground due to not staying up on his skinny body; they had nothing to hang onto. The parts of him not covered by the dirt stiffened Levi's, looked like a piece of dark leather left out in the sun way too long. He was walking toward me very fast and before I knew it, he was right in my face. I mean, literally, right in my face. "Hi!" he said, "My name's Eric Zimmerman!" Now, like most people, I do not like someone putting their face right up into my face like that! And just as I was thinking, "Eric Zimmerman, if you do not get your face out of mine, I'm going to make a nice ladies handbag out of your skinny little ass," I looked down and saw Eric's bony little hand outstretched to shake mine. That's when I looked in Eric's eyes and saw the simple sweetness. His eyes were dancing along with his laughter. He was in his own little world. Eric then said, "Love life huh, I love life too! I'm gonna' get me one of them "LOVE LIFE" signs and walk all over with it!" "Yeah, you do that Eric Zimmerman" I said, now laughing as well. Eric walked away still laughing and seemingly very much delighted with the idea of getting his very own "LOVE LIFE" sign!

After I left Eric Zimmerman, I got to thinking, I thought Eric Zimmerman was nuts, yet Eric Zimmerman loved my sign and thought it a great idea to walk all over the country with it just like I was doing. Maybe Eric Zimmerman wasn't the only nut in our brief encounter. That's the convenience of being nuts… we're always happy! LOVE LIFE with all your heart before anything else in your life and you may just find yourself being looked at by some, as a little nuts.

"Make sure your friends all think you might be a little nuts but have your neighbors convinced." ~ Steve Fugate

A Hug and a Beer

I was crossing the Shoshone Indian Reservation just outside of Fallon, Nevada. The temperature was past a hundred and felt like it was climbing. This was my first time walking in desert lands; I was on route 50, America's Loneliest Highway. I was a little anxious about the next fifty miles into the town of Cold Springs, the nearest water. There was a little store and gas station there and it would be my last place to stop before Cold

Springs. I was sitting on the ground out in front of the store having a couple hot dogs and my last ice cold drink for awhile. An old really beat up pick-up truck pulled up just to the right of me. I caught just a glimpse of a very big Shoshone Indian climbing out the passenger side. He had long black braids hanging out of a dust filled, once black cowboy hat. And he obviously had had a little too much to drink. I quickly looked away; I just didn't care to be bothered. I was in an unusual mood; I think I was more worried about crossing my first stretch of desert, than I was letting myself realize. The big Indian just stopped right in front of me, staring at me and my cart and my "LOVE LIFE" sign. I ignored him. And then he spoke, very slow, "What are you doing?" God, I did not want to be bothered. He repeated, "What are you doing?" "I am walking across America." I finally answered. Then he immediately and very matter-of-factly asked, "Why?" I was really in a funk and just didn't want to converse; I am certain that was the only time in all my walks I ever allowed myself to be in that kind of mood. I answered, "Because I've never done it before." He was not going to go away, he then says, "But why do you have that sign?" "Cause I love life!" I said my irritation showing. "Why?" He wanted to know. I told him that I just thought it was a nice thing to say. "But why?" he said, "And why are you walking with that sign?" Wanting the conversation with this drunken Indian to end, I finally said, "God told me to!" "No shit?" He said. "No shit." I answered. And with a stunned look on his face, he said, "I didn't know God talked to you white guys." I said, "Well, he talks to me." He turned to face his truck and the Indian woman at the wheel and yells, "Hey honey, God told this guy to walk across America and by God he's doin' it!" He turns back to me and says, "By God I'm buyin' you a beer!" "By God I'll drink it!" I answered. A few minutes later he handed me an ice cold beer. He said, "By God I'm going to give you a hug!" And I said, "By God I'll take it!" He gave me a big bear hug and walked off laughing. Now I was in a great mood and ready to tackle the desert. Hell, all I needed was a hug and a beer... by God!

I've limited my bad days to three minutes and it has been a long time since I've had to use the whole three minutes ~ Steve Fugate

Justice

I was walking through the town of Montrose, Colorado and the morning was beautiful. As I walked down the pleasant tree lined street, a lady was walking toward me pushing a baby stroller. I couldn't help but notice how very beautiful the little girl in the stroller was. She was absolutely gorgeous, with coal black hair and big dark eyes. "Snow White" came to mind. I remember thinking though that the child seemed a little old for a stroller. She looked to be maybe six.

The child's mother started the conversation by inquiring about my beautiful "LOVE LIFE" sign (always a good conversation starter) I started telling my story. Something about the black haired little angel caught my attention, it seemed as though the movement of her little head and her beautiful dark eyes did not coincide. I bent down to the little one and said, "And what is your name precious?" She did not respond. Her mother spoke up, "This is Justice." And then she added something that seemed a little odd to point out, "She was given that name at birth."

And then my world was rocked. Mother, very matter of fact says, "Justice has permanent brain damage, when she was an infant, her father threw her against the wall." I instantly blurted out, "May he rot in hell!" I was the father of two; I was out there walking the Nation because I had lost one. I had only one left, my little girl; my beautiful and precious little girl. How could anyone do this?! Shocked is a very inadequate word for that moment. But I did manage to regroup and say, "I'm sorry, I had no right to say that." The mother disagreed with me, for she very calmly said, "Why of course you did."

She told me she had concentrated much energy over the past few years on that same mindset. She said the realization came to her though, her anger was wasted energy and she found something else to channel her energy toward. She and a group of other courageous young mothers had just returned from a weekend visit to the state prison where the natural father of Justice was incarcerated. They went there because he was going up before a parole board. In her words, again very calmly spoken, "We were there to make sure the scumbag stayed where he belongs." And he did. Thank God they were successful. This group of courageous women joins forces whenever necessary and uses their energy to keep other dangerous people in prison.

I was preparing to leave and just had to say, "God bless you!" A very proud mommy grabbed the moment and said, "Justice knows about God, God and the angels." And bending down toward the real angel, she says, "Honey, show the nice man where the angels are." I could see no way she could comprehend that suggestion or for that matter, any suggestion. Mommy repeated several times, there was no response. I saw a proud mom trying to show off her little girl's abilities. You know how they never say "dada" or "mama" when you want them to. My heart was breaking, watching that oh so proud mommy trying to persuade that precious little darling to point up to where angels are said to dwell. So I bent down real close to little Justice, and with my finger pointed skyward, I said, "Sweetheart, can you show me where the angels are?" A sweet delicate little hand reached out and gripped my finger. Mother was satisfied, and I was changed. I just didn't know how profound a change it was, not yet.

Over the next few months I became more and more aware of what I was supposed to be doing. I am now convinced; when Justice gripped my finger, I received a life changing transfusion.

Slow Down!

I was in Kansas, and it was hot. For the last two days I had been suffering from chafing in the groin area, commonly referred to by us guys as, "crotch rot." Well, while eating at a diner earlier in the day, I was talking with the cook and he told me he heard that the heat index was already 101 degrees. I mentioned that I would have a miserable day walking due to my chafing problem until I was able to get to a store to purchase some medicated powder. The sympathetic cook told me that he had just the thing and went into his kitchen. He came out with a one-gallon Zip-loc bag filled with cornstarch. "Here," he said, "This'll fix you right up. Works better 'n any damn drugstore stuff!"

Later in the day as it became even hotter, my little problem started becoming unbearable. I was looking for a place to step off the road and address the problem with large amounts of cornstarch. There was another problem; there was nothing to hide in or even behind of, to treat myself, to powder my behind, if you will. In Kansas, they jokingly say that their state tree is a telephone pole. The highway was straight and there was neither tree nor building in sight. And there was lots of traffic so I definitely needed some concealment.

Finally, I spotted a little gas station off in the distance. As I approached the much needed oasis, I was stopped by one of a group of migrant Mexican workers who were standing around refreshing themselves from a day of hard work in the fields. He spoke English, however, with a very strong accent, "Hey, watchyoo doin' muhn? Watchyoo sign for muhn?" I was in a huge hurry and really did not want to engage in conversation at that moment. I was in a lot of pain. I answered, "I'm just reminding everyone to love life, that's all." He nodded and asked, "Watchyoo name Muhn?" At that moment I felt my old Appalachian Trail 'trail name' to be quite appropriate and told him, "No Clue." And not wanting to be rude, I explained, "Hey man, I can't really talk right now I've got to get to the restroom real quick, I will talk with you some more after I come out." As I started for the door to the gas station, the inquisitive Mexican stopped me with, "No muhn, the baffroom in the bach muhn." "Oh, thank you." I said, and headed for the rear of the building.

To my anguish, both the men's and women's restrooms had "out of order" on the doors! The building was located fairly close to the totally straight highway which made it difficult to not be seen by the numerous automobiles driving past. But I was desperate, I moved as close to the building as possible and dropped my drawers. I reached into the one gallon Zip-Loc bag, came out with a handful of cornstarch and slapped it on my behind. I can now relate as to why an infant coos when powder is applied to its behind. It felt wonderful. I wanted to assure the job was done thoroughly, so I quickly grabbed another handful and applied it to the front part. I then pulled up my shorts as quickly as possible and headed for the front of the building so as not to draw attention to myself. In my joy of a powdered butt, I had forgotten just how light cornstarch is and how it fills the air when using. I stepped back around to the front of the building to where the inquisitive Mexican and his friends were laughing. "Hey No Clue, you gonna' haff to slow down muhn!" "What?" I answered dumbfounded. In a fit of laughter, he said, "you gonna' haff to slow down muhn, dey's smoke comin' out you ass!" The guy standing next to him, also laughing, said, "No muhn, it too late muhn, dat's white smoke muhn! You dun blowed up you motor muhn!" This brought even more laughter from the two. I didn't care, my butt was powdered, I was coo-ing, and good to go! I don't always plan on making people laugh, but it sure is nice when it happens.

Somebody's Daddy

Just outside a little community not too far east of Kansas City, Missouri, a gentleman yelled for me to cross the road where he had his tailgate down with a spread of Hardees breakfast sandwiches, biscuits & gravy, two large coffees, lots of those little cups of cream, both sugar and sweetener packets, orange juice, a banana and an apple. He said, "My daughter called me this morning, said she saw you walking in the rain on her way to work and said, Daddy, that's somebody's daddy, will you go feed him and make sure he's okay, I would want someone to help my daddy." He went on to say, "That's my little girl, we raised her to be that way. I gotta back 'er up. Didn't know which breakfast sandwich you'd prefer, so I got 'em all. I gotta big bag of snacks for the road for you too." Yes, I am somebody's daddy.

Two Curious Girls, One Not

I had just walked into St. Genevieve, Missouri where I was planning to catch a ride on the ferry across the Mississippi to Illinois when a car pulled up with three young women, probably all in their early twenties. The two young ladies in the front were excited about my sign and insisted I tell them all about it. The young lady in the back seat however, seemed to have no interest at all. In fact, she seemed aggravated at me and every time I gave her the common courtesy of looking in her direction from time to time, she would turn her head away. I was not deterred at all due to the excited questioning coming from the other two. This was my first trip across America and I was still having a hard time telling of my son's suicide and I became very emotional. I told everything in detail, of how my son's self-centered decision had near destroyed the lives of me, his mother, and sister. Of the horrible pain it had caused his other relatives and friends. I told of how I was coming to realize that the pain would never go away completely, that I would just have to adjust to living with it. I started crying when I told of how I didn't want any other parent to ever have to go through the living horror I had to face after my only son's suicide. The young sweet driver told me she wanted to take my picture and would I mind waiting while she went home to get her camera. I told them I was walking to the ferry dock that was still a couple miles away and I would look for them.

About 45 minutes later they found me and the driver emerged from her car with camera in one hand and a twenty in the other. I immediately started protesting and insisted the money wasn't necessary. She kept walking toward me and when she got close enough to me, she got a very serious look on her face and she whispered, "You have to take this money, please!" She was motioning back toward her car with her eyes. I could see that there was more of a motive than just handing me the money. As she handed me the money, talking very fast, she whispered to me, "Look, you may very well have saved our friends life! She tried to kill herself just a few days ago and has been under watch at her parent's since being released from the hospital. Her parent's reluctantly let her go with us for a while today because we are her best friends. On the way to my house to get the camera she started crying and apologizing to both us and saying over and over that she had had no idea the pain she was causing! She was really hurt by what she was ignorantly doing to the people who care about her!" And as she was telling me where she wanted me to pose for the pictures, she sneaked in another whisper with tears in her sweet caring eyes, "Thank you sir!" That little girl in the back seat was certainly blessed with two fine friends. That "LOVE LIFE" sign, many times causes just the right people to stop.

"I've encountered way too many in deep despair when all they had to do was disconnect from society's conforming herd mentality and quit trying to fit in with everybody else. There is a stick of positive dynamite within each of us ready to be lit when we find our very own intrinsic innate individuality and break from society's herds."
~ Steve Fugate

The Shoes

Just a few miles outside Evansville, Indiana I stopped to call my daughter and let her know I was okay. I tried to speak to her at least every four days to keep her from worrying. The first thing she asked, "Daddy, how are your shoes?" I didn't want her to worry so I lied and said they were fine. The truth, the soles were nearly gone and the gravel was coming in. After I reassured her, I continued on my way to Evansville. My stomach was growling in anticipation of a meal at Mickey D's. I called their $1.00 double cheeseburger, "McFilet Mignon." Sure beat the hell out of Ramen noodles! I didn't have any money, which really didn't matter; my needs just always seem to be met, in every way.

A lady pulled up beside me in a beat up old car and commented that she liked my beautiful 'LOVE LIFE' sign. She told me that God had put upon her heart to give me some money. She told me she was very shy and bashful by nature so this was quite hard for her to do. I told her I did not accept money unless the giver heard my story. She listened and I accepted the money. Now I could get my "McFilet Mignon."

Once in Evansville I located the nearest Mickey D's. A police officer on duty in the restaurant asked if he could join me. He proceeded to ask questions about my walk. We were deep in conversation when I looked up from my "McFilet Mignon" and there in front of me was my timid benefactor. I had not seen her for nearly an hour and as is in most cases, I thought I would never see her again. She forgot all about her shyness and blurted out, "Thank God I found you; I saw your "LOVE LIFE" sign outside. I disobeyed God, I really did. I disobeyed God." I am totally confused and thinking, "This cop is going to arrest both our goofy butts." So I said, "No ma'am, you did not, had it not been for you I would not be here eating." "No, no," She said, "God told me to buy you a pair of shoes and I gave you a little money instead. Now tell me your shoe size and I'll go buy you a pair of shoes." To which I responded, "No ma'am you do not have to do that, I'll be fine." The cop then, instead of cuffing us together, said to me, "You better do what she says 'cause you don't wanna' piss off God."

She took my shoe size and said she would be back in within thirty minutes. I filled the officer in on the whole story and even though he getting off duty, he insisted on staying around to see if she would indeed come back with the shoes. True to her word, she returned in a half hour. In her hands was a pair of New Balance running shoes! On the box I saw a $79.95 price tag. I could see she probably didn't have a lot of money, and feeling bad I said, "Ma'am, you really should not have spent that much money." She said, "I didn't, I only had $50.00 but I felt this to be the pair God wanted me to get. I told the salesman at Foot Locker what you were doing, what I was doing, and he let me have them for what I had on me." I thanked her profusely and then was forced to say, "Ma'am, I don't want to look the gift horse in the mouth but these shoes are a half size off and if you tell me where the store is I'll walk there and exchange them myself." She looked me straight in the eye and said, "That's the pair He told me to get; you put 'em on and they'll fit." And then she left. The cop looked at me and said, "I thought you said she was shy?"

I put them on and wore them all the way to the end of my journey at Cape Henlopen State Park in Delaware. They were the best fitting pair I wore during the entire 4,858 mile journey.

"Your daily life is your temple and your religion. When you enter into it take with you your all." ~ Kahlil Gibran

Indiana Rescue

Just outside Canaan, Indiana and walking in a cold drizzling rain. I was in an area where I just could not find a good place to pitch my tent and as a result I was walking in the dark. I usually avoided this situation; it is way too dangerous, as the drivers just cannot see you well at night. An Indiana state trooper stopped and said he barely saw me and was concerned about my safety. I explained my situation to him and told him I was trying to make it to the next little town, Canaan. He said I was nearly there, within a half mile. He told me the only thing in town was a little country store and it did serve sandwiches. He advised me to use extreme caution and that he would tell the owner of the store that I was on my way in. He was not sure what time they closed and he wanted to ensure that I was able to get something to eat.

I made it to the little store about thirty five minutes before they closed. For some reason the lady who owned the store was very curt with me. It was obvious she didn't care for me being there. I asked if she could make me a sandwich, she said it was too late but there was a pre-made bologna and cheese sandwich in the cooler. I don't particularly care for bologna, but hey, when you're hungry... As I was paying too much for my sandwich I asked the lady if I could sit at the tables they had in the rear of the store. Even though she was still thirty minutes from closing, she snapped a very adamant, "No!" And as she was putting my change on the counter, I said something I know I shouldn't have said, "Lady, the state of Indiana has been wonderful to me, please don't ruin it." She turned immediately to the phone on the wall behind her and started dialing. Oh Christ, I thought, she's either calling the police, her seven foot tall husband, or her son who was probably seven and a half feet tall. At any rate, I went out the door, grabbed my stuff and took off as fast as possible. I was hoping to find a place quickly to avoid any confrontation with cops or giant family members.

About two blocks, I came to a really old Methodist church. I immediately headed up its drive toward the back. What I found was a cemetery on a hill with not even one flat place suitable for pitching a tent. The building was an old brownstone with a metal fire escape lit up by a naked light bulb under a metal shield. I sat down on the fire escape in the cold rain and started eating the very old sandwich. I started to feel sorry for myself, but I caught it and did not allow myself to go there. I knew self-pity wouldn't change a thing, it never does. So, there I sit in the cold and I decided to sum up my situation. I looked out at the tombstones and decided that Mr. Oliver Jones' grave might be a little more level than the rest. So, Mr. Jones it would be; I would pitch my tent atop Mr. Jones.

Within minutes of having accepted my situation, out of the corner of my eye I saw the light of headlights shining into the graveyard. A car was coming up the driveway to the church. I started getting my response together in my mind for whoever was after me. To the 7 ft. tall husband or to the even bigger son, I would say, "I am so sorry for my tone of voice toward your wife/mother, I was tired and not thinking clearly, please forgive me, I meant no disrespect." To the policeman I would apologize and hope for the best. I was thinking that at least I would be warm in jail. I still really did not want to go to jail though. The vehicle came around the building with its headlights directly on me. It was a fairly new Jeep Cherokee. The small (not 7 ft.) bearded driver got out and walked toward me. "We thought you might have come up here, my wife and I saw you earlier walking into town, but we were on our way somewhere else and couldn't pick you up at the time. We were wondering if you would like to spend the night at our home, get something to eat and clean up. My wife can do some laundry for you too, if you like." I was stunned! But not too stunned to grab my gear and get my little ass inside that warm jeep in record time.

My hosts were Harold and Lilly. They were both nurses. Harold and I talked for a long time covering an assortment of topics, one being whether a God truly existed or not. The next morning I left with a clean body, clean clothes, a full belly, and Lilly prepared a sack full of food for the road. Hartley drove me back to where he had picked me up. As I was preparing to exit his Jeep, he told me that when he and Lillian first moved to the Canaan area, they decided to attend church. After just a short while they realized it was not what they were seeking and soon left. He went on to explain that one lady and her family controlled the church and it was obvious that all matters of the church went the way she dictated. And then as I was stepping onto the street he said, "You know that woman who gave you a hard time in her store? She's the one at the church."

"I don't do church, years in business taught me to eliminate the middleman whenever possible. The middleman not only causes the price to rise, it greatly reduces the chance of actually meeting the real producer of the product" ~ Steve Fugate

Walk through DC in the Daytime *not* the Nighttime

On my first walk across America I attempted to use The American Discovery Trail as my route across. From having successfully hiked the entire Appalachian Trail I was accustomed to how organized it was. It was marked approximately every one tenth of a mile with a white blaze painted on trees and rocks, it was nearly impossible to get lost on it. Not so with the American Discovery Trail, in spite of having purchased the official American Discovery Trail map set. I was getting lost so much, I was forced to follow correlating highways most of the time.

I was in Washington D.C. on a bike trail in a city park designated as part of the American Discovery Trail. I was delighted I had finally got back on the official trail. And then, like so many times before, the trail ended with no more markings. I accidentally found the street I was supposed to be on though. It was starting to get dark and I did not want to get stuck in the middle of D.C. with nowhere to camp. And once again, my American Discovery Trail instructions failed me. The street I was on did not take me where the instructions said it would! Not wanting to be stuck in the residential area I was in, I began walking toward a busier area that I could see several blocks in front of me.

I came to a bus stop where several people were waiting, they were all black, as most of the population of D.C. is African American. As I approached with intentions of asking for directions, a young black woman quipped regarding my "LOVE LIFE" sign, "Love life huh? I'll love ya' baby!" A couple of people chuckled. A hooker maybe, or just wanting to get a laugh? I don't know and I didn't care! It was approaching night fall, and I was lost in a large city. A large city with probably the highest crime rate in America. And, I didn't have even enough money to take a cab, let alone for a motel room. I directed my question to one particular man, "Sir could you tell me please, will this street take me to Route 50 and out of the city?" It became quite obvious I had a made the wrong choice, when he answered, "Whadda' fuck ya axin' me fo... ders a police station right oer der muthafucka'!" as he pointed just a few buildings away. I thanked him and headed for the police station.

The police station was locked! I knocked on the door a few times and there was no response. I probably should have been more persistent and kept knocking until someone came to the door. My independent nature I guess? At any rate, just as I was leaving the police station, a taxi pulled up next to me. The black driver motioned me over to the passenger side door, " Hey man, ya' look lost, ya' alright, ya' needs a ride man?" I explained that I didn't have cab fare, but I could sure use some directions. The gentleman gave me perfect directions to where I needed to be. I thanked him and I expressed my concern at not having enough time to get there before nightfall. He then said, "Look man, ya sees that big brown buildin' down there.. dats a church, it'll be across from Mickey D's. Well, behinds that church is some kinda ol' Civil Wars fort or sumpin' likes that. Anyways, I'm thinkin' ya' can find someplace to maybe sleeps down there or sumpin?" I thanked him over and over! He said, "It's okay man, you just take care of yoself, okay?" I told him I would certainly try and headed for the church.

It was dark by the time I reached the site where the Civil War earthen fort had once been. It was on a knoll and I could see the lights of private residences in back of it. There were spaces in the walls where cannon once were. Now, the stone floor was completely covered with a layer of broken wine and beer bottles. There was a fairly level area of grass nearby where I could even pitch my tent.

Just as I started to pitch my tent, I heard the voices of some young girls. It was four teenage black girls and they were asking each other what they thought I might be doing. They seemed really nervous about my presence. I decided to take the initiative and approach them to make sure they knew I didn't mean them any harm. I went up to them and told them I had walked there from California and was walking across the United States. Just as they were relaxing a little, realizing I wasn't some weirdo, up walks three young black males. They were there to meet with the girls and the last thing they wanted to encounter was some old white guy getting in their way. The biggest guy starts in on me. "Wadda' fuck ya' doin' 'ere man?" He snapped. And another asked, "What's ya white ass doin' here man?" I don't mind telling you, I was scared shit-less! A white man in a hidden area of an all-black neighborhood, facing three young black men who all could have played football and were street wise and tough. And they were pissed! They were pissed because I was messing with their plans of scoring with the ladies and, I was white! I acted as if the young men weren't angry at all and I continued telling my story to the ladies and my new audience. I immediately let them know that I was walking because my beautiful baby boy had killed himself. I made a point to keep referring to my son as my baby (not a difficult distinction for me to make). I've never known an African American that wasn't a loving mommy, so I was working on the girls maternal instincts. I told them he was my only son and that my walk was also for my healing. At that time, I still couldn't speak of my son without tears. My strategy worked. The biggest male told me I had to leave there, and all four of the young women yelled at him in unison, telling all of them to leave me alone. One young woman said, "Dat man done loss 'is baby... you all jus' betta leab 'im alone!" The young men were speechless now. It was obvious what they were after, and now, the girls were getting upset with them. Finally, the bigger guy, the obvious leader, started asking me questions as if he were really interested in what the hell I was doing. And then he really decided to score points with the ladies and he gave me two dollars and told me to walk down to Mickey D's and get me two burgers. He told one of them to go with me and make sure no one bothered me. He even said, "We'll watch yo shit fer ya' man." The girls were now swooning over him... he was not stupid. He liked what they had more than he disliked what I was, thank God!

When we entered that restaurant of nothing but black people, it was instant looks and just as instant, making sure they were not staring. I have no idea who those guys were, but one would have to be an idiot to not know they carried clout in that neighborhood. My body-guard watched me like a hawk while I ordered my two burgers. He insisted on carrying them back for me, other than that we never spoke a word to each other. But I knew he would not have let anyone bother me. After we got back, the seven of them went over to the other side of the earthen fort and went down the knoll a little and out of my site. I heard them giggling and laughing every once in a while.

I got my tent pitched and was trying to sleep. It was a Saturday night, and there were the sound of sirens and gun shots all night long. In the Nation's capital! I was still concerned for my safety, I was in a bad spot. I found myself starting to really feel sorry for myself due to the situation I was still in. I still had to walk out of there the next morning, a quiet Sunday morning, when all the good people are still sleeping. I found myself not being able to sleep. I was frightened, I kept thinking of different scenarios, "What if those three young blacks later decided to come back and get the white guy?" And, "What if some other black people found out I was there and wanted to hurt me because I was white?" Out of fear, those kind of thoughts were in my mind most of the night. And then, sometime towards morning a sobering question popped into my thoughts, out of nowhere, "What if you had been a black man in earlier Selma, Alabama, or Jackson, Mississippi, in the same situation you are now in, only surrounded by whites." I didn't want to look at the horror that someone other than myself might have had to face. I only wanted to look at my own situation, right now! I couldn't believe it, there I was, in possible danger, and I was having to look at the absolute horror of racial prejudices. Because of my present situation I came to realize, I would not have wanted to be a black man in a white world prior to the enforcement of The Civil Rights Act in America. Maybe the reason there are so many Blacks in the District of Columbia is they went there to feel safe.

I woke up very hesitant about still having to walk out of the area I was in. I left around 6:00 am after the gunshots, and sirens, subsided. I walked past the police station, still locked and no activity in or around it. I continued on a couple of blocks following instructions of the kind taxi driver. I heard some yelling and cursing from across the street. Out of the corner of my eye, were three young black men, all staring and yelling obscenities at me from a laundromat. I never changed my pace and I don't think they knew I even gave them a glance. I'm somewhat street wise myself. I continued on toward the nice looking residential area I could see up the street. The three decided for some reason, not to harass me any farther. I had to consider, no one burned a cross in front of me, I certainly never had a rope placed around my neck, and I had not been physically harmed in any way. An hour or so later I found myself walking through a delightful and normal looking neighborhood, all black. Many people were coming out of their homes all dressed up and headed for church. Most all greeted me a cheerful good morning.

Careful What You Ask For

You know that phrase, "Be careful what you ask for." Well, I disregarded it and paid the price! I was somewhere in Eastern Maryland getting very close to ending my first walk across the United States. I found myself longing for female companionship. I was convinced I needed me a female companion and that was the only thing really missing in my life. I actually said this, out loud even, "Hey God, I want me a woman! And ya' know what, I ain't never had me no redhead. I want me a redhead." And after even deeper thought, I added, "A redhead with big tits, and hey, if she has a little money, that would be okay too." I swear, I really said that.

Well, I finished my walk across America and had been home for about three weeks and I spotted this beautiful redhead at a dance I went to. And guess what she had? Yup, this gorgeous redhead had big tits. I had actually met her once at another dance just before I left to walk across America. She was then seeing someone else, so I hadn't pursued my interest in her. She recognized me also and knew I had just finished my walk across the country. We started conversing and I was totally charmed by her. After the place closed we went to a restaurant where we drank coffee and talked until 3:00 in the morning.

The next day she called and invited me to her place for sushi. When I arrived at her beautiful three story beach house right smack on the ocean, I realized that I had even been granted the part about "if she has a little money..." Wow, I now had the perfect woman which I had personally ordered. We started spending lots of time together and I spent many nights at her home. One (two) of her biggest assets I discovered had received help from a doctor's scalpel. That was fine with me. Here in Florida, we rednecks call it a "lift-kit." You know, like what you put on your four-wheel drive pickup truck to raise it up higher. They (the trucks) get a lot more attention when you raise them up higher. I also discovered her resources came from having married a gentleman much older than she. Not long after marriage, the older gentleman had succumbed to cancer. That had been three years before and she was still in a legal battle with his children over his vast holdings. She also told of how she had to explain to him that he couldn't possibly really love her if he wanted her to sign prenuptial agreements. He agreed, and at the time so did the other fuckin' moron, the live one, sitting right there in front of her.

I spent three months with her and I spent more money on her than I had spent on even the poorest woman I had ever dated. While we were dating she was in my office one day and spotted my new, really nice and expensive treadmill. "Oh Steve honey, I need one of those so bad, do you think I could borrow that for a little while?" "Well of course you can honey," said the schmuck. Had I said, "Buy your own, bitch," I would still have a very nice treadmill (now I have to walk all over the United States for exercise). Upon our breakup, she insisted I had given her the treadmill as a gift. Now I'm going to let you see what a schmuck really is (even New Yorkers will be shocked!) and divulge this; she actually said to me after many, many, very expensive flower arrangements I had sent to her three story beach house, "Steve honey, these flowers are very nice, but there is coming a time when you might want to start visiting jewelry stores." Yup, and the schmuck dated her for about three more weeks and then *she* dropped the schmuck.

It took me all of about two to three weeks to get over her. It probably would have been sooner had I got my damn treadmill back. She did, however, give back a gator head from a large gator my son Stevie and I had gotten together. She had borrowed it to show to her family. She insisted on giving that back because she said it reminded her of just how unrefined I really was. Unrefined means I never made it to the jewelry store.

For some strange reason I no longer had any desire to have a relationship, was not missing female companionship, and was quite happy being all by myself. And I started happily planning with my daughter my walk around the states. I started walking Vero Beach's beautiful long boardwalk (a treadmill would have been nice) both mornings and in the evening. It had been several months since the relationship had ended and while I was doing my evening walk, out of the corner of my eye I saw a white Porsche Carrera, pull up very close to the board walk and just behind me. From the Porsche came a familiar voice which said very softly and sweetly, "Oh Steve," I caught just the slightest glimpse of red hair and I remembered the voice having told me she was planning to buy herself a new Porsche after her legal battle was over. I never stopped, I never even turned around, if I never learned another thing walking the Appalachian Trail, and across

America, I learned to never ever go backwards. And then I went home and searched the want ads for a used treadmill. Oh, the red hair was real.

My "LOVE LIFE" Walk around America

Say you're driving down the road in the worst state of mind you may have ever experienced; you just cannot chase the negative thoughts out of your mind. It is so very severe you may actually be entertaining thoughts that both everything and everyone would be much better off without your presence in the universe. All of a sudden you see something really odd walking down the highway toward you. It gradually comes into focus. You cannot believe what you are seeing. It is some weirdo with the words "LOVE LIFE" over his head! "Love Life" is at the very opposite end of the emotional spectrum of life from where your thoughts are at that moment. And you are so desperate you may think, "Hey, maybe this guy knows something, maybe he can help me." See, no one really wants to die when they're in those dire straits, they just can't see beyond the pain. It is an absolute intrinsic desire within all of us to live, no matter that they are thinking suicide to be the only way out. This is my "ace in the hole" if you will, when confronted with someone talking of ending their life. I know that somewhere within them is that desire to live.

Or say you're driving to work on a Monday morning and feeling like it is most definitely a Monday morning and you see some bozo walking toward you with a smile and a wave, and over his head is "LOVE LIFE". I bet you smile! Bet you could even have a good day because of seeing that sign. From causing one to let go of worry and dread by the perspective contained in those two simple words, all the way to, "Mending the broken heart before it stops beating" is the reason I kept walking.

So, a year and a half after walking across the United States, my little girl, Shelly, and I decided the first walk accomplished so much, I should do yet another walk and she would again help orchestrate it. Thus, I decided to walk with my "LOVE LIFE" sign again, this time I set out to walk the perimeter of the U. S. I started what ended up as a 9,727 mile journey of two years and two weeks on Saturday, March 8, 2003 from the southern terminus of the Florida Trail on Florida route 94 in the Big Cypress Swamp. Again, my beautiful daughter helped orchestrate my walk. Here are some stories from my 9,727 miles of walking around the U.S.

Why?

It was Saturday, March 15, 2003, exactly one week after I had started a walk around the U.S. from the Florida Trail terminus just west of the Miccosukee tribal lands.

Murphy's Law was alive and well, nothing was going to plan. I had just received word from my friend Larry Pesin that our pro-bono public relations firm had just deserted us. I made a joke of it, saying, "They must've been doin' one of those Readers Digest vocabulary enhancement quizzes and found out what pro-bono meant!" We both laughed it off, but I was starting to wonder if there was really any sense to me doing this walk. I hoped for a sign of some sort to show me if I should really be doing this walk. I really was starting to think I may be wasting my time.

I had told my daughter and a couple other people, "If I can be instrumental in saving but one life, the walk around America will be worth it." A young lady in her early thirties pulled her car up to me and got out. She walked up to me and said, "I had to stop and tell you that your sign has helped me so very much!" I had barely said, "Why thank you." before she turned, was in her car and gone! The next day, the same young lady approached me again and said, "I just could not leave Florida without telling you what seeing your sign did to me." She began telling me she was from Colorado and was in Florida visiting her two little girls for the first time since she had lost them in a fierce custody battle. Her story was a common one: she was suing for divorce because the father was never home and never showed the proper interest in family. But as soon as the divorce proceedings started, hubby all of a sudden had a change of face; he wanted custody of the girls. She was caught completely off guard. He had a great job and parents with tons of money who wanted those grandbabies. You could tell she was a very shy person and did not like confrontation. Soon after he received custody he left with the babies for Florida, where the grandparents were.

She then stopped talking and remained silent for a little while; as if she weren't sure she should share the rest of the story. She asked me to sit in her car with her and I did. When she did open her mouth again, she started sobbing. I mean, really sobbing! She started explaining to me between sobs, that, after visiting her babies a couple of days, she could not stand to leave them again and she felt she just couldn't live that way any longer. The day she had seen my sign she was on her way back to her motel room where she had already made all preparations for taking her own life. Through the tears she told me, "When I saw that sign, "LOVE LIFE" I actually had to turn around and go back and look at it four times. All I could think about after seeing the sign was if I took my life I would be depriving my girls of a fair shot at loving life." She was sobbing as she continued, "I became so ashamed of myself." My daughter was about her same age and my heart was breaking for her. She wrapped her arms around my neck and was thanking me over and over. And she said at least three times, "I cannot believe I am sitting here on a highway hugging a perfect stranger!"

I explained to her that my son had committed suicide and by walking all over the U.S. with "LOVE LIFE" over my head, I was trying to remind all that I encounter, we must love life. I told her she didn't have the right to take her own life, it didn't belong just to her. It belonged to her children, her parents, her siblings, and her friends. I also told her that others have a huge investment in her: love. We talked for a long time and about how she had no choice but to leave Colorado and move to Florida to be near her babies. We agreed that no matter where her babies were that is where she was going to live. She parted with a positive view that she was going back to Colorado with plans of quitting her job and moving to south Florida where her babies were. And I said to her, "And if that son of a bitch moves with your babies to Antarctica?" "Then I will move to Antarctica, by God!" She was smiling as she drove off. I gave her my daughter's phone number and they stayed in touch for a while. She did indeed move to Florida where her babies were. She had her answer right inside her the whole time; she just needed a little nudge because her intense pain had blinded her and caused her to come to a dark place where she "couldn't see the forest for the trees." And I received from her the little nudge I needed.

"I am ever learning to follow only my own heart, and in the process of finding the heart of me, I find an enormous amount of Love there for my fellow human being. I am in pursuit of a heart-governed mind." Steve Fugate

Just the Messenger

I was just outside Lakeland, Florida, and the newspapers were announcing the start of the Iraqi war. A reporter from the local Lakeland paper was interviewing me on a street corner. While we were talking, a car came around the corner and the occupant yelled out something. I didn't hear it; I asked the reporter if he had heard it. The reporter said, "they think you're protesting the war" We both laughed at how ridiculous that was. And damn if it didn't happen again that evening.

The very next morning I conveniently found an American flag at the side of the road that had blown off a car. Many were flying them at that time. I thought maybe this would keep the dummies from thinking I was protesting the war. I was walking through the parking lot of a strip mall later that afternoon, proudly displaying the American flag, flying over my beautiful "LOVE LIFE" sign. A couple just in front of me were entering their pickup truck. The man looks up, sees me and immediately gets a scowl on his face. He says to me, "I love life... but I love my freedom too!" Meanwhile, his wife is scrambling for the passenger door to get inside a fast as possible, knowing from experience that her husband was about to make an ass out of himself, yet again. I responded, "That's good sir." And with his skinny little chest popped out, he repeated, "I love my freedom too!" By now, his poor wife is scrunched down in the seat, totally embarrassed, paying for the mistake she made those many years before in choosing a mate. And I'm thinking, "I am getting damn tired of people misinterpreting my sign" I said, "that's good sir, I love my freedom too, and that's why I'm carrying this here sign!" The little woman had now completely disappeared under the dashboard. The little moron is now totally bewildered; he has to come up with yet more vocabulary! And he did, he added to the previous statement, "I love my freedom too... by God!" I would have been impressed, but he was pissing me off. I proceeded to explain to him, "Sir, I'm going to give you some advice that can change your whole life, when you get up in the morning, the very first thing you should do, reach back and ever so gently... pull your head out of your ass!" He just kind of grunted, jumped in his truck and slammed the door! I made my mind up right then and there; I was never going to worry again as to how others might perceive my beautiful "LOVE LIFE" sign. I personally feel it is a nice suggestion. What one thinks after they read it, I have absolutely no control over. I'm just the messenger.

"Let's just Love one another and be so confident in our own Life's choices that we need not expect others to make the same choices we did. Respecting, that their choices felt just as right to them as did our choices to us."

On a Sunday after Church

In North Florida, April 2003, but weeks into my first walk around the U.S. It was about noon (church letting out time) and a car stopped. A man in red pants with a white belt to match his white shoes, and a belly hanging over the white belt, but not quite yet, reaching the white shoes, got out of the car, approached me shoving toward me, a small pamphlet, and said, "Here, I got something you need to read." It was a religious tract. I said, "No thank you sir, I do not need to read that." He tried one more time and I yet again told him no. In a huff, he said, "I feel sorry for you!" And I said, "I feel sorry for you." I lied. How in the hell would he know what I needed to read? I guess he thought a man walking down the road with a sign, "LOVE LIFE" over his head just could not have his shit together as much as a fine church goer like himself. And I was dressed a lot better too.

But moments later, a Mexican lady and her little boy of about 9 years-old, stopped their pickup and she asked in a very strong accent, if I needed anything. I told her no thank you, but she kept insisting, asking me could I use a ride, want a cold drink, or something to eat. I finally said yes to a drink and she had the little guy hop in the bed of the truck and get a couple cold Pepsi's from a cooler. After offering me a ride again, she told me they were on their way home from church, saw me and turned around to check on me. She said, "You know, the bible it say, sometimes we meet angels and not know it, so I turn around to see you need help, I not take any chances!" It was me who met an angel. It was a very rural area, I wonder was it the same church both she and Mr. GQ attended?

Load the F'k Up!

I was but a few weeks into my walk around the U.S. and walking U.S. route 98 just east of Carrabelle, Florida. It was getting late and I had started looking for a place to pitch my tent. Not an easy task as I was in an area of very nice homes looking out at the Gulf. I finally saw a very large empty wooded stretch of land between two homes. I waited until there was no one around to see me and made a dash for the woods! I couldn't see either of the houses for the trees so I felt pretty safe and started looking for that perfect spot. Then, all of a sudden: the dog! A dog starts barking like crazy. A woman yells out, "Sic 'im boy, sic 'im!" So I start crashing through the woods headed back for the road. The lady was yelling, "Sic 'im boy, bite that son-of-a-bitch!" When I hit the road I was running as fast as I could with the heavy pack on my back and I could still hear that lady yelling for her dog to bite my ass! Within moments of getting to the road an old car stopped and the driver said, "Load the fuck up!" And that's exactly what I did. The driver was Malcolm, and his passenger was Marjorie, his girlfriend. Malcolm said, "It's a good thing we saw you, you don't need to be walking in this area this late, there's nothing here but a bunch of rich fuckin' assholes! They'll have ya ass put in jail." I told them what had just happened and thanked them for rescuing me. Malcolm was shaking his head acknowledging that he wasn't surprised and said, "They're all assholes, nothin' but fuckin' assholes here."

They took me to Marjorie's home where she and Malcolm lived and asked me to have dinner with them and spend the night. Malcolm started praising Marjorie's cooking skills and told me she was the finest cook he had ever seen, "A fuckin' chef she is," stated Malcolm. Malcolm was one of the roughest edged people I've ever met. He was beyond scruffy lookin'! He hadn't shaved in days and his clothing was filthy. Marjorie, on the other hand, was neat as a pin. She and her home were spotless. She told me she had grown up in Martha's Vineyard. Now Malcolm most definitely had not grown up in Martha's Vineyard. Malcolm had grown up in Lafayette County, Florida working on ranches and farms. The walls were adorned with buckles, trophies, and pictures from his rodeo days. He took down some he was particularly proud of and showed them to me. He told me, "Yep, I rodeo-ed 'til I was about forty two, 'til they made me fuckin' quit. Man, I used to love it when I hit a good purse a ridin' a bull or bronc, man there ain't nothin like goin' into town with twelve to fifteen hunert in yer pocket." I asked him if he was ever injured badly. Up came his shirt revealing a huge scar from being gored by a bull. He had to pull down the waistband of his jeans to reveal the whole scar. Marjorie let out a gasp and yelled, "Malcolm, for God's sake go take off them long john bottoms so I can wash them!" They were filthy! "They ain't dirty!" yelled back Malcolm. He seemed adamant about not changing his long john bottoms but she did talk him into going to wash his hands before we ate. While he was in the bathroom, Marjorie told me they had been together for 15 years. She said, "We are different as day and night. I struggle constantly to make him keep himself and his clothing clean; it's just the way he is. But I have never met a finer, or bigger hearted man in my life; he has always treated me like a queen." That's because Marjorie is a queen.

Malcolm was absolutely correct about Marjorie's culinary skills, our meal was awesome. After eating, Malcolm showed me a picture of him on a U.S. Navy PTF2 patrol boat. He was firing a fore aft mounted 50 caliber machine gun. "That was taken in Nam." Malcolm told me. "Weren't you guys the ones who sometimes took the Navy SEALS in for many of their operations?" I asked. Malcolm snickered, "Hell, takin' 'em in weren't shit. We took 'em in at night. Weren't nobody better at stealth than us." He further explained, "We took 'em in a bunch a times. Weren't never detected, not one damned time. Now, goin' in and gettin' those crazy sonsabitches was a whole 'nother story. The whole fuckin' Asian world was after their asses when we had to go in an' git 'im! It was usually just before dawn, but it looked like fuckin' daylight 'cause that sky was lit up with all kinds a shit bein' fired at them boys, uh, and us, I might add!" Malcolm then looked at me real serious and said, "The pucker factor was very high with all that shit a-comin' in and aimed in our direction." Marjorie interrupted and said, "Malcolm, why don't you show Steve all your medals, I think he would enjoy seeing them since he was in the navy too." I acknowledged that I would like to see them. Malcolm pondered for a moment and said, "If they had given me the damn things before I left Nam... I'd a-placed 'em on the bodies of the friends I lost." He never did show me the medals. Malcolm continued telling me about extracting U.S. Navy SEAL's after their missions, "And as if it weren't fuckin' bad enough gettin' their crazy asses outa' there, some fuckin' asshole Admiral or General decided they could get more prisoners to interrogate by givin' them crazy assed SEALS a day of liberty for each prisoner they brought back. Holy shit! I mean, we would take 'em in with one to two boats at most and would have to come back sometimes with twice as many to haul all the fuckin' VC prisoners those party-happy assholes would capture. They would have 'em tied together with strips of clothing, vines, and all kinds a' shit. They told me, when they ran outa' stuff to tie 'em with, they told 'em to just hold on to the other, and if that other was missin' they would shoot the one supposed to be a holdin' on to 'em. I never once saw a prisoner act up; they never took their eyes off those SEALs. They was scared to death of 'em. I never saw a SEAL mistreat one though." He said that anytime he was out on the town, as he put it, and a SEAL recognized him or any of his fellow crew members, the SEALs always insisted on buying their drinks. He said, "Those guys always let us know they appreciated us for comin' in to git 'em." Malcolm ended his story by telling me that they had to discontinue the prisoner for liberty program because they were bringing back more POW's than could be processed, and grinning real large he added, "Hell, 'em SEALS woulda' spent all their time a partyin' instead a fightin'." Marjorie put together some great leftovers for me and they drove me back to the highway the next morning. A few weeks later, over the phone with my daughter, I asked had she called the people I listed, to thank them for having helped me. She said, "Yeah I did dad, this one guy after I told him why I was calling said immediately, yeah, I told him to load the fuck up! I couldn't believe that was the first thing he said to me, dad." I could believe it, and so would Marjorie. My daughter added that Malcolm was very concerned about me though and wanted to know how I was doing. Not all saints hold crosses out in front of them.

Just Listened

I was in Mississippi, not too far before Natchez, sitting in a restaurant around 6:00 pm; I looked out the window to see one of the most obese men I had ever seen, slowly and arduously getting out of his brand new and very expensive truck. I believe he was about my same age. He used a walking stick to get himself to and up the three concrete steps to the door. It took him an awful long time. He finally stepped through the door and after looking all around, looked in my direction and still out of breath, said to me, "There you awh, I been a lookin' for yah. Saw an article in the paper on ya, luckily I jus' spotted yull sign a leanin' 'gainst the wahl he-ahh." He walked on over to my table and asked may he please sit and talk a bit. He told me that he had several acres nearby that would be a great place for me to pitch my tent and that I could shower, do my laundry, and have breakfast the next morning. He said that he really needed to talk with me, that it was very important he do so. I took Earl up on his offer.

While sitting at a table on his veranda lookin' out over his beautiful property, drinkin' sweet tea served to us by his very attractive and only slightly overweight wife, he started talkin'. He explained to me that when he and the pretty wife first married, he had started a pest control business. He said that after much hard work and sacrifices, their business became quite lucrative. He told me he had been able to live a very good life. Earl told me he loved living the good life, but had loved it way too much when it came to eating. He then told of the operations he had gone through in the last year or so for clogged arteries and of concerned doctors trying to save his life. He said his doctors had told him they had done all the operations they could do for now and were watching the way he would respond to medicines and diet. His wife and son had to take over managing the pest control business.

Earl's pretty wife came out and without any words, walked out to the edge of their property and began a very brisk walk around the property lines. She was making her second pass around and Earl nodded toward her, sighed and then looked at me with a forlorn look I could never forget. Two men just looking into each other's eyes, no words. His look said it all: he had not touched her in God only knows how long. Still looking straight into my eyes, he said, "I've killed myself Steve. I've eaten myself to death." And nodding toward the direction of his wife again, said, "She's but waitin' fah me ta die. I got no one ta blame; jus' me."

His wife served me breakfast on the veranda the next morning, she said, "Good mornin," and that was it. I believe it was a banana Earl had. He told me doctors had him on a very strict diet but that it wasn't difficult at all for him to not eat a lot anymore. Without saying it in words, he was insinuating it was much too late. He told me how to get back to the highway and said, "Steve, I thank yah suh, I really do." I told him, "Please do not give up, it is never too late to fight back for your Life!" I took a lot of deep breaths and did a lot of sighing thinking of Earl as I walked on down the road with the words, "LOVE LIFE" over my head. Never give up. Never quit!

Fort Apache

I was on state route 260 in Arizona within the Fort Apache Indian Reservation. I had stopped at a little store and gas station for a drink and snacks. I was sitting outside talking to three little Apache children who had been asking me questions about my walk. I thrive on such encounters. Out of the corner of my eye I saw an older Apache man watching me; he was probably in his mid-seventies. After the children left, the old gentleman approached me. He had grey-black hair pulled back in braids, he was very distinguished looking. He asked what I was about and said he was taken by the fact I showed much patience with the little ones. He told me of the success of all five of his own children. He attributed it to the fact that he kept his family out in the country and away from the cities. He said they were raised up to not forget their ancestral ways. I told him my story and he told me how much he appreciated my "LOVE LIFE" sign. We talked for quite a while longer. When we were ready to part, he took my hand, gripped it hard and with tears in his eyes, he said, "I am proud of you!" It was so humbling; I hadn't expected to hear anything like that. And again he said, "I am so proud of you!" I just stood there speechless, and with even more tears flowing, he said, "I am so very proud of you!" I couldn't believe his reaction to me and my story; it really caught me off guard. He turned and walked away, shaking his head.

The next morning, in Show Low, Arizona, a young man asked if I would mind coming to his office for an interview for the local paper. After the interview I told him about the old Apache man crying and thanking me three times. The young man pulled away from his desk with a very solemn look on his face and then looked down at the floor for a moment. When he raised his head back up he said, "I know why he did that." He hesitated a moment, he seemed to be struggling to continue. He said, "Last year, over thirty young Apache men took their own life."

Litterbugs Suck!

A newspaper reporter once asked me if I was going to lobby for my cause when I reached Washington D.C. I told him if there was anything I would lobby for, it would be the death penalty for litter bugs. I mean, hey, I have to look at that crap strewed by the roadside for miles. And the way I see it, you would probably only have to kill a couple of them. Can't you just picture this scene: two or three immature people riding around in their car drinking beer, down goes the window, an arm cocks back to toss his empty out onto the roadside for you and I to look at, and one of them yells out, "Hey man, don't throw that out man. They fried Bobby's ass in the chair last year for doing that!" Littering would become a thing of the past. I guarantee it.

Okay, so now you know how I feel about littering. I was barely 25 miles into the state of Wisconsin on U.S. highway 2 during my walk around the U.S. in 2004. I was just sauntering along loving life and suggesting the same to everyone else with my "LOVE LIFE" sign. All of a sudden I look up and was just able to duck as a large pizza box goes flying past my head. The box was full of paper and it was flying everywhere. Three young guys in an older white Cutlass zoomed on by me laughing and jeering. I was infuriated: I was stunned that they would try to harm me like that for no reason. As I stood there, I said out loud, "God I'd like to see those little bastards caught!"

It was about two hours later and a deputy sheriff pulled his car up beside me. He asked for some identification and then said, "Actually, I've been looking for you, did someone throw something at you earlier today?" I couldn't believe it. I told him yes. He continued, "Can you describe to me what was thrown at you?" "Yes sir!" I said, "It was a pizza box and it was full of trash." he then asked me if I could describe the car they were in. I described the car to him. He had his radio mike in hand and said into it, "go ahead and book them, we have a confirmation." I just stood there totally shocked. The deputy explained to me, the car behind them had indeed been close enough to witness what had happened, and called in with their tag number. He said the dispatcher said the gentleman had been totally irate when he called on his cell phone. They apprehended them in the next county he said. He was quite pleased they had been able to catch them, he said, "That's the reason those kinds of morons pull that stuff, they figure they're going to get by with it. This time we got 'em." He also told me, "Actually, the idiots have already confessed to littering anyway, they said they did not throw a pizza box at you, that all they did was throw out some cigarette butts. Duh!"

I asked him if the state of Wisconsin had a stiff fine for littering, I was hoping they did. He said unfortunately they did not, but that it was left up to the discretion of the judge. A few weeks later I was approached by a guy from the area where the littering incident occurred. He told me he had read in his local paper about three men throwing trash at a man walking down the road with a "LOVE LIFE" sign. He said they were each fined $750.00 apiece for littering. He also said they were charged with some sort of intent charge, but he couldn't remember what it was. And he said he had heard that the judge really chewed them out. Cops love this story, and so do I. If you litter our beautiful country you are void of any self-respect, and… you're an asshole.

Keep on Telling Them

I was in a good sized town in northern Ohio; I had called the local paper and told them what I was doing. They asked me to stop by their building to be interviewed. I was sitting in the office of a young lady reporter, maybe 30 years-old. She was stunningly beautiful. I couldn't help but think about how wonderfully blessed this young lady was. She had looks, a great personality, and obviously a great job. Her expertise at interviewing was as good as any of the interviews I've had. All in all, she was a delight to be around. She allowed me to fully express myself and I was able to really relay the devastation brought about by the self-centered act of suicide. As usual, when the interview was over, I asked that she send me a hard copy of the article. As we shook hands I expressed how I admired her for her obvious accomplishments.

A couple weeks later I was on the phone checking in with my friend Larry Pesin, who was helping orchestrate my walk. I asked if that particular newspaper had sent a copy of the article. He said that yes he received it but that wasn't all that was with it. He then said, "The reporter included a letter to you; are you sitting down?" I'm glad I was sitting down because I could not believe what was in that letter. He read, "Dear Steve, I am so grateful that you walked into my office. I just had to let you know how your visit changed my life. Prior to that day, every single day was a day of hell for me. Every night I worked on getting up the courage to kill myself. I constantly was thinking of the best and easiest way to do it. I had no idea at the time, how very selfish I was being! Thank you." The letter went on and told of how she was intent on pulling herself together. Wow, I had no idea! See, I guess I'll just have to keep on telling everyone to Love Life.

"Nothing is more positive and powerful than Love. Love defeats all negatives in Life. Love defeats all fear. When fear is gone Love may then flow freely." ~ Steve Fugate

We Never Know Who

I was in a New England state sitting in a little roadside park, part of an old one-room school house restoration project. A car pulled up and an older lady got out and walked up to me with food in her hands. She explained that she and the driver, her daughter, had spotted me earlier. She insisted that they return to her home and prepare some food for me. She was so excited about my beautiful "LOVE LIFE" sign. And in an accent I guessed to be German, she kept telling me how very wonderful my sign was. She told me she was born in 1935 and that she loved life very much. I thanked them for the food and they left. Later that evening the mother and another daughter stopped alongside me and gave me more food, Again, the sweet mother applauded my "LOVE LIFE" sign and kept telling me what I was doing was just truly wonderful. She had insisted the daughter join her to meet me and see my sign. The next morning the same lady came up to me with more food, and this time she had her granddaughter with her. She explained that she had insisted the granddaughter meet me. The young lady asked if they could give me a ride. And before I could give the usual, "no thank you." the grandmother interjected, "oh no sweetheart. No, this man must walk and display this sign!" She then took my hand and just kept rubbing and patting it as she again praised what I was doing. As I was telling her how much I appreciated her kindness, and while still holding hands, her coat sleeve pulled up, revealing numbers tattooed on her arm. She was 9 years-old when WW II ended. Only God knows what that little Jewish girl saw, the things that made her Love and appreciate her gift of Life so very much.

She just loved. She loved what I was doing! She loved her two daughters and her granddaughter and wanted them to understand how important it is to always Love Life! She loved me enough to feed me! She loved a stranger because I carried a message she fully understood the importance of. She helped me learn, don't complain, just Love Life.

Poetic Justice

I was in Waco, Texas and staying at the home of a couple who had invited me down to escape the foul winter weather in the state of Washington. It was certainly a nice reprieve from walking in snow blizzards in the Cascades. I had been in their home for a couple weeks when I found myself becoming more and more a captive audience for my hostess's father-in-law. He was some sort of spiritual adviser and had his own church. They believed in out-of-body experiences and lots of other mystical and so-called spiritual stuff. I personally will believe in anything one can prove to me. I really try not to discredit anything I haven't investigated. The father-in-law though was of the type who felt one should believe in all he believed just because he said so. In other words, "He was a total pain in the ass." Wanting to be a respectful and appreciative guest, I endured his preaching.

One day, while boringly enduring another of his lectures of pure dogma, he pointed to a chair and said, "I can become the same molecules as that chair and enter that chair as a part of it." "Damn," I thought, "this asshole really is nuts." He stood there looking at me as though I should fall down and worship him, and was obviously anticipating my astonished and revering response. My response was, "Why?" I could see he was exasperated by my honest answer. I'm sure, behind that smug look was the thought that he should have known better to expect anything other from someone like me. In layman terms, this means he did not have an answer as to why.

My hosts had a nine-year-old son who had a musical presentation going on at his school. The parents were unable to attend and they asked me to take the young man and attend on their behalf. Of course, I complied. The event was a tribute to military marching compositions, featuring the works of John Philip Sousa. There was a large Air Force base near the school. The show was a joy to watch; of course the children were precious. The Guru of Chair Molecules was present to watch his grandson perform. For the finale of the program, they chose to honor the military members and veterans in attendance. They did this by asking each person qualified to stand as the march pertaining to their branch of service was played. Upon standing, one of the young participants would bring a certificate of appreciation to them, along with a very sweet, "Thank you."

I couldn't help but notice Mr. Spiritual Advisor was squirming in his chair. I then remembered an earlier conversation with his son and the mentioning of "conscientious objector" and something about Canada. The reason it was vague in my memory, I had decided years before, I had no right to judge those who took that route. I have a couple good friends who did so; none of my business. I was 17 when I volunteered and had no thought of Viet Nam or anything else. Later in my tour, I did volunteer for Nam at least a couple times though. I am now glad they never sent me. Anyway, each military march they played, the more he squirmed in his chair. He was quite obviously uncomfortable in his present surrounding, maybe he had not fully come to terms with his past decision, or perhaps he had distain for the military. When they played the marches for the Air Force and Army, several stood up and the little ones delivered the certificates. And then came the best of them all, the Marine Corps hymn, "Semper Fidelis," it was all I could do to restrain myself from standing instead of waiting for "Anchors Away." I looked past the squirming Guru and scanned the auditorium for proud marines… there was but one. And (she) was standing right next to Oh Squirming One. She was very short of stature, but certainly not short of pride. She looked around, saw she was the only Marine standing and made up for it with her display for "The Proud, The Brave, and The Marines." She pushed her chest out as far as she could and stood so erect and so very, very, proud. By God, she was a Marine! It still gives me goose bumps when I picture that little lady looking so very tall. Now he really squirmed. And then came my turn, "Anchors Away" blasted out and that is exactly what I did. My ass shot out of that chair like a rocket. I don't think I out did the little Marine but I did my very best. I was proudly standing there waiting for the sweet little girl to bring me my certificate of appreciation and I saw that she was struggling to get past the Guru of Chair Entering and so I gave her a helpful suggestion, "Just give it to him, honey." And she did. He had to hand me my certificate of appreciation. He was trying to become a part of *that* chair, not with his mind though, but with his ass. If I never gained another thing from my four years, four months, eighteen days, four hours, thirty six minutes, and seven seconds in the U.S. Navy, I will always be satisfied with that moment of poetic justice.

Didn't Get Scalped

While having breakfast one morning in a little café along Rt. 2 in Montana I was answering questions from some locals. You just don't see a guy walking down the road every day toting a sign over his head that says, "LOVE LIFE." All of them warned me against walking across Native lands of the Blackfoot Tribe. They explained to me the Indians were not good people and would rob and possibly even kill me for a few dollars to buy drugs and booze. They also warned me not to walk through the Blackfoot town of Browning at night. One man warned that they are a very dangerous people and said, "They aren't like us."

I took what they said with a grain of salt; I had walked across many Native lands and had never been treated poorly. Quite to the contrary actually, many were the times Native Peoples would stop to offer up prayers for me. Many stopped and said, "May the Great Spirit be with you." I have been in their sweat lodges, smoked pipe with them, and spent the night in their homes. I had been given tobacco pouches and even had tobacco spread in honor of the message I carry. So, the Native Peoples had always welcomed what I was doing. I explained this to the locals but they insisted the Blackfoot were dangerous.

The next morning I entered Browning, Montana; and within an hour I had been invited to stay in three different homes. I declined, as I had saved up money for a motel room of which I was way overdue. I most generally preferred a motel room to a private residence. I had more privacy and didn't have to worry about imposing. I was also given food and as on all lands of our First People, which I walk through, I was asked of my "LOVE LIFE" sign often, and wished well.

I found the Blackfoot to be a wonderful people and a fine looking people as well. I found a lost billfold alongside the road belonging to a Robert Kickingwoman. I turned it over to the Blackfoot Tribal Police. The officer assured me he would find the rightful owner. I had to laugh when he said, "Yeah, there are a lot of those Kickingwoman around here." I said, "They are knock down gorgeous, I don't care if they kick." he smiled real big and said, "Yeah, they are hot huh?" He also answered my question of Blackfoot or Blackfeet, by explaining that the tribes in this country mostly preferred the name Blackfoot, and that most of the Canadian tribes generally went by Blackfeet. He said that "Blackfoot" is the English translation of the word siksika, which means black foot, because of the dark colored moccasins the people wore.

Several weeks later at Bemidji, Minnesota, I met the former Chairman of the White Earth Tribe of the Ojibwe people, Doyle Turner, who is also an Episcopal Priest. Doyle is a fine looking Ojibwe man with long braids and a very distinguished and wise look about him. I related to Doyle how some white people had warned me of the possible danger associated with encounters with our Native Peoples. When I told him one man had said, "They aren't like us." Doyle chuckled and responded with, "You know that's quite the compliment really." I concur.

That's a Good Sign

I was in front of a little strip mall, near Eagar, Arizona. I was waiting for the return of a kind young man who had gone to his father's junk yard to see if he could find a couple old bike wheels for me. I really needed replacements for the old ones on the cart I pulled behind me. I was sitting there on the sidewalk leaning up against the wall of a hardware store and I heard someone shout, "There he is! There's the love life guy!" I turned my head to see two ladies with four children. The kids were probably eight to fourteen years old. They were all laughing and one of the women said to me, "We saw you walking on the highway yesterday, and you changed our whole day. "Actually, you saved our day!" chimed in the other lady. They told me their story. The two ladies were sisters and there had been bad blood between them for years. They had decided just a few days before via the telephone to try to end their differences. So, two days before, the one living there in Arizona had picked up the other who had flown in with her two children from Florida. They said things were going a bit rocky on the road to reconciliation. And then, the previous day while riding down the road, the children got into a pretty bad argument in the back seat. Each mother took the side of their respective off-spring. The two sisters started arguing. An hour or so later, though the arguing had stopped, you could cut the tension with a knife they said. No one was talking at all and then one of the kids said, "What's that?" They all looked straight ahead to see me walking down the road toward the traffic with a big, beautiful sign over my head, "LOVE LIFE." All of them read it aloud as soon as they were close enough. All of them started laughing. The two sisters began telling me how silly each of them felt for allowing the dissension to take place. They thanked me for showing them what they were supposed to be doing instead of harboring bitterness. That sign did it.

Bill in Arizona

I was on an Arizona highway walking toward the traffic as usual and displaying my beautiful "LOVE LIFE" sign as usual. A man pulled off the road in front of me waiting until I came up beside him. He introduced himself as Bill, and told of having been observing me for days. He said he had wanted to approach me earlier but kept talking himself out of it. He admitted his self-arguments, I had heard them all before from others.

"He's just a homeless guy, why bother?" and, "I don't know anything about him he could be a criminal." And so on.

He made some small talk and then became real serious; it was plain to see he was distraught. He started pouring out his story. His wife, his childhood sweetheart succumbed to cancer two years before. He was left with a thirteen year old daughter. He belonged to a strict fundamentalist type Pentecostal church. To help deal with his grief he became very involved in the church. There was a lady there who immediately started showing interest in Bill and his daughter. He was thinking of how much his little girl was going to need a mother. And even though his little girl didn't like her, they became involved and were soon married.

They had been married a little over a year and he was miserable. His daughter was miserable and hated the new step-mother. Also, he found out soon after marriage, she had been married several times before. He told me he was full of guilt because he wanted to divorce her. She didn't want a divorce and told him it would be a sin and she went to their pastor. The pastor told him to just keep praying and God would work it out and divorce was not an option or he would be doomed for eternity if he left that loving and innocent Christian woman!

This man totally broke down in front of me. He was sobbing; he was in such turmoil and pain! What terrible stress he was under; trying to do what he was told God wanted and what was in his heart! He was spilling his heart out to a total stranger at the side of the road. He began telling why he had stopped me. A lady in in his church, a friend of his deceased wife, told him of seeing me and my "LOVE LIFE" sign on the road. She said, on seeing me she thought of him and felt that I may have encouraging words for him. She told him this after he had seen me more than once himself. He went on to say that he too had felt very strongly to stop and speak with me. He said he took her words as a sign of confirmation and so... here he was.

He began to question me, "Are you a man of God?" "Yes I am." I answered. I figured since I believe in a creator, higher power over the universe, this was a legitimate answer. "You pray and have God in your life?" Bill asked. "Yes." I assured him. He seemed to be struggling to put his mind at ease that it was okay to be confiding in a stranger. "Are you born again?" He asked. "No, but I am working on that one." I said. That answer seemed to satisfy him. He began crying again and said, "Please help me! Please!"

I said to this poor broken man, "What do you, deep down in your heart feel that YOU need to do?" He couldn't answer, he just shook his head. I went on, "Do you really feel that God will punish you for trying to bring peace to you and your little girl's life?" He finally stammered out, "No I don't!" I looked him right in the eye and said, "You know a whole lot more about what you and your little girl need in your life than that pastor does! You made a mistake, you were in a weakened state of grief and you made a bad choice. You were under the pressure of having to raise a teenage daughter by yourself and made a bad decision... that's all. You and your daughter deserve to be happy." That poor desperate man was absorbing every word I uttered! I went on to say, "Now go undo your mistake and get a divorce. You and your little girl get on with your life." I just felt so much Love for this man! (I have to confess though, I really wanted to say, "Now go throw that bitch the fuck outa' your house!")

Bill immediately calmed down. I reassured him that it would be fine with God and that everything would work out for the good. I told him to go on and enjoy life! We stayed in touch and Bill went on to get a divorce. As I came to know Bill a little better I realized he was a well-educated and intelligent professional. It is amazing what emotional strain can do to one. Bill insisted on donating money to my walk and he told many that I had helped him. One night he called and said, "Steve, you know how you have been used to help stop some from taking their own life? Well, you have done it again!" He started relating the story. His daughter was being abused by the step-mother. She was afraid to tell him, afraid he wouldn't believe her. She had only recently made him aware of the abuse and that she had been thinking suicide as the only way out!

"The "Godless" are they who are good-less, even though they may be members of churches and make a great profession of faith in God. The "Godly" are they that are goodly even though they make no profession of religion. The complainers and bewailers are the faithless and unbelieving. Those who deny the power of good, and in their lives and actions affirm and magnify the power of evil, are the only real atheists." ~ James Allen

Porsches in Jerome

I had just left Cottonwood, Arizona, headed up the mountain to Jerome, and was on a pay phone in front of a convenience store when about ten Porsche's of different styles pulled into the parking lot of the store. I am a car lover and I never recognized those particular body styles. So I excitedly excused myself from the phone to go take pictures of those new Porsche's. I had taken four or five pictures of the mysterious autos when a big man wearing plaid Bermuda shorts and black dress socks approached me. He looked like a Canadian on vacation in Florida. Instead, he was German and working for Porsche. He came toward me very fast and very angrily demanded, "You give me camera!" To which I said, "No, I will not give you my camera!" He demanded again, and again I said, "No!" He then reached for my camera and repeated, "You give me camera now!" I said to him, "If you touch me or this camera, I am going to knock you right on your ass!" He stopped reaching toward me immediately (funny how that works) but he kept insisting I give him my camera. I then said something I never dreamed I would ever say, (felt kinda' good) "look buddy, this is America, I am an American and you cannot take my camera away from me in this country! Now, I don't know how they do it in Germany, but your ass ain't getting my camera!"

Another of the German drivers approached me, his English was better and he was not hostile. He explained to me that the cars were prototypes and were there in Arizona as part of their testing. The cars had not been officially released to the public. There was a testing facility located near where we were. This I could understand, not yelling and trying to take my camera. I realize that auto manufacturers have to guard their new designs from being stolen. But the Bermuda shorts and black socks German guy, wouldn't shut up and just kept saying, "You give me camera!" His associate was trying to handle the situation with diplomacy, but big mouth would not hear it. Not only was diplomacy foreign to him, he had very poor taste in choosing clothing, how could he possibly choose the right words? He came past the nice German guy, and reached for my camera one more time. This pissed me off, so I started taking pictures again. The nice German guy, gets in front of the Bermuda shorts German guy, to keep us apart. I am still taking pictures and the Bermuda shorts German guy, starts jumping up and down in front of me waving his arms to block the pictures. I then, raise the camera over my head to get the shots without his flailing arms in the way. Now he's jumping higher, and the nice German guy, is jumping higher too. So, I, of course, responded by jumping higher than both, and taking more pictures. So now, all three of us are jumping up and down in the parking lot! It was great. Walking the country all alone as I do, you must seize every opportunity for entertainment so as not to become bored.

The nice German guy, finally figured out that I could be just as big an asshole as the Bermuda shorts and black socks German guy, and so now aimed his persuasion attempts toward his associate. They both walked away toward the very innocent Porsche's. Victory was mine! I have since seen what I believe to have been prototype cars, being tested in that same area, which were so well camouflaged that no distinction of design could be seen. Maybe I caused that, I sure hope so. I just Love being me, I never get bored.

"My memory is terrible I must be losing my mind, probably the result of having given so many a piece of it over the years. ~ Steve Fugate

It's the Love Life Guy!

2003 in Yosemite, I was sitting on a curb taking a break, watching four rock climbers on a sheer rock face. One climber, a young lady, was obviously fairly new to big wall climbing. The three young men were yelling out instructions to her. She may have lacked experience but certainly not courage, not at that height. I was sitting there in awe and admiration of their courage and ability. I was straining to hear what they were yelling to the novice. Then I saw that all were looking down in my direction, they were yelling across to each other, "Hey, it's the Love Life guy!" Made my day! They stopped their car later to talk with me and laughed hard when I gave my definition of tenacity, "Tenacity is having enough balls to start something you were too stupid to quit when you realize you shouldn't have started it in the first damn place."

Grazing in the (Wheat) Grass

Due to limited access sections of U.S. Highway 101 in California I could not walk straight into Oregon following that route. I was forced to take an obscure route into Oregon and then double back into California before I could continue on highway 101 and follow Oregon's gorgeous coastline. The obscure route took me into the very small community of Takilma, Oregon. There were no businesses, only scattered houses. I came to a fork in the road and there were no signs directing me as to which road was the one I wanted to continue on. I yelled at two guys delivering firewood and asked them. They both looked at me and then turned back to their work as though I had said nothing. So I chose a road on my own, hoping for the best. Almost immediately I saw two young men getting out of their car and headed for their house. I yelled at them, "Hey, will this road take me to route 199 so I can get back to California?" They looked at each other and shrugged, then turned back to me and said, "Sure." It was not reassuring at all but I continued on.

As I continued down my chosen route I saw a very small lady, not over four feet, I'm sure. She was bent over in small plot of very thick grass that was up to her knees. As I got closer to her she raised up. "Where are you going?" She said in a very shrill voice. Remember that little woman in "Poltergeist?" Well, that's who she kind of looked and sounded like. When I looked at her to answer I could see grass stain all around her mouth and, she was holding a wad of grass in her hand. In the 60's there was an instrumental tune called "Grazing In The Grass" and it immediately popped into my head and provided the proper soundtrack for this strange scene. I really had to control myself not to laugh and not to dance as well, as it was a great dance song. I told her where I was going and she told me I was going in the wrong direction and the road I was on dead-ended up in the mountains. She told me the exact way to go. I thanked her and started to turn around and head in the right direction. She noticed I was looking at the grass in her hand, "wheat grass." She said. "You can live on just this; it's almost all I ever eat." She then started expounding on the many attributes of wheat grass. And then while thrusting the bunch in her hand toward me she said, "Here, taste this." I really didn't want to, but hey, she did put me in the right direction, so I reluctantly took a bite of it. It was kind of sweet tasting but it still tasted like grass to me, and I had no plans of ever trying to live on it. I then heard a grunting sound. I looked behind her and there in the doorway of a very small one-room cabin stood a man that had to be over seven feet tall. I think he may have been the largest man I've ever seen. He was dressed in all black leather motorcycle gear. And he had patches and pins all over his black leather vest denoting that he was part of a

Christian motorcycle group, "Bikers for Christ," I believe it was called. And he may also have been the drunkest man I had ever seen. I could barely understand a word he was trying to say, but I did make out something about God and Jesus. The little woman glanced over her shoulder at him and then back to me and said, "He's an alcoholic." "How can you tell?" I quipped under my breath (being a natural born smartass.) She didn't hear me (good); she had immediately started praising wheat grass again. Then the seven foot, drunken, Christian biker motioned for me to enter the very small shack. I managed to make out a few words; he was opening up their home to me for the night. That was my cue to leave; I was not going to spend the night with a seven foot tall drunk Christian biker and a grass eating midget in a very small one room house. The scene was unusual, to say the least. But hey, they were both very kind and kept me from going the wrong way.

The next day, back on U. S. Route 199 and headed back into California, near the state line, I headed for a restaurant just off the highway. A hippy looking young lady was hitchhiking just in front of the restaurant and asked about my sign. After asking me where I was coming from, I told her I had just left Takilma. She raised her eyebrows and said, "Now that is one strange little place! You didn't happen to run into the really big black biker dude with all the Christian patches on his jacket did you?" I told her that I did meet him and she said, "Bet he was drunk huh?" After ordering my food at the counter inside the eatery, the owner struck up a conversation with me being curious about my walk. After finding out I had been in Takilma, guess what he asked? Yup, he said, "Hey, did you see the big drunken Christian biker dude with the little bitty weird woman?"

You know, in Takilma, two people blatantly ignored me; two others gave me wrong directions probably knowing full well they were doing so. They all looked to be what I think most of us would call normal and average looking. The big drunk gentleman and the very small lady not only stopped me from going miles in the wrong direction, they offered their home to me for the night, and grass to graze in. Let us all just live and let live and Love Life with all our hearts.

"Because I've learned to Love and appreciate my own gift of Life so very much I'm now enabled to Love and appreciate the precious lives of my fellow human beings." Steve Fugate

Don't Drink

On a Saturday in a little café, in a very small strip mall, at a small town off U.S. highway 2 in North Dakota as I was having breakfast one morning, I noticed a man probably in his late thirties ride up on an old bicycle. He hadn't shaven in a few days and quite obviously, had not combed his hair yet. His face had that look: he was an alcoholic. There were maybe ten other patrons inside the café whom all appeared to be farmers or ranchers. They all greeted the bike rider as he came in and all seemed to have a respect for him. Three of them told him they had work for him and to check with them when he could. He told all that he would do the specific jobs for them starting Monday. He came over to my table and asked if he could sit with me and told me he had seen me with my sign earlier.

During breakfast he invited me to his apartment to take a shower and do my laundry. I of course, jumped at that chance. We walked over to his little apartment as he pushed his bike along. His place was in a very old large boarding house. As soon as he opened the door to his spotlessly clean apartment, he pointed to a large glass punch bowl full of change and insisted I get my quarters out of it for the coin operated in house laundry room. He said he had plenty of detergent I could use and then opened up his refrigerator and grabbed a beer. It wasn't 9:00 am yet. It wasn't long before that was empty and he had another one in his hand. We sat and talked while my clothes were washing and drying. I lost count of the beers he drank while I was there, had to have been a twelve pack at least in about two and a half hours. One time, as he sat back down from his trip to the fridge, and was popping the top, he told me, "Look, I was nine years old; it was New Year's Eve, my 18-year-old brother, who I adored, came into my bedroom and woke me up. He said he wanted me to see something in the living room. When I got there, he said, "I'm tired of this shit Billy!" He then stuck a shotgun in his mouth and blew his brains out!" He then looked up at me, there were no tears, but the pain was evident to anyone with a heart, and he asked me, "Are you going to tell me I shouldn't drink?" "Absolutely not!" I responded, "I tried to drink myself to death when I lost my son and it didn't work for me, it only made it much worse, but I have never worn your shoes." He looked down at the floor for a long time and when he finally raised his head, he said, "Thank you, I appreciate that."

Hell no, I was not going to tell him what he should do! I have no idea how I would have handled that horror in my life at nine years old. I saw his face full of pain; I thought about him the next few nights… what in God's name do you say to that kind of pain? I just tucked him away in my heart along with the others I don't really have words for.

"When I learned to get my eyes off me and onto others, miraculously it seems, my own problems began to disappear." ~ *Steve Fugate*

Anishinabe

I was walking along just enjoying the beauty of the north woods of the Chippewa National Forest, somewhere between Bemidji and Grand Rapids, Minnesota, on U.S. highway 2, when all of a sudden, out of nowhere comes, "Hi there, how are you!?" Holy crap! I damn near had a heart attack. I actually yelled out, "What the fuck!" as I turned around to see what had just completely shattered my solitude. Not to mention near ending my life. There, not three feet from me stood a laughing Nelson Johnson, of the Odawa tribe of Indians, part of the Anishinabe of Manitoba, Canada, and member of the Three Fires Council. "Where in the hell did you come from and how in the hell did you get that close to me without my knowing you were there?" (I really was surprised; because in the years I had been walking alone around the country my senses had become much more in tune to my surroundings.) Nelson said while chuckling, "I'm an Indian." So, I wasn't as in tune with nature as I thought. Nelson's laugh helped heal my wounded pride.

Nelson explained to me that he was walking from Roseau River First Nation, Manitoba, to The Bad River Reservation of the Ojibwe People in Wisconsin. About 500 miles. He said he was due there on June 8, for the Spring Ceremonies of the Three Fires Society, and was on schedule. He explained to me that he was representing the Three Fires Society of the Anishinabe Nation, Manitoba, on the Healing Journey, a sacred journey to promote personal healing and to bring attention to the everyday mass destruction of Mother Earth. He explained that the destruction was through violence, racism, war, pollution, alcohol, drugs, and negative attitudes. Nelson, while sprinkling tobacco on the ground from a pouch, said, "Negative energy has caused much injury to Mother Earth." He explained to me that his people of the Anishinabe Three Fires Council, believed that a change to positive attitude would cause unique happenings throughout the universe. "Every day as we walk" said Nelson, "Prayers and tobacco will be offered for personal healing, a healing for Mother Earth, and healing for all races." He stopped, sprinkled some tobacco and said, "Positive thinking will set things right."

He gave me the tobacco pouch he had been using and asked that I sprinkle tobacco as well on my journey as I walked toward the meeting place of the Anishinabe Three Fires Society Spring Ceremonies. I said, "But won't you need this pouch? And just how do you know if I'm going near the Bad River Reservation? That's still a long ways from here." He said, "No, I have other tobacco pouches, anyway, I'll see you again at the Spring Ceremonies, you will be there, you will attend." I said, "No shit?" Nelson was smiling large. "They will love you. People will contact you along the way and some will bring you more tobacco. You stay well. You are walking in the right way. There is light about you." He walked with me until his wife came and picked him up for the night.

I was indeed brought tobacco and several times food was included to keep up my energy as I sprinkled tobacco for the healing of Mother Earth as so requested by my friend, Nelson Johnson. Several different times during my journey to the Ojibwe Lands, I was met by Ojibwe and other Native Peoples who would give me directions and confirm I was headed the right way. A couple of weeks later as I walked down the gravel road surrounded by forest, to take me to the gathering of The Three Fires Society, at least three times, tribal members walked out of the forest to check on my legitimacy for being there. I'm sure the "LOVE LIFE" sign was enough proof, but they still asked my name and as soon as I told them, I was free to continue. They are very guarded about their ancestral ways of sacred customs and traditions. The gravel road leading down to the shore of Lake Superior was very long and as I was starting to feel I would never get there, a car pulled alongside me and Nelson Johnson emerged from it smiling large and said, "It would only be right that I walk the last mile with you my friend."

Nelson had been right; they loved me and my beautiful suggestion to Love Life. I felt nothing but Love from a most beautiful people. The ceremonies were held in a huge lodge framed with tamarack pine, sometimes called lodge pole pine. I was allowed to witness some ceremony but was restricted from others. My voice recorder was taken from me while I was in the lodge, to assure none of their sacred rituals were stolen. Even their own people are not allowed to record or photograph. They thought that there were approximately 5,000 in attendance and Nelson said I was the only whiteface there, again, smiling large. I witnessed some of the ways of a most beautiful people. Nelson invited me back the next year but unfortunately, I was unable to attend.

You Are My Story

Early on in my walks, I thought I should try and get all the media coverage I could. I walked into MANY newspapers and was mostly turned down. But I did get a little over a hundred of them. Mostly small ones and a few bigger ones. I no longer seek them out, I haven't for years. Usually, these days, someone sees me on the road and calls their local paper. I was in Northern Ohio in 2004 on a walk around America. I was in a good sized town and so I approached the local paper for a possible interview to help spread my "LOVE LIFE" message. In spite of the fact, more than one local resident I encountered, told me their newspaper really sucked. I called the paper on a Monday and they set up a time for an interview the next day. So, I had to spend the night in a motel I really couldn't afford. I showed up next morning at the exact time I was told. I was then told they had decided it was not a story they wanted to run. I took a deep breath and then said something I would never say today, I said, "I doubt you will run any story today as important as my message." Always listen to the locals, the newspaper sucked.

No more than ten minutes after leaving the newspaper, walking up a hill, to my left, just above my head, and but a few feet from me, an older Jeep Cherokee slammed into a parking space! Scared the crap outa' me! Out jumped a very pretty dark haired young lady and ran toward me. She said, "Thank God I found you! I work at the newspaper and just happened to look out the window and saw you leaving with your sign. I ran downstairs and asked what you had wanted. They told me you were about suicide. I asked them to please let me clock out for a few minutes as I just had to talk to you!" After telling me she was 18 years-old, she told me this. "Me and my boyfriend since grade school, graduated on Saturday. He told me, being as he was leaving for college, he wanted to break up with me!" She said her heart was crushed and she had never felt such pain! She continued, "I jumped in my car and just started driving really fast and all I could think was that I had to drive into a tree or a wall or something! And then, I saw your "LOVE LIFE" sign. It was a big slap in the face!" Now she is sobbing, and she said, "I just had to let you know. I just had to! Thank you! And I am so sorry my paper wouldn't do your story." And I said, "Sweetheart, I do not need them. YOU are the story!" And while trying to catch her breath and stop crying, the little sweetheart said, "They suck anyway." And I've never personally sought out media coverage since. Hers, is the only kind of story I'm interested in now.

"I want to mend the broken heart while it is yet beating." ~ Steve Fugate

Do Too! Do Not!

It was a beautiful Sunday, a spring morning and I was walking in Northern Ohio. Near Akron, I believe. One of those new Harley Davidson V-Rods designed by Porsche zoomed past me. They were newly released then and I thought they were just beautiful. But moments later, the fine looking machine rolled up beside me. He had turned around to check out my "LOVE LIFE" sign. I said, "Good morning sir!" He was a nice looking man, maybe forty and sporting a well-groomed beard. He very softly said, "Love life huh? I hate life." "No you don't," I answered. "I do so.," he said. "You do not!" I came back with. "Yes I do!" He replied. "You do not!" and "I do too!" and again, "Do not!" I swear, there we were, two grown men standing out in broad daylight arguing, "Do too!" "Do not!" like two little kids. I finally broke the chain with, "You do not hate life, 'cause, if you did you wouldn't be out here this wonderful morning on this beautiful new bike enjoying the wind in your face." He seemed to ponder what I said and then he answered, "I don't know how I could ever love life." I told him, "Look, someone or some situation has hurt you very badly. You have to forgive and forget and go on, that is how you will begin to love life again." He just nodded his head and said, "I'm not sure." "I am," I said. "You go on and realize that you do and are loving life. You let that hurt go and let it die in the past where it belongs. You go love life." He actually smiled a little and said, "I'll try." And then he turned around and rode off on that beautiful machine, the bastard!

"Love your Life constantly and create a state of positivity that no negative dare try and penetrate. ~ Steve Fugate

Perspective

Christmas Eve, 2004, I was walking in the Outer Banks of North Carolina near the town of Elizabeth City. A gentleman stops his car alongside me and wanted to know why I was carrying a sign that said, "LOVE LIFE." So I told my story. I could see that he was very touched by what he heard. He asked me if I would like to join him and his family for

Christmas. At first I declined, explaining that I usually spent Christmas alone when out on the road. The reason: it was just too hard on me emotionally and so I hid from it. But he would not let it go and kept insisting I go home with him. I finally said yes.

They had a very modest home in a remote area. His wife was lovely and gracious. His little boys were five and nine and were good looking little guys. They were both intelligent and were both quite well mannered. They both had cancer. The five year-old had recently been diagnosed as in remission. The nine year-old however, began explaining to me his dilemma as to what his final choice would be for the "Make a Wish Foundation." He was quite happy. He said to me, "The doctor told me I could die from my disease, but I'm not afraid because I have the best daddy in the world and he would never let anything bad happen to me!" Daddy was standing in the doorway behind him and the tears were streaming down daddy's face.

Christmas morning, the two giggling boys woke me up. They had to, I was sleeping on a mat near the tree, next to the gifts. They joyously handed me my very own Christmas gift. It was quite humbling. They were living on a single income; one parent has to stay home. They were strapped by medical expenses and they have to face *that* fear every day. They still put their own problems away long enough to be kind and generous to a perfect stranger.

I stayed three days, the father and I became quite good friends. He drove me back out to the highway and sent me on my way. I left with a pack full of food and a heart that would never be the same.

A few days later on New Year's Day, I stopped for a big treat I had promised myself. I had put back money for this big day. Staying in a motel was always a big treat; I usually camped alongside the road somewhere. This motel stay was really going to be special though. I am an avid Florida Gator football fan. They were playing Miami in a bowl game, and I had been unable to watch even one of their games all year. I checked into the motel after I insisted they prove ESPN was available through their cable service. I was so excited. My first Gator game in a year! The game started at 7:30 pm. I made all the preparations; ran (really ran) to the store for beer and potato chips. I took my shower and then got all snuggled in and was catching up on scores from other games. About 7:00 pm the motel owner knocked on my door and in broken English, starts explaining that due to remodeling and so the all new electrical power unit could be installed, they would be cutting off the electricity that evening! He told me I could leave then and he would give my money back. He kept saying over and over in his strong Indian accent, "I very sorry, I so sorry!" It was already dark, I was walking, where was I to go? I was very disappointed and quite upset! About ten minutes into the game, lights out!

Next morning, I am prepared to tell the owner he should give my money back and I was not happy with the way he conducted business. I would chew him out proper. I reached into my pack to retrieve my receipt, and came out with something much unexpected. Those two precious little boys had put a picture of themselves in my pack. I sat and stared at it quite a while. A football game! I was genuinely ashamed. I was upset over a stupid football game. I took my key to the front desk and while the owner was being yelled at by two other guests, I apologized for having been curt the night before. I told him I sympathized with his problem and that I knew it was out of his control. I did not ask for money back. He was very thankful and insisted I take ten dollars back. Perspective... perspective.

Dick!

I was in a little town in South Carolina; standing just in front of me was a very skinny and strange little guy with a very scraggly and long beard. He was holding a stack of pamphlets. The closer I got to him, the stranger his demeanor. I looked around to see where he might have laid his "THE END IS NEAR" sign. As soon as I was close enough, he stepped right in front of me and I had to look directly in his face. I swear, I think his eyes were spinning. He asked, "Do you love life?" I grunted, "Yeah." I almost said, "No, I'm carrying this sign for someone else, you screwball," and walked on by. He reached out to hand me his propaganda, I glanced down, and "What Is God's Real Name?" it read. I declined to accept it and started to continue on. "Don't you care what God's real name is?!" He asked. And instead of simply saying, "No," and continuing on past him or taking the pamphlet and saying I would read it later, I made the decision to show the mentally ill how really intelligent I was and said, "You are probably going to tell me his name is Yahweh, right?" And with eyes seemingly spinning even more now, he defiantly yelled, "His name *is* Yahweh!" Finally realizing my mistake, I stepped around him and started forward. He jumped right back in front of me, of course. Now the strange little guy is really upset as he accuses, "I'll bet you don't even believe in Yahweh?" And yet again, I put myself on his level and said, "Actually I do believe in a supreme being." He shouts, "What do you think his name is then, if it ain't Yahweh, huh!?" Then I really added fuel to the fire and said, "I don't know what his name is and I don't really care." His face turned so red he looked like he would explode. I figured I might as well go ahead, light the fuse and finish 'im off, so I said, "I've cussed him out and called him all kinds of names and I don't think he gives a damn what we call 'im, just as long as we're a callin'!" He went nuts. Well, nuttier. He yells at me. "How would you like it if I didn't call you by your real name, huh?" I stepped around him, finally showing enough sense to ignore him and walk on. Instead of following me, he decides to just yell louder, "What's your name, huh?" I kept walking and ignoring, he of course kept yelling, "what's your name? Is it Dick?" he asked, really loud. "That's it!" He screamed, "Your name is Dick!" I know I asked for it, I engaged him, but it was still embarrassing. I already had enough attention with "LOVE LIFE" mounted over my head. Now I was in the middle of town with this skinny little weird looking guy yelling as loud as he could, "Hey everybody, that's Dick!"

It sounded even louder as he yelled, "Yup, there goes Dick!" And, "Hey Dick!" "See ya' Dick!" and, "Goodbye Dick!" I kept on walking and he kept on yelling, "Hey Dick!" Probably until I was out of hearing range. He's probably still on that corner yelling, I think I still hear 'im sometimes, "Hey Dick!" And I also hear, "If you had simply taken the little guy's pamphlet and respectfully listened to him a minute or two, you probably would not have been so embarrassed, Dick!"

"To follow one's heart, one must learn to discern images perceived with eyes of colored irises from ones perceived by the eyes of our heart." ~ Steve Fugate

My Corner to Corner Shelly Walk

On February 17, 2005. I was walking on U.S. highway Rt.1 in Daytona Beach, Florida. It was a delightful morning. I had spoken to my daughter only days before and we were both excited that my walk was nearly finished and I would be home in only three weeks or so. She and my three- year-old granddaughter would be driving down to South Florida from their home In Holiday, Florida to pick me up. It was a cheerful thought knowing I was only about 150 miles away from my little girl. I couldn't wait to see her. That morning the Daytona Beach News Journal had printed a story on my walk from an interview they had done with me the day before. There was a large picture of me with my sign alongside the article. So people were recognizing me and several were yelling, waving, and honking their horns. That kind of event always made me feel good and made for a great day. This time it felt especially good as I was in my home state!

My cell phone rang, I looked at the screen and seeing it was my sister calling, I was delighted! "Hey sis!" I shouted with glee knowing it was my adorable sister. I heard these words, "I do not want to be the one to tell you this!" Of course, fear gripped my heart. "Oh God!" I said, "It's mom isn't it? That's the only thing it could have been judging from the despair in her voice. It had to be the death of a loved one. And it had to be my mother because I had already lost my only son! There was just no way could it be my other child, my last child! I can still hear her next words screaming inside my skull, "It's your little girl honey... your Shelly is gone!!" How surreal! Cars driving by with people yelling and horns blowing and, "your Shelly is gone!" I felt like I was in slow motion and everything else was going super-fast past me! I had been there before! What In the hell am I going to do... how can I possibly handle this? My head was screaming and my heart was bleeding! I could hear my sister calling out from my phone over and over, "tell me what to do honey!" and, "Are you alright!" Finally I put the phone back up to my ear and yelled, "Hell no, I'm not all right!" and I hung up. I was in pure agony. My sister called back and said, "Please tell me what you want me to do honey!" I knew I wasn't being fair to my sister, I had to give her an answer but I didn't have an answer! Once more, my life was over! I just stood there with my mind frozen in disbelief... finally some words came out of my mouth, "call Larry damn it!" It seemed forever before I finally remembered Larry's phone number. Larry was my friend Larry Pesin who had been helping me orchestrate my walk and the chief reason for its success. I had called Larry nearly every week for the past two years while walking around the U.S. Moments later my friend Larry called, he was at the airport In Mexico City preparing to fly home to Florida from a business trip. I just started screaming to Larry that my little girl was gone; my precious, beautiful little girl was really gone! Larry said to me, "Steve, you have got to get it together!" "There is no fucking getting it together!" I yelled and then hung up on my friend! I had no Idea what the hell I was doing. This was my last child; she was all I had in the world! She was really gone... both my babies were now gone! My phone rang again and Larry simply said, "Steve, someone is coming to get you in just a few moments. Someone will be calling you, and all you have to do is tell them your exact location. My dear friend Larry had called a limousine service to pick me up and drive me to the West Coast of Florida where my lifeless little girl was waiting for her daddy to say goodbye. My sister later called Larry and told him how much our family appreciated what he had done for me, and Larry said, "He's my friend."

As I stood there in a trance of grief and anguish waiting for my ride, I automatically started trying to accept what had just happened to me. I simply looked skyward and these words came out of my mouth, "Both of them, you have to have both of them?" I loved both my babies equally, but if one death hurt worse than the other... it had to be the death of the only one I had left. Something else flashed into my mind as I stood there. Months before, while walking through Northern Ohio, a man saw my sign and insisted he had to relate his story to me. He told me of his wife leaving him and their two little boys without a word. As he was telling me his story my cell phone rang, it was my daughter. I apologized to the gentleman and suggested that perhaps we would see each other again. He told me he felt strongly to tell me his story. He said very matter of fact that he would see me again. I talked with my little girl for quite a while and then walked on into the little town. I had forgotten all about the man and his story. I came to a little bar and grill, knowing they usually have the best sandwiches, I went in to eat. Typical of a bar, when I first entered it was dark and I couldn't see well. I sat down at the end of the bar directly in front of me. I ordered a beer and asked for a menu. Someone said, "I've got that beer." And there sitting facing me just at the corner of the bar, was the guy who had been telling me the story! I couldn't believe it. He simply said, "Told you I would see you again." He went right back into telling me his story. He said that not long after his wife left, the three year old was accidentally run over in their driveway and killed. He saw the whole thing, he watched his baby boy die in his arms. Years later he was at his girlfriends' home and received a phone call telling him his 33-year-old only son had just died of a massive heart attack. He said he grabbed the side of the kitchen bar and he gripped it as hard as he could. He said he looked up and he screamed, "Father, thank you for the time I had with my two boys!" He said his girlfriend started yelling at him and said, "What the hell is wrong with you? How can you say something like that at a time like this? You should be asking why you!" He said he turned to her and said, "Why not me? Do I want it to happen to someone else instead?" This guy was for real, he really did that! Why in the hell was this guy so adamant about telling me his story? The recollection of his story helped me accept the horror once again... why not me? I never want this to happen to anyone else. And over my head was my answer, what I was preaching to all, I had to push on and... "LOVE LIFE"!

Figure 7. My little girl, Shelly, with her little girl, Cassie.

Can Change Only Me

There is only one person in this life we can change, and that is ourselves. Worrying about what anyone else does is a total waste of time because we cannot change them. But you can change yourself; you can change yourself into someone confident and strong enough to allow no one else's attitude or actions to deter you from being you. All the things we go through in life are but sculpting tools used to shape us into a better person. We all have the ability to handle all our own problems. The bad things we've had to face in our life become tools for making us a better person by converting them into lessons on how to better understand ourselves. Understanding ourselves and looking at our own faults to correct, instead of the faults of another which we cannot correct, make us much less judging and much more understanding of those others. This is the only way to a genuine pure Love and respect for all our fellow human beings, instead of just the words saying we Love all others. A good person is a person who *really* loves others. We become a better person when we stop the self-pity, the blame, and let go the anger and move forward, forward toward maturity. I never started maturing until I saw these truths. I was 54 years old when I started really maturing.

Had I allowed self-pity to persist in my life after the deaths of both my children, I would either no longer be on this earth or I would have gone completely insane. The single hardest thing I've ever had to do in my life other than bury my babies, was to convert my heart wrenching pain into a positive energy directed at others and away from myself. The world is changed each time one of us gets our eyes off ourselves and allow our real purpose in life, love and concern for our fellow human being, to come forward. Please, LOVE LIFE.

As one Somewhat Enlightened Perhaps?

In 2004. Walking in New Jersey not far from New York City and looking for a motel because it was dark, a small SUV stopped in front of me and out jumped a gorgeous blonde, dressed in all black with a black feather boa around her neck. She was all excited and saying a whole bunch of stuff all at once. As soon as I answered her question as to why I walked, telling her of my son's suicide, she said, "Come on, lets load up your stuff up and you must go with me into the city to hear this guy speak, I have two tickets, come on, let's go!" And I said, I'm not loading my stuff in your car because I'm walking around the U.S. and *that* would be defeating my purpose." She was not deterred. She kept asking and I kept saying no. She also said she would let me spend the night at her place to shower and do my laundry. Hard to turn that down, so, we loaded all my stuff into her car. She said she was nearly out of gas and had to pull into the gas station at the bottom of the hill. As soon as she said that, we ran out of gas! Being as we were not quite in a spot yet where the car would roll down the long, steep hill freely, I jumped out and gave a push. She yelled out that she would meet me in the gas station. There I stood while a wacked out blonde in a black feather boa was driving away with every single thing I owned! Maybe she wasn't really out of gas I was thinking!? But, she coasted into the gas station, gassed up and we went to hear some guy speak.

About a week later, on the phone telling my friend, Larry, about the encounter, he asked was she really pretty and did I really tell her no four times. After answering yes, he said, "You need to come home Steve, we need to talk!"

On the way there, she shared with me that about four years before, she had been riding a very large horse with her darling four-year-old little boy propped in front of her. Her precious baby boy somehow fell from the horse onto his little head and was killed. Oh my God! Oh my God… the absolute horror she had suffered.

She never told me what he would be speaking on, she knew, she just hadn't told me. She just said she had two tickets to hear him. She told me his name that I have since forgotten, but I remember saying it sounded vaguely familiar to me at the time and asked if he were a Buddhist. She said she wasn't sure. Anyway, he sat on the stage with his legs crossed wearing very loose fitting linen clothing and he spoke very softly and certainly had an air of calmness about him (the way of one somewhat enlightened perhaps?). About thirty minutes into the lecture, mostly about death being part of life and how we should all view it. He was basically categorizing all death to be viewed the same no matter the physical connection. She and I turned and looked at each other and we both rose from our seats and as politely and inconspicuously as possible, exited the theatre. We looked at each other again just after we exited but we never discussed our leaving or why, ever.

Seven years later, in 2011. In a motel lobby in a small California town just east of Sacramento on a walk across the country, a very nicely dressed gentleman sat down across from me and began inquiring of my reason for walking. I had observed him earlier as he kept going behind the counter and having conversation with the younger man, also of either Indian or Pakistani descent, who was obviously the proprietor. I first thought he might possibly be his father. The gentleman spoke very softly and very intelligently. He had a very calm demeanor and I am fairly certain he was a student of some eastern religion and/or their philosophies. After hearing of the deaths of my children, he very softly and seemingly to me, very humbly (the way of one somewhat enlightened perhaps?) told me that there was indeed a way to look at death and then handle the grief accordingly, no matter the kinship of the loved one. That's the way I perceived it. I then explained that having had the experience of losing parents, and a sibling, I felt that no death is as equally devastating as that of your own child. He then proceeded into a very nice and very quietly spoken explanation (the way of one somewhat enlightened perhaps?) of the proper way to view death and the grief attached to it. I had heard this before.

I listened to him quite a while, as he was pleasant to listen to. And then it dawned on me why he seemed to be talking around my belief there is no greater pain than losing one's child. After it appeared he had fully explained his outlook. I very calmly looked at him and said, "You do not have children, do you sir?" Though I believe I saw a slight glimmer of surprise in his eyes, he answered, very quietly and most sincerely, "No sir, I do not." I then said, also very quietly and most sincerely, "I feel then, that disqualifies you from this topic of conversation." The very fine gentleman became silent. I waited for his words in response, they did not come (the way of one somewhat enlightened perhaps?). After but a moment in silence, I asked yet another question, "Are you skilled as an electrician?" And as was his manner, he answered again, very quietly and sincerely, "No sir, I am not." To which I very respectfully said, "Neither am I sir, so we will not be able to have a discussion on electricity either I suppose." He smiled ever so sweetly and then changed our topic of conversation (the way of one somewhat enlightened perhaps?) to the number of miles I'd walked and so on. I smiled as well; it had been a pleasant exchange.

Your child comes from your womb, from your loins; your other loved ones have not that connection to you. It is by design; you will never love your parent as much as your parent loves you. We can lose, a parent, a sibling, and a spouse. Those three all have the same thing in common, they came not from your womb or your loins. The philosophy that one size fits all, allows not for the beauty of individuality. Life does not do group therapy. We are not born collectively, we are born one at a time… as individuals.

"I believe a truly unique individual stands alone and away from the herds because they have no fear of being alone. They are confident within themselves and totally self-reliant. The mavericks of the world are not followers of groups, parties, and creeds devised by someone else somewhere in time; they listen to a different drummer, the beating of their own heart." ~ Steve Fugate

Scarecrow

I was just outside Coshocton, Ohio in early spring. A concerned lady had stopped to tell me the temperature was going to drop unusually low that night. My summer sleeping bag was good for about 40 degrees so I knew I could be in for a miserable night. And I knew I couldn't build a fire in the mostly farmland, I was in. I found a rise where I would not be seen from the highway if I pitched my tent close to the fence. There was plenty of soft dry grass for a trick I'd used before. So I began stuffing the grass between my outer clothing and my long johns. I looked like a scarecrow when I finished and I cared not. I snuggled into my tent hoping I was prepared, when my cell phone rang and a lady who had stopped earlier, said she and her husband were out on the road trying to find me so I could spend the night in their home after they took me to an 'all you can eat' restaurant!

I've never taken down a tent so fast in my life! I was pulling tent stakes as fast as I could and grass was flying everywhere as I emptied my clothing of the impromptu insulation. I guess you could say, I was un-stuffing myself so that I could go stuff myself! I ended up staying three nights with Mike and Ruth of Coshocton, Ohio. See how good Life is when you set your mind to help others. Just Love Life, Life deserves it.

Salt Barn

I was just outside of Canton, Ohio in an area called Sugar Creek Township. It looked like rain fast approaching and so I was looking for a cover of some sort. I spotted the perfect one, a Quonset hut open in the front and half filled with a salt and sand mixture used on icy roads. A sign said it was the property of Sugar Creek Township and there was no trespassing. Just opposite of the "salt barn" was a small building, a sign said it was the Sugar Creek Township Maintenance Dept. There were two men in a little office, Mike and his one helper, Rick. Mike told me I could bed down in one of the salt barns. I had coffee and cheese doodles with them, an Ohio thing maybe? I shared my story and Mike shared that only recently his young son-in-law had taken his own life.

After Mike and Rick left for the day, I made my bed in the salt barn and out of the pouring rain and settled in. I was reading a paper Mike had given me. When a car pulled up in front of the open faced salt barn. A young lady, maybe her early twenties, got out of her car. She walked within 15 feet of me and just started sobbing! I realized that Mike must have told his daughter who I was, this was the little darling who had just lost her husband to suicide. I ran to her and just wrapped my arms around her and held her while she sobbed. She started trying to apologize for her break down, I stopped her and told her to let it rip! She was screaming out, "He did it right in front of me, he shot himself right in front of me!" All I could do was hold her, and love her. She continued screaming, "I was a stay at home mom, and I have lost our house! I have a new baby boy, what am I going to do?" I just kept holding her, she held on tight. I can't describe how much love I felt for that precious heartbroken child. I didn't have her immediate answer any more than I have anyone else's. But I do have love, so I just loved her. I was holding my little boy and my little girl. I did share with her though that I had found an inner peace in my solitude and a retreat from my grief. I told her I feel we all have our own answers inside of us. Sometimes it is very deep inside of us and we need an outside source to help find it. And that, there is a universal power waiting to help us. All we have to do is realize it does indeed exist and cry out to it, thus giving it credence. And we can absolutely achieve a peace and self-assurance that all will be well ... no matter the circumstances. She eventually stopped sobbing and screaming. I told her I loved her very much.

The next morning as I hiked down the road, Mike and Rick pulled alongside me in their work truck. Mike said, "You talked to my girl last night, thank you, I think she really needed that." She has called me since and says I helped her and she was coping much better. I didn't do anything special. I do not have anyone's answer. But this is what can happen when we open up our hearts to everyone, to strangers.

"I call what I do trail therapy, and like all other trails, it goes both ways." ~ Steve Fugate

You Will Not!

I wasn't far past Edinburgh, Pennsylvania headed for New Castle, when a man, probably in his mid-forties, pulled his big refrigerated truck over next to me. He exited the truck and walked up to me. "You love life, huh?" he asked, and before I could answer, he added, "Man, I do not love life." By now his lips were trembling. I motioned him to the other side of his truck away from the traffic, for more privacy. He started crying, "Man, I don't wanna' live anymore."

The desperation in the man's voice was certainly obvious. I told him firmly, "You are not going to kill yourself" "But I just don't want to live anymore." he said. I continued on, "Let me tell you who I am and why you are not going to take your life." I went on to tell him of my son's suicide and my daughter's death from an accidental overdose. I told him I carried "LOVE LIFE" over my head because I wanted no one else to stop loving life long enough to do what my son and daughter did. I could see I now had his attention somewhat. I told him also, "You didn't meet me by accident." I could see a little surprise in his face and he had calmed some. He started telling his story.

He had been cheating on his wife of many years and he got caught. She left him and was now suing for divorce. She only recently had moved in with a new boyfriend. And she would not even consider his pleas for her to forgive him and give him a second chance. He was devastated. He mentioned suicide again in saying, "I just don't want to live any longer." His head was hanging in self-pity. "You know," I said, "We really don't have the right to take our own life; it doesn't belong just to us. Our life also belongs to others, those others who love us. He seemed to consider this a little, and then said, "I guess it would really hurt my 19-year-old daughter and 22-year-old son." That's when I really let him have it with both barrels. And I really had his attention this time with the tone of my voice, "Who in the hell do you think you are? Why do you think you have the right to destroy your children's lives? To end those two kids right to a happy life? How very self-centered of you." He was shocked, to say the least. I never gave him time to react any farther, I would not shut up. I continued, "You can do anything you want in this life except hurt others and what you are considering will absolutely devastate the lives of others." He just stood there; I don't think that is what he wanted to hear from me.

Still not giving him a chance to speak, I related an incident which had occurred in Maine while I was walking around the U.S.: I was exiting a convenience store when a gentleman approached me. He pointed to my "LOVE LIFE" sign leaning against the store and asked if it were mine and what it meant. I told him of my son's suicide and what I was about. Now this very well dressed man had just stepped out of a brand new BMW and on his wrist was a Rolex watch. He looked like a successful man who obviously had his act together. He looked at me and tears were streaming down his face. He said, "My father killed himself when I was only 12. I don't know why he did that to me." The gentleman told me he was 62 years old. Fifty years had passed and this man was still crying. His father had filled him with guilt and broken his heart permanently.

After telling the story, I asked him, "Now you still think you have the right to cripple your babies emotionally for the rest of their lives?" He could not answer, he looked totally confused. I had caused him, just for a second, to stop wallowing in his own self-pity. I did not let up on him, I continued, "Listen, what my little boy did to me, his mother, his sister, his other relatives and all his friends, was extremely self-centered. He didn't realize it; he left this world ignorant of the devastation to other lives his suicide would bring."

I looked the truck driver right in the eyes and said, "But you sir, will not be leaving ignorant. No sir, I have just educated your ass. You will be taking your life knowing full well what you will be doing to your babies and your other loved ones. Yup, you will be leaving in a full state of pure self-centeredness." He only looked at me briefly and then down at the ground and said nothing. He was no longer talking of his woes and killing himself though. I repeated, "You will not kill yourself." He answered, "I'm not sure." But he was certainly not as adamant about his decision to commit suicide as he had been a few minutes before. I told him he would be okay and that he had all his own answers on the inside, just like the rest of us. That he had to consider the feelings of his loved ones and friends. That if he would always try to put all things in perspective, he could have a much better chance of coming to terms with his pain without hurting others. I again said, "You will be okay and you are not going to kill yourself." I gave him my card and told him to call me anytime. He still had his head down as he walked toward his truck. But I was pretty sure he had had a change of heart. I felt a real love in my heart for him. I have an experience I wish to God I did not have. But I do have it and I have come to believe that I have it for a reason. I'm a survivor of a suicide and I but tell my side of the story.

A few months later while visiting friends in Maine, I was listening to all my voice mail calls. My cell phone had been out of service for a few weeks. There was this call, "Hey, I'm the truck driver in Pennsylvania that stopped you. I just wanted to let you know I took your words to heart. You uh, you were right. I realized how wrong I would have been. Things did get better and I am trying real hard to adjust to life and just take it as it comes. Jus' wanted to say thanks!"

"If you are 70 years-old and your mama is still alive, you are her baby, whether your butt likes it or not. You do not have the right to take your own Life it doesn't belong just to you, but to your loved ones as well." ~ Steve Fugate

Model T

Near Slippery Rock, Pennsylvania, I was looking to find a convenience store or restaurant for coffee and breakfast. I try to kill two birds with one stone when I can and ask to charge my cell phone while I am eating. I came upon a little country store. As I was unloading my backpack and beautiful "LOVE LIFE" sign, I glanced in the window to see the owner/operator staring at me with a scowl on her face. I entered the store and asked the stern- faced lady if she had coffee. She nodded her head and pointed to an area behind me. As I was preparing to pay for my coffee I inquired as to the nearest restaurant. "Three miles straight ahead," the owner said. There were two men standing to the left of me, and one of them said, "She can make you a mighty fine breakfast sandwich right here." I looked at the owner and asked if she could prepare a sausage and egg sandwich for me. I'm fairly certain that she was giving the gentleman who had just spoken, a dirty look. She simply nodded and I told her then that I would like to have one. She came out from behind the counter and started for wherever it was she prepared food. As she passed by me I said, "Oh excuse me ma'am, would you mind if I plugged in my cell phone and charged it while I am eating?" She turned and replied, "No, you cannot." I was certainly surprised; I couldn't remember that ever happening before. One of the men spoke up and said, "Ann, it doesn't take hardly any juice at all to charge a phone." But the lady remained adamant about not allowing me to charge the phone. I told her very nicely I would then, have to cancel the sandwich and explained that when walking time is very important and I conserve time by doing two things at once. I told her I would simply walk the three miles to the closest restaurant and charge my phone there while I was eating. The store owner was clearly aggravated that she had made the 15 ft. trip for nothing. One of the gentlemen offered to take my phone to his house and charge it for me. I thanked him and declined.

No more than five minutes after I started walking again, a young lady pulled her car over and walked up to me. In her hand was a fresh made turkey sandwich made with thick slices of turkey with lettuce, tomato, and mayo. She was very excited about giving it to me; she explained that it had been intended for her lunch. She insisted on my taking the sandwich with the explanation that she would just buy something else at her work place. The sandwich was delicious: I had just finished eating the sandwich and I noticed off to my left an old man under a carport working on a Ford Model T open touring car. I yelled out a, "Good Morning" and he turned and motioned for me to cross the road to where he was. He immediately began telling me the history of his car and the entire history of Ford Model T's. The wonderful machine had been in his family since new and still had some of the original paint on it. An uncle of his, a doctor, had purchased it new and used it to service his patients in the area. My new friends name was Chuck Dickey and he had been born on the property we were standing on, in 1919. Chuck was 89! He was a big man and seemed to be in perfect health. Chuck was delighted with my Love

Life sign and said he thought it to be a good endeavor. He then demonstrated his own compliance with my sign when he stated, "I'm going to crank 'er up and we're going for a ride." I had heard stories of people who actually had their arms broken while trying to hand crank a Model T! Chuck bent down to crank and explained to me, "I'll probably have to give 'er a couple cranks before the one that'll actually start 'er." Sure enough, she started putting on the third crank! Chuck was smiling big; you could see that he got joy every time he cranked 'er up. As he was removing tools and other obstructions from our path, I remembered my cell phone. "Hey Chuck" I said, "Would it be possible to charge up my cell phone before we leave?" "Not a problem!" He yelled over the sound of the "Tin Lizzie." Chuck then proceeded to uncoil and walk a 100 foot extension cord around old car and tractor parts and then through a window of his small home. When he came out of the house from plugging the cord in, he rubbed the palms of his hands together a couple times signifying he was finished and said, "There, no problem!" He took me on a guided tour of the beautiful Pennsylvania countryside, most of which had changed little or none, according to Chuck. The interior of the "T" was surprisingly quite confined. So, every time that Chuck used his elbow to emphasize something, making sure I acknowledged it, it hurt like hell! But I didn't complain, it was all part of the wonderful experience.

Once back at Chuck's farm which had been in his family for three generations, we toured the farm property. He had several antique tractors and later in his home he proudly showed off his restored collection of cast iron tractor and farm implement seats. Chuck had been a pilot since youth and had delivered air mail. His father had actually delivered mail by air when they picked it up via a hook from a tall pole while flying and not having to touch down. Back at his house as Chuck handed me my fully charged phone, we both agreed we had enjoyed ourselves tremendously.

I left the company of Chuck Dickey with a bounce in my step and gratitude for the store owner who wouldn't let me charge my phone. Chuck had explained to me that he had already worked on his "T" for a half hour and that he only worked on it about an hour each day. If I had eaten a sandwich at the store while my phone was charging, I would have not met Chuck, and I would not have enjoyed a fresh turkey sandwich! Thank God for the lady's bad mood, or perhaps she was always like that. That's really none of my business and I'm convinced that had I become angered and brooded over her attitude, I would not have been so blessed. I have, by the way, learned this fact the hard way. I do indeed reap what I sow. Over the next few days, every time I felt the soreness in my left side, I smiled and thought of the smiling and laughing Chuck Dickey elbowing me and most definitely getting his point across.

"Giving, a means of transportation for Love." ~ Steve Fugate

"Sheppy"

Near Emlenton, Pennsylvania, went into a restaurant called "Fat Chaps" for breakfast, there wasn't anyone in sight. I started saying, "Hello" over and over and still saw not a soul. Finally, out came this delightful little lady named Sue. She was the owner of Fat Chaps restaurant. I asked if I could charge my phone while eating. She showed me where to plug in my phone and then yelled to her waitress," Hey, I'm going to be over here talking to Steve and having my coffee." She then sat down across from me, leaned over and said, "Now, tell me your story." I shared my story and then my curiosity had to know how her restaurant came to be known as "Fat Chaps" because I saw no one that fit the description of being fat. She said when she was purchasing equipment from an out of business hotel and Pizza restaurant in Pittsburgh, she noticed their now defunct sign and said, "Can I buy that too?" So, she bought their "Fat Chaps" sign. She said she loved taking shortcuts and was then no longer concerned with having to come up with a catchy name for her new restaurant. Sue and I traded stories for quite a while. She told of her dog she had when a child during WWII.

The dog's name was "Sheppy." She called her story a love story. It truly touched my heart. Here is Sue's wonderful story of Sheppy:

"My dog Sheppy was a beautiful mixture of Alsatian Sheppard and St. Bernard. I don't remember where she came from. I was in a four room school house in the sixth grade. Shep and I spent our days running the fields chasing rabbits and hunting adventure over and under the rocks! Our limitation was our seven acre farm, equipped with 2 horses and 40 chickens! People didn't interest me in the least. Only the guests Shep and I ventured to indulge were my life.

One time, my Shep went to a neighbor's place and killed a few of their chickens. Yes, I was sorry and I think my parents had said they were sorry and replaced the chickens. I walked up the lane to the school that next day and then came down that same lane but a few hours later absolutely devastated! The principal had called an assembly of all the grades, called me forth and proceeded to expel me from school until I had gotten rid of my dog, Shep!

NOTE: I asked Sue why he did that and she told me that as near as she could remember, the school principal was simply very good friends with the neighbor who lost the chickens. She also thought that possibly the neighbor was of some status in the community. She was but a little girl, she never looked beyond the fact that her beloved Sheppy was taken from her.

The dread consumed my life! I was given three choices by my parents: 1. To put Shep away. 2. Find her a home. 3. Enroll her in the army. This was the time of WWII and there was a training camp for dogs 40 miles east. Pleading never gave way to any good results so I chose the third option.

My mother and I drove newly U.S. Army enrolled Sheppy to her new environment. "You may return to visit her in two weeks." we were told. In exactly two weeks my mother drove me back to the camp only to hear from the officials, "She was able to jump our fence and get out. We found her though and have added 18 inches to the height of the fence. So, come back in another two weeks and you can see her." Do I need to describe my feelings? Two more anxious weeks went by and we once again visited the camp. By the way, just writing about this brings up years and years of pent up emotions remembering those words of the official on our second visit, "She escaped soon after you were here and we haven't seen her since, so very sorry!"

The way home was a constant search. My mother and I went to every house in the sparsely populated area to ask. It was all to no avail. Very near to our home was our veterinarian and my mother suggested we stop and inquire with him as our last stop for the day. The vet told us a dog had wondered in just recently, an awful looking thing he said. And it certainly wasn't Shep he added. I asked may I see him anyway and he led us to the kennels. There lying on the floor was a very thin, dirty, and haggard looking dog. As soon as the door was opened I dropped down to the floor to hug and love my Sheppy!

We had to carry her to the car; she had run 40 miles to home. I do not remember the words, the days, I but remember my heart... my Sheppy was home!"

Look Over Some Things...

May 11, 2007. Looking for a place to eat, I went off the main route, Rt.6, and into the very small town of Roulette, Pennsylvania. Roulette had one store, a little store/restaurant operation. As soon as I took off my pack and beautiful "LOVE LIFE" sign, a handsome young man greeted me at the door with an ice cold Mountain Dew. "Here," he said, "You look a bit parched." He had one of those smiles that can come only from a wide open beautiful heart. He certainly made my extra effort to find the store well worth it. He told me to go on in and get me something to eat. He then turned back into the store and said, "Honey, fix him something to eat please." There was a beautiful young redhead conducting the business of the very busy little store. She had that same smile and attitude, she was his wife. She would not let me pay for anything. I had just sat down when I heard the thundering roar of an obviously "hopped up" car squealing the tires for what seemed like forever. I glanced out a window just in time to see a white Camaro scream past. An old man was sitting at the table across from me reading his paper. He winced at the noise of squealing tires and engine roaring. Shaking his head, he looked over his paper at me and said, "That was your host. He does that constantly. It's his hobby." He continued, "we all just accept it 'cause he's such a fine young man, and anyways he keeps all the roosters awake for fifty miles." "Well he sure woke me up," I said, "Yeah, me too," he said, and went back to his paper.

Push on and Love Life

I firmly believe that because each and every one of us is so truly unique one from the other, that each of us is equipped from within with our own answers in Life. If one can but push past the tears and the ache in their precious heart, there is a place of rest within. A sanctuary within which allows us to deal with the pain in our own special and unique way. A unique way hard-wired into our very being already there waiting for a great act of faith to be shouted out into the wide open ears of the universe: "I Love Life!" You are then telling the universe how much you do truly love and appreciate your gift of life and that you are then trusting that everything will be okay. And it most assuredly will get okay. Anything short of love and appreciation for our beautiful gift of life is a negative and negative never accomplishes anything and serves absolutely no good purpose. We are all created equal in our rights to the universal laws, those laws of life. It is about Love ladies and gentlemen, only Love, Love, and more Love! Over my head as I walk, the two most powerful words in the Universe have been put together, "LOVE LIFE."

Push on and love the gift of life we've been so wonderfully blessed with my friends. When we awake and feel that sweet, sweet air on our upper lip we have indeed been gifted another day. Realize the miracle of that moment first and foremost and grab onto it and hold onto the beauty of our precious gift of Life. Give that moment precedence over all other thoughts that are attempting to cause us to put the realization of the beauty of our being alive yet one more day in second place. Absolutely nothing is more sacred than our gift of life. Hold onto the moment as long as it takes for the realization of the beauty of life to supersede and conquer all negative thoughts and simply Love Life.

Crazy Indian

9/6/07 Near New Castle, Pennsylvania, a guy yelled at me from across the street and asked if I could use a cup of coffee? "Yes sir!" I said. I then ran to his front porch where we talked through three pots of Starbucks coffee. His name was Al and his wife was Laura. Al belonged to the Tuscarawas Tribe of Indians, a part of the Iroquois Nation. Al's Cocker Spaniel pup was named Anahmush-manito, which means dog spirit. We talked about life and a lot about the Native Peoples and about my proud connections with them as I have crossed their lands. Al had been sober for twenty six years. He said he was referred to as the "Crazy Indian" when he was drinking. He said, "I decided to get sober so I could enjoy my insanity. It has been a lot more fun this way. I really am nuts and it's a lot more fun now that I can remember doing the crazy shit I do." We had a lot in common, in my heavy drinking days, I was once called, "Crazy Steve." True story. As I was leaving, Al presented me with a beautiful tobacco pouch decorated with partridge feathers. So glad he offered the coffee, so glad I accepted. So glad neither of us ignored the moment, and instead, grabbed the moment. And this is how we Love Life. Love Life, grab the moment.

Respect

In Kingsbury, New York, as I was walking by an open garage, a repair shop I think, a guy about my age with a beer in his hand stepped out and yelled, "Who in the fuck hired you to carry that fuckin' sign around?" I immediately crossed the road and entered the garage where five other men about my age were standing around drinking beer. Just before I entered I heard, "Damn he's coming over here!" The original speaker had taken a seat in the back and I fixed my eyes on him to answer his question. I said, "No one hired me to carry this sign sir, I do it all on my own. I lost my little boy to suicide and my little girl to an accidental drug overdose. I carry this sign so maybe I can remind your children or grandchildren to never stop loving life long enough to do what my two did." The guy in the chair gulped hard and was squirming in his seat. I continued, "We know for sure that several young people have not taken their life as a result of meeting me and this sign. One side of this sign represents my little girl and the other side represents my little boy. I will tolerate no disrespect." A voice to my right said, "Nor should you!" I handed the gentleman next to me my card and said, "Gentlemen, I thank you so very much for listening, have a good day." After I had stepped out of the garage, from behind me I heard, "Damn!"

A couple hours later a guy pulled up beside me and in a strong Hispanic accent said, "Hey muhn, I love you sign muhn. Dees is what is all about muhn!" I said, "Thank you so much my good man, I needed to hear that." See how easy I am to get along with. The people I worry about impressing the most are my two children.

"Love your Life, it mystifies and stuns the assholes just long enough to get past them." ~ Steve Fugate

F'k Cancer!

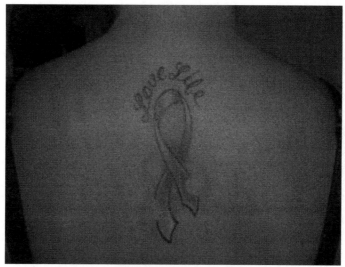

Figure 8. Amber 's tattoo.

I was on Rock City Road, heading south just outside Saratoga Springs, New York. A young man stopped his truck next to me with total disregard of traffic behind him. He had on a Yankee's cap covering up a bald head. He leaned over his passenger and said, "Hey, I gotta' tell ye' something buddy, I got cancer! I woke up this morning feeling all bad and depressed and scared. Then I saw you walking down the road with that sign and it made me realize, by God I love life!" And as I handed him my card, I answered, "Yeah, well, fuck cancer! You have every right to love life! You don't have a damn thing that can't be beat, cancer gets beat all the time. And by God, you're going to beat it too." "And with a big beautiful smile on that too young face, he said."Yes I am, I am going to live!" His friend in the passenger seat was nodding his head in total agreement and began pumping his fist in the air saying, "Yeah, yeah! Fuck cancer!" I said, "You've still got life, hell, you can beat anything." The traffic was starting to line up behind him and a horn or two blew. We kept on cheering and all three of us were pumping our fist in the air and saying, "Yeah that's right, fuck cancer!" And as he was driving away he said, "Yeah mister, you're right, Fuck cancer and I am going to live!" "Damn right you're going to live, fuck cancer!" I yelled back. I watched them go down the road; both were still pumping their fist in the air and surely, they were still shouting, "Fuck cancer!"

A few days later I retrieved my email and found this, "Yesterday you met a young man on the road in a gray Ford truck. He has cancer. He said you gave him hope. He is my son." And in big bold capital letters, "THANK YOU!"

Over a year later in December 2008, the young man's new wife contacted me. They had just recently married, that September. The wedding had been postponed by RJ after he was diagnosed with cancer. Amber wouldn't hear of it for long, she insisted they get married anyway. She said her husband, RJ, was suffering from Hodgkin's Lymphoma, a very aggressive disease. Amber told me, the day RJ and I met on the road, he was scheduled to be in treatment but he had contracted a mild cold bug and couldn't be treated as planned. She further explained, he became very depressed that day until he saw me and my "LOVE LIFE" sign walking alongside the road. "He always took another route than the back road he chose that day to pick up his friend." She said, "I know you and RJ met for a reason:" She also told me, "Since you inspired him so much I decided to add "Love Life" to the tattoo I had already planned for him, I thought it a perfect fit. 'Cause really, no matter what, you should just love life." How very intimate and loving. That tattoo, a beautiful little billboard proclaiming love and encouragement from an adoring and dedicated young wife. Probably every night and every morning RJ is reminded with so very much love, to love life and fight back. RJ is still with us. Evidently RJ is a fighter and is fighting back hard. He certainly married a warrior.

I got this message June 8, 2013, from RJ of Cohoes, New York: "Steve I'm not sure if you remember me. But we crossed paths in Rock City falls New York outside of Saratoga about 4 years ago. I was the young man with stage 4 cancer and your love life motto is tattooed on my wife's back and has become the catch phrase to my life and for my family. Thank you for everything. I can't put into words how much our encounter meant to me. It may possibly be the reason I am here today. I was having a very difficult time that day understanding why my life was going the direction it was. The way it all worked out with my passing you on the road and something telling me to stop and talk to you. It truly is destiny. Just so you know I am now in a durable 4-year remission. Thank you again and good luck." That "LOVE LIFE" sign has done some really cool shit!

Susan Bergier

I met Mark in 2004 walking U. S highway 1 in Maine, he loved my sign and we became fast friends. So much so that a couple weeks later he drove down one night and met me in Massachusetts so he could introduce me to his girlfriend, Susan. She was a delight! He invited me to his home in Maine in 2007 as part of my corner to corner "Shelly Walk." In the month I was there Mark spent hours and hours taping conversation with me to be later used on the "Hearing Voices" program aired on National Public Radio. I had been told before my visit that Susan had cancer. Had I not been told, I would have never known it by her actions.

About two weeks after leaving their home, Mark and his lovely girlfriend, Susan, stopped by on his motorcycle and treated me to dinner in Lincoln, New Hampshire. They brought this poem they wanted to share with me:

Pied Beauty

Glory be to God for dappled things.
For skies of couple-colour as a brindled cow;
for rose moles all in stripple upon trout they swim;
Fresh-firecoal chestnut-falls, finches wings;
Landscape plotted and pieced - fold, fallow, and plough;
And all trades, their gear tackle and trim;
and all things counter, original, spare, strange;
Whatever is fickle, freckled, (who knows how?)
With swift, slow; sweet, sour; a dazzle, dim;
He fathers - forth whose beauty is past change:
Praise Him. ~ Gerard Manly Hopkins

This poem makes me happy, reading it is a delight for me. They drove over two hundred miles to deliver that poem to me. Susan said, "We laughed, giggled, and sang all the way!" While helping me to memorize the delightful little poem, the three of us giggled and laughed some more.

I had walked miles proclaiming Love Life and felt I did indeed Love Life. Then I spent time with my friend, Susan Bergier, who was dying of cancer. I watched Susan, with earphones on her sweet bald head, learning a new language! She never dwelled on herself, being more concerned of the affect it was having on her loved ones. She taught me a new language: speak love and concern for others no matter your circumstances, and stay busy. Susan lost her battle less than five months after I was blessed to have spent time with her in Maine. During that time, she and Mark decided to marry. This is what her husband, Mark, wrote the day he lost her:

"More than anything, Susan believed in people, and because she believed
in people so completely, she never felt that anybody let her down.
That's a comfort to me, who knows how much more I could have listened
instead of talked. Now, Susan, I'll try not to let that happen anymore, with all your world
of people."

The simple words on Susan's stone say it all:
November 1943 – December 2007
What a Woman

Big Wheels, Little Wheels

Walking on Rt. 202 in Buxton Maine, I walked by a residence with a small sign saying it belonged to the Buchanan family. Two large gates were barring their driveway. The gates were made of old steel wheels of assorted sizes and styles welded together. Each wheel was painted a different color. A large sign over the wheels said, "Big wheels, little wheels...we are all significant! We can all make a difference!"

Greater Pain

In Maine, near Ellsworth, I met "Doc," after I asked if he was the owner of the beautiful custom Harley I was admiring. After hearing why I was walking "Doc" revealed that he had lost two children also. His two boys, 17 and 15, were killed in a fire in Manchester, New Hampshire, in 2000. The older son ran back in the house to try to save his little brother. A fireman by the name of David Anderson was killed trying to save the two boys. And "Doc" was there and could do nothing but scream. The stories I hear folks! There is always someone who has been through more than you and I have.

I Needed a Sauna!

My good friends, Mark, and Susan, from Maine, drove down to where I was on the road in Massachusetts and treated me to a great meal and a motel room. A room with a sauna! When Mark came down from their room the next morning to say goodbye, he exclaimed "Damn we didn't get a sauna in our room!" I found out later, when he was checking in, Mark had told the guy at the front desk what I was doing. After he left my room that morning, he asked the same guy when checking out why they didn't get a room with a sauna as well. The guy said he figured with all the walking I was doing I needed it more than they did! Mark roared in laughter.

Notes on a Guardrail

Near Millerton, Pennsylvania, I came upon a cross at the side of the road up against a guard rail, obviously the spot where someone had lost their life in a car wreck. It read, Tasha Marie Woodard - 1/31/92 - 1/19/07. On the guardrail were several hand written notes denoting visits from mommy, "You are still my angel," "I love you so much baby girl." and so on...there were many. I cried as I stood there knowing what mommy was going through. I left my card on the guardrail and later heard from the mother's sister-in-law telling me that the car Tasha had been killed in was driven by her brother, Scott, who lived

About a year later, the mother herself, Debra, called me and left a message on my voice mail, the first words out of her mouth were, "Please help me, please! I can't breathe and I can't live!" I was walking in a little park in Illinois when I got the message; I spotted a park bench and grabbed a seat so I could listen to this precious woman as long as need be. Between sobs she explained to me that she had recently lost her son Scott as well, he had accidently fallen from a cliff! We talked a very long time. We both knew I couldn't ease her pain. She just wanted to speak to someone who knew exactly how she felt and could but relate to her.

Not even two years after the call, Debra's sister-in-law, again called, telling me that Debra had just died of cancer. She never fought back at all, I was told. It is extremely difficult to fight back and to Love Life. But it is the right choice because it is what our lost loved ones want, for they Love us too.

Push on and Love Life

I firmly believe that because each and every one of us is so truly unique one from the other, that each of us is equipped from within with our own answers in Life. If one can but push past the tears and the ache in their precious heart, there is a place of rest within. A sanctuary within which allows us to deal with the pain in our own special and unique way. A unique way hard-wired into our very being already there waiting for a great act of faith to be shouted out into the wide open ears of the universe: "I Love Life!" You are then telling the universe how much you do truly love and appreciate your gift of life and that you are then trusting that everything will be okay. And it most assuredly will get okay. Anything short of love and appreciation for our beautiful gift of life is a negative and negative never accomplishes anything and serves absolutely no good purpose. We are all created equal in our rights to the universal laws, those laws of life. It is about Love ladies and gentlemen, only Love, Love, and more Love! Push on and love the gift of life we've been so wonderfully blessed with my friends. Over my head as I walk, the two most powerful words in the Universe have been put together, "LOVE LIFE."

Push on and love the gift of life we've been so wonderfully blessed with my friends. When we awake and feel that sweet, sweet air on our upper lip we have indeed been gifted another day. Realize the miracle of that moment first and foremost and grab onto it and hold onto the beauty. of our precious gift of Life. Give that moment precedence over all other thoughts that are attempting to cause us to put the realization of the beauty of our being alive yet one more day in second place. Absolutely nothing is more sacred than our gift of life. Hold onto the moment as long as it takes for the realization of the beauty of life to supersede and conquer all negative thoughts and simply Love Life.

My Elvis Sighting

Just east of Springfield, Illinois, a big truck pulling a trailer loaded with feed corn started pulling over to the side of the road as soon as he saw me. I thought he was going to go into the ditch he got so close, he was still not completely off the highway. A big black gentleman climbed down to the road with lots of grunts as his big pot belly sticking out from under his hole-filled tee shirt, bounced up and down. His face was filled with a most beautiful smile! "Hi there, I been a lookin' fer you! My name is Elvis!" I said, "Elvis like in Presley?" And with a wonderful laugh and shaking his head he said, "Yeah, my momma, she just loved Elvis!" I had the feeling he would have preferred another name, but whatever his momma did was the right thing, and okay with him. When he spoke it was as if he would break into laughter any moment. I was instantly very comfortable with him. He said, "Now y'all climbs up heah in muh truck heah and we gonna go on up the road a bit." And he started climbing back up into the cab as if I had been properly told and now I would simply do as he said. He never stopped smiling and chuckling. I said, "Sir, I do appreciate the ride offer and all, but I'm trying to walk from corner to corner of the U.S. with this here sign and if I take a ride, that kind of defeats my purpose." I might as well have said nothing at all. He insisted I get in his truck, "You looka' heah now," he said, "I'm a gonna' take ya up the road just a few miles where there's places to eat and stuff for y'all. And there's an ATM there and I'm a gonna' draws out some money for ya." I said, "Sir, I do appreciate the offer, but I am okay and I really don't need your money sir." Without hesitating even a second, he said, "Now, I didn't axe you whether you needed it or not now did I?" "No sir." I said "But…" He didn't let me finish and began explaining, "Now you looka heah now, it ain't really nunna you bizness what I does wit' my money, now is it?" "Well, no sir, but…" He cut me off again and said, "Now you ain't gonna' cheat me outa' my blessin'! I feel like the Lawd is a wantin' me to gives you a certain amount a money and by the grace of God, I'm gonna' do it whether you thinks I should or not!" He continued to laugh. Elvis had a real special way of getting his way.

Well, I was properly chewed out, chastised by a man smiling and chuckling the whole time. I climbed up in his truck and down the road we went. He explained he had seen me on the way to pick up his first load of corn for the day. He said when he saw me he just knew God wanted him to bless me. I said, "But…" one last time and was yet again, laughingly chewed out for it. We talked of giving, God, loving life, and lots of other things pertaining to life. He had a bible beside him that had been reduced to just a pile of tattered pages. He told me he had grown up in Mississippi, after I said he didn't sound like he was from Illinois. He spoke of giving, of love and understanding for his fellow human being. He was a delight to be with and converse with. In the parking lot next to the ATM machine, after he had given me the amount of money he insisted on, he gave me directions to all the services I might need. Then he grabbed me and gave me one of the best damn hugs I ever had. And that was my Elvis sighting. I'd hang a velvet painting of that Elvis on my wall any day.

The Ice Man

Wednesday, 12/12/2007, near Mack's Creek, Missouri, I stopped in the Star Dine-In Restaurant where Wayne Clinton and Joshua Greene paid for my breakfast and asked me lots of questions about my walk. Later, two ladies, both named Kelly, stopped and talked. One Kelly said she had a teenage daughter that is suicidal and into drugs. She thanked me for listening.

It was approaching dark and even if there had been motels in the area, I had no money. I was so used to walking in the rain and cold all day, I really hadn't noticed that my clothing was now completely covered in ice. Kind of scary when you are just sauntering along in a drizzling rain and you look down and you are solid ice! I didn't like the thought of camping in that condition so I knocked on the door of a farm house and asked to bed in their barn for the night. They were an old couple and obviously frightened and told me no. I was in a very rural area and becoming more than a little concerned. I passed a couple more homes but no barns. I came upon a church with a porch on both the front and the back. I decided to camp on the front out of the wind even though it could be seen from the road. Just before I blew up my sleeping pad, I decided to try the front door of the church, it opened and the heat was on! I let myself in and filled out the guest register and proceeded down stairs. There was a washer and dryer so I did my laundry. I found a can of ripe olives and consumed them with gusto. I made myself a nice bed on the warm carpeted floor and slept very warmly. I left them a note about the olives and told of having done my laundry. Thank you from the bottom of my heart Branch Memorial Seventh Day Adventist Church in Mack's Creek, Missouri, for leaving your church unlocked! I left my card but I never heard from them. May very well have saved my Life. If that couple had let me stay in their shed, I would not have ended up in a toasty warm building for the night.

Line Shack

2008, In Arizona, Donna and Mary Lou, on their way home from grocery shopping, stopped and wanted to know what I was about. They warned me of an approaching storm that was to drop a foot or more of snow in the mountains. They told me of an old line shack nearby that was no longer used by the ranchers. They suggested it would be a better place to weather the storm than my tent. They offered to drive me to the line shack and I took them up on it. They gave me extra water and Donna raided her groceries and gave me several slices of fresh from the deli prime roast beef. They both gave me their left over lunches from an obviously upscale southwestern cuisine restaurant, delicious! And I was very appreciative that they both apparently ate like birds, I had plenty of food. They dropped me off at the abandoned cabin and said they would not leave until they saw me make it to the cabin door. I trudged about 150 yards through hardened snow over a foot deep. As soon as I reached the door of the line shack, I heard Donna beep her horn in farewell. Mary Lou had ridden horses over nearly all of Arizona. Said she was founder and editor of The High Country Informant, a newsletter of history and personal genealogies of Arizona. She sends them all over the world, she said. The line cabin certainly showed the neglect of years without use. The door was jammed open and both windows were completely missing from each end. There was also a large hole in the roof where the stovepipe once went through. I found an old door, an old mattress, and some pieces of tin to cover the openings where the windows had been. I also found, out back, near the dilapidated cattle pens, an oil drum that had been used for burning trash. I rolled the drum back to the cabin and placed it on a large piece of tin just under the hole in the roof. I trudged around in the hard crusted snow and was able to collect a large pile of aged mesquite and discarded poles once used for the corrals. I then broke off a juniper bough for a broom and swept out all the rat droppings to make a place for my sleeping mat. I built a wonderful fire in the oil drum. Even though the storm never made it to my part of the mountains, it did get quite cold. I stayed toasty warm all night thanks to Donna and Mary Lou. The two of them also gave me a history lesson on their beautiful state of which they both were so very proud.

Happiness Use It or Lose It

In Jerome, Arizona, I stopped to see my good friend Dave "Doc" Loomis. I met Doc when I passed through Jerome in 2003 during my walk around the U.S. I remember well as I walked up the mountain toward Jerome, a beat up, really old, piece of shit Japanese car pulled up next to me and this man in his late 60's jumped out and started yelling, "You could have written my book! You could have written my book!" He was so excited that he forgot to put the car in park and it damn near went over the mountain before he was able to reach in and get his foot on the brake.

He then continued pointing at my sign and saying, "You could have written my book, you could have written my book!" He was referring to the book, *Happiness Use It or Lose It*, which he had just finished writing. In front of Docs little house was an old blue school bus with a large wooden sign on its roof consisting of a large finger pointed skyward and proclaiming, ART STUDIO UPSTAIRS. I stayed with Doc several days and we talked long as we walked his beloved dogs visiting hidden waterfalls and old Indian ruins. He told me the reason he had written *Happiness Use It or Lose It*, was to explore why so many severely disabled people are full of the joy of life, while others, far more capable and even wealthy, find life frustrating, worrisome, and at times intolerable.

Doc's formal education was vast, to say the least. He graduated with honors from Williams College in 1956, in his junior year he was tapped for the Gargoyle Honor Society, which chooses 20 members in each junior class. In his senior year he was the president of the Williams College Chapel, and a member of the Washington Gladden Society. He received a theology degree from Union Theological Seminary, New York in 1960. He earned a Master's Degree in Human Development from Harvard University in 1965. He served as chaplain for the University of Maryland from 1965-75. He was a union organizer for three years, and a minister of the Presbyterian Church in Bowie, Maryland, for seven years. He was awarded a Ph.D. in 1982 from the University of Maryland. But Doc said to me, "I never learned nearly as much in all those years as I did when I took a job as a pre-kindergarten teacher for a year, and when I worked in Prescott, Arizona, for 10 years with the developmentally disabled, and I trained them to perform basic assembly work." He used his education on behalf of some of the least able people in our society; those with severe mental and physical handicaps.

Doc celebrated the life and happiness he wrote so eloquently about in his book. He turned his Jerome yard into a miniature golf course, an obstacle course of hilarious sculptures that were made of the junk that people threw away. His monument to Deni the Woodworker, his beloved companion, was a wall made of hundreds of heart shaped rocks. I've helped him add to that memorial as we would look for the stone hearts on our walks. The front yard sign greeting people as they went back and forth from Jerome, after me and Doc's first meeting, "Love Life."

Four years after that first meeting, in 2007, I walked up to Jerome again to see my friend. I walked around the old dilapidated blue school bus, knocked on the front door of his very small one room house. The door opened up and there was Doc's smiling face and he said immediately, "Stephen, how are you? The coffee is ready, and would you prefer dry cereal or oatmeal?" I spent three days with Doc. We walked yet again in those Arizona Mountains several hours each day with his three dogs. We went to ancient ruins and Doc took me to a place he had found recently. It appeared to have at some time been a ceremonial circle for some ancient tribe of our First Peoples. Doc surmised it had possibly been an ancient Medicine Wheel. Medicine Wheels are ceremonial circles of stones used by our Native People for healing, spiritual rituals, prayer, meditation, and as visual reminders of higher principles. Perhaps that very circle where Doc and I sat on rocks arranged so; those many, many years ago could have contained dancers of the Navajo, the Hopi, or even the Apache. The most likely builders Doc explained were the Yavapai, but could date back as far as the ancient Anasazi and Sinagua tribes. They are considered actual physical connection points to the Spirit World. Medicine Wheels are representations of the Sacred Hoop and remind us that all things are equal and connected in the Web of Life. We talked long sharing our thoughts and just had a grand time.

Doc told me once, "Happiness is a self-chosen state of mind rather than a cause-and-effect formula" He chose this quote by his good friend Madame Maria Aberdini, who was born without legs, her feet attached to her torso, as the introduction to *Happiness, Use It or Lose It*:

[The reason I'm so happy is that I love life, yes, LIFE, just as it is. What an unbelievable feast, steeped in realness, mystery, drama, possibility, spontaneity, agony, ingenuity, uncertainty, challenge. Yet many starve, deeming life too messy and perilous to savor, their fare limited to items they expressly order.]

My friend "Doc" died at the age of 75 from complications of cancer July 12, 2010. Just a few weeks before we lost him, he called and told me, "Don't ever stop doing what you're doing, don't ever stop telling others to love life. I love you Steve." Damn!

Machetes

I was in Fontana, California, (near San Bernardino) and getting ready to cross more desert country. Out there in that arid territory, when you see a stand of trees off in the distance, it almost always means there will be a dwelling in the middle. I look for the little oases hoping to ask for water thereby keeping full bottles at all times. I became seriously dehydrated and in dire straits three times and so I have a real phobia of running out of water. As I was approaching just such an oasis, I saw a Mexican man just in front of me with a machete in his hand, "What can I do for you?" He said, in pretty good English. Call me timid, but machetes make me nervous. I held up my water bottle and asked if I could please have some water. He smiled real big, introduced himself as Moses and asked that I follow him. When we walked beyond the trees, I could see that he and two other Mexican men were cutting a small growth of sugar cane. Moses asked what I was up to, the sign and all. I explained to him and he immediately insisted on getting a chair for me and a homemade burrito he had left over from breakfast, and two apples. He made sure all my water bottles were full and then went back to cutting sugar cane. While I was sitting there, another of the workers walked up with an 8-foot piece of sugar cane and offered it to me. I told him I did indeed appreciate it, but it was way too heavy for me to lug around. And with one swipe of the machete he cut it in half for me. He showed me how to peel back the cane to get at the sweet center core. In very broken English, he explained, "you, uh thirsty, huh?" and he demonstrated by placing the end of the stalk at his mouth, "you suck; is good!" He said. He and the other two were smiling broadly; they seemed to be delighted in taking a small break from their strenuous labor and to be of help to a stranger. When I left, they all three shook my hand and wished me well. Moses kept asking if there was anything else they could do for me. He said to me, "Man, I always want to help the people who want to help people." I gave him my card and as I turned to walk back to the highway, I could hear those sharp blades cutting through the cane. I like machetes.

Very early the next day, Friday morning, I got a call on my cell phone. It was Moses wanting to know how I was doing and how far I had walked. I explained to him that I had not gone very far, as the wind was fierce and hindering my forward progress. We both agreed that the wind would probably die down as the temperature became hotter. Moses also told me that I should be very near the U.S. Border Patrol check point and could get fresh water.

Doing Stupid Shit

I was walking toward Indio, California, where I was planning on refreshing my water at the U.S. Border Patrol checkpoint there. The wind worsened and a sandstorm became my new concern and just as I was preparing to cover my face with a bandanna, an old white Chevy S-10 pickup pulled over in front of me. I was delighted to get a ride out of the blowing sand. I threw my stuff in the truck bed and opened the door to see a young Mexican man smiling broadly. He said, "Man, you're too old for this shit." I'd known him but seconds and could see already, we thought a lot alike. His name was Tony, he was 20 years-old and on his way to Los Angeles to sell his truck and purchase another to sell. He explained that used vehicles were one of his means of income.

We pulled into the U.S. Border Patrol checkpoint but a few minutes later, I told Tony that I had become pretty well known to the Border Patrol along both our southern and northern borders. I had even been given a U.S. Border Patrol shoulder patch. He was not listening to me at all. His mind was on other things much more important to him. Tony reached out his identification to the Border Patrol Officer. "Where's your driver's license?" Asked the officer. "Why do you need that?" Asked Tony. "Because the nice California Highway Patrolman standing over there wants to be sure you are complying with the laws of the state of California." And of course, me, you, and the officer, now know that Tony is probably not in possession of a legal driver's license, right? "Please, may I see your driver's license sir?" Repeats the very courteous and equally determined officer. "Uh, I don't have it on me sir." stammers Tony. "Why?" asks the officer. "Well, uh, see, I, uh, had this ticket I never paid and I---" The officer cut Tony short with, "Is your license suspended sir?" Well, uh, yeah." Tony was able to get out of his mouth. The BP hails the California Highway Patrolman over to our truck. He was a huge man probably in his early fifties. The first thing he says upon seeing me and my "LOVE LIFE" sign, "Hey, I see you gave this man a ride, good, good, real good. I saw you this morning sir in all that sand and hoped someone would give you a ride." The CHP took the papers that Tony did have on him and said "Now, if you are telling me the truth sir that you have but one ticket your driver's license was suspended for, then I'll just write you another ticket and let you go. That is, if the gentleman next to you has a valid driver's license, 'cause you sir are not driving away from here." He then asked for my driver's license and I proudly gave him my Sunshine State driver's license.

He went back to his patrol car to run checks on everything. Tony said to me, "Man, did I do the right thing by picking you up. But now I'm going to have to pay another ticket. Damn, damn, why do these things keep happening to me?" And I sarcastically answered, "Cause, you neglected to pay the original ticket and you are now driving without a driver's license." He was looking at me as if I had just happened upon some great revelation about life when the CHP yelled for him to come over to his vehicle. I saw the CHP being very stern with Tony but also seemed to be sympathetic toward his dilemma.

Oh, and by the way, also going on right beside us, a drug sniffing dog had picked up the scent of suspected drugs in an old mini-van. The older Hispanic occupants were sitting on a curb shaking their heads and claiming, "dey perscripshun, dey is perscripshun!" After a few minutes Tony and the CHP walked back over to the truck. The trooper still had not checked the validity of my license, and so Tony and I waited for that process. "Man." Tony says, "I can't believe it, he only gave me a citation, I think it is because I picked you up man!" I then saw the CHP walking back toward us so I stepped from the truck to assume my new driving responsibilities. When from behind me I heard a stern command, "Sir, would you please step back into the vehicle!" I turned to see the BP motioning for me to get back into the truck. I immediately leaped back into the truck. See, in my world, whoever has a loaded gun has authority over me. The CHP now walks up to the truck with my driver's license in his hand and so now I get out of the truck to change sides. The handler of the drug sniffing dog says something to the CHP and so the CHP is now giving his attention to the dog handler.

Now, you have to realize there is a lot going on at this checkpoint and a lot of noise. But I am out of the truck again and from the Border Patrol's finest comes, sterner and louder this time, "Sir! You must get back into the vehicle!!" And adhering to the laws of my world, back into the truck I jumped, again. The CHP and the dog handler had obviously decided to the huge relief of the occupants of the drug sniffed van, the drugs were indeed prescription. Now, the CHP looks at me and says, "Sir, you will have to get behind the wheel of the vehicle to assume driving responsibilities," looking at me as though, he was amazed I hadn't been able to figure that out on my own. This was just great, now I have conflict with two authority figures with loaded guns. I said, "Sir, I've been trying to but, I--" He never heard me and the BP who yelled at me was doing something else and so, I assumed my driving responsibilities. Sheesh!

So I was now driving down CA. RT. 86 headed toward Los Angeles and Tony is now my passenger. I had told Tony my story and he said to me, "Man, you probably will not believe this, but, last week when I was eating Chinese food; my fortune cookie said I would soon meet someone who would give me advice that would change my life! I have been looking at everyone I've met since then and I think you're the one." Now there's some pressure. Thanks, Tony!

He began telling me how he felt he was walking on a sharp edge and could easily fall off at any time. He explained how things just seemed to keep getting worse for him and he didn't know how to stop it. I said. "Oh, I can definitely help you with that Tony." Oh please!" pleaded Tony. "Okay," I said, "are you really ready to hear this," "Oh, yes sir." He said. "Okay," I said, "stop doing stupid shit!" And Tony said, "Well, er, I, uh…" And I interrupted with, "and stop making excuses for doing stupid shit!" We had a long and meaningful discussion, so much so, I missed my exit by about twenty miles! Missing your exit in a car is not a big thing, twenty extra miles on foot, very demoralizing. Tony called me late that night on his way back home to thank me. And I asked a stupid question, "Did you pay off that ticket so you can get your driver's license reinstated?" "Uh, no." said Tony. Over the next few weeks Tony called me about four times. The last time we spoke, after I asked him if he had a driver's license yet, as I did every call, and again, as Tony did on every call, he said, "Not yet." And so, I said, "Tony, you're still doing stupid shit." Tony said, "Why'd you say that?" I said, "I'm so sorry, I don't know what came over me Tony." We changed the subject; he was such a likable kid.

Thermos or Toaster Oven?

Figure 9. Walking California with thermos from FPL.

In 2007, on the other side of Four Corners, California, my gallon jug (once containing milk) was half empty and even though I had another four liters in my pack, I wanted to make sure I had a full supply of water, knowing this was my last chance for a few miles. I stopped at the FPL Solar Electric Generating Systems facility, which consists of acres and acres of solar elements. I walked up to the security gate and there was no one in sight. I did see an intercom system and so I pushed the talk button. A voice asked me what I wanted and I explained to him about needing water. He informed me that I was not allowed to enter the facility and he was not allowed to leave his post.

During my walks, I have experienced dehydration three times; twice, very seriously. I suppose I have developed a fear of ever again going to bed thirsty, it is a terrible experience. So, I answered with, "Sir, are you going to deny me water?" He didn't say anything for a moment and then, "Let me see if I can get someone to take my place for about five minutes." A few minutes later, a large heavy set man between 45 and 50 came walking toward the gate. I immediately introduced myself and he told me his name was Homer. He was shaking his head, but smiled when he asked, "Now, I want you to explain to me why I should walk all the way back to that building to get you water and then walk all the way back here." And I asked, "Does that FPL on that sign stand for Florida Power and Light?" "Yes sir it does," answered Homer. I explained, "I paid Florida Power and Light for electricity for both my home and business for well over thirty years down in Florida. I figure your company owes me big time." Homer said, "No shit! Thirty years huh, that's a long time." Reaching over the gate for my water jug, he said, "I'll be right back."

A few minutes later, here comes Homer with my gallon jug in one hand and a one-gallon insulated water cooler in the other. Homer lifted my gallon jug over to me and said, "Here's your water and I filled this other one with ice for you." I said, "You sure you want to give me that nice container?" He answered, "I figure you earned some kinda' little gift of appreciation for being a preferred customer for over thirty years." I thanked Homer and asked some questions about the huge solar conversion plant. He told me it was the largest of its type in the U.S. and one of the largest in the world. I told him I was certainly surprised to see a Florida based company in California. Homer said, "I don't give a crap whose name is on my paycheck, would you?" Homer smiled big and wished me well. I thanked him once more for the nice customer appreciation gift. Next time, I'm going for the toaster oven.

Heirs to the Throne

Not far out of Susanville, California, a gentleman stopped his van, got out, walked up to me and introduced himself as His Highness, Hannibal Two Moons Gray. He told me that Hannibal in Hawaiian means, "Man Who Walks with God." and that the Two Moons was his Native American name. He was an interesting appearing individual, maybe 5' 8' and 160 pounds, dressed in a white pull-over shirt, black leather vest, black pants and black boots. On his head of shoulder length gray/brown hair was a very large dark gray toboggan cap that came to a point. He had a snow white, well-groomed full beard. And he had a wonderful smile that went along with the complete calmness and self-confidence he displayed. His self-confidence was surprising in light of the fact, the things he started telling me.

Hannibal told me he had been married nearly forty years to Her Highness, Likaleialani Lampura (Kukonu,) who was the rightful heir to the throne of Hawaii. I don't make judgment friends, I only listen. He went on to tell me his wife was born January, 1953 in Lahina, Maui to parents of royal Hawaiian blood, her mother, Leilani Kaplani Ahila Kukoni, and her father, Keith Koa Kamahaha Kukonu. And people ask how I keep from getting bored out on the road.

He told me his wife's parents were fourth cousins. I'm used to that, I'm from Kentucky. My parents were fourth cousins as well, no royalty though. He said that both parents and child were forced out of Hawaii by the U.S. government and escorted to the mainland United States, aboard a U.S. Navy ship by the American C.I.A.-- No, I have not been watching too many Discovery and History channel programs -- and taken to Los Angeles, California. His claim is that this was done in order to prevent the former country of Hawaii from re-establishing as a country with its royal heirs and then rejecting statehood.

Later, I received several calls from his wife, referring to herself as, Her Highness, Likaleialani Lampura Kukonu. She said she had until 2010 to reclaim her throne and that both the past presidential administrations had done all they could to prevent that from happening. She said she had been in exile since coming to the U.S. and had never been allowed to return to Hawaii. She explained that in the last few years they had been watched even more carefully and were living in poverty because of it. She said she felt the present administration could help her and she was trying to get in touch with the president but the C.I.A. would not permit it. She sincerely pleaded with me to get her story out.

They said they would send me much more proof and copies of documents to verify their story. As soon as they came up with the money to mail out the package. I don't judge folks, I only report. It is my duty as a guy walking the roads of America with the words Love Life over his head to bring you the stories shared with me as accurately as possible.

The last time they called, I was told that three former presidents call sometimes just to harass them. Likaleialani pointed out that George W. used a pay phone but George H.W. and Bill Clinton did not. They asked me to put their story in my book and I told them I would and so: great, I've walked over 40,000 miles of the U.S. never having a hair on my head harmed and now I could be assassinated by the C.I.A. for divulging the existence of the rightful heirs to the throne of Hawaii. They later sent me a stack of documents and letters like an inch or so thick. And I have to say, they looked real important and authentic. Hey, I just tell the story.

Struble Ranch

Figure 10. Cowboy Ben Struble, Struble Ranch.

And I had the absolute honor of meeting cowboy, Ben Struble. I crossed into Oregon just beyond Doris, California and stopped at the only place I had seen for miles in which to dine. It was a cafe/bar and as I entered I was greeted with a smile and hearty hellos by the only other patrons in the place. The gentleman, dressed in a dust-covered black and white, fancy, but old western style-shirt, and a dust filled black cowboy hat with a toothpick sticking out of it for emergency cleaning, introduced himself as Ben Struble and the lady to his right as Missy, his wife. They commented on what a beautiful day it was and I told them I was enjoying walking in such weather. Ben said "Walkin'? And Missy said, "Hey, you the guy with that "LOVE LIFE" sign over your head? I saw you yesterday walkin' into Doris." And then Ben started asking me questions while Missy went looking for the waitress/bartender to give me some service. I liked Ben right off, he just had that air about him, you know, some people just seem to have a comfort zone around them. He asked meaningful things like the ages of both my children and how long ago had I lost them and things like that. He introduced me to the barmaid and two biker friends who came in a little later, none had the same enthusiasm over meeting me as did Ben.

Ben asked where I was going to spend the night, as it was already late afternoon. I told him I would find some place, I always did. He told me there were irrigation canals on both sides of the highway for the next few miles and he didn't see how I could possibly find a spot this late in the day. And then he said, "Hell, if dogs don't bother ya', you can pitch yer tent at my place and I'll run ya' back out here in the mornin' before we start brandin'. My place is on the California side but I'm helpin' a guy with his brandin' on the Oregon side tomorrow." He told me a friend of his had just butchered four buffalo and had given him plenty of meat and they were going to cook up buffalo burgers. And of course I accepted the offer.

We walked out to Ben's old and very beat-up '84 GMC pickup truck with a dog pen containing seven Bloodhound/Walker Hound mix dogs all baying with excitement at Ben's appearance. Ben said, "I love dogs as good as anything and there are two more at home, so if ya' don't like 'em ya' need to speak up now." "I love dogs," I told him.

So we drove back into California and then a few miles to the entrance of his ranch. He was pointing out the lines of his 7,000 acres by pointing to one ridge and then to another. He said his son had recently given up his job as a civil engineer in Washington to come back and run the ranch and was now living on what Ben called, "the home place." On the way to his ranch, at least two people called him and he invited each out to meet me and eat buffalo burgers.

He called his wife, Missy, who had left the bar before us, and told her he was having me over for the night and some friends for buffalo burgers. This was all news to her, and all she said was, "Okay, I guess I'll break out that bottle of fancy tequila we got and you better get some limes and some fresh lettuce and tomatoes for the burgers."

Ben simply turned the truck around and headed into the town of Doris to pick up some things to go along with the buffalo burgers and the fine bottle of Tequila. I waited outside the store and got acquainted with the seven friendly hound dogs.

Ben's place was a large mobile home with a large porch running the length of it. The railings had actual antique wagon wheels built into them and there was a saddle sitting on one section of rail. There were peacocks and hound dogs everywhere and a huge ram of some exotic sheep species with huge horns, named Douglas. And they all follow Ben as he walks the property. Missy says it was even more fun to watch before they got rid of the turkeys and their 25 year-old mare that was abducted by a wild stud that frequents the ranches stealing mares to build his harem. Several of Ben and Missy's friends showed up for buffalo burgers and to meet the strange guy walking around the country with a big "LOVE LIFE" sign over his head. Ben said, "Hell, we never get company, I had to go out an' get some guy off the road to get my neighbors to come visit with me." One cowgirl had asked what kind of boots I preferred and after telling her I wore Danner's she referred to me from then on as the "Danner Dude".

Many of the people at the little gathering came up to me at different times and said something like, "You know, you could not have run into a finer man today," or, "You will never meet any finer and real people than the Ben Struble family." One gentleman told me he considered Ben Struble one of the finest men in that part of the country. And all those things were said before that fine bottle of Tequila was opened. The fresh buffalo meat was wonderful and the Ben Struble stories were abundant.

There was the time in his much younger years when one of his hounds was tangling with a bear, the bear had the hound in his grasp and was crushing him. Ben got caught up in it and was trying to shoot the bear with his pistol without shooting his beloved dog and when he wasn't able; he accidentally shot and killed his dog. On another occasion when one of his dogs was fighting with a mountain lion, Ben, not wanting to make the same mistake twice and kill his dog, tried to get the pistol as close to the lion's head as possible. So close in fact, that the lion was able to grab the pistol and Ben's hand into his mouth. The situation stayed that way for several seconds as Ben was afraid the bullet would go through the lion and into his dog (did I mention Ben loves his dogs?) Finally he pulled the trigger and this time it killed the intended and not his dog.

And there was the time that a sheriff's deputy stopped Ben in front of a local bar and wanted to give him a sobriety test. Ben kept assuring the deputy he was not drunk. The deputy insisted he was drunk. A friend, Deb, who was there those many years ago said, "Hell, he may have let him go but Ben kept givin' 'im shit. Kept sayin' he wasn't even close to drunk and he didn't have the right to stop him." Deb said that at no time did Ben become upset or even raise his voice. She was laughing when she said, "that's just Ben, and that's what was pissin' off the cop." The officer gave him a breathalyzer test and took Ben to jail. Deb followed behind and got him out immediately. Ben decided to fight it and so it went to court. In the court room it was shown that the breathalyzer test did not sufficiently show proof of enough alcohol to justify a drunken driving charge and so the judge said, "Dismissed." But Ben said, "No sir, it is not over yet, it said in the paper that I was drunk and I wasn't. I want that corrected." The judge told the stenographer to make a note of that and see to it that it was indeed corrected. After the article appeared in the local paper with the correction and apology to Ben, one of Ben's friends reprinted the article on fliers that proclaimed at the top, "BEN STRUBLE WAS NOT DRUNK!" and posted them at all the local bars.

The next morning, after the little get together, Ben came out to the travel trailer he and Missy insisted I sleep in and treat as my own home, with his chaps and spurs on, getting ready to go help his neighbor brand his calves. Ben said, "Steve, you are welcome to stay as long as you like, I really don't care, we have enjoyed having you here." I told him that if possible and they didn't think I would get in the way; I would love to watch them do the branding. It was decided that because Missy had already started fixing me a huge breakfast, that she would drive me out a little later to watch the branding process and take some pictures.

After breakfast, Missy and I set out for the corrals over on the Oregon side where Ben would be helping to rope the calves for branding. I was excited after arriving, seeing all the cowboys and cowgirls on their horses with lariats in hand taking turns to enter the corral to rope and brand the calves. My excitement was soon quieted as Ben's friends came up to Missy telling her they had been trying to reach her to let her know that Ben had been injured petty badly after his horse was spooked by the rope going up under his tail and had thrown Ben off. When we got across the corral to where Ben was sitting with a bag of ice on his left shoulder, it was obvious he was hurt badly. He said he was okay as long as he didn't move around.

We waited a few moments to let the nonprescription pain pills they had given him, take effect. I took some good pictures of the branding and then to my horror, I watched the same thing which had spooked Ben's horse happen to his grandson's horse. The horse panicked and made the situation even worse by causing the rope to drop down and wrap around his hind legs. Everyone was yelling instructions to the 15 year-old cowboy as his horse was panicked, bucking and heading straight for the downed calf which was being branded. Several cowboys jumped in front of the calf and began waving their arms in the air and yelling to shoo the spooked horse away from the calf and the ropes connecting it to the two horses and their riders. And then, just as sudden as it happened, somehow, the horse just stepped out of the coiled rope. I couldn't believe it. If that horse had fallen into that calf and those ropes, I shudder to think. The young man stayed in total control, and at one point while the horse was still bucking, I'm certain I saw the young cowboy grin.

Missy and I walked Ben to the truck and Ben said, "Steve, I hate it that you didn't get to see the brandin', you are welcome to stay, someone will drive you back to my place later I'm sure." I declined, I thought it would be rude to not make sure I was doing all I could to see that my kind host was going to be okay. On the way to the hospital at Klamath Falls, Oregon, Ben said to me, "ya know Steve, now that I'm a little older [Ben was 64] every time I fall now, sumpthin' breaks." I said, "Yeah, I guess when you were younger and stronger, stuff wouldn't have broken when you came off that horse." Ben replied, "When I was younger, I wouldn't have come off that horse." And that's what I saw in his grandson.

Just as we were about to pull into the hospital parking lot Ben said, "Ya' know I'm starting to feel a lot better, I don't think I really need to go into the emergency room after all." Missy said, "Well Ben, we're already here so I think we should at least get a doctor's opinion." "Well, okay I guess, but I am feeling better," insisted Ben.

Ben was making little jokes and staying quite positive as they escorted him to one of the treatment rooms in the emergency room. He was telling the nurse how he didn't think anything was broken and she said they would check anyway. Missy came out after a while and told me that he had landed so hard on his shoulder that the first and second ribs had cracked and that his left lung had literally popped upon impact, putting a hole in it. Within about thirty minutes after entering the hospital, the lung had started to collapse. They had to insert a tube into the lung so he could breathe properly. Each time Missy came out to update me, she would tell me how positive he was and of some quip he had made. Not long before we left she came out and surprisingly, did not give an update on his little quips and quick sense of humor. I asked, "Well, don't tell me his mood has changed." "Completely, they just told him he will be in overnight." she said.

Back at the ranch, Missy told me a few more stories of Ben's escapades and told how Ben and his two brothers and one sister had been orphaned by a mother who, "Just went kinda' crazy, I guess," is the way Missy described it. She said after his father found out about it and was able, he took his kids out of the orphanage and did the best he could to raise them. The boys were pretty much on their own by 14 or 15, Missy said. I asked Missy about a framed newspaper article on the wall with the headlines:

"COWBOY'S CORPSE BURIED STANDING UP! CRIPPLED COWBOY WANTED TO WALK INTO HEAVEN."

"That's Ben's brother" she said, "He was a guide for Robert Redford on a horseback tour of the remote lands in Colorado and Utah that Butch Cassidy and the Sundance Kid, with their 'Hole in the Wall Gang,' had hid out in." The story was featured in the November, 1976 issue of National Geographic. There was a picture of Jimmy Dale on the wall which the National Geographic photographer had taken. I began reading the June, 1992 newspaper article:

Bull ropin', bronc bustin' cowboy Jimmy Dale Struble was buried with his boots on - standing tall in his grave.

The hard living, bighearted cowpoke hated to take anything laying down, least of all death. He wanted to enter the hereafter on his feet wearing his favorite cowboy hat... and his buddies didn't let him down.

In a simple ceremony in a country cemetery, Jimmy was lowered feet first into his grave, so he could meet his Maker standing up - as a cowboy should. "He was a cowboy to the core." Said close buddy Eddie McEllery. "He was a dying breed. He was loud, boisterous, big-hearted, and the best horseshoer to ever set foot in this valley."

Jimmy, 49, spent the last seven years of his cow-punching life in a wheelchair, paralyzed from the neck down. He died of lung problems after spelling out his burial wishes to his friends. His paralysis stemmed from a broken neck suffered in a fight in 1986 in Hanksville, Utah. Jimmy and another guy slugged it out over who was the better roper. "Jimmy owned a bulldog named Buster, when Jimmy got mad, Buster got mad." said Dan "Boon" Burns. "Buster jumped the other guy's dog and all hell broke loose.

"Jimmy was thumpin' the other guy real good when the guy's buddy picked up a baseball bat and bashed Jimmy on the head breaking his neck."

"I loved him like a brother." Said Burns, who took care of Jimmy after his paralysis. "But even I could get a bellyful of him in about 5 minutes. Jimmy was an off-the-wall individual. When there was nothing left to be said, Jimmy would say it."

Jimmy loved country music and lived a rough life drinking beer and trapping wild game. He never met a horse or a bull he couldn't ride.

"And when the beer came out, you better get the hell out of there if you couldn't stand the heat." Glenn Younger said, "cause like it or not, there was gonna' be some fightin'." Friends say Jimmy made them promise not to bury him lying down. "He hated sittin' on his butt for seven years and he didn't want to be buried that way." said Younger.

"He was used to roping steers, breaking and shoeing horses, hunting bear and trapping coyotes."

"He was a hard-headed country boy - make that heavy on the country boy."

Several dozen of Jimmy's neighbors, friends, two brothers, two daughter's and other family members waded through boot-top-high snow to carry out the crippled cowpuncher's last wishes.

Before they closed the coffin, Jimmy's brother Clifford, put a pocket knife in the deceased man's hand. "In case he wants out of there, he's going to need a good knife," he said. Jimmy's saddle-draped casket was loaded into the back of his best friend's pickup truck and driven down the road to Glade Park Cemetery in Grand Junction, Colorado. A friend sang the last yippee-yi-ya, yippee-yi-yo of "Ghost riders in the sky" as tough talking cowboy's pushed their hats lower on their foreheads - to hide the tears in their eyes. Then they looped their lariats around his coffin and lowered it vertically into the grave. ~ Jack Alexander, Staff Writer Grand Junction newspaper

Damn, it certainly ran in the family. I spent the night out in my little trailer home, took some pictures of some more peacocks, dogs, and the ram. The next morning Missy and I headed out to see Ben before I got back on the road. Missy never went back to see Ben after she and I had left the day before, she kept saying, "Ah, he's gonna have lots of friends with 'im, he won't be alone at all, you can be assured of that." On the way to the hospital, she was a little more honest about her reasoning, "I can't stand to see 'im hurtin' like that and not being able to do what he wants and not bein' with his dogs." A tough cowboy needs a tough woman. Ben's got one. They're both just as big hearted as they are tough.

In Ben's room, just as Missy had said, there were two visitors and there had been a steady flow of them since he had entered the hospital. He thanked me for sticking around and staying with Missy and he also thanked me for helping him to get his neighbors to come visit him. I told him I didn't really think it was me at all, that it was more likely, the buffalo burgers.

Ben got out of the hospital a couple days later after they felt it safe to take the tube out of his lung. I will miss those fine people back there on the California and Oregon border. Damn, what an experience it was. All I have to do is to continue to love life and I will continue to run right smack into those that also love life. Thanks Ben, thanks Missy, and by God, thanks to you Jimmy Dale Struble for refusing to lie down.

Love, the Healing Energy

At Madras, Oregon, I met up with Bill Sawyer who had lost his 18 year-old son in a head-on car collision on U.S. 97 during the Thanksgiving holiday season the year before. He rode his motorcycle down from Portland, Oregon to meet me and talk. We met up that morning in a very small city park and were sitting at a concrete picnic table.

Bill and I spoke a long time and every once in a while a 54 year-old homeless lady name Pam would approach us and ask if she could buy a cigarette from Bill. He gave her one each time she asked, without charge of course. Eventually, a Mexican lady named Lupe, came up to our table and said she just had to know about the sign. I started telling my story and introduced Bill and his tragedy and why he had ridden down to meet me. Lupe could see this was going to take a while so she sat down at the table with us. Pam, seeing another woman at the table then garnered the courage to join us. Lupe started telling of her problems with an alcoholic daughter. Pam then started telling of her battle with low self-esteem and depression. There were tears, there was also laughter. And some of the wittiest and surprisingly wise remarks were made by sweet little Pam. We all just automatically were responding to the needs of each other. Broken hearts were being mended. Bill said some truly beautiful things to Pam about how to achieve and maintain a high self-esteem, and it helped her; I saw it in her face. Lupe was the first to leave, having to go to work. She expressed regret at having to leave. She took my card and said she intended to call the local paper at Madras and ask them to run my story.

Pam stayed a little while longer; she explained she had recently gathered up enough courage to ask for some help and that some local people were helping her. Bill and I gave her a little money and she immediately said, "Oh, that's not the reason I was here. I'm not begging for money, that's not the kind of person I am." "We know that," we both assured her. She finally accepted the money and with a big smile on her face she said, "I'll get something to eat now, and I really like slushies." She was just so very sweet.

Pam left to get something to eat and Bill and I stayed on a little longer. Bill reached in his wallet and pulled out a picture of his beautiful son Daniel and handed it to me. He said, "I would be honored if you could take this picture of my son with you on the rest of your journey. I think Daniel would really like that." I was honored; I placed it in my wallet between the pictures of my two beautiful children. Bill and I said our goodbyes, both thrilled to have made a new friend. And I headed out to take care of some things I needed be to get done while I was in a town.

A few hours later, walking out of town, just out of the corner of my eye I saw a lady sitting on the grass under a large shade tree. I didn't recognize her at first: it was Pam. She had cleaned up and changed clothes and her hair was all brushed back. She looked sweet, she looked pretty. She yelled out as she held a large plastic drink cup high in the air, "Hey Steve, I got my slushy! Thank you and tell Bill thanks too!"

The next morning a car stopped and a lady got out and told me she was a reporter for the local paper in Madras. She said a lady with a very strong Mexican accent called and suggested they do my story. I then told her of the gathering of Lupe, Pam, Bill, and myself. She looked up at me from her writing and with eye's real wide, she excitedly said, "I saw you, you were at the park! I was stopped at the light and I couldn't quit looking over at the four of you. I kept wondering what you all could be so deeply engaged in. I remember thinking I would love to have time to go over there." You felt the energy ma'am. She felt the energy of love as it mended the broken heart.

"Only Love puts the broken hearted back on path to the beauty of Life and only Love of Life can light the way." ~ Steve Fugate

Farmer Mike

In 2009 at Grass Valley, Oregon, inside the Grass Valley Country Store and Deli, I met a young man working there who simply called himself Farmer Mike. He had a long, very well groomed ponytail that went to his waist. He gave me a large container of potato salad he had just made after I told him what I was doing and had given him my card. Later that day I was hopping around the little camp ground where I had my tent, looking for some shade where I could sit and use my laptop and be able to see the screen. It was a little awkward but hey, Doug, the manager of the campground let me camp for free. But anyway, a big 33' motor home pulls in right beside my little bitty tent and stops. And Farmer Mike, whose hair is now loose from the pony tail, steps out of the motor home and says to me, "come over here please, I need to talk to you." So I went up into the big motor home with him. He said, "I have never met anyone before who has had so much bad stuff happen to them and then turn it around and do such good things with it." I said thanks. He went on. "Someone who walks as much as you shouldn't have to sleep on the ground all the time, I brought this here for you to use." He explained to me that he had picked the RV up for a very low price. He also said he lived on a nearby ranch at no charge and said he was very blessed and felt he had to pass it on. He started to walk off but turned and said, "When you get finished with your walking, please don't forget the people you're helping, stick with them, okay?" I answered, "Absolutely!" He smiled, walked over to the campground office, paid for two nights and then walked off toward town.

"Love Life, to help assure there is always a large supply of wonderful people and the good Karma to reward them with." ~ Steve Fugate

Cameras are Evil

Somewhere between La Pine and Bend, Oregon, while I was stopped talking to a full bearded cyclist wearing a homemade jumpsuit, whom, had memorized the entire Christian bible, and was proving it to me, a car stops and a couple jumps out shouting, "We know you! We know you! We know you from Blairsville, Georgia! We work with Winton Porter at Mountain Crossings!" Mountain Crossings is an outdoor outfitter store in the Walasi-Yi Center, the only building the Appalachian Trail actually passes through in its 2,175 miles from Springer Mountain in Georgia to Mt. Katahdin in Maine. I didn't recognize them at first, but it came to me later. They had both thru-hiked the Appalachian Trail in its entirety like myself, it was Jen "Princess Brat" and Jimmy "Alpine" Ingram. It was wonderful, like seeing family. They could only stay but a moment, they were trying to get to Klamath Falls, Oregon to look at property before nightfall. Jimmy asked the guy on the bike to take our picture with Jimmy's camera and the guy's face just froze in a look of pure fright! Jimmy said, "Oh, you don't touch electronic equipment?" The guy just grunted. Jimmy must have been familiar with whatever religious cult he was from, for he simply said, "Okay," and lifted his camera up in front of us and took the picture. I'm not going to join that cult because I like my laptop and camera phone too much.

Your Children are Your Happiness

In 2009 I was camped in a small trailer park in a small town in Oregon. I was sitting under a tree to eliminate glare on my laptop screen. From a travel trailer about 200 feet away, came very loud yelling and then a young man no more than 11 years-old, erupted out the door with his mother right behind him. The little guy, extremely upset and crying, was yelling, "Why is he living with us anyway! That's our money mom. That money is for me you and sissy. He's awful, he don't even work and you buy all his beer with our money, I hate him!" And mom yelled back, "I have a life too, I need to be happy too!" With head down he started walking past me. I started a conversation with him, telling him about my walking. He became interested and we talked some. He never mentioned his encounter with his mom though and soon walked away. Again, with his precious little head hung down filled with things an 11 year old shouldn't have to be dealing with. My heart was breaking for him. Hey dad's and mom's, your child is an extension of you! You do have a life for sure, and you do have the right to be happy. But guess what, so does your child. And you have to make sure this wonderful and precious other part of you has happiness in their life too. If you want to find out just how much a part of you they really are… lose one! And because they are a part of you, making them happy will make you happy. How I wished I could have told the mother to throw the bum out and go get her little guy and wrap her arms around him and Love him! Love your children with all your heart and with all your actions. Our children are our path to the beauty of life. Oh how I miss my two, my Stevie and my Shelly. How I love them!

"Flipped Off," Kindly

2009, in Sedro-Wooley, Washington, I was approached by a man and woman who were both covered with beautiful tattoos, and asked if they could take my picture. They were Tim and Lise Sconce of Tiny Tim's Tattoo's in Sedro Wooley. Lise, asked if anyone ever treated me harshly and I said, "Not really, other than someone giving me the finger every once in a while. Actually, that hasn't happened on this trip yet; I'm kind of disappointed, it has become kind of a badge of honor for me I think." We said our goodbyes and I went across the street to a convenience store. As I was leaving the store, I heard real loud, "Hey Steve!" I looked up and Tiny Tim and Lise, from their Harley's, were both holding those tattooed arms up high, and flipped me off! Now was that thoughtful or what! Just brings tears to your eyes don't it. Yet another random act of kindness and reason to Love Life!

A Cutter

Near Toppenish, Washington, a young man stopped and inquired of my sign. He said he was 24 and made real good money working at the wind farms. He asked what my sign had done for me, had it changed my life. I told him it has changed my life so much that I think the letters comprising the words; "LOVE LIFE" had actually dripped down from the sign and entered through the top of my head. Then He told me he had attempted to take his life about three times. He hung his head down and said, "But I don't do that anymore." Then he raised the shirt sleeve on his right arm and said, "Now I do this!" Up and down his arm were several cuts and burns, some, the size of a coke bottle bottom. He continued, "I do self-mutilation."

I said, "I am absolutely thrilled that you did not take your life. I can see in your eyes and hear in your voice, you are a very sensitive and caring individual. You are the ones that are most likely to attempt to end your own life. And the irony is, you are the very ones the world needs the most. We need the sensitive ones like you, who have a heart open to others, who understand how bad it can get." I told him how he didn't have the right to take his own life as it did not belong just to him. I told him of how we can do anything we want in this life, especially in this country, except hurt other people. And suicide, I explained to him, goes way past just hurting others. It completely devastates the lives of those left behind. You just don't have the right to do it! I looked him in the eyes and I said, "Ya know what, I love you!" That made him pull his head back, his eyes got big and just stared at me. I went on, "Yeah, let me tell you how a perfect stranger can love you like that. See, I can no longer give to them all the love I have for my two babies and it has to go somewhere, so I put it toward the children of others who are still alive and can receive it." I could tell this touched him.

He then said to me, "Well I promise I am never going to try to kill myself again." "Fantastic!" I said, "Now, about that stupid shit you're doing to yourself for attention?" I kept talking; I didn't really want an answer from him yet. "You know, DNA is really a fantastic discovery, it has proven just how completely unique we are one from the other. Of the billions of people inhabiting this world, we are all uniquely individual one from the other. This is a friggin' miracle." His eyes enlarged again and he said, "I hadn't ever thought about that. Wow." I continued, "Now, if science has proven that each one of us is different one from the other, doesn't that make us unique then, from each other?" This time I let him answer, and he said, "Well, yes, I guess it does." And I said, "Then why do you have to get attention by cutting and burning yourself?" He hung his head and said, "I guess I should stop it, I guess I should listen to all my friends and stop it for them." "No," I said, "You should stop it for you. Your friends have been telling you to stop it for a long time and you haven't stopped. When others tell you to stop, you simply go mutilate yourself again so they'll tell you to stop again. That's how you get the attention you mistakenly think you need." He started crying, crying hard. I reached out so as to shake his hand, but I didn't let go, I continued to hold his hand and explained to him again how the world needs the sensitive hearted individuals like him who are sensitive enough to understand the problems of others.

He kept shaking my hand and told me he really felt he was supposed to stop and talk to me and that he had been feeling an awful lot of guilt lately for what he had been doing to himself. With tears running down his cheeks, he said, "You really helped me sir, nobody has talked to me like that before, sir." Now the tears are running down my cheeks as well. The young man insisted on giving me some money toward a motel room.

Wrong Picture Man!

In Pullman, Washington, the home of Washington State University, the sister city to Moscow, Idaho, the Moscow-Pullman Daily News covered the story of my walk through their area. Geoff Crimmins, the photo editor for the paper had called me earlier and given me a two hour window of when he would show up to me photograph me as I walked out of Pullman. I was just walking along and heard from across the road, "You're taking the wrong picture man!" I looked across to my right and there were two big burly guys still yelling, "No, you're taking the wrong picture man!" I looked up in front of me and there was Geoff Crimmins taking pictures of me, but, running past him was an absolutely knock down gorgeous young blonde in skin tight pink shorts and tank top! The two big burly guys roared in laughter when I yelled out to Geoff, "No, you're taking the wrong picture man!" Ain't Life a blast?

Never Argue with a Drunk

Just south of Lewiston, Idaho, at a campground and river access, I approached a young man and woman who were next to their truck parked near the river. I approached them so as to ask them if there were a fee for camping in the area. I was new to Idaho and I always try to stick to the rules. I saw a bottle of whiskey on the tailgate of the truck and they sounded intoxicated. But I saw no one else nearby and so I decided to ask them. I said, "Hello, excuse me please." The guy, who was about 25 to 30 and about 6'5" tall, turned and said, "Hi and goodbye!" "Oops", I thought, "Wrong guy to ask!" As I was turning to leave, his girlfriend started to reprimand him for being rude to me. So the guy, trying to appease his girlfriend, made an attempt to be cordial; it was not a good attempt. He asked what it was that I had wanted. I told him never mind that it was no longer important and attempted to leave. He started yelling at me to tell him what I had wanted. Trying to appease him, I told him I had simply wanted to ask a question. He then said, "So, ask the fucking question!" And I said something I should not have said to a drunk man, "Sir, please do not speak to me in that tone of voice." Well, he came at me full force and shoved me, 55 pounds of gear hanging on my back and all. Down I went, I didn't have a chance with all that weight on my back, and I felt like Humpty Dumpty! And like Humpty Dumpty, I couldn't get back up again; I was strapped into all that weight. Then he towered over me yelling, "Love life huh, you don't look like you're fuckin' lovin' life now."

His girlfriend grabbed him and kept telling him to stop. Then I made another stupid mistake while lying there on my back totally helpless; I reached in my pocket for my cell phone. He grabbed my arm and the girlfriend took my phone. I do not remember ever feeling any more helpless in my life as I did at that moment. I begged for my phone back. I promised them that I would not call the police if they would only return my cell phone. My phone is my only connection when I'm out there on the road sometimes up to 100 miles or more away from anything; it has become very important to me. The girl eventually gave my phone back as she kept repeating that I had a problem and was a mental case. I did tell him that what he had just done was a very cowardly act. He just shrugged, I'm damn lucky he didn't kill me; I was already on my back for saying something stupid. They walked back over to their truck and left me alone. I was finally able to get my butt up off the ground. I didn't seem to be hurt too badly, other than a scratch on my elbow. The fall had broken my "LOVE LIFE" sign and the fiberglass rods which attached it to my backpack. And I had fallen right on top of my laptop which was packed in the back of the pack and so I was quite concerned about that.

I walked back toward the highway, trying to decide whether I should call the police or not. My dilemma being, these are the very type of individuals I want to help in life. I want to help troubled youth, not get them in more trouble. But as they were driving up the long gravel road toward the highway I decided I should call the police because of his drunken condition and I felt it my duty to get him off the road. I dialed 911 and gave the license number. They pulled them over while I was still on the phone with the dispatcher.

It was quite a while though before a deputy with the Nez Perce County, Idaho, sheriff's department, Jerry, came out to Upper Hogg Island, the campground on U. S. routes 95 and 12 where it all happened. He interviewed me and took pictures of the tiny scratch on my elbow. He asked if I was hurt anywhere else and I told him, "Nowhere else except my pride and my feelings." I couldn't help it, I choked up. The deputy saw it at once and very compassionately asked, "Hey, you okay buddy?" I answered yes and got it together. He asked me to go with him to where two other officers, another deputy and an Idaho state trooper had the couple in custody so I could identify them. When we got there I identified them. The officers asked if I wanted to press charges and I told them I did not because I knew the DUI charges would be hard enough on him. The two officers who had arrested him looked dumbfounded. I asked, "You did give him a sobriety test didn't you?" They had not. I had explained to the dispatcher that the driver was very seriously intoxicated and yet he had not been tested. Two hours had passed since the incident. They immediately proceeded to test him and he passed. He drove away. As they were driving past me, the young lady mouthed the words, "I'm sorry." Jerry, whispered to me, "Maybe she'll get rid of that idiot." "I hope so," I said. Jerry drove me back to Upper Hogg Island and as I was getting out of the car he said, "That guy looked damned intoxicated to me, and he has a history of violence." He also told me that because of what had happened, Idaho law says the guy would have to attend anger management classes.

There was a good side, I was able to take the really choice campsite my attacker had previously occupied and my laptop was just fine. The elbow healed in a few days, but it took a little longer for my hurt feelings. I had been bragging only that morning, "twenty three thousand miles and I have never received a scratch from anyone!" Hey, that's still not a bad record though. And the record could have remained perfect had I not broken a very well-known common sense rule, never argue with a drunk.

"We all like to be called stubborn I think. It gives us the distinction of being independent and we like that. Being stubborn can be an excellent trait. That is, if one has learned there are indeed two kinds of stubborn; smart stubborn and stupid stubborn. My dilemma is in humbling myself enough to fight my ego and switch to smart stubborn when I see I'm being the stupid one. It's tough, the stupid one is quite self-righteous." ~ Steve Fugate

"Poop-head!"

An older dark brown Mercury drove by me in Billings, Montana as I walked toward the Wal-Mart about a block up. An arm with a wide black leather wrist band with metal spikes sticking out of it went out the passenger side window just after the car passed me at a very slow rate of speed due to the traffic, and gave me the finger while voicing the words, "Poop-head!" Who in the hell calls anyone a poop head today? I hadn't heard that since I was about four. Anyway, I had reached the Wally World parking lot and was cutting across the lot when I spotted the old mercury, the get-away car, which had been used in calling me a poop-head. From the rear I could see that it was empty except for the front passenger seat. And with the window down and their elbow propped on top the door, I could clearly see a *big black metal studded leather wrist band.* The car was in my direct path to the store as I angled across the parking lot. Just as I got to the rear of the car, (I swear this is true) the passenger sneezed. I said, "Bless you!" as I walked by a very startled older female with purple and jet black spiked hair, with added facial piercing. Nothing though, not even all her personal body decorating choices, could take away from the shock on that woman's face when I turned around and smiled at her. A huge "poetic justice" smile.

The Rose

Just walking out of a small South Dakota town built atop a hill, about 4:00 in the afternoon, and I heard someone yelling at me, "Hey, gonna' need a place to stay tonight?" I looked up to see a very thin cowboy walking down from a small house perched on top the hill. His name was Darren and he had obviously been drinking. He told me everyone just called him "Slim" and that I was welcome to stay at his home. I told him I wouldn't mind pitching my tent in his yard. "Slim" said, "You can pitch it anywhere you want or you can stay in the house, just go on up and make yourself at home. I'm goin' to the bar and do me some drinkin' and do some karaoke, see ya later." And with that, he was gone. In front of his house he had piles of firewood bundles stacked on tables with a coffee can that said "donations" on it. While I was pitching my tent, several people came by and got firewood. It was the weekend and there were lots of campgrounds in the area. I took him up on his offer and entered his very small, very old home, and used his kitchen table for my laptop. On the walls were pictures of "Slim" on horseback and there were horse bridles and other tack hanging here and there. There was an old wood burning potbellied stove in the middle of his living/bedroom. I crawled in my tent at dark and still had not seen any sign of "Slim". About 3:30 am I heard someone helping him to his door. About 4:30 am I heard his back door open and "Slim" yelled out, "Man, its cold as shit out here, I'm gettin' wood for the stove. Get yer ass in here and get warm!" It was serious cold in my tent so, within a few minutes I was in that house. "Slim" fixed up some cowboy coffee, eggs, and a pound of bacon which I consumed with the gusto of a hound dog. "Slim" was still pretty well intoxicated and though he fixed himself a plate, he never touched it. I ended up eating his as well. Walking usually around twenty miles a day keeps me forever hungry.

Slim" had a very old hi-fi, probably from the early 60's and he had an Eddy Arnold record playing. I asked him if Eddy Arnold was still living, he said he didn't know. That's easy enough to find out I told him, I'll check it on the laptop. "Slim" said, "That may be the first one of them things I ever actually looked at. I hate that modern hi-tech shit! I think we'd all be better off without that crap." I chuckled at his comments and proceeded to find out that Mr. Arnold had indeed passed away only the year before. "Slim" was obviously impressed but wasn't going to admit it. "Is there anything else you would like to know?" I asked. At first he just grunted and shook his head no and then he said, "Hey, can ya see what Bette Midler is up to now?" And so I read him some of the latest news on her. "I always loved hearing her sing 'The Rose'." he told me. So, I clicked on a video of Bette Midler singing The Rose. We sat there watching and soon the tears were streaming down that skinny cowboy's face. Then I spotted one of her singing "The Wind beneath My Wings." Now we were both crying. I was thinking of my two beautiful babies and what my memories of them did for me. Of course I had no way of knowing what thoughts or memories it provoked for "Slim." And then he started talking.

He told me he had two sons, two years apart that he had to raise by himself. He said both boys were into football and polo. The oldest, he said, was a natural born athlete excellent at polo, his preferred sport. He talked and talked about the oldest son and how good he was at everything he did. And then he said, "But then he really screwed up." He looked down at the floor for a long time and with tears welled up in his eyes he continued, "See, he had been raised up with guns, he knew all about them. We had gone hunting his whole life. He was 16 and he knew better. See, what he did was, he saw a rat out there in the shed ya see. So he grabbed his huntin' rifle and tried to get a shot at it... ya see. Now that rifle had a scope on it ya see and he was in a small space and so he figgered if he was gonna' be able to get a good shot he would have to scare the rat out of the hole it ran into, see? Now he had already tried to get a shot so that meant the safety was off. So he laid the rifle down and then stretched out on his belly real flat like to look into the hole and try to spot the rat. Well, he musta' seen it in there and then reached his hand back for the rifle. He got the rifle by the barrel and began dragging it up toward himself. Now I don't know what that trigger caught on... but it caught on somethin'. The bullet entered just under his chin and then went on through. He was gone instantly."

I had already told "Slim" of my son's suicide. He looked at me and said, "Now there were some around here who said my boy killed himself. Horseshit! He would never have done that." I didn't ask "Slim" how he could have known such details of what had happened if no one else was present when the accident occurred. I also didn't ask him what the police report said. A few minutes later, "Slim" said he had to go cut some trees for someone and get some more firewood to sell. I packed up my tent, put everything on my back and walked on down the road with Bette Midler singing in my head, "You are the wind beneath my wings." Did I mention, I cry a lot out here?

Heart of the Native

I walked past the Little Bighorn battle field where Custer got defeated by the Oglala Lakota, Northern Cheyenne, and Arapahoe people, in a last ditch effort to protect their land (which had been agreed upon and duly recognized by the U.S. government as Indian land) from the gold diggers who had illegally trespassed on their lands and discovered gold. Just imagine if today the U.S government decided it wanted the land in Ohio, Pennsylvania, and New York, being occupied by the Amish people and started attacking and killing them to get it.

Somewhere between Busby and Lame Deer on the Northern Cheyenne lands I found a dead juvenile bald eagle lying in a roadside ditch, obviously having been hit by an auto. How very sad it was to see this beautiful bird lying there dead instead of soaring effortlessly overhead. Knowing how sacred the eagle is to the Native American and how valuable the feathers are to them, I pulled the body up to the side of the road where someone might spot it more easily and retrieve it. I was in a dead zone for my phone and so was unable to notify tribal police. The penalty for having eagle feathers or parts without proper permits is a $100,000 fine and imprisonment. And only our Native People are allowed permits. At Lame Deer I met Northern Cheyenne Brian Robert and told him where I had found the eagle. He said it would surely be long gone by that time. Brian was very interested in why I was walking. He spotted the very cheap compass which I had hanging off my backpack strap. Brian told me he had a very nice Suunto compass he wanted me to have. He also gave me a beautiful necklace which had been decorated in beautiful bead work by a Cheyenne friend of his. He showed me a design woven into it and explained it to be the Cheyenne Northern Star and told me the necklace was to hang my new compass from. I couldn't believe he was giving me such a special and valuable gift. Brian told me he appreciated my message and that it was much needed on Native Lands as they had very high suicide rates.

On both the Crow lands and Northern Cheyenne lands, many Native Peoples stopped to talk and inquire of my "LOVE LIFE" sign. This curiosity among Native People has been prevalent on all Native lands I have crossed. And I have crossed many, including; Lakota, Seminole, Miccosukee, Cherokee, Shoshone, Hoopa, Karuk, Yurok, Ojibwe, Blackfoot, Nez Perce, Apache, Hopi, Navajo, Chippewa, and Ojibwa. I have never been treated even slightly rude in any way by any Native Peoples while crossing their lands on foot. And most of the time I have been in very remote situations where I was quite vulnerable. I believe the curiosity and open heartedness of the Native People has been much taken advantage of, and sadly, has contributed to their downfall in our history.

A Fistful of Dollars

Not far from Lakota lands and headed for Pine Ridge Reservation, an old banged up Thunderbird pulled beside me with four people inside and they obviously had been drinking. They were probably Lakota considering the area we were in. The driver asked what I was doing and I told him. He then spotted my Northern Cheyenne made necklace and expressed that he would really like to have it. He held up his hand clutching some dollar bills and offered them to me for the necklace. I informed him it was not for sale. He said, "But you do not know how much money I am holding." I told him it did not matter, the necklace was not for sale, it was a gift from a Northern Cheyenne back in Montana and I could not part with it. He tried to persuade me to sell a couple more times when the woman in the back seat said, "He is not going to sell it, he cannot sell it, now give him the money." They all four started laughing and just seemed absolutely delighted that they were able to give me the money, necklace or no necklace. They gave me the three dollars, which I believe was their intent in the first place before the driver spotted the necklace. The Lakota people, like all our First Peoples, are special, they have hearts designed to give.

You notice a lot more when you're on foot, you move very slowly. The lands of our Native Peoples are always a pleasure to walk across. This is due to the fact most I have encountered are very curious, very kind, and extremely generous. I have certainly witnessed social problems on the reservations no doubt. The worst problem I've seen is alcohol. It has been my observation, the more the particular Native Peoples encourage and practice their ancestral ways, the fewer social problems they have. We are thousands of years removed from our ancestral ways, they are about a hundred years removed from theirs. A forced removal at that. No damn wonder they have social problems.

The Lakota People

I have a wonderful and dear friend, Elizabeth Garcia Janis. Liz is a child psychiatrist and author, who donates her time all over the world as natural disasters occur. This is her quote, which I believe she tries very hard to live by:

When all is said and done
and the dust has settled in,
I ask myself
did I feel all the love I was given.
Did I give life my optimum?
Did I love all my maximum?

Liz is a true giver; she has been known to pay the toll for the car behind her at toll booths. And she is a happy giver. She enjoys life as much as anyone I've ever met. She told me at her birthday celebration in New York City, "Steve, if you don't start having more fun, I'm going to take your 'LOVE LIFE' sign away from you!" And then she laughed and laughed. But I took her serious, and from then on I absolutely stayed aware of how important it is to have fun and enjoy life in all our endeavors. Liz is beautiful on the outside because she is so very beautiful on the inside. She is a knock down gorgeous Filipino princess who was then engaged to handsome Lakota warrior and sun dancer, Lawrence Janise. They met when Liz was volunteering her services to the Lakota people at Pine Ridge Reservation in South Dakota during a severe snow storm. They both said it was love at first sight.

My friend Liz told me that she had never met a finer people than the Oglala Lakota. She spoke of their spirituality, their family values, their generosity, and their honesty. I agree, as I've learned a lot about life's balance from them. Liz had notified me she would be visiting her fiancé, Lawrence, over the Labor Day weekend (2009). I was in South Dakota, and not that far away from Pine Ridge so we agreed to meet up.

I arrived at Pine Ridge a couple days earlier than planned because I literally was not able to walk in as originally planned. Lakota's will not let you walk. As soon as I left the Lakota- owned Prairie Winds Casino, cars started stopping and offering rides. I had turned down two rides already when the casino bus pulled up and offered me a ride. I really wanted to walk because I was running three days early on meeting up with my friend, Liz, I had about 30 more miles to go and figured a slow walk would narrow it down to only one day early. The Lakota bus driver said, "Come on man, get in the bus man. The hostess at the Casino restaurant told me all about you, get in here and tell me all about what you are doing." What the hell, I took the ride.

We had wonderful conversation, mostly about the Lakota people and their proud history, Sitting Bull, Red Cloud, Crazy Horse, Luther Standing Bear, and many more. I figured, what the hell, I'll at least walk the 15 miles from Oglala to Pine Ridge and arrive only two days early.

I went in the little store at Oglala and had a nice talk with the lady behind the counter. I told her that Lawrence was going to try to get me an interview with Tom Casey on KILI-FM radio "The Voice of the Lakota People" (North America's largest Native American owned radio station). I was sitting outside the store and a lady came out of the store and said, "Hey, I hear you are going to be interviewed by Tom Casey." I told her there was a possibility. Just then my phone rang and it was my friend Liz checking on me. The lady said, "Is that Tom, let me talk to him."

Just as I was ready to leave the store property, a group of young men called me over to their car and asked me to explain to them what I was doing. They had beer in the car with them and said they had plenty if I would like to go with them and "throw down a few." Before I left that store three more people approached me wanting to know what I was doing. This kind of curious questioning happens occasionally when I am walking through white communities, not every ten minutes.

Back out on the road for five minutes and I turned down a ride, another five minutes and I had to turn down another ride. About 15 minutes later there were three cars pulled over at the same time offering me a ride. Now remember, I am not hitchhiking and I am walking facing the traffic. Now I have three cars pulled over and trying to thank all for their offer but no thanks. One car had pulled into the opposite lane for me to be able to get in easier and caused us all to receive "the finger" from a car going the opposite way. Then a Lakota couple pulled up in a red pickup truck and the driver kept shouting for me to hurry up and jump in the back. There were soon three vehicles backed up behind them, what the hell, into the back I jumped. I'm sitting in the bed of that truck thinking about how fast they were going when they put on the brakes and came to a screeching halt in order to pick up a Lakota man walking down the road. He jumps in and starts telling me the history of the Lakota people. Within minutes the truck has to decrease speed rapidly in order to pick up yet another Lakota man walking. He also felt obligated to tell me of the Lakota people. And a third time the brakes take us from a rapid rate of speed to a complete stop as the three of us hang on tight and then make room for the third Lakota man who, as soon as he introduced himself to me excitedly shouts, "Look over here man, look over here! That's where Red Cloud is buried." Another man interjects, "The high school is named after him." One man asked, "Did you see the college yet, did you visit the Oglala Lakota College yet?" Another said, "Make sure you visit our Wounded Knee Memorial." When we pulled over in Pine Ridge for us all to unload, the three men all jumped out and each instantly reached in and grabbed a piece of my baggage. They all shook my hand vigorously and kept telling me places I should visit. It never bothered any of them that I was not Lakota, that it was my ancestors who took their land and tried to rob them of their customs, their traditions, and their pride.

In Pine Ridge I stayed at the pow-wow grounds. The grounds are an evening gathering place for Pine Ridge residents. They find a shade tree and park their vehicles (mostly pickups and mini-vans) and get out and gather to talk. I heard a lot of laughter. When they would see me under my chosen shade tree, they would smile and wave.

Sweat Lodge

Lawrence Janis, Lakota sun dancer, invited me to participate in a sweat lodge ceremony with him, his family, and friends. I helped chop up the wood and start the fire to heat up the rocks and had a wonderful time talking and listening to Lawrence. It was wonderful watching all his family and friends show up for the "sweat". They were loaded into pickup trucks and all arriving smiling and laughing.

I was very excited to have been invited to participate in this beautiful and sacred ceremony. However, a few minutes into the ceremony after they closed the opening, I experienced a slight problem, I felt I couldn't breathe. Two years earlier I had to exit from a sauna for the same reason. So, I had to bail. About 15 minutes after exiting, I was leaning against the hood of a truck feeling pretty bad over having to leave the "sweat" and I heard Lawrence ask that the door be opened again. Oh goody, I thought, someone else has capitulated and cannot take the heat. I was thinking that it would really be a reprieve for me if it was one of the young Lakota braves that were present. And sure enough, it was. It was a very young Lakota warrior; out stepped bare chested little three year old Wic'api, Lakota for Star, Lawrence's great nephew. Lawrence said, "When saying Wic'api, between the C and the A is a guttural sound in the pronunciation and the C is a ch sound. We just call him 'Choppy." So, "Choppy" outlasted me.

About 30 minutes later more Lakota gave up: the five to eight year olds. I was sitting next to Lawrence's mother, she reached over patted my knee and said, "You tried, and you are here." Her son-in-law came over to me later and said, "What matters, you are here." At the end of the "sweat" at least two others repeated the same to me.

About midway during the "sweat" ceremony Lawrence invited me to sit at the opening and address the participants and explain my cause, my purpose. During the whole ceremony I heard everything that was going on in the sweat lodge and enjoyed the singing in the enchanting Lakota tongue. I sat in the circle after "sweat" and smoked peace pipe. As Lawrence passed the peace pipe to me he said, "Your "sweat" comes in another way." A nephew of Lawrence came up to me and told me he heard me being interviewed on North America's largest Native owned radio station, KILI-FM radio, "The Voice of the Lakota," and that it really had an impact on the way he would look at things from now on. Lawrence and Liz took me to the site of Wounded Knee. I really do not know what to say as to how it affected me to stand there on that holy ground with a Lakota warrior, a descendant of the victims of that terrible atrocity. Certainly, I was honored, but there was such a sadness overshadowing the experience, an unavoidable and very important part of the experience I suppose. I've included this award winning poem by my friend Lawrence, exactly as it was when he handed it to me:

Figure 11. Lawrence Janis, Lakota sun dancer.

Pushed Down and Stepped On ~ Lawrence J. Janis

We are here, we survived
We got this far.
Our parents got us here,
Their parents got them here,
We got this far.
We were pushed down and stepped on.
When once we were free.
They put us on this place,
Called the agency.
They fenced us in... we had to ask to move.
And to push down and step on us harder.
They didn't let us hunt for food.
And if we did... we were labeled hostile,
And hunted down.
And to push down and step on us harder.
They gave us rations as they saw fit.
If we didn't do as they said,
They cut our rations and we were starved.
To push down and step on us harder.

They gave us a plow, a few tools, a horse and a cow.
And told us to live like them.
To push down and step on us harder.
After we started to adapt,
To try to live with a plow and a cow
They changed the rules.
To push down and step on us harder!
They started to act.
To take more land.
The allotment was a tricky plan
They took more land.
To push down and step on us harder!
They took our children away from us.
They put them in boarding schools.
They took the language
And split our families.
They took our pride.
To push down and step on us harder!
They put an outlaw on our religion.
We prayed in secret.
They broke our spirit.
To push down and step on us harder!
They gave us alcohol!
Fire water, to destroy each other!
But we forgave and we forgot.
And we fought and died for them, when the great wars came.
To push down and step on us harder!
They had to humor us.
They gave the anthro's, a study plan.
To come up with the New Deal.
To push down and step on us harder!
They put, another act.
The anthro's came up... with the IRA.
And the government took out the I... so we couldn't see.
We reorganized, we acted good.
We plowed and we hayed.
We lost our pride and we got it back.
They broke our spirit, we became more spiritual.
We are here... we survived.

We got this far.
To push down and step on us harder!!!
TO LIVE AND BE HAPPY, WITHOUT DRUGS AND ALCOHOL.
THE BLACK HILLS ARE NOT FOR SALE!!!!!!!!!!!!!!!!

LJ Janis (Isakip Kiya)

Perpetual Motion

2006, New Year's Eve day, in Ardmore, Oklahoma, I met Crazy Bill and he blessed me with a night in a motel room. A friend forever! Crazy Bill wasn't really crazy but you could tell he was a bit odd and he took delight in the name his friends had dubbed him with. And just how in the hell would I know whether one is odd or not? Bill was a welder who specialized in very ornate wrought iron spiral staircases. He took me to his welding shop where spiral staircases were everywhere in various phases of construction. Also inside his shop were several old dilapidated sports cars. One was a 1953 Porsche. While Bill was telling about the Porsche, my eyes immediately went to a contraption consisting of several piston operated arms in a circle mounted on a stand. "What's that?" I inquired. "That's a perpetual motion machine I invented," he stated proudly. "Uh, shouldn't it be moving?" I inquired. "It almost does. I still have to work out the bugs," he said with a very confident look on his face. He then showed me pictures of a 30's Bentley he wanted to purchase. He said that even though he really could not afford the Bentley he would continue trying to purchase it. He explained that it was much more important than eating. He said he always makes sure he still has money for beer and cigarettes for him and the missus though. Bill's quite the family man.

Before Bill took me to the motel room he had offered, he insisted on taking me to his home for dinner. He promised me a delicious burrito dinner. I was excited by the thought of a good home cooked meal. On the way to his house he said he needed to stop at the convenience store for beer and cigarettes as the wife was nearly out of her brand. He didn't say whether brand of cigarettes, beer, or both. I went into the convenience store with him and just as we were starting to check out he said, "Oops, I just remembered we only have enough for two" and he took off across the store. When he returned he plopped a package of frozen burritos on the counter.

"Crazy Bill's" wife was a very frail looking woman and a match made in heaven for Bill. She threw the three burrito packages in the microwave and then a package of frozen Tater-Tots followed those. Well, it was cooked in a home. We each had a can of "Bud" with our gourmet meal. Over dinner Bill mentioned to his wife he had made another offer on the Bentley. She looked over at me and said, "It will never run, it will never be fixed up, and he will never listen to me that he shouldn't buy it." "Oh," she then added, with what looked like a very sincere admiring smile, "Did you see Bill's perpetual motion machine?" Bill never looked up from the delicacies in front of him and seemed totally unconcerned with his wife's utterances. "Yup," Bill said, "don't wanna' offer 'im more, but will if I have to." His wife said, "You guys want another beer?"

Bill took me to a motel just out of town and said, "Let's go in here and see what kinda' deal we can get here. The owner is one of them guy's from India or somewhere like that, real nice guy though, I like 'im, he owes me a favor or two." He got an excellent deal, so good, I got the room for the next night as well. I spent New Year's Day in a motel in Ardmore, Oklahoma watching college football. Wonderful! And I got to see a perpetual motion machine! Love Life!

Don't Cuss Though...

Near Kansas, Oklahoma, I met Ike. Ike told me he loved Life with all his heart and that he was a thoroughly happy man! He said that after his first cup of coffee in the morning he immediately opens his first beer and then drinks all day long! "I thoroughly enjoy it." He said. "And, I smoke cigarettes all day too!" He added. He told me he was self-employed and never missed a day of work. He said that he was perfectly happy with his lifestyle and had no desire to change it. He explained that his two grown children though, were quite religious and refused to visit him because of his habits. "That part hurts." He said with a sigh, and added, "I don't cuss though." Ike insisted on buying my next meal. While chuckling, I said to him, "Well hell Ike, maybe they're afraid to get too close to you again and then have you die from all your bad habits?" He said he was in perfect health and had just had a complete physical. And then he said, "Anyway, Love ain't supposed to have any restrictions in it. I Love both of them and would never even think about telling them they are a religious pain in the butt." I really liked him, I told him I thought that was just a real shame. "I can handle it," he said, "I Love Life. I just have to wait 'til they learn the difference between judging and loving." Hmm??

Bonnie and Clyde

I was walking through Buffalo, Missouri in a cold rain and was fairly miserable, when a lady yelled from an old Lincoln, "Hey you need a place to sleep tonight?" "That would be very nice." I yelled back. It was Teresa and the driver was Tom, who she said was her dad. Teresa told me to put all my gear in and she would feed me, let me take a shower, and wash my clothes for me. Wow, now I'm a happy guy. Before I entered the car, I gave them a card and told them exactly who I was and what I was doing. As we were driving back through town Teresa started saying things like, "Now I want ya to know, we have six guns and they're all loaded. My dad is real protective of me and he won't hesitate to shoot you." I assured her none of that would be necessary. She told me she was aware of all the bad people there were out on the road these days. I told her again who I was and I told her that if she was going to be uncomfortable with me in her home I would prefer not to go there. I told her I would not be comfortable knowing I was creating such discomfort for her. She apologized and pleaded with me to please let them help me. And Tom explained that Teresa just worries a lot and that they would love to have me stay over. The rain was pouring down now and it was getting dark, so I let it go and went to her home.

Tom and I were sitting at the kitchen table eating tacos and just jabbering away. Tom told me he had known Teresa since she was a little girl. I thought he was her dad. Anyway, we're sitting there and Teresa is in her bedroom talking on the phone to her brother when, "BAM!" This loud noise goes off in Teresa's bedroom which was adjacent to the kitchen. Tom jumps up with me right behind him and we run into Teresa's bedroom and there she stands pointing at a 45 automatic lying on her dresser. The color had completely left her face. She started screaming at Tom, "You stupid son-of-a-bitch! I told you to never have a loaded gun in this house! [What happened to the six loaded guns?] I saw it laying there close to the edge and so I reached to move it farther up on the dresser and the fucking thing went off you fucking asshole!" Evidently, Tom had gone into the bedroom as soon as we entered the house. He had taken the safety off and placed the gun on the dresser so he could get at it in case the murderous man with the "LOVE LIFE" sign tried to kill them. The bullet went through one side of the steel door which led to the outside. Because of the angle it didn't go through the other side, but you could see the bulge where it almost had. Tom tried to lie and insisted the safety had been on, which of course is impossible. Teresa continued to yell at Tom and berate him until he threw his hands up in the air and left. Teresa, who was an absolute wreck, so I told her I wanted to leave. She said it would be fine if I stayed because her brother Alex would be over any moment and was staying the night.

Alex came over and he was very Mexican. Teresa was very not Mexican. Okay, so I'm thinking adoption until I accidently saw a kiss between the two, it was not a brother and sister kiss. Well, not in my family. Alex had spent some time in prison five years before, drank too much and was trying very hard to change his life he said. We spoke for hours after Annie Oakley went to bed and a few more hours the next day.

If that gun had been aimed in another direction it could have easily killed me or either one of the other two. And they had been afraid of me. The next day at a Dollar General store in Buffalo, a sweet young lady who worked there walked up to me and handed me a very large cup of hot coffee. She said she had seen me in the rain the day before and felt sorry for me. She said she saw someone pick me up in a Lincoln and that made her feel much better. She wouldn't have felt better had she known it was Bonnie and Clyde in the Lincoln.

Sylvio

Somewhere in Missouri, a seriously beat up old mini-van pulled up beside me, the driver was a very colorful young lady who called herself Sylvio. She was dressed quite unusual, sort of Amish looking, long dress going to her ankles, a heavy scarf tied around her head. But she was wearing very bright chartreuse shoes which looked like ballet slippers and they were over long, very colorful thick socks. There were two other people in the van and a pit bull. The other two, a guy and a pretty young woman, were both just as colorful in dress, and had lots of tattoos and piercing. The girl's hair was a purplish red. I saw that color once on a '37 Chevy coupe; it looked good on the little Chevy. Sylvio asked if I needed a place to stay for the night. She explained that she was currently staying in a place they called "the ghost town" with several other people who were all practicing a simpler way of life. She told me that she would be sleeping in her van with her dog and I could use her large tent. I decided I would take her up on it. She opened up the back of the van so I could place my large backpack in the back. I never even thought about the pit bull and simply tossed the pack up into the back. It evidently startled the dog and she attacked. Sylvio was able to grab her before she got to me. She snapped at Sylvio and brought blood on her hand. She grabbed her dog and flung her down on the ground and held her there screaming at her until she finally stopped snarling. I apologized for startling the dog. They all three told me the dog was always like that when she was around men. Sylvio said she would never own a pit bull again and that the dog had caused her numerous problems. I've owned pit bulls, never had one act like that though.

After arriving at the ghost town I met several of Sylvio's friends. They were all very nice but for some reason I felt a discomfort and made up my mind not to stay the night with them. Sylvio said she had to make a trip to the store which was back on the highway. I rode back to the store with her and told her I wasn't going to stay. She wanted to know why. She kept questioning my reasons; was I turned off by someone, was I nervous around strangers. I explained to her that it was just a decision I had made and I need not explain it other than it was a decision I had made, it's called following your own heart and I do it all the time. She seemed to like that answer and we had a wonderful time driving to the store.

She dropped me off at a stretch of woods where I could pitch my tent. Sylvio started giving me all kinds of natural stuff, soy milk, organic energy bars, and energy drinks. She just couldn't believe I preferred greasy hot dogs and burgers over the natural stuff. People are always worrying about what stuff will kill them if they eat it. I think what is killing them is the worrying about the stuff they eat killing them. Eat and be merry damnit. A few days later, Sylvio came by my motel room and visited with me about an hour or so. She brought me a chocolate milk shake. She gave me some more energy drinks. I really enjoyed her company; she was a sweet and giving person with a beautiful heart.

One of the things Sylvio mentioned a few times was character. She talked of the importance of always maintaining a high character content. That last visit in the motel room, she shared with me that she had a nice apartment in some fairly large city in a neighboring state which she maintained and would visit every so often. She said she had developed a good scam (her word, not mine) in that her old van made her look the part of being a less fortunate individual. Using that appearance and adding to it with her manner of dress, she would pull her van off the road at different places in a three state area and hold up a sign saying she needed gas money to get home to her family. She would tell them she was nearly out of gas and needed money for more. She said most felt sorry for her and usually gave enough to get gas and some food. There was not even the slightest hint she thought her actions to be wrong in any way. After all, Sylvio was of very high character content; she told me so. Just who am I to judge another. There was a time in my life when I thought the beautiful bright yellow flower, dandelion; to be a weed. Follow your own heart.

Solidod

Figure 12. My Apache friend, Solidod, with the horse named Solidod.

Solidod, that's her name, her only name. There she stood at my door but a few days after I returned to Vero Beach, Florida in May 2010, to work on my book, having recently finished my "Shelly Walk" from corner to corner of the United States. Full blooded Apache, 81 years-old, her eyes dancing around taking in everything, cautious, but confident, she said, she had felt led to my door. She lived in the same complex, but said she never walked in the area I was living and had not done so in some time. She was still standing on the walkway and looking into my little efficiency apartment and while pointing to the back wall, asked "How did you get that?" She was pointing at a wild sage bracelet wrapped with red cloth given to me and previously worn by my friend, Lawrence Janice, Oglala Lakota brave and sun dancer. She knew exactly what it was. As she also identified gifts given me by Navajo, Northern Cheyenne, and Ojibwe, which were hanging on my wall. Her parents were both killed by some white men in a jeep, in a remote area of a Nevada reservation (the reservation land later taken back by the U.S. government). They raped her mother, who had quickly hid her infant daughter under a mesquite bush when she perceived danger. The 3 day-old infant was later discovered by her grandfather; he called her a Daughter of the Sun and named her Solidod. The grandfather walked up into the mountains to die when she was ten. Her suffering was far from over, but she survived it all, even a gunshot that killed her unborn baby.

An old busybody neighbor in our community kept gossiping and spreading lies about her. Solidod went to see her one day and told her if she didn't leave her alone and start minding her own business, she was going to cut her fucking head off and put it on a stick in front of her teepee. She told me with a huge smile on that face full of hard earned wisdom, "You know, she has never bothered me again." Go figure. She is Solidod and she is my friend. In my mind, she is an American treasure! Her story, *An Apache Original – The Life and Times of Solidod* is incredible; she is truly a survivor.

Punctuation and Phooey!

September 2010, I was invited to speak to all the U.S. Army troops at bases in Anchorage and Fairbanks, Alaska. Assigned to me for my week there to handle scheduling, my meals, and transportation, were Captain Nathalia Howard of Columbian birth who had worked her way up from the enlisted ranks and Sergeant Katrena Edwards. Katrena, a young black woman from Louisiana who immediately upon my complimenting her name during our introduction, said to me, "Honey, you have no idea what kinda' crap I had to listen to bein' in Louisiana and havin' 'at name when 'at damn hurricane hit!" I loved her immediately.

Just as I was preparing to speak on my last scheduled talk to over 1100 U.S Army troops in Fairbanks, after being told not to expect over 10 or 12 to show up, I was asked by a civilian volunteer mental health professional who had heard me speak the evening before to not be so graphic in describing the way my son took his own precious life. I said, "No, I will not change that, I do not enjoy describing my only son's death, it breaks my heart to bring it to mind over and over. I do it for a reason." I know exactly what I'm doing and the impact it creates and I believe it works. She also asked me to watch my language. And as I gestured toward the crowd of well over 1100, as opposed to the previously estimated 10 or 12 individuals, I said, "Absolutely not, I'm going to add a couple juicy words because my math is obviously much better than yours." Captain Howard, who was obviously stunned, said to the civilian volunteer, in her strong Columbian accent, "Ma'am, Mr. Fugate, he no cuss; dose are punctuation marks." And Sgt. Katrena Edwards, just as stunned, and in her just as strong, southern accent, spoke up and pointed out that many in my audience had been to either Iraq or Afghanistan (as both she and Captain Howard had). And she finished her statement with one hand on her hip while the index finger of the other pierced the air for emphasis, "Ma'am, when that bullet goes flyin' past yor head, you ain't a sayin' darn and phooey!"

The civilian volunteer was replacing the duties of Capt. Howard and Sgt. Edwards and would be taking care of my needs for the next few hours as my speaking schedule had ended. I was dreading riding to the airport to catch the redeye with my civilian critic, but was rescued by my sweet friend, Sgt. Katrena Edwards. I watched as she called her husband back in Anchorage to tell him, "Baby, I'm gonna' be late gettin' back 'cause I'm gonna' take Mr. Fugate to the airport so he don't gotta' ride with 'at bitch, okay baby?" She was laughing when she ended her conversation and said, "my baby said he don't blame ya, he wouldn't wanna' ride with 'at bitch either!" I salute you Sergeant Edwards and Captain Howard for looking at how my message was received and the positive results, and nothing else. I still receive mail and calls from many of those young soldiers.

"I am learning to follow only my own heart, and in the process of finding the heart of me, I find an enormous amount of Love there for my fellow human being. I am in pursuit of a heart-governed mind." ~ Steve Fugate

My Joel Kody Walk

In 2011, I walked from Vero Beach, FL, to Surry, Maine, and then back to Cincinnati for a couple weeks to see my mother for the last time, and then on to Oakland, California, 5,317 miles. I called this walk, my Joel Kody Walk, in honor of a young man who lost his battle with depression and took his own Life.

Chicken Legs and Spiders

Outside the only store in Holopaw, Florida, at the intersection of U.S. 441 and U.S. 192, I was sharing an old cable spool as a seat with Rob. As I was just starting to take a bite out of the biggest fried chicken leg I ever seen, Rob says, "Now I ain't a wantin' to ruin your meal or nuthin' like 'at, but looka' this---" And before I could say, "Well, then don't!" he pulled up his shirt sleeve to reveal a big gaping raw hole in his arm from the bite of a brown recluse spider. And I then said, "Holy shit!" I asked how long ago he had been bitten. Rob said it was one week before and even though there was a lump as big as a baseball where he had been bitten, he didn't go to the doctor until the big hole appeared and started getting bigger. He seemed quite proud of it and held his sleeve up for quite a while as we both told stories of brown recluse and those we'd known who had been bitten. I out did him on the stories though, I once knew a guy who was bitten by brown recluse twice in a ten year span! Rob seemed impressed. I continued eating my big fat juicy fried chicken leg, loving my life and being so very thankful for how blessed I am for the numerous encounters I've had with Life's unique and oh so interesting individuals. We're all unique each in our own special individualities and deserve respect and love from one another.

Sheila of Haiti

Just out of Alatchua, Florida, a beautiful young woman stopped and introduced herself as Sheila of Haiti. Said she loved life and loved my sign. Sheila of Haiti was an absolute joy to be around. She gave me money and insisted I get a meal at Pearl's Country Store, just up the road. The ribs and fried okra were awesome! Sheila of Haiti called me a couple days later to check on me and just could not stop telling me how much she loved my sign, loved life, loved God, and how very much she loved me. Sheila still calls. I answered my phone yesterday to that sweet accent, "Hello, its Sheila of Haiti! How are you? I Love Life! I love you!"

"Love life with all your heart and watch your heart grow, it has to in order to contain all the love you will have coming your way." ~ Steve Fugate

Bad Back saved My Life

2011. I was experiencing chafing in my groin area even more than usual. It usually heals up after treatment with salves at night and medicated powder during the day. This hadn't been the case, so I decided to take a day off to allow it to heal. I got into Pearson, Georgia early morning and the Indian motel owner let me check in early. I got a nice clean room for $35.00! Clean, yes, but the ugliest damn room I ever saw. Screw glamour, it had a hot shower. And I must admit, it's prettier than the inside of my tent. As the owner was taking me to see my room, I asked if it was a 'no smoking' room. In that very strong Indian accent he said, "You serious, I try that already! My brother, he own motel, South Florida, he have "no smoking" room. He tell them, "no smoke," they no smoke. Here... everybody smoke! I say, "No smoke," they lie... they smoke! This Georgia... they smoke... everybody smoke... I give up!" I said that would be just fine and that I appreciated his honesty. Many a time, I've been guaranteed it was a 'no smoking' room and I smelled it the moment I entered. Hey, it was $35.00, no continental breakfast either.

Well, tomorrow morning came and I realized I wasn't going any damn place. The chafing I had been experiencing had become infected and there was a baseball sized cyst on my thigh in the groin area. So I stayed another night hoping it would go down some, it instead became the size of large grapefruit! So, I booked the room another night and came up with a plan, I would lance the cyst myself. So, I took the palms of my hands and slapped 'em with all my might against the sides of that cyst and holy crap! I let out a yell that scared me. I mean to tell ya' folks, by God, that hurt like hell! I'll skip the gory details. Suffice it to say, the cyst was now half the size it was. Then I found the name of a clinic in the next town, 14 miles away, Douglas, Georgia. My plan was then to get up real early and walk into Douglas and go to the clinic.

Well, so much for the idea of walking into Douglas. Besides finding a bump in my arm pit four hours later the size of a golf ball, my back locked up on me with muscle spasms. I could not move. A friend was on the phone with me about 5:30 AM and said if I didn't dial 911 that she would. I dialed 911 and the ambulance took me to Coffee Regional Medical Center in Douglas, Georgia. In the emergency room I was told that I had developed a staph infection and the huge cyst in my groin and under my arm had to be operated on immediately. Just before they rolled me in to the operating room the emergency room doctor came in and told me had lost his brother to suicide and thanked me for doing what I do. I spent six days in the hospital getting the best care I have ever received in a hospital and the best I've ever seen anyone else receive anywhere, the place was awesome. My doctor told me that there was probably no one on their staff, no matter their age, that wouldn't be willing to trade heart and lungs with me! That there walking is darn good for you. She also told me that had I tried to walk the 15 miles to Douglas, I may have very well have been found dead at the side of the road, whoa! Sure glad my back went out.

After being released from the hospital I went back to my motel room in Pearson and stayed for three more days before heading out again. It was damn rough at first and I had to move VERY slowly. Left Pearson, Georgia at 4:30 in the morning to resume my walk across America. My back didn't bother me until I had walked about eight miles, halfway. But, it was a mild discomfort and bearable. I rested in Douglas, Georgia and left early in the morning headed for Broxton which was only nine miles away. Though I felt pretty strong today, I have determined not to push it. I lost 11 days due to sickness, don't want that to happen again. I'm definitely Loving Life right now.

Love Heals

David and Tammy, stopped to talk to me near Dublin, Georgia. After telling them my story and why I was walking, David's eyes welled up with tears and he told me he had lost his only brother, Dale, to suicide less than two years before. David asked me if I would like to have a cold Mountain Dew from the cooler in the back of his truck and we moved to his tailgate and continued our talk for at least another half hour. We spoke of the horrible pain his brother had to have been in to have caused him to crush David's heart by removing himself from his life. We spoke of how important it was that he forgive Dale, as he was in so much pain he became blinded and didn't realize he was indeed being self-centered by not considering the absolute horror he was about to deliver to his parents, his siblings, and his friends. After we spoke, I walked up to the passenger side of the truck where his wife Tammy had sat patiently and apologized for having kept her husband so long. She smiled big and very sweetly said, "Oh, I didn't mind at all. Thank you so much!" There was a whole big bunch of love for her husband in that woman's eyes.

An Old Man in Pain

I was just walking into Milledgeville, Georgia, a very small in stature, old man spoke to me from across the road in one very strong Georgia accent, "wearyheadinfur." it sounded to me he was saying, I wasn't sure, so I said, "pardon me, sir?" He then walked across the road to where I was and repeated it and this time I correctly interpreted it as, "Where you heading for?" I told him and I also told of why I walked with that big Love Life sign over my head. The little guy just stood there for a few moments not saying a word, and then his eyes started welling up with tears, and just as some started flowing down that precious old face he blurted out, "I just lost muh wife!" I grabbed his hand so as to shake it and said, "Sir, I am so very sorry for you loss, God bless you, sir." Now the tears were really flowing and he said, "Forty-nine years, oh my Gawd, forty-nine years." I put my left hand on top of our hands and told him again how very sorry I was for his loss. He reached his left hand into his pants pocket and pulled out five folded-together one dollar bills, handed them to me and said, "Here suh, yer a doin' a real good thing." He then turned and headed back across the street to his old truck. Bless his precious heart, what pain he was in. We all need love.

Three Flags a Flappin'

In Athens, Georgia, I was expecting a visit from a Facebook friend and her husband, who were driving down to Georgia from Illinois to visit their daughter. There is a "loop" around the city of Athens and pedestrians are not allowed on it. I didn't have a map of Athens and no one I asked seemed to know how I could navigate back to route 441 on foot without getting on the "loop." I ended up going a few miles off course until I finally got some descent directions. We agreed to hook up at a Red Lobster I had been told was in my path. I was walking as fast as possible in the fierce heat under the weight of my backpack trying to get there in time to meet up with my friends.

A young black man with very long dreadlocks and a smile from heaven ran up to me with a big ice cold bottle of water and a huge bag of snack foods. He said, "Here man. I love your sign man. That is such an awesome sign man!" No sooner had he handed me the treats than a guy in an old beat up Ford Ranger truck with three very large flags mounted just in back of the cab came driving by us blowing his horn. The young man with me hollered out, "Hey Mathew!" The flags were: an American flag, an M.I.A. (missing in action) flag, and a Confederate flag. And all three were waving in the breeze. The driver turned the truck around and pulled up beside me. I asked him if I was close to the Red Lobster yet and he informed me I was still a couple miles away. He then said, "Heck buddy, we'll jus' throw yer stuff in the back here n' I'll take ya' thar." Also in the back of the truck was the largest dog I had ever seen in my entire life. And he had no hair. I asked what kind of dog it was and Mathew told me it was a German Sheppard. That dog never even slightly resembled a German Sheppard. Mathew said, "Jus don't startle 'im and ya better let me put yer gear in thar." Not a problem Mathew.

So, with my "LOVE LIFE" sign stood up in the back and the three flags flapping all around it, we whizzed in and out of traffic on Atlanta Highway in Athens, Georgia, as we headed for the rendezvous with my friends. No sooner had Mathew pulled out of the Red Lobster parking lot than my friends pulled in. A little later while dining in the restaurant, who should walk in but none other than the flag flyin' n' great big hearted Mathew himself, with camouflage cap and all. He just had to come in and check on me to make sure I had met up with my friends he said. Our waitress was a delightful young lady named Stacie. Stacie had lost cousins to suicide she told us and was active in suicide prevention at the University of Georgia where she was a student.

"Love fertilizes Life, the more we Love Life the greater our bounty from Life." ~ Steve Fugate

"Boogie," International Language?

At Newfound Gap, near Gatlinburg, TN, I was going to do a few miles of the Appalachian trail for old time's sake, but the weather forced me to turn back the next day. As I was heading back and about a mile and a half from Newfound Gap, I encountered three South Korean women coming toward me. All three were wearing cotton clothing and plain sneakers, not even a good running shoe. They had absolutely nothing at all with them, no food, no water, nothing. One of them spoke some English and the other two spoke none at all. The one asked me, "How far, end?" I answered, "Maine." She said, "Maine?" I said, "Yes, the state of Maine is where this trail ends." "How far that?" she said. "Two thousand miles," I answered. "What!? Two thousand miles! No, no!" She said. And I added, "Yes, yes, and, there are very serious thunder storms forecast for today also." "Oh, we maybe should go back, yes?" "Yes, you should most definitely go back," I said. At that, she turned and started to explain in Korean while motioning with her hands for her companions to turn around and head the other way. She said, "Boogie, boogie!" They flew back down the trail and I never saw them again. I had to chuckle at them, they were quite cute. But, I shudder to think what could have happened to them had they gone several miles and been caught in a storm. And even if they had cell phones on them there was no signal there in the mountains.

Cherokee People

I was walking through Cherokee, North Carolina, which is always a pleasure for me. As it is when I cross any of our Native People's lands. They always give me and my beautiful Love Life sign much more attention than I normally get walking through a community. I've walked across many native lands including, Seminole, Miccosukee, Shoshone, Apache, Hopi, Navajo, Hoopa, Karuk, Yurok, Blackfoot, Northern Cheyenne, Oglala Lakota, and Ojibwe. I have always been treated wonderfully. One fine looking Cherokee man, holding the hand of his five year-old grandson, came up to me and inquired as to what I was about. After I told him why I walked, he said "We lost three young men not long ago." He looked me straight in the eyes after he told me as though waiting for me to tell him why. He took my card and said he intended to give it to someone of importance in his tribe. I walked away from that incident with a heavy heart. I hear similar stories on nearly every reservation I have walked across. While walking on through Cherokee, in two different incidents, young Cherokee men who were performing dance in front of some tourist attraction simply stopped performing and walked over to find out what I was about. I love it! Both young men shook my hand and told me that I was doing a good thing. Nearly every Cherokee I saw either waved at me or blew their horns as they drove by.

Stop Blowing up Stuff!

Just outside of Cherokee, North Carolina, a young man stopped his truck to inquire as to what I was doing and why. He became very excited when I told him that I had now walked over 27,000 miles of the U. S. He said in a very strong Tennessee accent, "Hey, ya think I might hook up wit' ya sumwhar' and walk wit' ya some?" I told him that may be possible one day. He liked that. He had a wonderful smile and I liked his excited curiosity about everything. He told me his name was Mark and he asked would I like to spend the night at his house with him and his little dog and take a shower. Shower is the magic word for me, I jumped at the chance. His house was a few miles from the road I was traveling, but he assured me he would bring me back out to the highway the next morning. The home was high on a mountain in a Cherokee community called Towstring, the only residential section in the Smoky Mountain National Park. It was grandfathered in when the National Park was formed.

Mark's house sat upon a ridge nearly atop the mountain; he said a Cherokee woman rented it to him at a great price. As we sat on his front porch he told me he was 23 and that he was curious about everything and had been that way his whole life. He said he had become curious about explosives and how easy they were to make. He told of how he had really become fascinated with them and kept experimenting with blowing things up. One day, he said, he rigged up his homemade explosives on a large boulder to see if he could blow it up. He said that it did indeed blow up. And unbeknown to him, he said, "The damn law happened to be flyin' over in a helicopter and saw the explosion. Well, next thing I know, they're at my house with a search warrant and found all the stuff I had and I went to jail for 11 month's!" He went on to say, "I stopped blowing things up." I agreed that was a good idea. As he was telling me how he wasn't very close to his family and how his older brother was a pain in the ass, a car pulled up. "Damn, that's my brother Benny," Mark said. Brother Benny had his wife, 3 year-old daughter, and 2 week-old little boy with him. They just started unloading their luggage and Benny says, "You said if I had no place to go to come to your house." Mark said, "Hey, looka here at the new guns I got!"

I pitched my tent in Mark's yard and sat out in the yard and watched the two brothers go from rifle and handgun fondling to a 30 minute video game session at an earth shaking volume. While sitting on the front porch talking, all of sudden Mark says to Benny, "Hey, let's get them weed whackers and clear this here property." Benny never had time to answer yea or nay before Mark was handing him one of the two heavy duty gas powered weed whackers. As they were standing at the point where the front yard became nearly a sheer drop off, I asked Mark, "How are you going to trim the drop off, are you going to tie a rope to your waist and work your way down while Benny holds the rope?" They both looked at me like I was just plain stupid. "Hell Steve, it ain't like it's straight down or nuthin' like 'at?" Mark said while shaking his head at me. So, I looked down it again, all I knew, by God I wasn't about to do it. The two of them attacked the extremely steep slope, slashing through the weeds and anything else in the way with those noisy machines and moving down the slope like the worlds loudest and fastest eatin' mountain goats. I never saw either look down to check their footing, not one time. Upon reaching the bottom which was covered in weeds well over their heads, meeting the drooping branches of the numerous trees, it became a race to see who could cut down the most the fastest. They were swinging those screaming machines up and down, first cutting the weeds and then attacking the tree branches. I had never seen anything like it in my whole life. They continued the attack with motors roaring and the weeds, limbs, leaves and dirt flyin' in the air! I swear, when they finished, no more than 30 minutes after they started, that mountainside yard which had been completely grown over, looked like a well-manicured city park. I do believe young and crafty Mark was making sure his older brother earned his keep.

The next morning as I was loading my gear into the back of Mark's pickup, he yelled out the door to me, "Hey, will these weigh ya down much?" He was holding up two cans of "Bud" in his hands. I declined with a no thanks, and he looked totally bewildered.

His Brother Broke His Heart

Near Goode, Virginia in Owens Market, as I was ordering breakfast, the young lady taking my order asked if I was the guy walking who had lost both his children that she had seen on TV. She told the others working with her and then told me that she would cover my meal. While I was eating, another of the young ladies came up to me and slid her hand under my plate and said, "Here, this isn't much. I have a son who suffers from depression. I live in daily fear. Thank you for what you're doing; you're doing something." She was crying as she left my table. I stopped about three miles down the road to get a soda, took my pack off, leaned it against the store wall and my phone rang. I walked around in the parking lot engaged in my phone conversation and then walked back to where my backpack was, and attached to my Love Life sign was a crisp $20 dollar bill. I looked all around and saw no one; the giver was nowhere in sight

As I was leaving Roanoke, Virginia, a man stopped me to ask of my Love Life sign. As soon as I mentioned my son's suicide he said, "I just lost my brother to suicide, man." All he could do then was look down at the ground and shake his head. When he tried to talk, he choked up. He appeared to be embarrassed because he just couldn't form the words to explain that horrible pain in his heart; so he changed the subject. "You take donations man?" and handed me some money. He never said another word, turned and left. His brother broke his heart.

Clydesdale Chickens

In Pulaski, Virginia, on a Saturday morning out in front of a very small wooden building proclaiming over its door, "Full Gospel Church" I saw several people standing around stacks of wire cages containing assorted varieties of chickens and pigeons. On one of those large portable signs with the flashing lights along the top, next to the cages, were the words:

WEDNESDAY: GOSPEL SING AND CHICKEN SALE
SATURDAY: CHICKEN SALE

I stopped and chatted awhile and received excellent directions concerning my route and was told interesting things about the birds. You know those chickens with fat legs that have feathers all the way down to their feet, the ones you always see at county fairs, a friend of mine calls them, Clydesdale Chickens.

Asteroid Hitting Earth 11/11/2011!

Just out of Roanoke, Virginia, a man stopped and said he just had to talk to me. He pointed to his Chevy Blazer full of his belongings and said his wife had thrown him out the day before. He then proceeded to tell me that God was all over him and directing his life. Sorry, but it looked to me, more like *his* wife was the one directing his life. He told me God made him stop to tell me that a huge asteroid would hit Earth on 11/11/11. He didn't say, but I have to assume, it would probably be hitting us at either 11:00 AM, or 11:00 PM. I just like keeping things in order. He asked my opinion of the profound prophecy he had just given me from God and I responded, "Horseshit." He then reached into his truck and came out with a tabloid that he held up right in front of my face so that I could see the proof he was indeed a prophet, with the headlines, "ASTEROID WILL HIT EARTH ON 11/11/2011!!" The last tabloid headlines I had read were in the supermarket line back in 1990, "500 POUND CHERNOBYL CHICKEN!!" And there was a picture, just terribly frightening. My son Stevie though, then a senior in high school, bought it to put inside his locker door. He probably would have put the asteroid headline there as well. I suppose I should have notified my friend Mike Guzo, who had just dropped me off from a delightful stay with him and his lovely family. Mike is coordinator for emergency services in the Roanoke area. I'm fairly certain such an event would fall under his job description. Is Life entertaining or what! Don't ya just Love it!

The Blues

Figure 13. Playing the Blues.

At Bedford, Virginia, near the Goodwill store in a strip mall, I was using an outside electrical outlet to recharge my phone and laptop when I watched a very cosmetically challenged 1964 Plymouth Valiant pull into the parking space in front of where I was standing. Out stepped Randy, a man about my age. He was carrying a much worn guitar case and a folding chair. After he pulled a beautiful and shiny steel guitar from its case, he placed the open case in front of his chair, obviously as a container for appreciative listeners to drop money into. He played the blues; played them damn good: He told me proudly that he never learned to play until he was 25. I told him I loved the blues and asked was he familiar with Roy Buchanan. He said he loved his rendition of the Peter Gunn theme. I agreed. We both agreed on what a true tragedy that such a talent as Roy Buchanan had taken his own life in a jail cell. I told him I had seen Albert King live and was right up front watching the blues legend perform. Randy expressed envy, said he had most every album Albert King ever made. He strummed that fine instrument continually as we talked. A young black man walked up and placed two dollars in Randy's guitar case. "Good blues man, real good, thanks," he said. A guy stepped up next to us and started singing the blues in one of the most talented voices I've ever heard. He said his name was Charlie Frazier and after I complimented him on his beautiful voice, he said, "I bought my first house with this voice." He went on to tell us that he had worked with Chuck Berry, Bo Diddley, The Drifters, Gary U.S. Bonds, John Lee Hooker, and the Chantels. After singing along with Randy in a couple more songs, Charlie excused himself saying he had to get a prescription filled. A few minutes later Charlie rejoined us with a bottle in a brown paper bag under his arm and I then realized it was a Virginia state liquor store he had gone into. Charlie left after a while. Randy and I discussed the

147

beauty of a Love Life attitude and had some laughs as he strummed his steel guitar and thanked those who threw in mostly change and an occasional dollar or two. A little boy being watched by his mother came up and threw in some change. Randy looked up at him and laughingly said, "Thank you, I do believe you made my quota for the day and I now have enough that I can go home now!" The little boy looked up smiling big at a smiling proud momma. Randy watched me as I unplugged my electronics and prepared to depart and said to me, "Is that all you need, man, a little shot of electricity from time to time? Now that is freedom, man." Charlie called me the next day; thinking I might still be in the area and offered to share some of the best black bean soup and cornbread I would ever eat in my whole life. I wish I had stayed around. Randy and Charlie gave me my real shot of electricity.

Spencer Dimmitt

Just outside Ulysses, Kansas, It was getting dark and the temperature was dropping as well. So I was looking for a tent spot. There are few trees in this area to hide behind so I just walked deep into an open field covered with a new dusting of snow. Someone saw me and called the police. Deputy Terry Maas showed up. After he checked me out, he told me it was fine for me to camp there. Deputy Maas told me he had lost three friends to suicide while growing up in Nova Scotia. One was very close, he said. After conversing for a while Terri said he had friends that wouldn't mind at all chipping in with him to get me a room. I told him that would not be necessary; I was used to sleeping in the cold. "Wouldn't you rather have a room?" Terry said he was worried about me and how cold it was getting. He made some calls to friends, loaded up my gear and took me to a motel in Ulysses after he went to Mickey D's so I could buy a McFilet Mignon (double cheeseburger) for a dollar.

Deputy Terry Maas was at my door the next morning with four huge breakfast burritos. Then he took me to get an item I had left behind in the field, when he picked me up. He then took me to a place called The Fuel Barn and bought me coffee. Later that morning I was about a mile out of Ulysses and fighting fierce winds when Angie stopped. She said she had seen me walking a few weeks earlier, in either Missouri or Illinois and wanted to know my story. I told her, and she said she did not think I should fight the wind all day, that I should let her get me a room. It really was useless walking against the wind, and saying no to Angie, so I accepted the offer and Angie took me back to the motel I had just left and I ended up back in the same room.

Okay, the next morning Deputy Maas picks me up again for coffee and takes some pictures with me. Later in the day, I had actually made it two miles out of Ulysses when a truck stopped and the driver said, "Where in the hell are you a goin' and what the hell you a doin?" I told him and he informed me he was Spencer Dimitt, owner of the Fuel

Barn in Ulysses and that Deputy Terry Maas was one of his best friends. He also informed me that the weather was turning worse and that I should stay at his home just up the road in Johnson City, Kansas. Spencer and I hit it off immediately.

Not only did he let me have the run of his home in Johnson City, he took me out in the snow covered prairies to see whitetail deer, mule deer, and coyote. Until you have driven across a snow-covered west Kansas prairie at 50 miles an hour in order to cut off at every turn and stay alongside for as long as possible, the most beautiful and largest whitetail buck I've ever seen in my life, you just have not witnessed wildlife at its most beautiful. To watch that magnificent animal at that speed with such grace was truly an incredible experience for me. It was also truly incredible that we lived. My head hit the top of the roof so many times it just quit hurting after a while. Spencer never spilled his drink one time, either. Riding with Spencer Dimmitt is not for the faint of heart. Spencer bought me new gloves and gave me a new micro-fleece jacket he had. He also made sure I had money when I left, said he really believes in what I'm doing.

Just outside of Trinidad, Colorado, I stayed in Spencer's other home up in the mountains. He made sure plenty of food and plenty of firewood was there for me not to mention, the bottle of fine "Single Barrel" Kentucky Bourbon (just in case I ran out of firewood he said). When Spencer was telling me about the house and that I could stay there as long as I liked, he added, "Now there ain't a TV there." And I said, "Perfect!" It was spectacular there with the fresh fallen snow. A herd of elk walked right past the house every night.

A few days after I had left Trinidad, Spencer called me and said, "There is a serious blizzard comin' and you can't be walkin' in it, I'm comin to get ya'." He wouldn't hear no. He drove about 300 miles staying just ahead of the blizzard. I hadn't told anyone but I was worried about a deep chest congestion I was experiencing. I knew it wasn't good to be in those single digit temps and sleeping on the ground. Spencer picked me up and drove me to Pagosa Springs, Colorado where we got a room in a very nice resort and we soaked in the 108 degree mineral springs as often as possible. The chest congestion started breaking up and was soon gone. It was a wonderful time spent with Spencer, we had great conversations, and we became fast friends. Spencer once again insisted I have enough money on me to continue with.

"Let us Love our Life, that precious gift we're endowed with at birth, until Love becomes the most prevalent part of who we are. Let us Love Life until we Love before we look, Love before we talk, and eventually, Love before we think; then, we are on path to a heart governed mind." ~ Steve Fugate

Young Navajo Man

I love walking through Native Lands, the curiosity and the total lack of fear to approach and question is always a delight and the Navajo are no different. Several Navajo people had stopped to talk. In just two days of walking through the Land of The Navajo, here in Arizona, I'd encountered five stories of loved ones lost to alcohol. The oldest of which was 33 and the youngest 30. Three were their children, two were brothers. The youngest was the brother of a beautiful young Navajo woman, Traca, working the front desk of a motel I was checking into. The tears poured as she showed me a picture of the precious little 4 year-old daughter of her now deceased brother.

A young Navajo man slammed on his brakes when he saw me. Gordon told me that he certainly did not love life now and couldn't see anything worth living for anymore. Just four days before on Christmas day, he caught his wife of five years in bed with another man. Just months before, he lost his little brother to alcohol and just two weeks before, his brother's one-year-old daughter accidently choked to death. I told him that my son's suicide started my walks; I told him that stopping to talk to me couldn't be just a coincidence. We talked about his uniqueness in the universe, about the absolute honor of his being born a Navajo and his beautiful ancestral ways. We talked of his loved ones, and how he would crush their hearts and destroy their lives if he took his. We talked of the beauty of the gift of life; he told of the joy he got from riding his two horses. We talked of how we have to push on and Love our gift of Life no matter what and how a Love Life attitude gives us an individual power from within. A power that gives us the strength to resist, and to not allow anyone else's actions to control our emotions or our reactions. I asked Gordon, "You could never have done to your wife what she did to you could you? He said that no, he could not. I said, "There are no levels down here. There are but places. No matter the worldly position of status one has reached, there is no level over another. The only levels are those achieved within each, our own place. When someone does a wrong to us, something you know you could not do to anyone, this means that person has not yet grown into a place of wisdom and maturity in that area of Life as we have. Forgive them as soon as possible, and let the incident leave your mind. When we allow someone else's actions to control our emotions even slightly, we have succumbed to that person's level in that we are allowing them to alter the level we have achieved within our place. This of course makes us no better than the other person, it but means we have obtained a wiser and better understanding of that level in the understanding of Life. This strengthens our place within taking us toward self-contentment, which is, the beauty of Life.

Gordon promised me that he would go to be with his family, he promised he would concentrate on chasing away all negative thoughts and to concentrate instead on how wonderful his gift of Life truly is. He thanked me and as we shook hands I capped my other hand over his, I told him that I love him. Gordon had a surprised look on his face after I told him I loved him. "You're wondering how a stranger is capable of loving you," I said. He nodded yes. And so I explained to him that I no longer have my two children to give my love to, and so I have an overflow of love that I can give to the children of other parents in emergencies when they are unable to be there. He smiled at that. Still holding on to his very rough and calloused hand, I made him promise to me as a proud Navajo man, and give me his Navajo Oath to never again entertain thoughts of taking his own life. He said, "I promise. You have helped me. Thank you. You be safe out there, friend." Later, after I related this story to someone and they asked, "Is there such a thing as the Navajo Oath?" I said, "There is now." From the look on Gordon's face when I asked him to give me his Navajo Oath, I'd have to say there is.

Who's Nuts?

While savoring my senior citizen coffee at McDonalds in Portales, New Mexico, an old gentleman walks up and very cheerfully, says, "Good morning." I responded, "Good morning and how are you sir?" "Could be better" he said, "Everyone tells me I shouldn't put a combination lock on my door. But damn, it's not like it's on my house, it's on a damn storage shed." I just nodded my head. He continued, "Apple cider vinegar mixed with baking soda seems to help me a lot. I thought about putting magnets next to the combination locks. Have a good day." And out the door he went leaving me sitting there with a totally bewildered look on my face, I'm sure. "You have a good day too, sir," I mumbled to myself. Outside a few minutes later the same gentleman approached me as I was putting on my backpack and preparing to leave. "Where you headed?" He asked. "San Diego," I answered. "Hmm," he said, "There's a trucking company right here in Portales that goes to California, S&L, I believe it's called. They have reported scorpions dying from cancer, that's why I always wear this here cowboy hat. Damn sun's not getting me!" He wasn't wearing a cowboy hat; he wasn't wearing any kind of hat. He must've been nuts? Probably the exact thoughts of passerby's as they drove by me early that morning, sitting on the side of the road on a big rock dry shaving and then brushing my teeth in 29-degree weather. The old gentleman seemed just as happy as I was, go figure. Soon after that, when people would ask me how come I'm always so happy and in such a good mood, I began answering them, "That's the convenience of being nuts, you're always happy."

His Ashes Sparkled

After returning home from a walk across the United States, I called my "Joel Kody Walk," at the chosen tranquil spot on the beautiful Indian River Lagoon, my friend

Sonya, and I, stooped down on the water wall so as to not allow an eastern wind to disrupt our intentions. I asked had she ever done anything like this before, she, like me, never had. I opened the container given to me by Joel's mother to spread anywhere I felt to do so, during my walk dedicated to him. I held it just above the water and emptied the ashes of young Joel Kody, who had lost his battle with depression and took his own life. I said goodbye and told him it had been nice having him along on my journey. Sonya said, "Look his ashes are sparkling!" Because of the light reflecting off Joel's remains as they slowly sank to the bottom, he did most definitely sparkle. I feel I owe it to the memory of Joel, to the memory of my own two precious children, and to the memory of lost children and loved ones of way too many others, to continue to "sparkle" with a love of life to spread to others for as long as that Life may continue. Sparkle, radiate Love, and let us mend the broken heart while it is yet beating.

"Let's face this new day for what it is, a new gift to replace the gift we received yesterday. It is an even better gift than yesterday because it is brand new and fresh." ~ Steve Fugate

Giving and Receiving

When I first began my cross-country walks, I refused to take donations. I would save up all the money I could and be frugal with it. Well, when one is in a hail storm and sees a motel to escape to, screw frugality! In reconsidering my decision to not accept money, I came up with two reasons to start accepting money from others: One, in not accepting an offer of money from another, I was denying that person the self-satisfaction of helping, and of being a part of my walks. Two, I was going to starve to death!

Still stubborn though, I added to the fact that I never ask, (never have, never will) a stipulation that I would not accept a donation unless the giver listened to my story as to why I walked. Then, one day, a man obviously having difficulty walking, came up to me and handed me fifty dollars. I explained my requirement and he said, "Listen, I don't need to hear your story. It's obvious you're doing a good thing with your ability to walk. I'm not even 40 yet, and my ability to compete in marathons and ironman triathlons has stopped because I now have a rare bone disease attacking my hips and legs… I just want to be a part of your walks!" Wow! I ended the 'have to hear my story' stipulation right then and there.

Another man, I was telling, that I not only never ever asked, I had actually turned down offers of money from some whose attitude I did not particularly care for, then asked me, "What if someone offered you $10,000 dollars, would you turn that down?" I answered, "I have no idea, no one has ever offered me that much, why don't you try it and let's see what I do?"

Here are just a few of the many acts of kindness that I was gifted with during my walks of this beautiful and wonderful country.

"Random acts of kindness come from a loving and giving heart reacting from a message that heart telegraphed to the mind in that moment the eye witnessed another in need and then acted. Perhaps our goal should be that our hearts remain in that mode at all times." ~ Steve Fugate

YOU enjoy Life!

Once in a very remote area in Utah I saw a rock atop a piece of paper and picked it up. Under the paper was a folded twenty and on the paper, "YOU enjoy LIFE!" If you're wondering if this made me cry, the answer is yes, absolutely.

Brie and Merlot

In Yosemite National Park, a young man stopped who had just catered a wedding and gave me two bottles of Merlot and some fine Brie. Later, a young family from Kansas stopped, and thinking I was homeless and needy, like many do, mommy very sympathetically asked, "You need anything sir?" I innocently said, "Yes, would you happen to have a corkscrew? I really need to open a bottle of Merlot to go with some fine Brie I have." By the look on their sweet faces, I saw *that* was not the answer they had expected.

Just Kindness

In Worchester, New York, a lady in a really beat up old car pulled up and offered me five crumpled up one dollar bills. She said, "Here, please take this and buy yourself something to eat, I used to be homeless." I told her thanks but that I was not homeless. She insisted that I take it anyway, and said she would still like to help. I reluctantly took the money. Her eyes were sweet and she smiled real big when I accepted the money, glad I took it.

It stormed all day with a lot of lightning and I sissied out and took a motel room at a little spot in the road called, Howe's Cave, New York. The motel was the Holiday Motel. I asked the lady at the desk how much? She said, "fifty dollars." She took one look at my face and said, "How much can you pay?" I offered $40.00. She said, How about $35.00?" "That'll work." I answered. While she was ringing it up she said, "I made it an even $30.00; if it were my motel I wouldn't charge you at all." I thanked her very much. I asked what time the restaurant opened. She informed me it was the only place to eat for several miles and unfortunately it was closed on Mondays. She seemed really bothered by it and so I assured her it would be fine as I had eaten a big lunch. Later that evening she knocked on my door and handed me a Burger King bag with a whopper, fries, and a large soda. I tried to pay her for it but she refused. When you walk all day with at least forty pounds on your back, you are always hungry. I inhaled it.

"Kindness is the shadow of God in man." ~ Kahlil Gibran

Laconia Bike Week

I walked through Henniker, New Hampshire, the only one on earth the sign says. All day long I kept seeing signs "FREE FOOD at The Tent." The annual bike races and motorcyclist gathering at Laconia, New Hampshire was going on. "FREE FOOD" was then emblazoned in my brain. The next day, it rained all day and as I was passing a big tent at the side of the road I saw a huge sign, "FREE FOOD FOR BIKERS." And it was under a tent, out of the rain. I knew it was meant for the many bikers on their way to the annual Laconia motorcycle races. I looked over and saw a tall biker with a long white beard and braided long white hair. We just stared at each other for a moment. I knew I wanted some of that free food, I also knew I was not a biker: how do I get the free food? I spoke first, "I'm not a biker [as if that were not obvious] but I would be willing to pay for some of that food (I could get $1.35 worth anyway,)" "Come on over here," he said. "I'll charge you the same thing I charge all the other people: nothing." I ate hot dogs and Sheppard's Pie till I could eat no more. He told me I could spend the night under their tent and out of the rain. I took him up on it and I joined in and helped to feed the numerous bikers who stopped and indulged. I also helped them feed breakfast the following day before I left "The Tent" with my belly full of food and kindness. It was a Christian biker group and they had been feeding the bikers for over twenty years without charge. Not one person at any time tried to talk to me about religion, nor did I see any of them talk to anyone else about their beliefs.

Let's just Love one another and be so confident in our own Life's choices that we need not expect others to make the same choices we did. Respecting, that their choices felt just as right to them as did our choices to us. ~ Steve Fugate

David's Place

I went in David's Place the Barber Shop at Gardiner, Maine, for a haircut. As David Oxton, the owner was unfastening the cape from around my neck, he said, "Now you can tell folks that you got a free haircut in Gardiner, Maine." I said, "But sir, I have the money to pay." He said, "I don't care if you are a multi-millionaire sir, this haircut is free!"

Trail Magic

As I was sitting on the curb in front of a c-store eating a sandwich in the town of Hanover, New Hampshire, a young man, an Appalachian Trail hiker, sat down beside me. He introduced himself as Jeb from Harrisburg, Pennsylvania, and said he was doing his last thousand miles of the "AT" and had started in Pennsylvania on this last part of his 'section hike' of the entire trail. I delighted him when I said I was a 2000 miler and had done all the "AT." He asked about my "LOVE LIFE" sign and I explained. For the next 15 minutes or so he remained silent. As he rose to put his heavy backpack on and continue his quest toward Mt. Katahdin, he handed me a five dollar bill and said, "This isn't much, but maybe it can help you save some more lives." I said, "Yes it is much, it is a great amount coming from someone who has to watch their money the way you do. Thank you!" I knew how frugal you have to be to stretch the money for that long journey. Jeb is typical of the type of young person you will find hiking that beautiful 2,175 mile footpath to healing. He's the reason I encourage all, and particularly, our young people, to hike the "AT".

Take My Son With You

Walking through Maine on my walk around the United States in 2004, a man pulled up beside me, handed me a bag and drove off. The bag contained two twenties, two ham and cheese sandwiches, a cold milk, a Hershey Bar, and a picture of his beautiful son with a note telling me he had killed himself at age 27 and, "How I wish my son could have heard your message! Please keep doing what you're doing! My son loved to travel, I hope you don't mind taking him along with you." Did I mention, I cry a lot out here on the road?

Nice Encounter

Walking in downtown Schenectady, New York, about 4:30 pm, a lady walking past me looked up at my sign and said, "Thanks, I needed to see that, it's been a rough day!" I said, "Thanks, I needed to hear that, it's been a rough day!" We both laughed.

"Love is the lubricant to make the world turn smoother." ~ Steve Fugate

Good Karma!

In Warren, New Hampshire, a lady at a store called the Warren Mall, turned me down when I asked if I could please get some water from the spigot at the side of her building, but said she would sell me a bottle for a dollar. And she was quite curt about it. I'm a low budget operation; I am not going to pay for water if I don't have to. Like I have said before, every time someone is not so nice to me something else really good happens to me. Not 30 minutes later, a car pulled up beside me, I heard a loud whoop and turned to see a very well-endowed young lady thrust her front half out the window, pulled up her top and revealed all. New Hampshire certainly is lovely that time of the year!

It Don't Mean a Thing

A man got out of his car and said some people at the restaurant I had just left in Carrollton, Ohio, had told him about me and that I was walking in honor of my children. He was crying as he told of having recently lost his son to suicide also. He pointed behind me and said, "See that big mansion up there on that hill, that's my daughter's, she's just been diagnosed with terminal cancer. None of it means a damn thing does it mister?" "No sir, it does not." I replied. He thanked me for walking with "LOVE LIFE" over my head. He just needed to talk to someone that he felt might possibly relate to the pain he was in. He placed a fifty dollar bill in my hand and insisted I take it. To help heal your broken heart be ever alert to help heal another's broken heart. I've a tool I wish to God I did not have. I have the tool of, perspective. If I can Love Life after losing both my beautiful children, most anyone can.

One Tough Lady

I found a lady's purse just outside of Indianapolis with all her credentials and driver's license. I called her; she was delighted and came immediately to retrieve it. Just a little more than a couple hours before, as she was crossing a parking lot to a drugstore to get a prescription filled, a man had grabbed it. She was 88 years old (same age as my mother) and he threw her against a car! She had just put a hundred dollar bill in the purse to pay for her prescription. I felt terrible for her. But she said, "Hey, I'm 88 and this is the first time anything like this has ever happened to me, and we just have to let things go and go on." She told me not to feel bad and offered me a ride through Indy which I turned down. She insisted I take ten dollars though, which I finally accepted. As she was walking back to her car she turned and with a big smile, said, "Oh, I really like your sign. I Love Life, always have."

Little Town with a Big Heart

Early morning, cold and anxious to get to warmth after a night of rain and keeping dry in a leaky tent, I was headed into Whitewater, Kansas. A lady stopped: I asked if there were a restaurant in town. She pointed me toward Mom's Café and said she wanted to buy my breakfast and then drove off. In the café, "Mom" asked if I was the guy walking and then slipped me a good sum of money and said she was told to give that to me. After a wonderful breakfast and some of "Mom's" homemade strawberry-banana preserves, I was followed out the door by a young lady who wanted to hear my story. She told of not always making good decisions in her past but now she was able to Love Life. She too, insisted on giving me a donation because she believed in what I'm doing. But minutes later, a lady stopped to give me a half gallon of apple juice and four bags of animal crackers. A sign says, "WELCOME TO WHITEWATER, KANSAS. THE LITTLE TOWN WITH A BIG HEART." I concur.

Big Hearted Shaun Patty

In El Dorado, Kansas, "Hey!" I heard from behind me. I turned and there stood Shaun Patty with two large cups in his hands. "I've got hot chocolate or coffee for you, take your pick or have them both:" I took the chocolate and we talked at length. I left Shaun and went looking for a place to tent. I found a place behind an empty building next to a McDonalds: hot coffee in the morning! Later, car headlights directly on my tent woke me up. I heard, "Hey Steve, you awake? Been lookin' for ya, come on man, I'm gonna' take you to a motel and outa' the cold." It was Shaun and two of his little boys. Shaun had gone on his Facebook and gathered more money from friends, enough to get me a room. Tagan, his 5-year-old, insisted on carrying my "LOVE LIFE" sign into the motel for me.

Crop Dusters

Near Jonesboro, Arkansas Just after walking past an airplane hangar at a crop dusting company, a young man pulled his truck along side of me and explained that and he and some of the pilots he worked with had just seen me walk by the airplane hangar they were in. He told me that some had seen me earlier walking with my sign and they all had decided that because I wasn't asking for anything they wanted to give me some food. He said, "Beins' you ain't a carrin' one them damn 'Will work fer food signs' we figgered you was alright and not jus' another one of them sorry lazy asses tryin' to get sumpin' for nuthin'." Well, he then hands me two plastic grocery bags filled with cans of soups, stew, Chinese meals, etc. It all probably weighed at least 15 pounds. He seemed very proud of he and his friends decision to feed me and I hated like hell to tell him I couldn't carry all that weight. I ended up taking only half of what he offered and he seemed to be satisfied with that. I ate a can of the beef stew and gave the rest to a road worker a couple miles further down the road that seemed delighted to get it.

Liquor Bars in Churches?

After speaking to a congregation of about 50 people in a church at Great Bend, Kansas, they took a "love offering" for me and presented me with a much needed and very much appreciated, $43.00. That same day, just up the street in an Eagles Lodge, at the bar, over beers, and I swear this to be true, we actually were, discussing a belief in God; three people donated $75.00. Maybe they should put bars in churches? Hey, do the math??

I Help People, he said

Near Sedalia, Missouri, a guy pulled up beside me in a brand new, really nice truck and asked if I wanted a ride and I told him no thanks. Then he said, "Look, I would like to help you out; I would like to get you a motel room." I didn't have to ponder that decision long. Once in his quite expensive truck, he told me that he had to stop at the medical center that he managed. He was inside but a few minutes and when he came out he handed me a large bag full of energy bars. And before I could get out a thank you, he reached his hand out to me and said, "Here's a hundred dollars, this should help you out." I was stunned, to say the least. I said, "Sir, are you sure? That's a lot of money." It was a stupid thing to say and by now I should know better, knowing that people giving want to give and are joyful in doing so. The gentleman said, "I don't mean to brag Steve, but this is what I do, I help people whenever I get an opportunity. I have been very blessed in my life and so I pass it on." He took me to a very nice motel and purchased me a room. Before he left, he asked if there was anything else I needed. The hundred bucks sure came in handy two days later; I was caught in a terrible storm and was able to get another room.

Don't Argue with Mamie

In Crowell, Texas, Mamie stopped and asked where I intended to spend the night. After I told her I would be sleeping in my tent she insisted on getting me a motel room. She sternly said, "You will not." and insisted on getting me a motel room. And before I could utter a second "No ma'am," I was in a motel room she purchased. She was very insistent on the matter. The next day I was invited into Shaw's Pharmacy for coffee and good conversation with Mike Shaw and friends. They all asked where I spent the night and when I told of Mamie's persistence they all chuckled in agreement that you don't say "no" to Mamie.

Christopher Ryan Lee, Caliente, Nevada

In Caliente, Nevada, I came out of a C-store where I had asked about the price of a motel room. A guy walked out of the restaurant next to it and asked if I was hungry and offered me to come in the restaurant and join him and his wife for a meal. I told him thanks but I had just ate and that it was not a meal I was looking for but a cheaper motel and asked if there was another in town a little cheaper. He immediately pulled out his wallet and handed me a $100 bill! Kim said he loved my sign. I told him why I walked. He then told me he had lost his oldest son Eric in a car wreck at 32 and about 7 months later, their other son, Christopher, killed himself on his 30th birthday due to intense grief for his brother! Kim later sent me a picture of their son's tombstones because of the words from a song Christopher had written which were on his stone, "Did you learn to listen, to listen with your heart, did you learn to love your fellowman, did you do your part" Kim wrote below the picture, "The words from this one taught me to do what I did today when I saw you walk by the restaurant, I am trying to love my fellow man as he did, he was one of the sweetest giants anyone ever knew. He stood 6 foot 6."

Christopher Ryan Lee

April 23, 1977
April 23, 2007

Did you learn to listen,
to listen with your heart,

did you learn to love
your fellowman,

Did you do your part?

Worlds End
Christopher

Figure 14. Christopher Ryan Lee

You One Who Do All Work

In 2011. At Hawthorne, Nevada I got into town late and dark was closing in on me. There are usually not a lot of places in a town to pitch a tent and I was trying to avoid getting a motel room because I only had $50.00. After looking around for a suitable tent site, I realized I was not going to be able to tent, so I decided to see if I could talk a motel clerk down to $30.00 or at least $35.00. The first motel told me they were booked but that the Hawthorne Motel should have a vacancy and it would probably be $32.00. Great, I would go to the Hawthorne Motel. I thought I followed directions precisely, but try as I may, I could not find the Hawthorne Motel. As I walked through the motel section, very tired, and in the dark, I decided to try the Holiday Lodge. It looked like it would certainly be in a price range higher than the 30's though. The owner of the motel met me at the front desk. Looking around at the surroundings, I figured I had little chance of getting a room within my budget. But I was one tired puppy and I had to try. I presented my card to him and told him why I walk and I then said to him, "Sir, I would certainly appreciate any kind of break you could give me on a room." In a very strong Indian or possibly Pakistani accent, he said, "How about it free?" I said, "Excuse me sir?" He very straight faced said, "Free, I give you room for free." I was blown away. I kept thanking him over and over as I fought back the tears. The kind gentleman said, "Why you thank me, you one who does all work: You one who carries the important message." I still thanked him even more and he said, "That's good, now go get in room and rest from the cold." That put a smile on my face for sure and the thought of it helped me to endure the next night at Walker Lake where I couldn't find a level spot for my tent so I made my bed on the concrete slab in the entranceway to the outhouse. There were three walls to help deter the wind and the wind was blowing away from me so the smell wasn't all that bad. And just before I laid down, I saw a herd of wild horses running in the distance, just beautiful. Now go Love Life and get your just rewards.

Laptops, Wine, and Cowshit

In Washington, a man in front of me on the highway had pulled into the driveway of his family's ranch and was sitting there on the tailgate of his truck waiting for me to approach him. His name was Sarn, and he wanted to know exactly what I was doing. We talked awhile, after I told my story he told that he was a rodeo cowboy just returning from a weekend of bronc riding, bull riding, and calf roping. He told me to throw my gear in the back of the truck that he wanted to take me up to the house and refresh my water and see if he couldn't find me a few things to eat for my long stretch before I got to the next town. He came out of his house with water and a peanut butter and jelly sandwich, a variety of energy bars, some real good cheese, and a full bottle of California Cabernet Sauvignon and a corkscrew. He offered to let me stay in his cow pasture for the night and I accepted. I found a spot where there was not as much Cowshit, and pitched my tent. I sat there eating cheese, sipping the Cabernet Sauvignon, and occasionally shooing away a curious young bull so he wouldn't step on my nice laptop and possibly interrupt my Broadband connection. I hate peanut butter and jelly sandwiches, one of the most common foods given me out on the road. I never say anything but, "Oh thank you so very much." And sometimes I've had to eat them.

Thought I was Stealing Stuff

In the Pamida store at Tarkio, Missouri, I was walking around in the store trying to figure out how to buy stuff to keep me warm on the cold nights in my tent and I had very little money. Everything I wanted to buy just cost too much, so I settled on buying two of those pull down knit caps for only $2.00 apiece. The strategy was to put them on my feet and roll my sock tops over them so they would stay on during the night. I had been wandering around in the store for a long time, these kinda' decisions do not come easily. A lady stepped in front of me and said, "Sir is there something I can help you with?" By her tone of voice and the look on her face, I could tell she was concerned with the fact a guy with a backpack sitting in front of their store had been wondering around inside for a very long time. See, nearly everyone upon first seeing me decides that I am a homeless wanderer. I handed her one of my cards and told her who I was and why I walk. I could see the look in her eyes change. She introduced herself as the store manager. She told me she was extremely sorry for the loss of my children. We talked a very long time. Shana had spent ten years in the army and said she had really loved it. I had to ask why she would give it up already having half her time in before retirement. She told me, "I had the opportunity of an instant family consisting of two little girls, both under three that needed a mother, and a wonderful man." "What a great decision." I said. She told me to go to the isle where they had the sample sized products and pick what I wanted. She also told me to get several packs of beef jerky for the road. Instead of paying, she had me sign a form and said, "You didn't get much, are you sure you don't need anything else?"

Sweet Texas Girl in Washington

In the town of Skykomish, Washington, I spent the night at a hiker's hostel; it's only a few miles from where the Pacific Crest Trail crosses at Steven's Pass. That evening, I went into a little bar called the Whistling Post. The bartender asked if I were hiking the PCT and when I told her what I was doing, she said, "Holy shit!" I told her that's what all Texan's said to me after they found out what I was doing; she was indeed, from Texas. She told me that less than two years before, her boyfriend had committed suicide. We talked about it and she was trying to listen but she was so busy with other customers, it was difficult for her. Evidently she heard more than I thought she did. The next morning at the front desk was a birthday card for me and a big batch of homemade cookies, the card read:

Happy Birthday Steve!
Here are some cookies I made for you. God bless you!
Your story touched my heart! Suicide of a loved one has
been my biggest trial by far. Thank you for reminding me
to Love Life, which I try to do every day. I am going to pass
your story and website to everyone I know! Please stop in
and visit Skykomish, WA if you are ever back this way.
Happy Birthday from Delana
(I'm the Whistling Post bartender from Texas who said "Holy Shit!" to your story)

No Ugly Showers

Leaving the delightful little town of Twisp, Washington, I was walking past the Blue Spruce Motel and saw a strikingly beautiful young woman tending to the flowers in the motel yard. Her baby daughter was in a stroller watching mommy. Mommy looked up at me and said, "Hey, you need a place to stay tonight? I have one room that hasn't been remodeled yet and it has an ugly shower, I can let you have it for the night." I said, "Thank you, yes. There is no such thing as an ugly shower." The shower was beautiful. As was Nicole's heart. She brought me several frozen dinners that she said had been left by previous guests. She also brought me Pepsis and fresh peaches. She gave me the room for two nights. She told me that God had blessed her and delivered her husband from drugs and saved her marriage. She said she was just giving back.

Cheapest pair a Boots Ever!

My boots I started out with in California finally wore out on me, rocks were starting to come in from the worn out bottoms. My right shoe always wears out prematurely because my foot had to be re-attached after a motorcycle wreck in 1969. So I didn't want to hit Danner Boots up just yet for a new pair because it's really not their fault the one boot wears out so fast. The left boot was still in great shape. (Danner Boots are awesome.) So, I thought I would buy a very cheap pair to get me by for a while and then hit Danner up for another donated pair. In Monroe, Washington, I saw a shoe repair store which sold boots, Quality Boot & Repair. Sometimes shoe repair places will sell used boots, so I thought I would give that a try. The owner, Kevin Pease, looked on his shelves and did not have anything used which would work for me. And all his new boots were high quality like Red Wings. I just couldn't afford to pay $200.00 and up. But Kevin and I talked for a very long time and had a great time laughing and cutting up. He said the slow economy was really starting to hurt his shoe sales. After I left, I walked into a grocery store and found a pair of boots for $19.00.

Later that night, Kevin called to see if I was still in Monroe. He asked me to come by his store and see him before I left. I went in the next morning and Kevin, as soon as I walked in, he looked down at my new boots and said, "Man, that's the cheapest made pair of boots I've ever seen in my life." Kevin told me that he and his girlfriend had checked out my website the night before and they had decided they just had to help me. He was apologizing that he hadn't caught me before I bought the cheap ones. I told him it was great because now I could give something as well, I would just drop them in the Goodwill box or something. Kevin was so picky about making sure my new boots fit just right and would be comfortable for me over the long haul. He picked out a beautiful pair of waterproof Red Wing hiking boots for me! They probably retailed for around $200.00.

While I was trying on my new boots Kevin started getting real busy, he made two big sales while I was still in the store. I called him a few hours later while walking down the highway to let him know how wonderful the new boots were and he told me he had one of the best days the store had had in quite a while! He said, "Thank you, you brought them in." I said, "No I didn't, it was your heart that brought them in." As I was walking out of town I spotted a Goodwill box and popped in the pair of boots.

Strawberry Fields Forever

On a back road on my way over to route 11 for my walk into Bellingham, Washington, I had to walk by fields and fields, of ripe strawberries. The smell was overpowering and had my mouth watering. A car pulls up beside me with two smiling young ladies in it. "Hi," they said as they handed me a full quart of fresh picked strawberries. "We work for Sakuma Brothers Market Stand and we all wanted you to have these." No sooner had they pulled away and another vehicle pulled up with two different young and pretty smiling girls. They handed me a small bag and one said, "Here, they forgot to bring you the shortcakes!" While they were still there, a pickup with two young men pulled up and greeted the three of us. One young lady said, "They work with us too." I said, "Did you guy's bring the whipped cream?" I'm not so sure they needed whipped cream, those were some of the best strawberries I had ever eaten and the homemade shortcakes were indeed the best I had ever eaten in my life.

Fearless Red Fox

In Legends Restaurant (Beverly's, as locals call it) in Stonewall, Colorado, Beverly taped up my broken glasses for me. I Told Beverly of just getting out of my tent at a hidden spot between Weston and Stonewall, and of seeing the most beautiful and largest red fox I'd ever seen, no more than 20 ft. from me, that acted as if I weren't even there! Beverly said she was most likely the fox workers at the nearby New Elk Coal Mine had been feeding for a long time, said she had become quite a pet to the miners. I mean, that fox walked right by me as though I were not there. It was pretty cool. Later, I met LeRoy in front of Stonewall Lodge and RV Park. LeRoy was staying in a cabin there with his wife who was a foreman at the New Elk Coal Mine. Said she had recently transferred from another Colorado coal mine where she had been in a near fatal mining accident. LeRoy's wife had him bring me a piece of her just fried chicken. I met Fred, owner of the lodge, who told me a severe storm had been forecasted for the area and he said, "Now, if you get caught in a snow storm just up the road at Cuchara Pass, you will die!" Then he added, "I'm not tryin' to scare ya' or nuthin'!" Uh... okay Fred?? He told me I could stand in front of his place and try to get a ride to Cuchara or La Veta, just beyond the Pass. I decided to try and get a ride. See, the way I figure it, if I'm dead, I'll be unable to walk the rest of the way to Oakland, California, reminding all to Love Life. So, I stood there in front of Stonewall Lodge trying to get a ride to beat the storm... *all day*! No ride and it was getting dark. Fred said he had just had a cancellation and he could give me a cabin for just the cleaning fee, $25.00. The cabin was wonderful and Fred's girlfriend, Penelope, brought me some good food to cook up and a nice red wine. The storm did not materialize and so I headed out for La Veta the next morning. I said goodbye to Fred and Penelope, who were preparing to leave for their winter home in Ft. Myers, Florida! Grrr! Always Love Life my friends and you'll find all the good stuff just up the road or right around the corner.

On the road to La Veta, a guy stopped his truck beside me and while reaching his closed hand toward me, said, "Here, your sign made me do some serious thinking yesterday about something going on in my life right now, thanks." He dropped a folded bill in my hand and then drove away. I opened up my hand to see a one hundred dollar bill! I had ten dollars left after paying for my room at the Stonewall Lodge. I never asked for a dime, I never do.

Kindness in New Mexico

In Hondo, N.M. at the only store in town, I spoke to a Navajo lady who said she took her little boy to the school bus stop near the store each morning and then waited all day at the store for the bus to return. She said their small ranch where they raised sheep and cattle was 25 miles from the bus stop. She explained that they could not afford the gas for two round trips every day. She was originally from the Ramah Navajo Reservation near the Arizona line.

I met Robert Leyva, a Mexican man who was so very proud of his home state of New Mexico! He pointed to the distant mountains and told me, "those are the Capitan's...and that big peak over there is El Capitan itself!" He named all the mountain ranges I would be walking through and past on my journey through his beautiful New Mexico. He gave me his business card, he worked for a beer distributor and it just said, "The beer experts"... I used to be one of those, only I didn't get paid for it. The Capitan Mountains are the birth place of the original Smokey Bear. He was a bear cub rescued from a forest fire in the Capitan's in 1950. He spent his life in the zoo at Washington D.C. as the real Smokey Bear.

As I was nearing Lincoln, N.M., Dale picked me up and took me on a guided tour of Lincoln, the town where Billy the Kid killed the sheriff of Lincoln County and where he escaped from jail. The town is almost exactly as it was in Billy's day. Dale pointed out things like the Tunstill's store and the building that Billy escaped from. Dale knew the history quite well, it was all very interesting. Dale said he was the most blessed man alive to live where he lived. He said he owned mountains on both side of the highway, I had camped on his land unknowingly. He said he loved the town of Hondo where he led the choir every Sunday morning in a little Baptist church filled with the sweetest people on earth. I think they are blessed to have Dale.

At the hardware store in Capitan, N.M. two of the employees helped me patch up my tent with duct tape provided by the store. The whole store gave me an audience earlier as I related my story and why I was walking. As I was leaving Capitan, John Cox, a deputy sheriff in Lincoln County, New Mexico, stopped and gave me two hot sandwiches and a big hot cup of coffee. We talked long and John shared with me the story of a miraculous healing of a brain tumor in his three year old son. We were both teary eyed. I was telling John how my new -15 degree sleeping bag was not even keeping me warm in + 32 degrees. He said that he had plenty of sleeping bags and immediately went back home and got me one. It was very heavy but I hoped to be able to handle the extra weight until I could pick up my new one at Socorro, NM. John gave me his card and told me to call on him for anything I might need! He stressed over and over, "Please do not hesitate to call me for anything no matter where you are!" Wow!

How to be Beautiful...

In a very small store attached to a house, very remotely located within lands belonging to our First Peoples, a young woman stepped through a doorway behind the counter, obviously attached to the living quarters of the connected home. I was once married to a very beautiful woman. I'm 70 years old, and I've seen many very beautiful women. I have never though, seen a woman so beautiful as she who stepped into that store. She was breathtaking! The two older women behind the counter gave a quick glance at her and then, but a moment, both ceased serving customers, looking away from their endeavors, so as to survey their surroundings. As though they were protecting her. There were three other male customers there. Two men about my age, who I could see, like me, had momentarily stopped breathing. But, also like me, had enough years to know not to stare and even, act as though we had not noticed, and then catch our breath. This is learned respect. The younger man though, continued to stare with mouth agape. The beautiful young woman gave none of us more than a glance, whispered something to one of the older ladies and then glided back through the door.

Having had given my card to the two ladies minding the store, I was later contacted by that beautiful young woman, telling me she had seen my sign outside through a window and had stepped into the store to get a glimpse at who would carry such a beautiful sign as "LOVE LIFE" on foot and through the desert. She told me she thought I was beautiful. The most beautiful thing in the little encounter was her heart.

I Want to Share the Wealth

Went to Charlie's Market in La Veta, CO to buy groceries for the night for my motel stay (YEA!!). Asked the lady at the very small deli section the price of the rotisserie chicken and struck up a conversation. Linda was a very sweet lady, with tear filled eyes; she came out from behind the counter and gave me a great hug (I collect hugs)! She put some salt in a small container for me because they didn't have the little take out packets. As I was waiting for the customer in front of me to settle up with our cashier, I started talking to the pretty young lady behind me. She told me her young brother-in-law, whom she cared for very much, had just days before, tried to take his life with pills and that he was still in care and under watch. She took my card and asked would I talk to him if she could get him to call me... of course I will. I reached for my wallet to pay for my groceries and the cashier, with a huge smile on her face, said, "You cannot pay for these, they're already paid for." I couldn't believe it! And as I was standing there in disbelief, the young lady that had been behind me handed me her change from her purchase! I went back to the deli and gave Linda another hug. She simply said, "You sure you have everything you need?" So I took another hug.

I know you've probably heard some others proclaiming the wonderfulness of life and how we all should embrace and love it, and you may have thought, "Well, it's easy for them to love life, they're very wealthy and have everything they need!" *That*, my friends, is not the case with me. I have no material wealth and I'm certainly not speaking from the gated mansion, I live in a travel trailer which was given to me. I am but speaking from my heart. Even though, when walking the United States, I often times do not know where I'll lay my head or where my next meal will come from, I have an inner joy, an inner peace. And like the wealthy, I always end up having everything I need. I Love Life, I Love my Life, therefore, I'm wealthy. Love Life with all your hearts my dear sweet friends, I want to share the wealth.

Babies and Fools

Just outside of Missoula, Montana, Mike stopped on his bike. He had already pedaled from Portland, Oregon, and was on his way to Ney York City. He said he had seen a newspaper article about me in the Orofino, Idaho; newspaper. We talked for a little while and then Mike rode off. About an hour or so after Mike left, I looked up in front of me and the sky was completely black. Lightning started flashing and each time it flashed it seemed to be getting closer to me. I've been in a lot of storms, but this one was looking much uglier than most. Just as the huge rain drops started to hit me I bowed my head and said, "Lord, this is an excellent opportunity for you to prove that old adage, God takes care of babies and fools." I looked up and a new Toyota Land Cruiser had pulled over in front of me. It was two young ladies from Spokane, and both were yelling for me to hurry up and get in. Just as I got me and all my gear in the sky just opened up. Rain, snow, hail, you name it, it all came down. We had to pull over twice and wait for it to subside. The slush was at least 8 inches deep on the road with a solid sheet of ice under it. That four wheel drive vehicle was sliding all over the place. In about a five mile stretch, you could barely see. I asked my rescuers to look out for Mike on his bicycle; I was really concerned for him. The hail was doing damage to the vehicle I was sure. The driver told me she had bought a whole sack of Arby's roast beef sandwiches at Missoula and I was welcome to the rest of them. They were still hot. God, did they taste good!

The storm subsided some and I asked them to drop me off at Stoney's Conoco station, about twelve miles from where they had rescued me. Mike was there, he said he had just made it in under the protective canopy of the gas station when the storm hit. It continued for a couple of hours with lots of hail and rain but it never did get as bad there as it was when it hit me earlier. I was telling the two cashiers at Stoney's about the severity of the storm and they both said that was normal weather for Montana. Three people behind me said they were from that area and they had never seen anything like it before. And particularly not in August. The people at Stoney's were wonderful to all of us waiting out the storm. There were several couples on motorcycles whom had sought refuge in the remote gas station as well. We drank a lot of coffee.

The Ballad of Sam McGee

Just outside of White Sulfur Springs, Montana, I saw a beautiful lake and it looked like camping might be allowed there. I spotted a travel trailer camped there and I approached it to inquire whether it was free camping or not. Felix came out of the trailer and we started talking. He told me there were no fees and he and his wife Mary had been there for a week. He invited me inside to meet his wife Mary and fixed me some chili. They were from a little town in Arizona called Baghdad. Felix started quoting poetry for me. He quoted several poems and a couple Robert Service poems, including the Ballad of Sam McGee. He quoted them all word for word. His wife Mary seemed to enjoy it just as much as I did. He recited them beautifully and passionately. It was wonderful. What an entertaining evening, on a beautiful Montana lake surrounded by mountains and listening to wonderful poetry. Beats the hell out of television.

Zion National Park in Style!

Kane County Deputy Sheriff Cate stopped about five miles out of Mt. Carmel, Utah to check on me. He was concerned about my route. He informed me that I couldn't continue on my intended route up 86 to Utah 14 to reach Cedar City because about four weeks before, an avalanche had destroyed a section of road 14 just five miles before Cedar City. He explained that the only other route was via Utah 9 through Zion National Park, which I could not walk through, not only because of the sheer danger of sharing the road with cars on the dangerously narrow road, but there were two tunnels that pedestrians are forbidden to walk through. So, Deputy Cate drove me into Mount Carmel Junction and offered to drive me through the park and drop me off where his jurisdiction ended. I hadn't eaten since the day before and where he would drop me off had no food sources. He told me to go ahead and eat in Mount Carmel Junction and he would look for me later and give me a ride through the park. He also informed me that hitchhiking in Utah was illegal.

So, in Mount Carmel Junction, I politely left a restaurant after realizing the menu was beyond my price range and headed for the Subway across the street. Kevin followed me out the door to find out what I was about and I explained my Love Life mission to him in detail. After my meal, sitting on a bench in front of Subway, Kevin came over to me and told me he was the tour guide on a very modern tour bus with French Canadians from Quebec headed through Zion National Park on their way to Las Vegas. He said he had asked his driver and the 25 to 30 French speaking tourists if they would mind giving me a ride: cool! Kevin incorporated me and my Love Life message into the tour. He told them my story and then took questions for me and translated my answers into French for them. I certainly enjoyed riding through stunningly beautiful Zion National Park in style. Some passengers applauded when Kevin told them I had said, "You do not have the right to take your own life, it does not belong just to you." I received apples, a bag of chips, a coke, and several pats on the back during the most luxurious ride. Just before the bus stopped to let me off in St. George, Utah, I shook hands with and thanked each passenger for rescuing me. After I had put my backpack and "LOVE LIFE" sign back on, several of the passengers stepped off the bus to take my picture. Kevin told me as we shook hands, "Life is about love; love is about what we do for others. Love life, my friend."

Giving Helps with His Pain

In a café in Valdez, Colorado, my waitress explained what I was doing and asked management if I could tent in back so as to grab breakfast there next morning; they said no. The sweet waitress kept apologizing; I shrugged it off because I always have hundreds of positive things happen after a negative. Barely one mile down the road, in Segundo, a gentleman sitting in front of Sam's Place, yelled and asked how far I was going. It was Randy James, the bartender. He said he owned the trailer across the street and that it was being remodeled but had electricity and heat. He said I was welcome to spend the night there. Then he invited me to the Christmas party Sam's Place was having.

There was a table of free food and everyone was just great. Met a great couple, Herb and Char, and Char's father. I met Randy's son, Jonathan. As I was leaving, a very hunched over man, David, came up to me, said Char told him what I was doing, he thought it a great thing. As he shook my hand, he slipped a $20 to me and said, "Here, I help out a lot of people around here, it helps me to deal with the pain I'm in." See why I've learned to shrug off the negative things and believe the positive is on its way.

"Giving, medication for the heart, get a lifetime prescription." ~ Steve Fugate

Most People are Just Damn Good

At Osage Beach, Missouri, in a Shoney's Restaurant, I introduced myself and gave my card to my server, Susan. Being the only customer, I sat with the manager, the cook, and the two servers. Four years before, Susan lost her 18 year-old son in a car wreck. With tear filled eyes she said, "It just never ever goes away, does it?" No, it does not. Robert, the manager, shared having grown up in foster homes and battling depression and winning, because he loved life, he said. Robert said my money was no good there. As I started for the door Susan handed me a Styrofoam container filled with even more food from the buffet bar.

"Give, give, and give. Giving of our self is a guarantee for happiness. No matter the pain suffered in life, it can all be overcome through giving. If you want to be happy in this life forget about yourself." ~ Steve Fugate

Cop Stops

I actually have not been stopped all that often by police. For the most part, they ignore me and drive on by. Most wave back when I wave. And most of the time when they do stop, it is because of curiosity. Sometimes though, they are told to check me out because someone has called in and said I looked suspicious. Fortunately for me, the officers I encountered were all smart enough to figure I couldn't be trying to hide too much, what with a big red and white sign over my head and all. No more than a couple of times have officers ever actually been rude. And even on the rare occasions when they were told to investigate me, they were nearly always concerned for my safety. And most times they even asked if they could do anything for me.

Not Seeking Political Office

In northern Ohio on Route 44, just south of Chardon, a plain-clothes officer who was following instructions stopped me. He told me someone had called me in as suspicious looking; maybe it's my mustache. Always before, after running my driver's license, I was always free to go. Not this time. Whoever called this time, had clout. Maybe it was the mayor's wife? The officer seemed irritated that whoever was on the other end of his radio, was not allowing him to release me and go on about his daily routine, and tracking down the real ax murderers. I proceeded to show him a letter of introduction from the honorable Mayor of Vero Beach, Florida. He still was not given permission to let me go. I could plainly see the officer was aware I was no threat at all. He was becoming very exasperated that he wasn't being allowed to use his own judgment, and let me go.

I then remembered having several copies of past newspaper articles with me. So I showed those to him. While holding one with a big picture of me, he talks into his microphone, "Look, this guy even has newspaper articles with pictures of him and that big sign over his head. When was the last time you saw a criminal seeking media coverage, huh?" It became obvious the dispatcher had a quick wit when the officer chuckled and said, "Yeah, you got me there, but I don't think this guy's seeking political office." I laughed too.

He was finally permitted to release me from his questioning. He sincerely apologized for having to stop me, he wished me well and told me to be careful. He was still shaking his head in disbelief of the bureaucracy interfering with his common sense.

Don't Jump!

I was on the bridge over the beautiful Quechee Gorge in Quechee, Vermont, and stopped in the middle to take a picture. As I was stepping from the bridge a police cruiser pulls up and the lady officer ask if I am okay. Across the street another police cruiser pulls up as a backup. She asked again if I was okay. I asked her what was up. She told me that someone had called in and said I had put my leg over the rail of the bridge and was preparing to jump. I told her that I did not at any time put my foot near the rail and I was simply taking pictures. I then told her about losing my son to suicide and why I carry "LOVE LIFE" over my head. She apologized for the inconvenience but said that a lot of people had chosen that exact same spot to take their life. I didn't ask her how many had "LOVE LIFE" over their head. She was just doing her job.

Movies Lie

In Nevada, 2003, a state trooper, after trying very hard to get reception on his personal cell phone for me, suggested I use the phone at a local brothel to call and check on results of tests recently done on my daughter to confirm she had MS. I knocked on the door of the brothel, no answer. I turned to leave and heard very harsh and loud, "Whadda' you want?!" Scared the living crap outa' me! I turned to see a woman that, well, uh, that movie, *Pretty Woman*, well, that's a lie. The prostitutes in the movie had sweet dispositions and they were *pretty*. I asked to use the phone; she handed me a remote and went back in slamming the door. I couldn't reach my daughter, so I called my friend, Larry Pesin, for help. I excitedly whispered, "Guess where I'm calling from, I'm in---" just as I started to say, "a whorehouse," there stood, *not* Julia Roberts. So, I finished the sentence, "uh, Nevada." Larry said, "What the hell's wrong with you, you've been in Nevada for weeks now?" Days later, I explained I had been calling from a whorehouse. Larry said, "Ya get laid?" "No, I bought food instead."

Nevada Highway Patrol

After Fallon, Nevada, U.S. Route 50 is called America's Loneliest Highway and I can testify to that claim. I walked many miles of it on my first walk across the U.S.A. in the summer of 2001. My loneliness was eased by Nevada Highway Patrolmen who would occasionally idle their cars alongside and talk to me. If they couldn't stop they would often use their loudspeakers to give me encouraging words.

Once past Fallon, Nevada, the towns are 50 to 80 miles apart. When you are walking, those stretches of asphalt can seem even longer, particularly in the summer when I crossed the state. You really can see for miles and miles. Except for the very rare ranch house seen from the road, there are no trees. What you see mostly is the heat distorting the miles and miles of asphalt. Then there is the occasional livestock hauler barreling down the span at high rates of speed, permeating the hot, dry air with the smell of various farm animals. Mix those smells with 103 degree temperatures and it's coming at you 80 miles per hour. It is a definite shock to the nasal passages. And though you can't see them, you can certainly tell when the truck is hauling sheep.

I was able to walk these stretches of desert highway because of the cart I had built. The cart I pulled behind me enabled me to haul as much as 70 pounds of water, my tent, sleeping mat, and other equipment. I made a hydration system by running aquarium hose from a five-gallon water cooler up the tongue of the cart and over my shoulder. Plus I had to add usually at least four one-gallon jugs for the longer stretches. Besides having a source of water right at my mouth, I always had shade immediately over my head. I had covered a 2 ft. x 2ft. piece of plastic sign material, Corplas, with Mylar. I then fastened this to my pack frame so that it was directly over my head. It worked quite well. For the really hot days, I also had a very lightweight umbrella that I had covered with Mylar.

Mylar looks like aluminum foil and is very shiny in that Nevada sun. I must have been quite the sight walking down the highway. And then, add to that, a big white sign with bright red letters proclaiming, "LOVE LIFE." That part of Nevada has a lot of open range where cattle graze freely. The sight of me stampeded more than one small herd. I certainly attracted the curiosity of the very few Nevada Highway Patrol Troopers I encountered. One in particular, Jake. Jake could not believe I was out there. He was incredulous at the idea of someone actually walking out there in the summer. Over a period of four days, when Jake would come upon me during his patrols of his assigned stretch of Rt. 50, he would idle his car alongside me and we would talk. He said he did not want to stop my forward progress. And we certainly didn't have to worry about oncoming traffic. Any other vehicles approaching could be seen way before they got to us. We had great conversations. Jake still shook his head and chuckled in dismay every once in a while; still amazed I was out there. He said he came across many cyclists taking on the trek, but no pedestrians.

One late afternoon, two pretty rough looking men in an old beat up pick-up truck drove by real slow and cursed me. After driving by, they both stuck their hands out their windows with that famous signal! They then slowed down, as though to see what my reaction would be. And, being in possession of some common sense, I gave no reaction. A few minutes later, they drove by very slowly in the opposite direction. They both stared menacingly at me. I stared straight ahead as though they weren't there. This unwanted attention had me concerned. I kept expecting them to return, not knowing what I would do if they actually got out of their vehicle.

After nearly an hour had passed, up drives a Nevada Highway Patrol Trooper. Man, did he look good. I was out of Jake's territory now, but this trooper was his friend. Jake had told him about me. As soon as he asked how I was, I related my story. I described the men and the truck as best I could remember. He looked at me and said, "You just described every vehicle and every man in the Nevada desert." He was quite concerned for my safety. He asked my plans for the night and I told him I simply got as far as I could off the highway and pitched my tent just before dark. Due to the terrain on that particular stretch of road, it would be difficult for my tent not to be seen. Especially if someone were to be looking for it.

My new trooper friend came up with a plan. We estimated approximately how much farther I would walk before camping for the night. He asked me to cut it short by an hour; there was a certain area he wanted me in, there was a small grove of trees where I could be hidden from the highway. He would be unable to be there at the exact time I camped, but he would at least know the general area where I would be. In the meantime he would look for the truck so as to question the two men. He advised me to of course, to make sure no vehicles were in sight when I went off the road to pitch my tent. He said he would give two quick toots of his horn as he drove by during the night, letting me know he was in the area.

I did hear the horn at least twice during the night. I slept well, knowing I was being watched over. The next evening the trooper stopped and checked on me. He said, though they had continued to look for it, they had not seen the truck I had described. It was a real good feeling knowing the Nevada Highway Patrol was watching out for me.

Concerned Citizens?

In East Helena, Montana, after I had pitched my tent and made camp I was approached by a police officer and an auxiliary officer saying they had been informed by a concerned citizen that someone was camping there. He told me that on occasion there were undesirables who frequented the spot and consumed their beer. I told him that I had just picked up all the beer cans and other trash and showed him the sacks I had put it all in. The officer looked at my card and told me he had seen me walking earlier and was convinced I was not an axe murderer or anything. He said that it was city property I was on and as long as I left the next morning, he saw no problem with me staying. As they were walking off through the trees I heard him say to the auxiliary officer, "I wonder why the concerned citizens didn't clean up the place?" That made me smile.

Lots of Prisons

In Colorado, near Canon City, I was looking for someone to ask directions to the Royal Gorge Bridge, I wanted to see the highest suspension bridge in the world, 1,053 feet. Someone instead approached me. "Hey man, what the hell you doin' man?" This guy was what I call rough looking. He really looked and sounded hard core. I answered that I was simply reminding everyone to Love Life. He acted as though I had not said a word as he asked, "have the friggin' asshole cops harassed you yet?" "No one has bothered me." I answered. "Well, they will," he said. "They're all assholes around here; they stop me all the time. For no reason at all! I never do anything wrong." It is my personal opinion the man had no idea the definition of the word innocent. I had already been warned that this area had a higher concentration of prisons than any other area in the whole country, including the federal ADX Super Max Prison. I mentioned this to Mr. Mother Teresa and suggested that might be the reason the police check him often. I pointed out that due to the large number of penal institutions in the area the police were probably required to check out everyone and often. I suggested that it was probably not just him they were singling out. "Hell no," he said. "That ain't got a damn thing to do with it. They're just assholes, and that's all!" If I were a cop, I would want a heavy chain fastened to his leg and keep him staked out in a field somewhere so as to know where he was at all times.

Sure enough, later that day a Colorado Highway patrolman stopped me and checked my driver's license. I further volunteered newspaper articles covering my walk and the letter of introduction from my hometown mayor. The trooper then enlightened me. He said, "Sir, you are walking into an area more dangerous than most people will ever realize." I'm not sure what that meant. Maybe more prisoners escape than is known to the general public. He didn't elaborate, and I didn't care to know.

I told him, "I was expecting to be stopped soon. I guess if I was a cop in this area, I would stop old ladies in wheel chairs." And without smiling at all, he said, "We do." He further instructed me to be very careful over the next few days, to stay alert and conscious of my surroundings. He seemed genuinely concerned for my well-being. He then said a most reassuring thing, "Sir, you keep yourself very alert to what's in front of you and we'll watch your back for you." That felt nice.

I was stopped by three other lawmen that same day. I told the third officer how often I had been stopped already. He said he would see if he could do something about that for me. He was on his radio as he drove away. The very next morning, an officer was approaching me with radio mike in hand, and he went back on the highway, nodded to me and drove on by. That occurred once more that day. After that, the officers would only beep their horn or nod to me.

I Fought the Law and...

In the summer of 2008 I walked over Steven's Pass in the Cascades of Washington, which was a great event for me. In December of 2003, I was about 15 miles west of Gold Bar walking in knee deep snow and headed for Steven's Pass when a Washington Highway Patrol Trooper stopped me and told me I could go no farther, and as a matter of fact, I had to go back to Gold Bar. She said it was too dangerous and would be even more dangerous at Steven's Pass. She said she was going to flag down someone and ask them if they would take me back to Gold Bar. I was so pissed. I had been enjoying the absolute beauty of the snow covered Cascades. I said to her, "What if I refuse to take the ride?" She smiled and said, "Then I will follow behind you in my cruiser with the lights flashing all the way to Gold Bar while you walk." How embarrassing would that be? She won. Then she told me that I would have to hitch a ride from Gold Bar all the way to Leavenworth. She said it was too dangerous and she would arrest me if I didn't heed her warning. I capitulated because I have a rule in my life; if you have a gun you win. It took two days to hitch a ride. There was an Espresso Café and a bar across from where I had to hitchhike. The bar fed me three times and the young lady working in the café brought me hot chocolate quite a few times. Going through Steven's Pass in my hitched ride, I could see how very dangerous it would have been for me to attempt to walk through. This time when I walked through there were signs posted which were not there before, "No pedestrians". I assumed it was a winter time only rule and walked on through. I wonder if I was the cause of the signs. I hope so, what a distinction!

Policeman Delivers Poetic Justice

Just east of Toledo, Ohio, a couple stopped to inquire of my endeavors. As I was answering their questions a Lucas County Deputy Sherriff pulled up beside us and courteously inquired if everything was okay. A police officer doing his job, investigating something that he sees which is out of the norm. While the couple and I were explaining that all was well, a lady pulls up alongside in her car and said, quite harshly, while looking at me with obvious disdain, "Officer, I'm so glad you're checking that strange man out, I saw him earlier." The deputy said, "Ma'am, actually, I stopped to check on *his* well-being. It is the pedestrian and the hitchhiker that are most vulnerable out on the road." The man and his wife smiled knowingly at me. The officer said as he was pulling out, "Have a nice day."

The LOVE LIFE Bandit

Two Burlington, New Hampshire, police officers stopped me, said someone called and said I looked suspicious and needed to be checked out. They were courteous and allowed me to go my way after checking my Florida driver's license. I figure there must have been a rash of robberies in the area by an old white male on foot with a forty five pound pack on his back and a large red and white "LOVE LIFE" sign over his head. This had happened before on my walks, so obviously he has terrorized other states as well. I hope they catch him soon.

Big Hearted Florida Trooper

April, 2013, Just in front of a Wal-Mart store in Tallahassee, a couple pulled alongside me and the gentleman driving asked, "Was your AT trail name "No Clue?" I said that indeed it was. He said we needed to talk and he got out his car and explained who he was. He was Florida Highway Patrol trooper, Ken Kelsch who now taught at the academy here in Tallahassee. He asked if I remembered a Florida state trooper who stopped to talk with me near Port St. Joe Florida. I did remember him and what he did for me. He said I had helped inspire him in his desire to thru-hike the Appalachian Trail, which he planned to do in seven years upon retirement. Here is the story of my first meeting with trooper Ken Kelsch.

In 2003 near Port St. Joe, Florida, Highway Patrol trooper, Ken Kelsch, stopped. I asked of nearby motels and he said there were two: the very nice Port Inn, and the other, a dump. I explained that even a dump was more appealing than my tent; it was getting dark and I had walked over thirty miles. He insisted on taking me the two miles into town. The trooper was obviously concerned that I may have to spend a night in what he kept calling a really cheap motel. And I kept insisting that was exactly what I was looking for. He told me it just wasn't a nice place. I couldn't seem to get through to him: it was all I could afford. I finally told him that I appreciated his advice but it was nearly dark and I had to get on my way and off the highway. As I started to leave, he said to me, "Hey, let's see if we can squeeze your gear in my patrol car (Camaro), 'cause you aren't going to make it to Port St. Joe before dark." I accepted the ride and asked that he take me to the cheap motel. He never answered. We pulled up in front of the Port Inn. It was a beautiful and elegant looking old building. I immediately interjected, "I cannot afford this place, please direct me to the other place." "You don't want to stay there." He said very matter of fact. "Let's go in and find out just how much it is, you may be surprised." I knew it would be a waste of time, I knew what my finances were. And I was quite worn out from walking over thirty miles. I just wanted to lie down.

The trooper walked up to the front desk in the beautiful charming lobby, and said to the very nice lady, "I would like to get a room please." He turned toward me, sensing I was about to object, and gave me the look. You know the look, that look only an experienced officer of the law can give. The look said, "It is finished, please be quiet, you are going to get the ticket." "Okay," from my mind, because I knew that look. Just as he was about to hand the lady his credit card, he said, "Excuse me just a moment ma'am." He stepped away from the counter and motioned for me to follow him. After we had gone just a few feet, he whispered to me, "Could I please see your driver's license?" I had to laugh, I said, "Yeah, that wouldn't look too good if you put up one of "America's Most Wanted" for the night." He seemed embarrassed at having to do it, he apologized and proceeded to call it in on his hand held walkie-talkie.

He asked the lady if there was any food available, knowing it was Sunday night in a small town and everything would be closed. They only offered Continental Breakfast, so she set me up with some fruit and cereal. The trooper said he would check on me the next morning with his wife. He said he wanted to hear all the stories I could tell him.

True to his word, he knocked on my door the next morning; his lovely wife, Pat, was with him. He said, "We are here to pick your brain," and laughingly said, "We're going to get our money's worth." We sat out on the front porch of that wonderful old inn and chatted. His wife Pat, found me out on the road later in the day, after school hours, so that their daughter, Brooklyn, could ask me some questions.

Some Things Said, Some Things Noted

Uh Oh… the day before I left on my first walk across the U.S. in 2001, a friend of mine, a renowned Christian minister, said to be prophetic, handed me a piece of folded up paper. She told me not to open it until I had started my walk. I opened it up while being quite miserable walking across a Nevada desert in 105 degrees. It read, "The journey is my home." Aw Shit!

Weed or Flower?

As a guest in the home of a friend in Maine, I offered to mow his grass while he was at work. He told me that would be nice but to not cut the dandelions. The whole yard was covered with dandelions. There was one little patch where even the grass barely grew, so I mowed only that. That evening, my friend commented that I did a nice job mowing his yard. Just who in the hell am I to judge a weed from a flower? I now see the dandelion as a beautiful golden flower.

Why I Accepted Donations

When I first began my cross-country walks, I refused to take donations. I would save up all the money I could and be frugal with it. Well, when one is in a hail storm and sees a motel to escape to, screw frugal! So, in reconsidering my decision to not accept money, I came up with two reasons to start accepting money from others: One, in not accepting an offer of money from another, I was denying that person the self-satisfaction of helping, and of being a part of my walks. Two, I was going to starve to death!

Still stubborn though, I added to the fact that I never ask, (never have, never will) a stipulation that I would not accept a donation unless the giver listened to my story as to why I walked. Then, one day, a man obviously having difficulty walking, came up to me and handed me fifty dollars. I explained my requirement and he said, "Listen, I don't need to hear your story. It's obvious you're doing a good thing with your ability to walk. I'm not even 40 yet, and my ability to compete in marathons and ironman triathlons has stopped because I now have a rare bone disease attacking my hips and legs… I just want to be a part of your walks!" Wow! I ended the 'have to hear my story' stipulation right then and there.

Another man, I was telling, that I not only never ever asked, I had actually turned down offers of money from some whose attitude I did not particularly care for, then asked me, "What if they offered you $10,000 dollars, would you turn that down?" I answered, "I have no idea, no one has ever offered me that much, why don't you try it and let's see what I do?"

Blasphemer!

You know you're well into the Bible belt when you come out of a Tarkio, Missouri, Dollar General Store and you find a humongous family bible placed on top your backpack. It was a brand new bible. I took it into the store and asked the employees if they might know who put it there. None seemed to know who it might have been. I asked if I could leave it with them and if they were to possibly find out who left it, would they please explain that I appreciated the gesture but just couldn't handle that much extra weight. It felt as though they were all staring at me as I left the store, I was expecting to hear at any moment, "Blasphemer, blasphemer!"

No Door to Knock On

In New Jersey, after telling a Jehovah's Witness I wasn't interested, then tried to back up her actions by saying what she was doing was biblical. She said, "You know, the bible tells us to go door to door." I said, "I know the scripture well, it also says that while you're there to cast out demons, heal the sick, and raise the dead. Are you doing that too?" "Of course not!" she answered. "Oh, so you're just doing the easy stuff?" I came back with. She immediately retreated to her car. Another Jehovah's Witness stopped me out on the road and as I politely tried to let her know I wasn't interested, she said to me, "Jesus said for us to go door to door and spread the gospel." To which I said, "I don't have a door ma'am." I walked on down the road with "LOVE LIFE" over my head, and maybe she found someone with a door. Personally, my religion is my individuality.

Damn Fool

In Pennsylvania, three men walked out of a barn where they had been working and inquired of my "LOVE LIFE" sign. One gentleman, Harold, the father and grandfather of the other two, was 98 years old. They told me of a man who had recently passed by their barn intending to cross America walking only backwards. I asked if he had told them why because I had read that it had already been done before. The father and son said he hadn't given them a reason, just said he was going to walk backwards the whole way. Shaking his head, Harold said, "looked like a damn fool to me, kept havin' to look over his shoulder to see where he was a goin', damn fool." Gotta Love the basic wisdom from a simple observation of a 98 year-old!

The Express Lane

To Love Life is to use the express lane to the beauty of Life. Loving one's gift of Life immediately takes us out of the congestion of traffic in the slower lanes with the big trucks hauling blame, anger, spite, judgment, greed, and worry. It's not always easy passing some of those trucks because we've become so accustomed to using some of their cargo we have come to believe them necessary in Life. One of the biggest trucks is loaded with fear; really give it the gas when you pass so as to pass the one in front of it too, its carrying doubt. And when your express lane temporarily ends, instead of dealing with those big trucks, simply pull into the first rest area until they pass by. Your engine will be cooled and stronger, enabling you to pass the next caravan of big trucks even easier than before. And no matter how tiring the trip seems, you will eventually reach your destination... the beauty of Life.

"Love Life, and pass those who may not, go around them for now, eventually they may be riding in your draft." ~ Steve Fugate

Mine, Mine!

Just out of Canfield, Ohio I was walking down U.S. Rt.224 and for no good reason at all I suddenly veered left to the guard rail about seven feet away and looked down in the ditch. Just about three feet away, resting on its edge against blades of grass was a one hundred dollar bill. I swear it! The first thing I did was look over my shoulder to my left and then to my right, I suppose to make sure nobody was watching me to take it away from me. I then proceeded with a forty-pound pack on my back to leap over that guard rail like a gazelle. I picked it up and with the bill clutched tightly against my chest, I again sneaked looks over my right and left shoulders, "Mine, mine, mine!" It was so faded and cracked from exposure it looked to be counterfeit. A bank back in Canton assured it was indeed legal tender. It came in real handy.

Deep Stuff

Just before I left for my first walk across the states, a local church's children's minister asked me to speak to her class of five to seven year olds a few Sundays. First question on my first visit from a darling little girl, "How do you use the bathroom?" After getting my composure back and answering, "I go into the woods." "Yuck!" she said. As did several other little girls and, of course, all the little boys thought it was cool. After my walk started, I would sometimes call the class and they would put me on speaker phone and after a Sunday phone call, the teacher would have them write me little notes and then send them to me at one of my pre-scheduled mail stops. In my tent one night in a very remote part of Utah, I was reading the letters from the little ones I received that day. They were all sweet and said cute things and many drew pictures of me, you could tell it was me because they all drew the little cart I pulled behind me. One note from one little fella' said this, "I pray to God you get to where you feel you really need to get to when you get to there and get what you want to get when you get to get there to!" I couldn't believe it. You could certainly tell by the printing it was done by a 6 to 7 year-old but how in the world did he come up with that? A few days later when sharing the note with a friend, he said, "Man, that's deep."

Margaritas and Cigarettes

In West Plains, Missouri, at a little café where I was eating, I met John, who insisted on driving me over to his house and showing me his Model A Ford collection. We climbed up into his big Lincoln Navigator and as soon as we entered he attached the breathing apparatus to his face. He looked at me and said, "This is from having a Margarita in one hand and a cigarette in the other for most of my life." His three Model A's were all restored beautifully and I enjoyed looking at them. John was a very nice person; he was very lonely though. I spent a few hours with him as he drove me around West Plains and showed me the sights. He just needed someone to talk to. So, talk to people. It's a great way to give when you do not have riches. Probably more helpful than money.

Gotcha!

An older dark brown Mercury drove by me in Billings, Montana, as I walked toward the Wal-Mart about a block up. An arm with a wide black leather wrist band with metal spikes sticking out of it went out the passenger side window just after the car passed me at a very slow rate of speed due to the traffic, and gave me the finger while voicing the words, "Poop-head!" Who in the hell today, calls anyone a poop-head? I hadn't heard that since I was about six. Anyway, I had reached the Wally World parking lot and was cutting across the lot when I spotted the old mercury, the get-away car, which had been used in calling me a poop-head. From the rear I could see that it was empty except for the front passenger seat. And with the window down and their elbow propped on top the door, I could clearly see a *big black metal studded leather wrist band.* The car was in my direct path to the store as I angled across. Just as I got to the rear of the car, (I swear this is true) the passenger sneezed. I said, "Bless you!" as I walked by a very startled older female with purple and jet black spiked hair, with added facial piercing. Nothing though, not even all her personal body decorating choices, could take away from the obvious shock on that woman's face when I turned around and smiled at her. A "poetic justice" smile.

No one's Religion Please.

In Utah, a gentleman asked if I had any religious affiliations. I told him I believed in an Infinite Spirit of Love, Life, and Wisdom, not manmade religions. He asked, "Have you tried Mormonism?" I said, "Sir, I lost my only son to suicide, I never know when my next meal is or where I'll lay my head at night. Yet, I have a constant joy in my heart and I love life with all my being. What can your religion give me I don't have?" He said he couldn't answer that. I thanked him for his honesty.

"Tell me nothing of your religion, show me only the Love you claim your religion has taught you, I'll choose my own teachers, as did you." ~ Steve Fugate

Walking with Buffalo

The Black Hills of South Dakota, called *Paha Sappa -"Hills that are black"* by the Lakota people - are truly beautiful. I walked into Wind Cave National Park and was excited about the opportunity to walk amongst the buffalo. I had barely entered the park when I saw a huge bull and several cows crossing the road in front of me. It was so exciting. Just after I spotted them, a park ranger, Fred, stopped to check on me and find out for his own curiosity what I was up to. I was worried that he might not allow me to walk among the bison, but he assured me it would be okay. Fred told me to simply give them plenty of space and the warning sign for danger was if the buffalo stopped wagging its tail and instead raised it up in the air. Also, if one were to keep staring at me and lowered its head in my direction: get the hell outa' Dodge! Well, I saw a small herd and was able to get some pictures but not nearly the close up shots I wanted. I still had about three hours to walk through the rest of the park so I figured I could still get a good close up shot of a large bull. And then, up pulls Fred, again. "What's up Fred?" I cheerfully inquired. It seems that Fred had second thoughts and decided he would look really bad if I was trampled to death by a herd of wild bison. I pleaded with him but to no avail. So, Fred drove me the remaining five miles to the park gate; as we drove out I saw several large bulls that I probably would have walked by. My dad walked with some buffalo once and I had always wanted to experience the feeling he described to me, that it left him with. Fred's an asshole.

Some Russian Guys

On 97 near Liberty, Washington, a guy with one of the blackest beards I've ever seen stopped across the road from me and offered me a ride. He spoke very broken English, he explained that he was Russian but had been in the U.S. for twenty years. He told me that in the former Soviet Union, he and his whole family had been persecuted for their Christian beliefs. He said he spent three years in a Siberian prison, his brother spent six years and he had uncles who had spent as much as twenty years confined and even tortured for their beliefs. He pulled up his left trouser leg to reveal a horrible scar next to a terribly deformed looking knee cap. In his strong accent, he said, "This is what the Communist did to me for being a Christian and for not going to Afghanistan to kill innocent people." Damn! He explained that 22 of his family members were now in the U.S. and they lived in a commune like environment there in Washington. He spoke very passionately and seemed very sincere. Now, I think I heard this right, I asked him to repeat it several times but the accent was so strong and he spoke so excitedly, I'm still not sure but it sounded like he was telling me that his father had managed to get his name on a list of people that Ronald Reagan asked to speak to when he visited Moscow. He said that the KGB kept constant vigilance over his father and would not allow him to speak to Reagan. And it sounded like he wasn't too crazy over Gorbachev. He asked once more if I wanted a ride and was absolutely amazed that I wanted to walk instead of ride in his car. He just kept shaking his head and asking if I was sure. He also asked if I needed anything else and then drove away.

The next morning he stopped again and introduced me to his brother. His brother, he said, was the one who had spent six years in a Siberian prison camp. They were on their way to Seattle to pick up a wrecked car to rebuild for a family member who needed a car. I've noticed that people who've experienced a loss of freedom in their lives really love my "LOVE LIFE" sign.

The Six Degrees of Separation

On route 50, "America's Loneliest Highway" in Nevada 2001, Bob Mottram stopped in total disbelief that I was alone in the desert with "LOVE LIFE" over my head. He was the outdoors writer for the Tacoma News–Tribune and put my story in the Washington paper. He also mentioned my story in his book, "In Search of America's Heartbeat – 12

Months on the Road". Eight years later on the road in Oregon he spotted me and yet again stopped his RV to find out what I was up to.

Near Lake Stevens, Washington, a guy stopped and asked if I needed anything. He said he always stopped for those he saw on the highway toting a full backpack, as he was a hiker. He told me he had hiked the Appalachian Trail in '99. This perked up my ears as I too had been attempting a thru-hike of the "AT" in '99. He invited me to McDonald's for some breakfast. I asked him what his trail name had been and he said he went by his real name, Mike. As we sat there he kept saying I looked familiar to him (he never looked familiar to me at all) and so we kept the investigation going as to whether we had crossed paths or not. Well, it turns out that we actually spent two nights together in the same cabin at Goose Creek Cabins near Blairsville, Georgia, close to the "AT" while I was recuperating from a severely sprained ankle. That sixth degree of separation is alive and well in my life. Now, when sharing my "AT" album and friends ask who the guy with the bushy white hair and beard is standing next to me, instead of saying, "Beats the hell outa' me." I can say, "Why that's Mike, hell, I'll never forget him."

I am the Groom

Walking down a beautiful part of route 9, near Acme, Washington, and passing by a beautiful large home with a gorgeous view of Mt. Baker, I was confronted by a very tall and slender young man stepping out of the entrance to the home. He looked like he had been sleeping on the streets for a week, he did not look like he belonged to that house. He excitedly introduced himself as Colin and asked me to follow him into the beautiful home. "You'll have to excuse the confusion" he said, "we're all busy preparing for a wedding this coming Saturday but it just isn't every day someone walks by with a LOVE LIFE sign over their head." He led me into a kitchen full of busy people and said very loudly, "Hey, this guy is walking the country with a big "LOVE LIFE" sign over his head! Is that cool or what!" Everyone applauded. His father immediately took my water jug and began filling it, and his mother put a plate full of homemade cookies under my nose. An absolutely beautiful young woman came down the stairs and I asked if she were the bride to be. She said yes. I thanked them for their hospitality but explained that I didn't want to add more chaos to what they were already experiencing and needed to make some more miles anyway. They all laughed and said goodbye. I was looking for Colin to thank him and he was out front on his cell phone explaining directions to friends flying into Seattle for the wedding, while on his knees picking and eating wild strawberries. "Are you related to the groom or the bride?" I asked Colin. "I am the groom." replied Colin. We talked a little while but he was way too busy taking care of last minute things for his wedding. He did have time to tell me he was getting married to the most wonderful and the most beautiful woman in the world! What a cool family.

From Rags to Riches

Just outside Bellingham, Washington, as I was walking past a very nice home, a very pretty young lady stepped out onto her driveway and asked if I needed anything. I told her I could use some fresh water. I told her my story and she went in and got her husband so he could hear my story as well. They were Peter and Michelle Parsons and they invited me in their home for the night. Peter was an engineer on a factory fishing boat out of Dutch Harbor, Alaska that fished the Bering Sea. He was waiting for the new season to begin. Michelle said she hoped he wouldn't be out for five month's like he was the last time. We had fantastic conversation over a dinner of fresh fish, a perk from Peter's occupation. Michele did my laundry and fixed me up with energy bars and both fresh and dried fruit for my next day's journey. I left there with full stomach, clean clothes and refreshed from a hot shower.

I was but a few miles from the home of Michelle and Peter, I stopped and stripped off my pack and ducked into the bushes to relieve myself. When I stepped back out, I saw two cold bottles of water next to my pack. Guess I had not been as incognito as I thought. As I was standing there enjoying one of the bottles of water, I heard, "You want something to eat?" I looked up to see a man about my age holding a plate full of fried chicken and vegetables in front of him. "I see you found your water, I live in the house just in back of us, but you can't see it for all the large bushes." He told me he was a Christian and that Bellingham has a lot of homeless and said he feeds all that he can. I thanked him and we talked awhile as he had become very interested in what I was doing.

It's "from rags to riches" out here on the road, one day I'm in a fine home spending the night and the next I have to spend an hour hacking out a tent space from the briars with my pocket knife. I ended up with a nice flat tent site and very well hidden from the passing autos though.

Next day in the Big Rock Cafe & Grocery at Mount Vernon, Washington, as I was paying for my purchases, Randy Audette the owner said, "Where you headed Mr. Love Life?" I told him I was going up to Blaine and then walking to Key West. He gave me permission to tent on his property. Great, no hacking with my knife and I have a place to get fresh coffee the next morning. He also let me sit at one of the cafe's tables and work at my laptop. The very cute bartender/waitress was bending down trying to help me find an electrical outlet and the zipper on her very tight jeans broke! "Damn!" she said, "Hey, anybody got some safety pins?" A couple female patrons looked in their purses to no avail. A few minutes later as she passed me on her way to a customer's table I saw she had solved her problem. She had taken four of those large black and chrome, very strong paper clips and clipped them up the front of her jeans doing the job of the zipper. I complimented her on her ingenuity. She just laughed, what a wonderful personality, she had not a care as to how it looked! She just had a job to do. I love women like that.

Free Entertainment

I was lost in Bellingham, Washington and had asked several people directions to no avail. I spotted a welcome sight, a kiosk with a sign over it which said, "Bellingham Info". Well, the map at the kiosk left me even more confused than I had been before. As I was standing there frustrated I looked up over the map and there was a sign which stated, "IF YOU ARE LOST IN BELLINGHAM BLAME THE FOUR CITIES THAT BECAME BELLINGHAM." I'm not real big on blaming things so I looked around for someone else to ask. I approached a lady walking toward me and asked if she could direct me to Broadway. She looked at me as though I was a leper, but she acknowledged that she did know how to get to Broadway and started giving me directions. I was about 15 feet from her and I took a step closer to her so as to hear over the downtown traffic. She frantically stuck her hands out in front of her and said, "Don't come any closer to me or you will have to get your directions elsewhere." I said, "Ma'am?" She said, "I'm serious, do not come any closer." I said, "Ma'am, are you infectious or something, do you have a contagious disease?" "That's it." she said throwing her hands up in the air, "You'll get no directions from me!" Don't blame me lady, blame those four cities that became Bellingham. God, I Love Life!

Hold Onto Your Gift of Life!

The evening I walked into Blaine, Washington, I met the young attendant at a convenience store. His name was Ryan and he was 28 years-old. He told me he had congestive heart failure at 26 years-old. The doctors told him that part of his heart was twice the size of normal. There was no one there but the two of us and he kept stepping out to smoke cigarettes. He told me that he drank as well. I asked, had not the doctors advised him to stay away from tobacco and alcohol? He said that indeed they had but the heart disorder he suffered from was hereditary and he said he figured it wouldn't matter one way or the other. I chewed him out with a whole lot of love attached. I can attach that love by visualizing my two babies and knowing they both would want me to use it to help others. He was such a sweet and sensitive young man. I told him the same things that I say to those who tell me they are considering ending their lives. I explained to him that he doesn't have the right to be that careless with his life, that it doesn't belong just to him and that he owes it to the people who love him to take care of himself and to try and live as long as he can. We talked a very long time and I do hope that my words had an effect on him. He did say he would try to start looking at his situation differently.

Grandma Loved Life Too

I was sloshing through a cold rain near Park Hills, Missouri, toting "LOVE LIFE" over my head and feeling pretty cold and wet. Because of the rain most cars had their headlights on and so I didn't notice that I was waving at a funeral procession. As soon as I realized it I stopped waving immediately. The procession was slowing down for an intersection, the window went down in about the fourth car and a beautiful young lady with a very sweet smile said, "My grandmother would have loved your sign." Rain, what cold rain?

Harold's Barber Shop

Figure 15. Harold's Barber Shop

I was somewhere between Sedalia and Lincoln, Missouri, when I spotted Harold's Barber Shop in a little strip mall just off the highway. Harold's Barber Shop was quite the experience. Harold was 85 and still runs his shop three to four days a week. I asked, "How much for a haircut, sir?" "$4.00," said Harold. Four bucks, I couldn't believe it. Waiting for the two ahead of me and getting to listen to Harold's stories was an added treat. Harold gave me an awesome haircut and even trimmed my eyebrows and mustache. He was very meticulous. I handed him a five dollar bill and asked if that would cover it. He handed me back a dollar bill and said, "We don't do that here." He placed my card up on his wall mirror with the LOVE LIFE side showing. Take a walk across this land of ours my friends and you will see some quite remarkable things and meet some of the most interesting and just damn good people.

A Nuisance?

While walking up the coast of Oregon, I was telling a lady who lived in a beautiful Oregon seaside area how thrilled I was to see seals for the very first time. She said they considered them a nuisance. "A nuisance?" say I, "How can they be a nuisance? They play with beach balls and stuff, clap their flippers together like they're applauding something, and they make cute little noises and stuff like that." She said, "Believe me, they are a nuisance!" And I said, "Hell, down in Florida where I'm from, we got 12-foot gators that snatch your ass up, take ya down and put ya in a hole under the mangrove roots 'til ya rot real good so they can eat ya easier; now *that* ma'am; is a nuisance!"

Brother Fish

Figure 16.

2009. On route 125 going into Strafford, Missouri, walking toward traffic as I usually do, there was no shoulder at all and very deep ditches on both sides of the road, so I had to walk in the road as close to the edge as possible. A very frustrated driver of an old green Ford pickup was getting tired of waiting behind the two other cars also waiting for oncoming traffic to clear so they could then go around me. He was shaking his head and holding his hands palms up, as to say WTF! As soon as the cars in front of him made sure they gave me plenty of room and passed me, the green Ford truck's motor was gunned and came straight at me. I ducked down as far as I could and that prevented the large extended side mirrors from hitting me. I looked up and a young lady was holding her arms out the window of the next car taking my picture. "Do you mind?" She asked. I said, "That guy in front of you tried to hit me." And quite unconcerned, she said, "Oh I saw that," and continued to snap pictures of the novelty with "LOVE LIFE" over his head. But a few hundred feet down the road, I saw the Calvary Mission Church, with this portable sign in front of it, "SHACKING UP WILL COST U HEAVEN - HOPE ITS WORTH IT!" And at the very bottom of the sign it said, BRO. FISH. I think maybe Brother Fish needs to change his sign to a more important community minded message, "IT IS NOT NICE TO RUN OVER OLD MEN ON THE ROAD!" I wonder if Brother Fish drives an old green Ford pickup truck.

LOVE LIFE Sign is Powerful!

A lady in North Florida, pulled up beside me and yelled, "Thank you!" And as she sped off she threw out a full pack of Marlboros and a lighter. Evidently, the message on my sign, "LOVE LIFE," inspired her to quit smoking and become a litter bug.

Thank you Sir!

In Maine, a lady came up to me, handed me an ice cream and a bag containing a sandwich and an apple, and with tear filled eyes, said, "My husband met you yesterday and after hearing of the loss of both your children and seeing the words 'LOVE LIFE' over your head, he went straight to our son and ended an ongoing feud between the two which had gone on for a few years. Thank you sir, thank you!"

Power of Love

Love is not just a word, Love is the term used to describe the most powerful force in the universe. Love is a term not to be used lightly. It may leave the lips a thousand times a day to fall straight to the floor if it doesn't first pass through a heart unblocked by the dividing forces of anger, blame, and hatred. The power of Love exhibited depends on the purity of that Love, on how diluted and polluted it has become by anger, blame, and hatred. Love never separates, Love never divides its participants. Where there is division there is no Love. We cannot realize and use the real power of Love until we understand the purity of Love.

Dumpster Diving

In Chester, Illinois, where a big sign proudly proclaims, "Home of Popeye," I tried to cross the bridge over the Mississippi into Missouri and was stopped by a "No Pedestrians" sign. Try as I may to hitch a ride across, I was having no success. I needed a sign to show I wanted only to cross the bridge. I spotted a garbage dumpster in the Illinois Welcome Center Park across the road. As I victoriously pulled my head out of the dumpster with an empty Mountain Dew 12 pack carton in hand, there stood a lady with tear filled eyes saying, "Sir, please, I'll go into town and get you something to eat." I explained to the sweet soul I was not foraging for food but had just found my much needed sign material. I still had to convince her though that I had in fact just eaten at a local restaurant. She didn't have a magic marker I asked to borrow, so I spent at least 35 minutes using an ink pen making sure it would be easily seen. Moments after I flashed my sign, "OVER BRIDGE," a car stopped. "So, my sign worked," I asked of the driver. "What sign?" said the driver. I showed him the sign and he said, "Nah, I always pick up everyone I see at the bridge." Sigh…

Hells Angels, on Religion??

On a late Saturday morning in August, in New Hampshire, I was sitting on a rock enjoying the babbling brook with the White Mountains for a backdrop and enjoying the glorious weather, when two Massachusetts Hells Angels pulled up on their bikes to throw down a couple beers at the tranquil spot. We talked mostly about the day-old Harley one was riding. Then one asked me, "Hey did you see that fuckin' sign back there, that, "Christian Camping?" Did Jesus have a certain way of pitchin' a tent or somethin?" "Yeah, I did see that sign, and I hope not, I camp most every night and I hope I'm not pitching my tent wrong," I quipped. He went on, "I bet they wouldn't let me fuckin' camp there." I agreed with him that they probably would not. The other Hell's Angel said, "Bet Jesus would've though." And I said, "Bet Jesus wouldn't have had his own special campground separating himself from everyone else."

Three Times Dead… I'm changing!

In 2011, just east of North Vernon, Indiana, on U.S. Route 50, Steve Leisure called me over to his "Sunshine Variety" open air thrift store. He offered me what looked like chopped figs sprinkled with something. "This craps really good for ya," he said. "Don't know what the hell that is on 'em, though; tastes good, so I don't care." They did taste good so I didn't care either. Steve said he was pronounced dead three times in his life and it drastically changed how he now viewed life. "You had one of those out of body experiences?" I asked. "Hell no. I just figured after three times dead, I should make some changes," he said.

Owls in Church?

In 2004, a Montana rancher let me tent on his land. He told me of his disdain going to church to please his wife. He said he didn't see why he had go into that building and out of the beauty he was in every day. Doing a sweeping motion with his hand, he said, "Right here is my church." He also told me he didn't like seeing all those, "Owls," he said. "Owls?" I asked. "Yup! When you walk in they all do this." He moved just his head, very slowly, looking over one shoulder and then the other, you know, kinda' like an owl. He continued, "They look just like owls, they just gotta' see who's showin' up for church; just a bunch a owls!" Looking down at the ground and shaking his head as though trying to figure it all out, he looked back up and said, "Why, two weeks ago, or there about, there we were sitting in that stuffy building, and the preacher was reading words spoken by Jesus himself, and he said, "My father's house is not made with hands." I whispered to my wife, "then why in the world are we in here?" He said she got mad at him.

Fame

In Missouri, outside a convenience store, I was having a hotdog, a huge cup of coffee loaded with French Vanilla Creamer, and counting my money. I had less than $3.00. Just as I started to put my money back in my pocket, a young man walked up and said excitedly, "You're famous! I've seen you on TV n' shit, you're all over the internet, and there's a documentary about you too." I looked down at my closed hand containing the money, started laughing and said, "so, this is fame huh, hell, I was expecting a little more than this. How ya' get that one with all that money and shit, you know, the one like Elvis and Michael Jackson n' those guys got, huh?" Now we were both laughing; hell, made me feel kinda' famous, know what I mean? Make people laugh, there's medicine in laughter. It can heal your woes big time. And... make you feel famous!

Polite Way to Say Kiss My Ass

In Lynden, Washington, near the British Columbia border in a store parking lot, an Indian man, impeccably dressed and wearing a gleaming white turban, walking toward a new gleaming black Mercedes SUV with a British Columbia license tag, saw me walking across the lot with "LOVE LIFE" over my head, and cynically said to me, "I do not think you Americans know anything about loving life, what could you possibly tell me about Love Life?" I thought a minute and suggested, "Never judge a population of 300 million as a whole." He never answered. His wife was maintaining a certain distance behind him as they walked, some specific religious sect they belonged to I guess. All I know, I'm still alive today because I never asked my ex-wife to do that.

I Love This

While walking facing the traffic with "LOVE LIFE" over my head in Oregon, a really beat up old car went by to my right and the driver stuck his head out and yelled, "You idiot!" I looked up to see the source, and then heard tires screeching! About three or four cars up, a car did an abrupt left turn. And paying more attention to the idiot with the "LOVE LIFE" sign and not the road in front of him, the asshole had to slam on his brakes, then sending him sideways and nearly ramming the next car. I walked past with my finger pointing over my head and backwards to my "LOVE LIFE" sign, grinning big.

My Friend, Hell No!

One morning, I was sitting in McDonald's working on this book when I realized I hadn't checked my mail from the night before. There waiting for me was an email from a friend I hadn't been in touch with for a few years. It read:

"Hello, Steve my good friend from so long ago. While I told hundreds of people about you and how proud I have always been to know you - little did I know that one day I would be reaching out to you for help? In early April I tried to hang myself. I just started seeing a psychiatrist and using heavy meds for sleep. Tonight, again, the overwhelming urge to try it again was upon my chest and I have not slept. I still have the undying support of my wife. What I would like to know is are you out on a trail somewhere and if so I would like to fly to that spot and have a serious man to man chat. My cell is ----"

Upon reading his message, I fired off an email telling him to get his ass to Vero Beach as fast as he could and that I would be calling him in mere moments. I put my stuff away as fast as possible and ran out to my van and called him. This friend is fairly well known throughout the country, not exactly a household name, but certainly a name many could recognize. He is extremely talented, successful, very well educated, has authored books, and produced several CDs displaying his numerous talents and genius.

My friend began telling me of a lawsuit against him and a battle that had been ongoing for a few years amounting to several hundred thousand dollars. An amount that threatened his and his wife's financial security they had worked so hard over the years to establish. He said he just got tired of the huge attorney's fees, the worry, and the long trying battle against a heartless foe who had done this sort of scam before, simply trying to get rich quick.

He said, "Steve, I gotta' tell you though, when I slipped that rope around my neck, a peace came over me. I couldn't believe how calm I felt about it. But for some reason I couldn't go through with it at that time. "

I cut him off with, "Well of course you felt at peace with it, you were about to end all your problems. No more worries! No, you were leaving all the worries with your wife and your son, with your other loved ones, and friends, along with totally crushed hearts. No, you'd be gone. *But* you would be leaving behind a trail of completely devastated lives." I told him of a 62 year-old man I met in Maine who, while sobbing, told me of having lost his dad to suicide when he was twelve." I told him that my son had gone out of this world ignorant of the pain he was leaving us with. I told him that, "By God you're not going out ignorant, you will go out now knowing how self-centered you are being and the pain you will be causing those you claim to love." I went on and on about the pain he would cause and that his life didn't belong just to him that it belonged to others as well, family and friends alike who loved him.

After a while, my good friend said, "Steve I know what you're saying is true, you are so right, but let me just interrupt but a moment and then you can go right back to chewing my ass out." "Okay, talk." I said. He told me, "Steve, after I wrote you that email last night, I went to your website and I read all night long, nearly finishing the entire site. I cried and I laughed. I loved the story, 'A Hug and a Beer'

And I saw what your son's suicide did to you and your family. I saw what suicide had done in the other stories you told. I became ashamed of myself for what I had been thinking about doing to my family. I left your website with a different outlook on my life. I went straight to my wife and apologized and asked her forgiveness. Thank you Steve. Now you may continue chewing my ass out!" I eased up on him... some.

Bad Moods are Selfish

In 2006, I stepped up to the counter at a convenience store in North Georgia, near Blairsville where I was then residing. "How are you?" I asked the lady waiting on me. She only shrugged her shoulders. "I'm doing great." I volunteered. She rolled her eyes, sighed, and reluctantly spoke, "Well I'm not." "Oh, I'm sorry." I said. I then asked, "Are you alright, is something troubling you?" "No more than usual," she replied with a smirk. She then added, "I'm just depressed, that's just me, I'm always like that." I smiled my best smile and as caring as I could be, I said ever so sweetly, "Oh, that's too bad you've become so centered on yourself and are making others around you miserable." Now I had her full attention. She looked at me as if I had not understood a word she said and so further explained, rather curtly, "No, it doesn't involve others, it's just me. I'm the one that's depressed. I never bother others with it." She was so sincere in her explanation. I explained to her, "Self-misery affects others just as self-joy spills over and lifts the spirits of those near us. When we are miserable it can cause those near us to also be miserable, this is why bad moods are so very self-centered." She then justified her mood with, "Well, I have had a lot of bad things happen to me." I smiled real big and answered, "I can certainly understand that, so have I."

She rolled her eyes as if to say, "Oh no, am I going to have to listen to this guy's crap?" I was not going to let it end though, I wanted her to be happy, and maybe I could help. I kept on explaining, "I have a joy in my life, and I love life. Even though I have lost both my beautiful children, I still love life." Now she was listening. I continued, "I lost my 26 year-old son to suicide; six years later, I lost my beautiful 36 year-old daughter to an accidental drug overdose." I could see instantly I had hit home, she had at least one child, I could see it in her face as she said, "Oh God; I am so very sorry." She was struggling with understanding this little debate we had engaged in; I could see this was a new concept for her. When I left she was giving me a smile. She had taken her focus away from herself via perspective, just long enough to make her smile. I must truly have a love and concern for my fellow human being to have risked having my eye's clawed out by a pissed-off southern girl in a Georgia convenience store.

"The two reasons a bad mood is selfish: 1. It restricts the freedom of others by possibly causing them to have to act differently in our presence. 2. It denies to others the beauty of who we really are." ~ Steve Fugate

Tough Yuma Cowboy

In 2009, early in the morning near Yuma, Arizona, just a few miles into California, an old beat up pickup truck pulled up beside me. The driver was maybe forty, skinny, and the face under the dust-filled cowboy hat was like leather and well-worn like the hat. He was staring at me hard and demanded, "Now you tell me what the hell there is about life to love?" I said, "Breathing." And he answered with, "Hell, it seems the more I breathe, the more miserable life gets." So I said, "Maybe you need a respirator." He chuckled with me. I continued, "Loving life is just something we as individuals determine to do; we simply make our mind up to love life and use the energy we've spent blaming it and put it toward loving it. Life is never our enemy; our attitude toward life is our enemy or our friend." He said a couple more negative things, life sucks, too many assholes, and so on. I cut him off and told him why I carry the sign. He said, "Damn, man! Damn! A feller shouldn't oughta' have to bury his children... damn!" He never offered any more complaints; we just stayed silent for a moment and then he spoke again, "Damn, I'm really sorry you lost your kids, man, you take it easy and be careful out there buddy." I said thank you sir and he drove off, still shaking his head at what he had just heard. Amazing what perspective can do; it's a tool that works well for me. I wish to God I didn't have it, but I do. It's a two-part deal for me; my heart aches every time I relate the loss of my babies, and is then relieved by the hope that possibly another broken heart is mended before it stops beating. I try to Love Life and allow "perspective" to create a balanced path to walk, with great appreciation for the Life I've been given.

A Plunger on the Appalachian Trail?

In 2006, I went back out on the Appalachian Trail, and did 340 miles from Springer Mountain, in Georgia, to Erwin, Tennessee. Not far from Erwin, I saw a young man with a plunger sticking out of the top of his backpack. Of course I had to know why one would have a plunger while hiking the AT. So, "Hey, what's up with the plunger"? He replied, "Would you have stopped and talked to me had you not seen my plunger?" I chuckled and agreed with his clever way of meeting other hikers. He really touched my heart though when he explained why he chose a plunger as his attention grabber: He explained that he had only recently finished med school. He told of the huge expense for his education and how hard his father had worked, the extra hours and so on, always making sure tuitions were paid and that all his needs were met. With obvious emotion in his voice, he told of how much his father encouraged him during the rough times. He proudly proclaimed, "My father is a plumber."

Ohio Mail Deliverer

April 4, 2007, near Nashport, Ohio, it got cold and was forecast to get even colder that night, down to 22 degrees. Screw that, I'm from Florida! A lady delivering mail pulled up and handed me a bag holding a bottle of water, a box of Girl Scout Cookies, and a pair of heavy duty winter gloves. She said she had seen me that morning and had returned home to retrieve some things she thought I might need. After I told her about my son's suicide, she shared her story with me. Her name was Deanne, she was 37 and she had just recently gone through a bout with severe depression. She said it just came upon her one day and no matter how hard she tried she just could not pull out of it. She told of a good husband and two great little boys, and no reason for her depression. She tried doctors and the medication helped some, but still the depression would not go away. Finally, she said she just cried out to God and begged for help. She said that she was now overcoming the depression and gradually returning to a normal life. She said she now wanted to do whatever she could to help others.

A little over two years later on 7/24/2009, I received this email: Steve, I am the mother of the mail lady Deanna that you met in Nashport, Ohio April 4 2007. Thank you for your words to her that day. I believe your words made a difference in her life. She just did a 20 mile walk in New York for Prevent Suicide. She had a hip replaced and needs another but did the whole walk. She Loves Life. Thank You.

What did I do or say to her that was special? Nothing, I but told of the loss of my two precious babies and she saw the pain, and then she saw that I still had joy, that I did indeed Love Life. That perspective obviously helped Deanna garner up some extra strength for her battle. All I did was force myself to Love my Life because there is no way I could undo the deaths of my little boy and my little girl. My children and I welcome all to use our story for perspective for encouragement toward finding your own inner strength to Love Life no matter your circumstances.

Push On

"Push on and love the gift of Life we've been so wonderfully blessed with my friends. When we awake and feel that sweet, sweet air on our upper lip, we have indeed been gifted another day! Realize the miracle of that moment first and foremost, and grab onto it and hold onto the beauty of our precious gift of Life. Give that moment precedence over all other thoughts that are attempting to cause us to put into second place the realization of the beauty of our being alive yet one more day. Absolutely nothing is more sacred than our gift of Life. Hold onto the moment as long as it takes for the realization of the beauty of Life to supersede and conquer all negative thoughts and simply... Love Life.

We're Not Odd

Just past Inglis, Florida, I looked up to see a lady walking in front of me. She was walking really fast so it became a challenge for me to catch up and pass her. It took me longer than I figured to catch up. When I got beside her and saw her face I was surprised at how old she was, she had to be in her 80's. She asked about my walk and after I told about my children, she shared that she had lost her husband Thanksgiving Day 2010 and just weeks later, two days before Christmas, her daughter-in-law killed herself. She said, "I walk off my pain." "Me too," I said. She said, "People think I'm odd." I told her that some think I'm a bit odd too. She said, "Why, you're not odd at all!" I asked did she not think it odd that a man walk all over the country with a big sign over his head. She said,

"No." "Then you, cannot be even the slightest bit odd," I said. We both laughed. We walked away from each other smiling big and still chuckling. What a great way for two strangers to part, what happens when both Love Life.

Pissed off Atheists

A man in California saw my "LOVE LIFE" sign and asked what I was about. After explaining my endeavors to him, he asked, "Do you believe in God?" "Absolutely," I answered. He then asked if I talked to all I meet about God. I told him that I do not. After he asked why not, I answered, "Because, I don't want the atheists to kill themselves either, do you?" He said, "No, no, of course not." I then said, "Well, if I start talking to an atheist about God, it just pisses them off, and if they're dead you can't talk to them about anything can you?" he walked away as if in thought.

Star of David

12/25/11. In Panaca, Nevada, I found myself in a situation I try very hard to avoid, dark falling before I find a tent site. I was walking through a field just across the street from the little convenience store where I had just had my hotdog dinner. I was trying to find a spot out of sight of cars and nearby homes. Trying to focus in the dark and find something suitable to get me out of my dilemma, I heard voices right behind me. It was a couple who told me their names were David and Star. Star said, "Yup, just think of the Star of David and you'll remember us."

They told me that I could maybe pitch my tent at their place if they could find room. When we reached their place I saw why they said they would have to find room. They were honest to goodness hoarders. It was like 3 acres of totally worthless stuff everywhere. I really looked around next morning, I swear, there was nothing of any real value. They were in their 60's and Star said they were newlyweds. She also told me they would let me stay in their home but there was no room. Hell, there was no room anywhere! David said that when they first married, they had 100 tons of stuff hauled away. "Really, one hundred tons, as in 100 times 2000 pounds, where in the hell was it?" I asked in astonishment as I tried to picture there ever having been any more junk there. David sheepishly said, "Well, I've collected a little bit more since then."

They both went inside a junked travel trailer and started emptying and rearranging so as to make room for me to use the little bed. There was no heat they said, but at least I'd be out of the wind and off the ground. The next morning Star brought me a piping hot bowl of oatmeal with cinnamon and brown sugar. God, it tasted good in that 20 degree desert cold. Star drove me back to the c-store apologizing the whole way for not having room for me in their home. Hey, I slept warm and didn't have to pack up my tent in that cold with numb fingers.

9 Year-Old Book Critic

I was sitting in my van facing out the open side doors, on my laptop and tackling the grueling task of rewriting my manuscript after professional editing. When little red headed 9 year-old Tyler appears and asks, "Hey, can we go walk in the woods today?" I told him I was really pressed to get the rewrite done and so not today. He promptly expressed interest and asked to see my manuscript. So I presented to him the stack of pages not yet corrected and Tyler asked what all those little pencil marks were. After explaining those were corrections Tyler blurted, "Wow, that's a lot a mistakes!" I justified by saying, "Well Tyler, It was done by a professional who knows much more about punctuation and grammar than I do." Continuing to look through the pages he did not let up, "I've never seen this many mistakes on anybody's paper!" he said, with eyes opened wide as though totally astonished. "This is my first book," I again justified. I then told Tyler I was really busy and perhaps we could walk in the woods the next day. He said okay and as Tyler was leaving, he innocently (I think?) took a parting shot with, "Man, didn't you go to school?" He then skipped across the road. He remains unharmed because his grandfather, Mark, is a good friend of mine.

Companion No Longer Needed

After my divorce in '96, I erroneously thought I had to have a companion for my life to be complete, so I searched the dating section offered by the local paper. A lady in Ft. Pierce sounded interesting, I gave her a call and we agreed to meet at a popular restaurant located between our two cities. She said she would be wearing some black so to identify her. She was in fact, wearing a long heavy black coat over all black clothing. Hey, to each their own, even if it is August in South Florida. And, strangely, she kept staring at my feet and continued to do so even after our introduction. I could tell she didn't like me. Good, I didn't like her either. We must have been driven by hunger or we would have ended it right then and there.

Inside the eatery, after being brought my fine Kentucky Bourbon, "The Woman in Black," while pulling a cigarette from a black purse I could've used for a year-long jungle safari, asked, "You gonna' drink that in front of me?" and I shot back, "You gonna' smoke that in front of me?" I'm telling you, we hated each other! But moments later, she leaned her head to one side and looking under the table, said of my very expensive boots, "What animal had to be killed for those?" "I have no idea," I said, "I paid to have it killed." Actually, they were from some kind of huge constrictor snake I was hoping would come back to life any moment! And because I'm a gentleman, I resisted asking, "And how many circus tents had to be destroyed for that coat?" Each realizing the other to be a complete asshole, we both concentrated on eating in order to end the agony as soon as possible. Her concentration was intense!

And I solemnly swear this to be true; as we were rising to leave the table and get the hell away from each other, she reached down, picked up the dish containing the liquid left from her coleslaw, and promptly slurped it down while standing there. Totally stunned, I said, "Nice, just really nice." At the door waiting for a table and looking straight at us was my good friend Deputy Sheriff Blue Bowling, with his gorgeous and classy new girlfriend. Unfortunately, my boots remained inanimate. I picked up the tab declining her offer to pay her half, as I wanted the full brunt of this valuable lesson. The boots are long gone but I'm still single.

Fault Lines

Speaking to a young lady in California about correcting my own faults after she asked how I became so positive about Life. She said, "Well, everyone has faults why should I try to fix mine? I said, "Here in California, there's the San Andreas Fault, which could one day cause great harm to many people. If you were able to correct it, would you not?" She said of course she would. "Well," I continued, "I've come to realize my faults can hurt others. It is impossible to correct the San Andreas Fault, but not my own."

We mustn't be afraid to look within for our own faults. This procedure is what makes us much more understanding of and receptive of others we think we see faults in. We are much less likely to judge others for faults after seeing the same or maybe even worse, in ourselves. Looking for and finding our faults certainly becomes easier when we realize that most our faults are in reality, assets for our personal walk through life. Yes, assets we were born with which have been wrongly molded and shaped into a use other than they were intended. Redesigned by us to fit our particular environment. This is why our faults are so difficult for us to recognize as such, we see them as just part of who we are. These faults must be recognized as assets to more easily be converted back into their original good purpose and to be seen by others as good. So, in reality, instead of finding faults, we are but remodeling our person back to its original design. The original design can then be used as it was meant, as a tool of love toward all others.

March 23, 2013 to June 20, 2015, I walked into all the 48 contiguous states. Some stories from my Zigzag Walk:

Red Wolf

Just a couple weeks before I left on this walk, somewhere near Vero Beach, Florida, I had a most beautiful encounter. Walking and daydreaming, on my way across a meadow toward a canal where I had been tracking a little gator, about two feet long, using a method of tracking I learned from an Ojibwa elder, he calls, "tracking and untracking," I just happened to look up and loping along just in front of me was one of the most beautiful things I ever seen. It glanced over at me and knowing it was a safe 200 feet away from me, it never increased its speed, it just kept glancing at me periodically as it headed for the woods and safety. However, it stopped at the edge of the Indian River Lagoon, maybe two football fields from me, sat and just watched me for a few moments before entering the woods. It was too large for a coyote, and smaller than a gray wolf. It was reddish in color. Its ears were larger than a wolf but smaller than a coyotes. I've seen hundreds of coyotes and a few wolves, in my travels. I couldn't possibly be looking at a red wolf could I? There are less than 200 and in only two places in the world. A very well monitored preserve in South Carolina and an island in the Gulf too far off the western coast of Florida for them to ever make it ashore. They once roamed Florida and much of the South. The Seminole, the Cherokee, and the Shawnee, spoke of them. A week later, as I was looking across a small stream at the little gator I had been watching, I looked up and about 100 yards away from me was my red wolf at the edge of the woods just staring at me. We actually stared at each other for about a full minute. My red wolf started acting nervous so I stepped to the right a few feet to be hidden by a tree line, the red wolf stepped back too. After but a few seconds I stepped back out from the tree line. And so did my wolf! It was awesome. One of the most beautiful incidents in my life ever. We just looked at each other for a few seconds and then my red wolf very slowly turned and walked into the woods. I never saw the hauntingly beautiful creature again. I saw scat and tracks for a while, but never again any fresh ones. My wolf was gone. Online I found a story, "Woman in Florida takes picture of red wolf in back yard." The picture could have easily been my red wolf! The sighting was about one year before mine. The lady lived outside Fort Pierce, Florida, probably about 20 miles from my sighting. I had been struggling with the decision to walk again. For some reason, my red wolf was the sign I needed. I started preparing for my walk.

Curly was an Outlaw

After I ate, at the one convenience store between Cross City and Perry, Florida. I went back outside to check my cooler to see if I needed more ice. As soon as I went out the door I heard a baby screaming as loud as I ever heard one scream. In front of me in an SUV was the baby in two of the largest arms I've ever seen on a man! They were covered in tattoos and he was patting the baby on the back. Mommy in the passenger seat took the child and the driver looked over at me and my cart. I said, "That's quite a set of lungs there." Smiling, the huge man said, "Yup, he's gonna' be a good one I think." I got some ice and as I was dumping it in I realized I could get the whole bag full in if I had someone to help by holding my cart level while I dumped in the ice. I looked over and saw the guy still watching me, so I asked could he possibly hold my cart level for me. He started getting out of his vehicle and I thought he would never get all the way out. The man was absolutely huge! He had a sleeveless t-shirt on and he was totally covered in tats. They were on his neck, they were everywhere. He apologized for being so slow getting out and explained he had some health problems. I immediately started apologizing and asked him to please forget about it that it was not really that important. But he insisted and said he really needed to get out for a while anyway.

We got the ice in and as he walked away from me I saw on the back of his shirt, "Support Your Local Black & White" I asked, "Is that Black & White as in Outlaws?" Without turning around and very simply, he said, "I'm an Outlaw." I told him I had known a few other Outlaws many years ago. I named them. Some he had known and others he had heard of. He told me his name was Curly. He was completely bald except for a very small pony tail; very low at the base of his neck. He had numerous small gold rings in his left ear. Curly told me he was from Peoria, Illinois. I gave him my card. As I walked back into the store to retrieve my phone from charging I noticed Curly behind me and held the door for him. As I was on my way back out I heard, "Hey Steve, come 'ere." I looked over to see Curly towering over the shelves as he was searching for snacks. He motioned for me to come around to where he was. He had a twenty folded up very small and said, "I want to help you with whatever it is you're doing." I told him I appreciated it very much. He said, "I know you do, just pay it forward man... pay it forward." I told him that I do pay forward. Curly said, "Yeah, I bet you do." Back outside he said, "Look man, you run into any of my brothers in your travels, tell 'em you know Curly... most of 'em know me." Love Life with all your heart my friends and you too will find caring in some unexpected places.

Old Florida Cowboy

I met Brad one morning in a gas station in Otter Creek, Florida, we were both having coffee. He was an old Florida cowboy. He was wearing a straw cowboy hat and his skin had most definitely seen many a day in the Florida sun. Brad said he was raised up in Pasco County, Florida and started chasing cows when he was just a boy back in the 40's. He said he could remember when Pasco County was nothing but cattle and cowboys. He shook his head as though in disgust and said, "Why hell, I remember when there weren't but 10,000 people in the whole county. I just read somewhere that there are now over 400,000 people there!" He shook his head some more and continued, "Why, where I grew up in the little town of Odessa, they're now startin' to call it North Tampa! I swear, that makes me sick to my stomach." He said he moved there to Levy County so he could breathe a little easier. As I got up from our shared picnic table he said, "Now you be safe out there and watch out for all them assholes on them damn cell phones, they'll run over ya!" He's right too, every time I have a close call, it's someone talking on their cell phone.

LOVE LIFE, my meaning

Love Life means just that, to love the life you have right now, the life which is in front of us right now and not one we wish it to be. To love life is to love the fact we are alive, that we have air to breathe. That we realize, before anything else is presented to us after we awake, that we have indeed first been granted the gift of life. I call it falling in love with the act of breathing. My key to a love life attitude is to look not for perfection outside me, but to find the perfection of who I really am inside me, the one I was created to be, the "I am." Who we really are is a calm and gentle soul. A soul that judges not, hates not, and angers not.

Serendipitous

I did 22 miles today. I saw an older Lincoln that looked brand new, pulled off to the side and waiting for me. The driver was really old. In fact his ball cap said he was a World War II veteran! He handed me a ten and said, "That's a good sign, you stay safe." As he was pulling out I was able to thank him for his service. He smiled. A young man, Steve, approached me as I was filling my cooler with ice and asked of my sign. I told my story and then proceeded to tell why I think everyone should Love their gift of Life. He said to me, "Man, this is like serendipitous man! I woke up this morning with the attitude that I was going to Love the beautiful day that was waiting outside for me. I left the house determined to have a great day. And then I run smack into you, how cool is that!"

Restaurant Closed, Hearts Open

5/1/13. This morning upon entering Repton, Alabama I was told the only restaurant was the South 40 located one mile off of my route on south 41. I hadn't eaten since yesterday so I went against my rule of never deviating from my main route and took the very hilly route out of my way. When I got to the restaurant there was a man working on something just in front of me. I asked if they were open and he informed me they were closed on Mondays! Talk about demoralizing. I couldn't help but show my frustration, I just dropped my head down to the top of my trekking poles and said, "Geez, I just walked here all the way from 84." The guy shrugged and I accepted the situation with a sigh and said, "Oh well." As I was struggling with pulling the cart over that same one mile of rolling hills, a new silver BMW pulled up beside me and the female passenger handed me a bag with 2 big fat turkey and ham sandwiches and a cold soda. It was the owners of the South 40 restaurant! The driver was the man I saw at the restaurant. He said, "I went in and told my wife we gotta' fix this guy something to eat and take it to him... come on let's go find him." If y'all are ever in the Repton, Alabama area, you have to go eat at the South 40 just because of the great people they are!

Jus' a Payin' Back

Near Bainbridge, Georgia, I heard the sound of something dragging behind me. Just as I heard it, I was passing by a gentleman sitting out in his front yard and waving to me. I yelled out and asked could he see something dragging from my cart. In that wonderful Georgia accent, he said, "Why the whole rear-ends a draggin' sir." That was certainly alarming, and when I stopped to check it out I discovered that my cart had broken at the axle! The gentleman said, "Bring it over heah to me and ah take a look at it. My knees are bad so ah don't move so well." His name was Bill Johnson, born in Plant City, Florida, and raised his whole life in Bainbridge.

Bill looked at my little pull-behind trailer over and said, "Take at thing apart and let's fix it. Ah got all the tools and lots a scrap metal." He moved very slowly through what looked to me like disorganized clutter, in a little building with a faded sign barely readable, "Bill's Bicycle Repair." He said he hadn't been open in years. We both agreed that his first two ideas would be way too heavy for my little cart. Then Bill said, "I think I got just the thing... if I can find it that is." He was gone for a few minutes and returned with a long piece of angle cut galvanized steel punched full of holes. "This hee-ah stuff ain't a gonna' bend." He said. We both tested it by trying to bend it and it would not budge. I had to completely disassemble my cart and Bill began giving me things to do and we proceeded to cut two pieces from the galvanized metal and bolt them on top the length of the two bottom frame pieces that had broken. About two hours later, the cart was back together and more structurally sound than it was before I met Bill Johnson. I offered him money and Bill said, "I can't take 'at, people do things for me all a the time. I'm jus' a payin' back." Bill brought me two ice cold orange soda pops and insisted on having his picture taken with me.

Love from an Alabama Road Crew

5/5/13. Near Silas, Alabama, I was kicking myself for not having taken the time earlier in the morning to wait for Dollar General to open so I could buy some snacks. Instead, I had to eat one of those boring Clif Bars, pretty sure the main ingredient is mud. As I was trudging up one of the hills on the roller coaster I'd been walking, I saw at the top of the hill three Alabama DOT trucks. As I got closer I could see one woman and three men in the trucks. They were watching me and just as I got up to the first big truck, all four got out. Each of the four were handing part of their lunches! One handed me a jar of peaches and some peanut butter snack crackers. One handed me a small pack of cookies and a beef jerky. Another handed me a can of Vienna sausages and some snack crackers. The woman handed me a can of potted meat and a pack of Ritz crackers. One man took off his safety vest and handed it to me. His friend said, "No, let me give him mine because it's a lot newer." I sat right down and started snacking to the delight of the four Alabama Department of Transportation workers. They said they had been watching me all morning as they passed me repeatedly and worrying about me walking a highway without a paved shoulder. They all four smiled approvingly as I put on my bright florescent green vest with silver reflective strips and an outline of the state of Alabama huge on the back stating ALDOT in the center of it.

Laurel, Mississippi

5/8/2013. Just before Laurel, Mississippi, about 11:30, I went into Walkers Dairy Bar for something to eat. The place was packed. I told the very efficient man at the order window who was very adept at handling the large crowd that I'd like a chili dog and a root beer. He said that would be $3.75 and asked did I have 75 cents. I did indeed and he handed me back seven dollars change. A few minutes later he looked over at me and said, "Here ya go sir." He handed me a paper tray with my chili dog wrapped in tin foil. Sticking out from under the tin foil I saw the corner of a ten dollar bill and I glanced up at him with surprise. He said, "We appreciate ya." Now all I had to do was get back to my table without bursting into tears. Ladies and gentleman, no matter how many times these kinds of thing happen to me, I am always touched by, and am in awe of, the goodness of our fellow human beings. So many express surprise at the many random acts of kindness which I encounter. A very common statement to me after I tell of an act of kindness is, "I can't believe there are still good people in the world." Perhaps the ones making such statements are conditioned as I once was by television, movies, and news media sources to just expect bad because I was shown so much of it and was then not looking for the good. I've walked over 40,000 miles of this wonderful country full of the most wonderful people and have never been seriously harmed. I look only for the good along with making certain I am treating all I encounter with that same goodness and respect.

Count Your Blessings

Keith pulled his Harley up to me after I watched him pass and then turn around. He said, "Man, I just really felt compelled to turn around and talk to you." I told him my story and he said that he could relate. I told him I was so very sorry for his loss and he started telling his story. In Goodlettsville, Tennessee on March 4, 1999, his home caught on fire from the upstairs where his two little boys, Seth, 4, and Ryan, 2 years-old, were sleeping. Keith and his father-in-law were both severely burned trying to rescue his babies but to no avail. He lost his baby boys. His 11 year-old daughter and his wife were downstairs and so were not harmed. Keith said, "Both my little boys died by smoke inhalation, they weren't burned to death, I'm thankful for that." Folks, I don't want to hear about three flat tires in a week… you know what I mean. Keith told me he now has four other beautiful children by another wife and said he is very thankful for what he has but said not a day passes he doesn't think of his two little ones lost. I told him I certainly could relate to that. I reached to shake his hand and he said, "No way man, I'm hugging you!" After the great hug he said, "Thank you man, thanks for listening to me". Love did that ladies and gentlemen. Love Life until you love all the human beings in life, not just in your Life.

Dialysis, Piece a Cake

5/8/13. Randall Dykes from Waynesboro, Mississippi, pulled alongside me as I was starting to cross the road over to Ramey's Grocery & Grill to grab something to eat. Randall wanted to know all that I was doing and why. After I shared my story he told me he stopped because he loved my sign and he handed me $10.00 and said he wanted to pay for my food. Randall said, "You know, it just don't get no plainer than that sir, you just plain 'ol gotta' love life. I was supposed to have died several times now and I ain't. They thought I was gonna' die when I was six when they had to take a kidney out, but I didn't... I'm still here. When my good kidney went bad I was told I would die but my aunt, God bless her soul, gave me a kidney. They thought I would die at each one of my two open heart surgeries and I didn't. My last open heart surgery killed my last good kidney and I'm on dialysis now, been off n' on it for 13 years now." Randall told me he has a precious 12 year-old little girl and a 25 year-old son that is just a great son. He said he has been blessed with a wonderful family. He said, "I truly do love life and I appreciate my time here every single minute. I was on the waiting list for a new kidney but they told me there was a huge chance that my heart could not take the transplant operation so I took my name off the list. Why should I take that chance and take a kidney from someone that don't have a heart condition like mine and cheat them outa' life. Heck, I've already been here for 51 years." He's telling this to a man 15 years-older than him, I was in total awe of his complete unselfishness.

He was laughing and smiling while we were talking, this was not an unhappy person. He was delighted after he asked my age and I said 66. He told me I was very blessed. I told him I knew I was very blessed with good health. He really laughed when I answered his question, "You must have serious strong legs sir?" with, "I can squeeze a rhinoceros in half with 'em." His attitude about life has made a difference in the way I now look at my own Life. Oh, and Randall said dialysis was a piece a cake.

Pure Love

Pure Love contains everything needed to mend not only the broken heart, it contains everything needed to mend the world. Pure Love contains wisdom, peace, freedom, respect, tolerance, understanding, beauty, gentleness, giving, kindness, and everything good and positive. The Love I speak of loses its purity when tainted by, anger, hatred, blame, complaint, greed, envy, spite, and all things bad and negative. In my mind, the epitome of human Love is exhibited when that precious newborn is placed in its mother's arms. Believe it or not, there is a Love even greater than that sacred event. It comes from the source which created that mother's Love. I found this Love completely on my own, without assistance from any manmade group. All I want is to be able to share the absolute beauty of what I've found. I have found the beauty of Life.

Collins, Mississippi

5/11/13. I made the decision this morning to walk through the town of Collins, Mississippi, instead of staying on the by-pass. Leaving town, I became concerned whether I should go straight or turn on route 49 to get me back to route 84 and to McDonalds. As I was crossing at a red light, I asked an old black gentleman stopped for the light if I were going the right way. He was turning right after his stop so I was keeping him from making his turn. Getting impatient he motioned with his hand for me to go on and get across so he could make his turn. I started to ask him again but he just motioned again for me to hurry up across. As soon as he made his turn, he pulled into a bank across the street and got out of his vehicle and walked up to the ATM. He was very crippled in one leg and the walk was obviously a struggle for him. He looked over at me and I tried to ask directions one more time but he turned his head away from me. Just before I had to make my decision of which way to go, I saw a gentleman sitting on his porch and he gave me the help I needed. Almost immediately after getting my directions, a car pulled alongside me. It was the gentleman with the bad leg. He said, "Man, I owe you an apology. Man, I was hurtin' real bad this mornin' and jus' goin' to get money to fill my prescription to help me sum wit' this pain man." Even though I told him it was okay and I now knew where I was going, he insisted on making sure I knew exactly where I was going. He explained to me, "Man, I got to thinkin' after you passed, man, that poor man don't know where he's at in a strange town and I said to myself, that jus' ain't right man... it jus ain't right. So I jus' had to turn around and find you sir. You love life too sir." I love all animals but we humans are my favorite! Had the gentleman not been in pain and impatient with me, I would not have had the honor of seeing a real man displaying real character.

A Pepper n' Crackers

On 5/12/13 I did 18 miles and ended up about 5 miles east of Prentiss, Mississippi in spite of being held up by rain. A young man in a 4x4 truck showing much more mud than paint pulled right up in the waist deep weeds alongside me and handed me a cold Dr. Pepper, a package of peanut butter crackers and said, "Here, now tell me yer story." I did and he said, "This world needs people like y'all a tellin' their story. Y'all ever come through Terrible Creek again; I'll bring ya another Peppa' and some more peanut butter crackas'." Laughing a delightful laugh, he pulled back onto the highway. I drank my Peppa' and ate my crackas'.

Friendship Baptist Church

In a little community called Friendship, after being in the rain for about a half hour I spotted the Friendship Baptist Church with the typical big overhang over the main entrance and headed for it for refuge. There were several cars there. There was also a funeral procession arriving at the adjacent graveyard. I always feel kinda' bad when I know all the grieving family members are seeing my "LOVE LIFE" sign... oh well. Anyway, I was under the overhang just waiting out the downpour when a man holding a little boy in his arms came up and asked my story. I told my story to Walter McLaurin and his 19 month-old grandson, Alijah Denzel. Walter asked me to tell my story to the handful of men in the fellowship hall. The men were preparing a catfish dinner for all the mothers in the church in celebration of Mother's Day. I told my story and the pastor gave me a plate filled with fried Mississippi catfish. Someone said, "ya gotta' give 'im some sweets man." So he heaped on a humongous piece of homemade red velvet cake! While eating I was thoroughly entertained by little Alijah Denzel who Walter said was named after Denzel Washington. Walter followed me out and just kept asking me more questions. He was a delightful gentleman. It soon stopped raining and I strapped "LOVE LIFE" back on and walked on down the road.

Waterproof, Louisiana

I walked into Waterproof and at Bubba's Grocery, Deli, & Gas, as I was checking out a good spot to park my cart while I grabbed a bite, a voice said, "Just leave it there I'll watch it for you." It was Waterproof Police Officer Mack Melton. He wanted to know my story and we talked awhile. Mack said, "Ya know what's really funny about Waterproof?" I looked at him and he finished with, "Our mayor's name is Mr. Flood, ain't that just funny as hell."

Just before I camped, Tensas Parish Deputy Sheriff Chris Goad pulled alongside me. "Hey," he said, "The sheriff was in the office when I went in after I left you and he asked me about you. I told 'im, heck I got his card, let's look 'im up. Me and the sheriff checked out your story for a long time. We saw where you got the key to the city of Canton, Ohio and Oakland, California too. It was really interesting and me and the sheriff really enjoyed it." He then told me where I could camp on some private property owned by the Chief Deputy's father. I said thank you to Chris and he really touched my heart with, "No sir, we thank you."

A Mother Teresa Story

May, 2013, near Monroeville, Alabama. Edith Ferguson, and her son John, stopped and wanted to know my story and I of course shared it. They offered their home to me and I politely said no because I was trying to get in a few more miles. A few more miles down the road at a c-store, a man called me by name and said his wife said he should meet me. It was Bill Ferguson, and he said if I would come to their home for the night, he would drive me back the next day. We had steak for dinner, got a shower and did my laundry: Life is good! They offered me a room in their home but I chose the privacy of my tent. The Ferguson family dropped me off the next morning. I started late because Edith insisted on fixing me a huge breakfast. A few days later they tracked me down to bring me some cough drops for my mild cold, Gatorade, and a sub sandwich.

Over a week later, the Fergusons came to my recue yet once again, bringing my lost map atlas they had found on the road back to me at Waynesboro, Mississippi. I had mapped out my entire route in the atlas. It had laid out in the elements for a week. Edith had gone to great measures to dry it out for me. She used a hair dryer and an iron, Bill told me. They brought me more cough drops, more Gatorade and another huge sub sandwich. They drove 180 miles round trip to bring me my maps.

Edith told me when she was a very young lady growing up in the Philippines, she decided to become a nun. During her training she was assigned to someplace in Rome. Whatever the place was Mother Teresa was actually there at the same time. She said she went in to tell her superiors that she just didn't think she could do it. She said, that Mother Teresa herself told her that being a nun was not for everyone and for her to go home. And that when the time was right she would find a good man, marry, and raise a wonderful family. She patted her precious young hand, and said, "Go on now and do not worry about it." The tears streamed down her face as she told me her special story... I felt honored.

In Transylvania

In Transylvania, Louisiana, where the water tower has a big black bat painted on it. There is a large Mennonite population there. I went into a restaurant for breakfast, the sign simply says, "the farm house @ TRANSYLVANIA." I told the waitress what I wanted and she said some lady had come in and paid for it already. While I was eating, the owner came over and told me the lady who paid for my breakfast had stopped to talk to me about an hour earlier. I barely remembered her stopping and our brief conversation. She said the lady had really been touched by my story. She said the generous lady had a troubled son who had been giving her problems for years and was now back in jail. I told her to please tell the lady thank you for my meal and that I will keep her and her son in my heart. They let me charge up my stuff, gave me bottles of water and a bag of ice. As I was leaving, my waitress ran out the door with the five I had left for a tip and just flat refused to accept it. She said, "I would like to help too please."

Just down the road at the Farmers Supply Company, owned by Mennonite Phil Schroeder, I spotted a bunch of rocking chairs on the porch that looked to be the perfect place to sit and repair one of my trekking poles. An employee said it would be fine and to take my time. The owner, Phil, came out and wanted to hear my story. It took so long to fix my stick I figured I might as well go ahead and fix all the problems I was having with the cart. When I went in to purchase the hardware I needed, Phil would not let me pay for anything. And he started helping me with my repairs. Each time he handed me an item I requested, while refusing my money, he would say, "Now you go back out there and take your time and just relax." He and his employee's kept bringing me cokes. I was there for nearly three hours and I accomplished much.

No Mustard!?

In the tiny community of Afton, Louisiana I went into a very small place called Double D's Barbecue. I went up to the order window with menu in hand, and mind finally made up on a choice. "I'll take the rib plate please" I requested. "Dat's only Satadeys." she said. I looked at the menu again and sure enough, "Only on Saturday for plate lunches" was penciled in at the top of the menu. After studying the menu again... thoroughly this time, I said, "I'll take the double cheeseburger all the way with mayo." She said, "You wants mustard too, right?" "No ma'am, I just want mayo." She shakes her head as if to say, "Y'all just have no idea about anything if you don't like mustard and mayo together." She then started making huge patties by hand, so I asked, "Ma'am can you cook those very rare for me please?" "You means you only wants 'em half cooked!?" and shaking her head again, she mumbled, "and no mustard." She hollered over while the burgers were frying and asked what sides I wanted. She said they never had the sweet potato fries I wanted, as was the answer for the next two sides I requested, which were all on the menu by the way. So I asked if I could have some potato salad and she said that would be okay. She finally handed me a huge double cheeseburger with everything on it. It was not the slightest bit rare, not even pink, but I'm telling y'all right now, that was one of the best damn cheeseburgers I've had in years! The lady, who, was the only person working in the eatery and doing everything herself, heads for the door and looking over at me says, "I'm going to the store next door and get your potato salad, I'll be right back." I told her the cheeseburger was filling me up and I really didn't need the potato salad. She said, "Okay," and went back to cleaning her grill. Now I ask y'all, is that laid back or what? I love it! Love Life my friends.

Alabama Kindness

I started one morning about 7:30 and was Loving Life just because I can, and because I was breathing air that didn't cost me a damn thing, nor was there a charge for the view offered by beautiful Alabama. Those beautiful Alabama hills were talking to me that morning. They were saying, "Yo ass ain't doin' no twenty mile day today honey chile!" A pretty lady pulled up beside me and while handing me a Styrofoam container with wonderful smells coming from it, said, "Suh, we saw y'all the other day in Dothan and we just wanted to help ya some, there's just not a big selection of restaurants in Elba... so hee-ah." It was crammed full of sausages, grits with cheese, sausage gravy, and the best darn biscuit I ever ate! There was an ice cold coke too. Around 10:00 am as I was entering Elba, with a very full belly, a man stopped and said he had recently begun following my walk on Facebook. He said, "You look like you can use a break." I told him I was doing great and that I wasn't quite ready for a break yet. He said, "If I give you the money specifically for a motel room, will you get a room?" I smiled big (I Love motel rooms) and said that indeed I would. He said he wasn't going to give me his name because he didn't want to be acknowledged on Fb. Smiling, he said, "You seem to tell all on Facebook." "Not if I'm asked not to," I said. I asked would it be okay to tell the story without his name and he said that would be fine. And that's why I only did a little over six miles that day. I enjoyed my day off and prepared to challenge the Alabama hills again the next day with a most vigorous Love Life attitude.

Loving Life in Enterprise, Alabama

In Enterprise, Alabama, one morning a truck pulled beside me and the guy started yelling, "Thank you! Thank you! Thank you!" He was pumping his fist in the air and continued with, "Yes, I love life! God I love life!" and, "I love you!" As he drove off he was still pumping his fist in the air and yelling, "I love life! Yes, yes, yes!" Wow! He was a very tall black man with a most wonderful smile and was driving a pretty new bright red Ford pickup. If you live in the Enterprise, Alabama area, I highly suggest you try and locate this man and then hang out with him every chance you get. I loved it!

Tallulah, Alabama, Picture Takin'

Walking through Tallulah, Louisiana, I encountered a group of men in front of the police station, the chief of police being one of them. One guy insisted the police chief let him take a picture of the chief with me. And *then* the picture takin' began! Each person there then decided they too wanted their picture taken with me, as did the original photographer. While I was taking a picture of the police chief, he invited Rev. Jones to be photographed with him. And then a detective came around the corner of the building and the chief insisted he get in the picture. Two more people were then invited into the group. The chief asked me a lot of questions and I watched the expression on both he and Rev. Jones' faces go from jovial to compassionate when I told of my son's suicide and why I walked. They all wished me well and safe travels. Rev. Jones shook my hand and said, "It's a good thing you do, I'll pray for you sir."

Old Friends in Louisiana

I left my room about 10:30 and started north toward Arkansas while watching closely for my friend Misty Clark and her two children who had a two hour drive north to Tallulah. Her husband Ricky was working in the East Texas oil fields and couldn't make it. Just outside town I heard a horn blowing repeatedly behind me, and of course I knew who it was, it was my friend, cute little Misty Clark, loving wife of my friend and proud husband Ricky Clark. Misty says this about herself in her Fb profile:

I'm a three-wheeler ridin, mud-diggin, hay haulin, log draggin, sawmill helpin, hard-workin, cow raisin, friend lovin, truck drivin, wife, mother, and tough as nails true blue woman! A small town girl, married for 11 years to the best husband in the world and have two wonderful, beautiful, kids! I love my family and friends, love gettin muddy and dirty on my three-wheeler, campin, bass fishin, trout-linin, snaggin, yo-yoin, jiggin & raisin my boxer puppies. We raise our own meat, haul our own hay, saw our own logs and raise our own garden.

I know she is indeed all of that, but that sweet lady was nothing but tears when she wrapped her arms around my neck and said, "Ricky said to take you and get you a motel room!" We loaded my cart in her truck and went back to the same room I had last night. Her children, 11 year-old Elijah and 8 year-old Rachael are wonderful! We spent several hours just goofing off and reminiscing about when we first met on the road on my first walk across Louisiana in 2003 while walking around the United States. Ricky joined us for a long time via speaker phone from the oil fields somewhere in Texas. Little Rachel loves to hug and added several to my immense hug collection. She entertained me during our visit making "LOVE LIFE" posters. She also wrote "LOVE LIFE" in the dirt on the tailgate of their white truck. I had a wonderful time with all my friends in Louisiana and I most definitely LOVE LIFE.

Love all Animals

Entering a grocery store in a small town in Mississippi, a gentleman in a red shirt, approached me, pointed over to where I had left my cart with the "LOVE LIFE" sign propped up so that all might see, and asked, "Does that Love of Life include animals?" "Of course it does, all animals are a part of Life," I responded. A few minutes later a young man, an employee of the grocery store came up to me with an ice cream bar, chuckled and said, "Here, some guy in a red shirt bought this and asked me to bring it to you." That ice cream was delicious, it was filled with good thoughts.

"Who is cruel to animals becomes hard also in his dealings with men. We can judge the heart of a man by his treatment of animals." ~ Emmanuel Kant

Love Will Spread

Love of Life is just the obvious first use of love to get our day started. Love will then spread out from there toward all in our path the rest of the day... that's simply the power of love. I believe when we try ever so hard to Love Life no matter what is in front of us then love precedes us. The light of love cannot shine from us unless we first turn on the light switch. Treat Life as a person you see in your room when you awake, reach over and grab them and make them to do exactly what you want to do that day. Repeat this daily until Life automatically does exactly what you want every day. You will eventually discover it was but your own reflection in the mirror, you'll recognize the smile.

Y'all Walks!

In Mississippi, I was sitting on my cart outside a c-store taking my ten minute break of every two hours. Two cars full of ladies had pulled up in front of me and one lady had ran over to the other car to greet them. The one out of the car looked at me and said, "Honey, do y'all ride that thing?" I chuckled and said, "I wish I could. No ma'am I pull this behind me as I walk the country. "Walk!" she said, "You mean honey that y'all walks! And y'all pulls 'at thing behind ya!" She asked why and I proceeded to tell my story. After telling of the loss of my children she just put both hands to her mouth in astonishment and was shaking her head. She said, "No honey, no, you lost both you babies!" She then came right to me, bent down, and placed her pretty black cheek right next to mine and gave me a firm heartfelt hug. I thanked her for her compassion. She walked over to the car and I heard her telling her friends, "This man here done lost both his babies!" The driver side door opened and out came another beautiful lady who promptly walked over and placed her arms around my neck! There is compassion abounding in this world. I left there crying. Love Life my friends.

Headin' for Memphis

May, 2013. Just past a spot in the road, Shelby, Mississippi, I got caught in an awesome storm for about 30 minutes. I got real wet but in no time was real dry and real happy. A pretty young woman in front of a convenience store, Courtney Stevens, asked if she could take my picture and interview me for the local paper, the Bolivar Commercial. While she was interviewing me, three youngsters came up to us and started asking me all kinds of questions. Courtney, wisely, just recorded the kids asking me questions and then added a couple of her own.

A young man and his wife came up to me after watching my interview with Courtney, and said they were the ones hitchhiking toward Memphis earlier in the morning that had hollered and waved at me. I remembered them; they had been sitting on all kinds of luggage holding out their thumbs. They introduced themselves as Jesse and Samantha. Jesse said, "I heard most of your interview sir. Me and Samantha have lost two children, they were both stillborn" I told them how very sorry I was for their loss. Jesse went on, "I lost two with my first wife also. My wife was six months pregnant with twins, and we were in a car wreck and she miscarried." Again, I expressed how very sorry I was that he had to suffer the horrible pain of losing four babies. Jesse said he and Samantha were trying to make it into Memphis and possibly find work. They were picking up all their stuff getting ready to go back up to the highway and try their luck again, and Jesse said to me, "Hey mister, will you keep me and Samantha in your prayers please, we really need 'em right now." "Yes I certainly will Jesse; I have you and Samantha firmly in my heart as of right now," I told him.

"Prayer is but hope from the heart generated by Love for the wellbeing of another."
~ Steve Fugate

The Same Pain

After doing 22 miles I was in my tent in an open field next to a rice storage facility in Boyle, Mississippi. Robert and Michele Mosley from Boyle said they saw my interview on the news on the Greenville station. They said they were hoping they would see me on the highway. They explained that today would have been their little girl, Robyn's 37th birthday. They lost her to a brain tumor when she was 30. They said what I was doing touched them very much and that they were inspired by the way I've chosen to handle my pain. I can't have my babies back, I can't take away the pain, so, I have to move onward and upward. What better way to do that than being able to influence others positively, including those who've suffered that same pain.

Myrt in Mississippi

One morning in June 2013 Myrt pulled her SUV up in front of me, got out and walked up to me and said, "I saw you on TV and I just drove sixty miles to give you a hug!" "Well, bring it on," I said, "I collect hugs!" She wrapped her little arms around my neck and started crying. She said, "You have touched me like you'll never know. You have inspired me so very much." She asked me was there anything she could do for me and I said no, that I was just fine. She wrote down her full name and phone number and said, "When you get into Clarksdale, call me and we'll come and get you and give you a place to stay for the night." She started heading back for her car and stopped, turned around and said, "Ya know, I love you." How sweet is that! I told her I loved her too. She then turned her car around and headed back in the direction she came. The responses I get never cease to astound me.

In Clarksdale, Mississippi, I called Myrt and true to her word, she came and got me. She took me to lunch and then to her home where we had awesome conversation. I just had to ask what inspired her so much that she just jumped in her car and drove 60 miles to hug me after seeing me on her local news. She told me that four days before Thanksgiving Day, her husband of 40 years calmly told her he was having an affair and wanted a divorce. Whoa, just like that, that's got to be a serious jolt for anyone. She said the divorce procedure has been extremely stressful. She said she hardly ever watches TV and never watches that particular station I was on, and she came upon it by accident. She said she wanted to click onto channel 5 and accidentally hit channel 6 that had my interview. She said, "When I saw "LOVE LIFE" over your head I said, that's it by golly, that's it, I've been stuck in this divorce stuff and it's just time to move on and get back to loving life as I always have!" She also told me she Googled me immediately and found the poem I had dedicated to my babies, "Tiny Dancers." That, she said, was the final push which made her say, "That's it, I'm going to go hug this man!" She truly touched my heart.

"Tiny Dancers" I wrote as a tribute to my children to assure them I am indeed learning, and that I am indeed allowing my pain to further my understanding of life:

Tiny Dancers

In a song, "Hold me closer tiny dancer"
A thought imbedded, in my heart that is.
I've two Tiny Dancers I no longer see.
Oh, just to hold closer,
but a moment, but a moment please!
My Tiny Dancers forever heart bound
making me reach way inside

so as to feel, so as to know,
to thine own heart be true.
Knowing life has placed all just right,
right where all belongs exactly.
Oh beautiful the mystery of life.
My Tiny Dancers on a floor unseen,
inside my being, turning, twirling, for me,
beckoning, come follow and see.
Watch as we twirl upon our dance floor
in a pattern of steps beyond your world.
Beyond pain lies the beauty of life,
a remedy within, upon a floor of glass
from which to watch... oh my,
the feet of my two Tiny Dancers,
Oh my... oh my.

"He's here for Us Man."

In Greenville, Mississippi, two black gentlemen, Fred Dotson, and his friend Sherrod Brothers, got out of their car to talk. Fred immediately said, "I want my picture with you and I want to hear exactly what you are doing and why. I want to hear everything you have to say, please." After I would say something or answer one of Fred's questions, he would say it again very slowly to his friend Sherrod. Evidently Sherrod had a hearing problem for he seemed quite bright otherwise. I was really touched by the patience Fred had with his friend, there was a sweetness about it. He wanted to make certain his friend understood every word I said. Fred said to me, "People like you are here for people like us man. You follow your heart man, that's why. Everything happens for a reason man, I just lost my sister to cancer man and it's killin' me man. God bless you man for carin' about others man." He looked at Sherrod and very slowly said, "He's here for others, he's here for us man." And with a big beautiful smile on his face, Sherrod said, "Thank you for doing that sir." I bet Fred shook my hand ten times at least, and nearly every time, he placed his other hand on top mine. It was a very touching encounter for me. I really admired the love and concern Fred showed for his friend Sherrod.

Police and Gatorade, Walls, Mississippi

In Walls, Mississippi, about four miles from Memphis, Walls police officer Lance Wade, stopped me with his lights flashing, checked my ID and asked my story. While they were running my driver's license, Lance pulls out his phone and said, "I gotta' get yer picture man." That made me smile. I asked if there was a Dollar General store in the area and he told me no but that there was a convenience store just up the road. I explained I can get Gatorade and PowerAde a lot cheaper at Dollar General. About ten minutes later Lance comes back, with his lights flashing again, and hands me a red Gatorade and says, "Sure hope you like this flavor." I thanked him and he left. About 15 minutes later officer Wade pulls up yet again, with lights flashing yet again, got out with a larger orange flavored Gatorade in his hand. He said, "I've got the camcorder going in my car, the department told me to get me handing you a Gatorade on film and for you to tell your story." Okay, so I did. First time that ever happened!

Let's Not Lose Him!

About two miles from Memphis, Jermaine and Tawanda Hudson from Ruleville, Mississippi pulled up and Tawanda started excitingly telling me they had seen me on TV. She said she wanted her picture taken with me. I told her that would be fine but I wanted a picture of her and her family as well. She asked her son, 17 year-old Ja'Marcus Davis, to get out of the car and have his picture taken with her and Jermaine. When Ja'Marcus stepped from the vehicle he had a backpack in his hand and I watched him slip it on his back. I couldn't figure out what he was doing and then I saw the tube running from it and into his stomach. Tawanda explained to me that her son has liver cancer and his stomach is filled with large tumors. They had just left St. Jude's in Memphis, where he gets chemo through an IV every 3 weeks and he also takes chemo in pill form. Tawanda said Ja'Marcus is starting to gain a little weight and the doctors are confident the tumors are shrinking. Ja'Marcus gets very tired they said after the treatments and he told me bye and went back to the car. Tawanda said she was not going to lose him! I couldn't help it; the tears flowed as I told them I would have Ja'Marcus in my heart and that I would ask all my Facebook friends to please have her little boy in their hearts for positive thoughts, prayers, meditations or whatever's! "Damn, he's only 17," I said on Facebook, "let's not lose him!"

Memphis

Walking facing the busy morning traffic heading into Memphis, I looked up to see a garbage truck with lights flashing nearly coming to a stop as all three occupants had their cell phones raised to take my picture. It was so funny! I gave them a smile and a wave and they all gave me thumbs up. What a way to start my day!

Just past Graceland a guy passed me walking extremely fast, I was impressed! He had to stop for the light so I caught up to him and complimented him on how fast he walked. He said that both he and his two sons are walk racers and that his sons actually compete. I had never heard of it before. His name is John and he is a massage therapist specializing in sports medicine, from Charlotte, North Carolina. He said he was in Memphis for a week with a pro-golfer client of his competing in the FedEx St. Jude Classic and that the tournament's sole beneficiary is St. Jude Children's Research Hospital in Memphis, Tennessee. The tournament is one of the oldest continuously-operated stops on the PGA. He asked what I was doing. We talked right through at least four "WALK" lights and then he said, "Would you be so kind as to let me donate to what you are doing?" Blew my mind! I said yes and he pulled from his jogging shorts pocket, a twenty dollar bill. Bless his heart. On down the Elvis Presley Blvd a couple miles and a big guy named Mark Hampton yelled out, "Hey, I'm a truck driver and I saw you in Greenville, Mississippi last week! Come on over here and we'll get ya a couple sandwiches and a cold drink." I did so and met all his friends who were volunteering with him doing work for the Memphis Community Life Center.

Halls, Tennessee

Near Halls, Tennessee, Tommy stopped and helped me get the night's motel room. His little boy, Neylan, was waving vigorously at me from the other side of daddy's truck. When I acknowledged him and spoke to him, Tommy said, "That's Neylan, and he told me to stop and give you some money." Wow. Love Life my friends. And uh, pass it on to your kids.

About two miles from Dyersville, Tennessee motels, I was rescued from the rain storm by a young lady. She stopped and said she had seen me on Facebook. She took me to lunch where her mother, and little brother, were waiting for her. You should have seen her mother's face when her pretty 22 year-old daughter walked into the restaurant with an old man who was a total stranger. The stranger part lasted less than five minutes. We were soon laughing and having a blast. By the way, not long after we entered the eatery, the hail started falling. Sure glad the young lady finally talked me into the ride. I had turned down one earlier about five miles out. On the way to drop me off at the motel, she and I had a great talk. The sweet young lady has had four miscarriages. Bless her heart.

Don't Thank Me Thank Him

Saturday before Father's Day, 2013 at Wickliffe, Kentucky, inside a c-store called The Trading Post, I began telling my story to the two clerks, a lady probably in her late fifties and a young lady in her early twenties. I tell my story sometimes several times a day and I've been doing this for many years now. But I guess Father's Day was pressing harder on me than I realized. After I told that both my babies were now gone, the older clerk said, "Today must really be hard on you?" and I absolutely lost it! I just stood there at the counter crying. I just couldn't keep it together like I always do. I kept trying to finish my story and I just kept choking up! I said, "I'm sorry, please forgive me." The older lady said, "It's perfectly alright honey, you stand there and cry all day if ya want." The younger one just had a sweet and understanding look on her face. I pulled myself back together.

About a half hour later, still in the store, I walked over to where I had my cell phone plugged in and checked the status of the charging. While standing there with my phone in hand, a very tall blonde man, maybe in his mid-thirties, and wearing a red t-shirt, walked up to me real fast and said, "Is that your sign and cart out there… here," and handed me some folded up bills before I had a chance to even answer. I caught glimpse of a hundred on the top and I said, "Oh, thank you sir!" He had turned immediately heading for the door, he never even turned around and with his index finger pointed skyward, he said, "Don't thank me, thank him." I put my phone back down to finish charging and headed for the door to tell him more how much I appreciated and needed his generous gift. Before I even made it to the door, I saw him get in his car and leave. I looked at the folded bills and there was $200.00. I asked the two clerks if they knew him, they did not.

Nicky's B-B-Q

One morning just outside of Clinton, KY I spotted a restaurant, Nicky's B-B-Q. I headed towards it hoping it would be opened and serving breakfast. As I walked onto the parking lot a gentleman came out the door and asked how I was doing, I asked him the same, we both said fine and then he said, "Have you eaten yet sir?" I told him that as a matter of fact I was heading inside to purchase breakfast. He said, "You'll not pay for it here, this is on me." I was obviously speaking to Nicky. Inside, my breakfast was wonderful, I charged my stuff, and the conversation with Nicky was the best! Nicky brought out a bag of ice as I was preparing to leave and dumped in my cooler. Again, he would not let me pay. If you're ever in Clinton, Kentucky, please stop at Nicky's B-B-Q and say HI to Nicky McClanahan.

Little Woman, Big Heart, Big Gun

A Kentucky Highway Patrol Trooper pulled her cruiser up in front of me and when she stepped out of the car I could not believe how small she was. She was petite. I would call her dainty looking, but that huge gun on her hip stops that description. Once she started talking I forgot about her stature. She was a very confident individual completely sure of herself. She had a terrific smile she greeted me with and then immediately said, "When I saw your sign, I knew I had to find out your story." As soon as I finished telling my story, she asked, "What is your philosophy, what is your creed, what do you tell people about suicide?" We talked for quite a while. As we shook hands and were preparing to leave, Trooper A. Ramsey reached into her shirt pocket and then handed me eleven dollars. "It's not much." She said, "But I want to help. There's a restaurant just up the road, get you something to eat with it." She was way cool! I met a guy in Bardwell, Lou, and I mentioned the trooper to him. Lou said he knew her and that she was an outstanding trooper who was firm but also fair. Lou said all the men he knew who had had dealings with her, have great respect for Trooper Ramsey. Love Life my friends above everything else it only gets better.

Small Kentucky Town

In a little place called Cayce (pronounced Cay-see), Kentucky, I sat in the only act in town, the Cayce Café, filled with farmers speaking of seeding, spraying, combines and such. They went behind the counter to get their own coffee. The cook came out between orders and laughs with them as she smoked her cigarette. The farmers were all big and muscular, except for one; she was a young lady wearing bibbed overalls that did not even begin to hide her beauty. She was sitting next to her father that she patted on the shoulder both rising and reseating; both times she left the table. He smiled each time. Love Life, get out and notice it and you'll do a lot less bitchin' about what you only see of it on the news. Could help get rid of some of the fear of Life the news causes also?

Second Thoughts?

Yesterday in Hickman, Kentucky as I was climbing a very steep hill, a lady going in the opposite direction stopped her car and said, "Here, I got you a Mountain Dew." I walked over to get it and she blurted out, "Do you *really* love life!" "I most definitely love life!" I answered. She said she lost her husband not quite two years ago and life was just too hard. She was obviously very distraught. I told her we needed to talk, that I could help change her mind about loving life. I asked her to please turn around and meet me at the top of the hill about 100 feet away, where there was a "pull over" across from the police station.

I walked to the spot and waited, she took longer than she should have to come back and meet me. Second thoughts I suppose. As soon as she pulled up I said, "You didn't meet me by accident." Christy told me she had passed me twice before getting up the courage to stop. I told Christy of losing both my babies. She was obviously moved, stating that she couldn't begin to imagine losing one of hers. She said that life was just getting to her. That it was nearing two years since she lost her husband, her childhood sweetheart she had three children with. She said she was just weary of having to do everything alone and of being alone. "Just everything!" she said, sobbing. I asked her, "What is the one thing that has you down more than anything else and keeps you from being able to have joy?" She instantly replied, "Losing my wonderful husband! He was only forty!" I said, "You obviously loved your husband very much." Crying, she said, yes she did. I said, "Your husband must have loved you very much too." "Oh, he did, he did." she said. I asked her had she enjoyed pleasing her husband and seeing him have joy in his life. Of course she said yes. I asked did she think he felt the same way about her having joy in her life. She said, "Oh yes!" I told her that my two children loved their daddy with all their hearts and they wanted my happiness as I always wanted theirs. I told her I felt it my duty to show respect to the memory of my precious babies by giving them what they would have wanted... my happiness. I told her she owed that fine man she was married to the proper respect by giving him what he would have wanted, her to love life once again.

I told Christy that self-pity is a useless negative which has to be converted into self-reliance. I told her my favorite quote by Kahlil Gibran, "Your pain is the breaking of the shell which encloses your understanding." I told her I knew it was extremely difficult to do, but it is just something she has to do to get her life back on track. I said, "You've got to take a stand on your own and just plain old, reach down, and pull yourself up by the bootstraps!" I asked her, "If your husband was here right now, what would he say to you?" Still crying, she answered, "He would tell me to get it together and be strong!" "Yup," I said, "he was indeed a good man!" Now go please your first and only true love by loving life with all your heart, no matter what!" She said she had never heard it put that way before and that she would try very hard to love life as she used to. I told her I would have her in my heart. She said, "You be safe out there sir." Love your Life my friends, just as it is right now. This will calm you down and clear the way for you to see things better and remove negative obstacles from your path with ease.

Brandi and Little Holden

6/25/13. In Kentucky, just across the Ohio River from Mount Vernon, Indiana. Chris, whose property joins the ballpark I was tented in, came over to see what I was doing there. I explained and he then drove me over to his house where I could charge my phone overnight on an outside outlet so I could grab it early this morning. Then about 9:30, four lovely young ladies came by to take pictures with me and gave me a huge piece of cake. They said they followed me on Facebook. About 10:00 Mary Jo and her daughter,

Deidra, brought me some lasagna. They too were Facebook friends. They started telling me of a young lady they knew who had recently lost her nine month-old little boy, Holden who had been sick from birth with seizures and how hard the little 21 year-old mommy fought for the life of her child. They said that the mother's sister, precious little Holden's aunt, saw my "LOVE LIFE" sign yesterday and said, "That's it Holden, I'm hearing you loud and clear baby boy... love life!" The story really touched me and I asked them to call me with the info on how to contact the young mommy who was facing the horror of horrors.

Tom Gibbs stopped and gave me a ride over the very narrow bridge into Indiana. Tom said his wife and daughter told him I would be needing a ride over the bridge and to look for me on his way to work. About noon, after I reached Mount Vernon, a car pulled over and two pretty young ladies got out to talk to me, a brunette and a blonde. The brunette, Brittany, said, "We've been looking for you, we're on your Facebook and we're friends of Mary Jo and Deidra." I said, "Great, they were supposed to give me info about a young lady who had just lost her baby boy." Brittany pointed to the little blonde and said, "You're looking at her, that's my sister Brandi." I immediately held my arms out and said, "Come here baby!" I stood there and just held that precious baby girl whose precious baby boy, little Holden, had died in her arms. As I was hugging her daughter, their mother, Katrina, emerged from the car as well. We all four were crying as we talked of little Holden. Brandi just kept hugging me. I just felt so very much love for that child and what she had just gone through. We must have been a sight standing on the street in downtown Mount Vernon, Indiana, all four bawling. Brandi said my words to her helped her very much.

Gateway to Happiness

Love Life, it truly is our gateway to happiness. When we show our appreciation for our precious gift of Life we are rewarded with inner peace. Inner peace brings joy and contentment. Only Love puts the broken hearted back on path to the beauty of Life and only Love of Life can light the way. The more real Love we're capable of giving, the more Love we're then eligible to receive.

Fight from Inside

On a Sunday, walking through Quincy, Illinois, an older lady in a really beat up early 90's T-bird drove past pointing at me all excited and saying something, but I was unable to hear her. There were wooden wedges keeping the power windows from falling down. A few minutes later she pulled alongside me. She had to be at least 80. Her hair was dyed jet black though. She offered me a ride which I turned down. She was very sweet and kept asking me was there anything she could do for me. She was very frail and just did not look healthy at all. And all of a sudden she said, "What would you do if six attorney's, two judges, and your family members turned on you?" I immediately said, "Forgive them and get on with my life." She said, "This has destroyed me." I said, "Fight back." She said that she was fighting. I said, "I'm not talking about that kind of fighting, I'm talking about fighting to get your joy back so you can love life again." She looked stunned, like she had never even thought about that. I told her I had lost both my babies and she put both her little skinny hands over her heart and told me how very sorry she was. Neither of us said anything for a minute, then she said to me, "But they have my money." I told her that I once lived with a girlfriend who was worth several million dollars. And that I became quite unhappy in the situation and just put my backpack on one day and left. I was 60 at the time and even though the backpack was at least 50 pounds, I jumped up in the air and clicked my heels together while climbing a steep hill! I was free, I got my joy back. She laughed with delight at my story. She really cracked up when I told her I was singing verses from that Paul Simon song, "No need to be coy Roy. Just hop out the back Jack! Make a new plan Stan. Don't need to discuss much, jus' get yourself free." I said, "Look, I'm not telling you that you shouldn't try and get what's rightfully yours, I'm simply saying, get your priorities straight. Your joy and having peace of mind is worth more than any amount of money. And when you are at peace within yourself you think much clearer and things just plain old go much smoother. Just forgive everybody and get your joy back." She just was totally delighted and said, "I knew I was supposed to stop and talk to you. I'm going to try, I'm going to really try. Thank you very much!" She offered me a ride one more time and then drove away smiling. I didn't give her some great revelation, I just spoke a simple fact that we all really know to be true deep down inside us. Life is so very simple, the reason I Love Life so very much.

"Many do not get to see the goodness in people that I see, because they're moving too fast. Objects do not blur when I walk past, nor do individuals. Slow down and give the eyes of your heart time to focus in on what the eyes of colored irises are seeing." ~ Steve Fugate

Posey County, Sheriff's Department Donation

Well, another first for me when Trinity Becker, of the Posey County Sheriff's Department came up to me as I walked out of the Dollar General store and said she had been looking all over for me. She said she was on my Facebook page and had told Sheriff Greg, about me and he said, "Well, go find him and find out what we can do for him." I told her I needed nothing and she left saying she had better get back to work. Later, still in the same parking lot while I was being interviewed by a wonderful young lady for the local paper, The Mount Vernon Democrat, Trinity, came back and handed me an envelope with money they had collected at the sheriff's office to buy me a meal at the China Buffet. The reporter took a picture of me accepting the donation. The meal was great.

Fuzz Patton and Freckles

Figure 17. Fuzz Patton and dog Freckles.

I was busting my butt one evening trying to make it to the crossroads of Illinois route 1 and Illinois 146 to make it to the only store to get some ice and something to eat. I got there 5 minutes too late, the sign in the window said they closed at 6:00. I was a bit disappointed… and hungry. I saw a couple guys at a huge garage across the street and headed over and asked if there was any place else to get food. There wasn't. I asked if it would be okay to pitch my tent behind one of the large buildings. The mechanic working the nightshift, Eric, suggested I pitch my tent inside an empty truck bay in case it were to rain. After I pitched my tent, Eric came over and asked if I was hungry, that he would have one of the coal truck drivers pick up something for us on their way in to have their truck serviced by Eric. I told him that would be great. When the food got there and I went to pay for my part, Eric and the driver who picked up the food both said no way. I tried to pay Eric once more and he refused. He said, "I want to help you, it takes balls to do what you do man!" Is there a thin line between "balls" and just plain ole being nuts?

Come morning I had the pleasure of meeting Charles "Fuzz" Patton and his really cool dog, Freckles. Fuzz has owned the tiny store and gas station at The Crossroads for 37 years. There was once a café too but Fuzz said it was just too much work for him so he shut it down. I had cheese Danish and coffee, Fuzz said the coffee was on the house. On the counter was one of those clear plastic containers holding hot cashews that the attendant scoops out for you with a special little scoop and puts them in a little paper bag for you. I told him I had not seen one of those in years. How cool is it that Fuzz thinks it important enough to keep doing it. He said that years ago, a guy used to come around and service them. Now, he said, he has to special order everything from a little company in Ohio. We talked about how much things have changed. We talked about how hard it is to run a business and lots of other things. I bought a bag of ice and some snacks for the road because Fuzz told me food was at least 15 miles away after I left there. Outside, after I took Fuzz and Freckles picture, Fuzz said to me, "Here these are for later down the road." He handed me one of those little bags stuffed full with warm salted cashews. Freckles licked my other hand... I was good to go. How can one not Love a Life so filled with such wonderful individuals.

The Pain Killer, Giving

June, 2013. Five miles south of a little place called Ridgeway, Illinois. I made it to Reeds Grocery at Cave-In-Rock, IL. Rose Reed, the owner, let me charge my laptop and phone. You just would not believe the breakfast buffet Rose offers up for just $5.00. Rose and I chatted off and on during my three hours there hiding from the rain and charging up me and my stuff. Rose lost two of her sons, to cancer, and to a heart attack, seven years apart. Rose knows pain, but Rose is a very happy person. She would not let me pay for my breakfast. Giving can be used as a pain killer, I prescribe it.

It is more about giving when we truly Love Life than simply loving our own Life and giving but to ourselves. Yes, go Love your life and enjoy all it offers us. But, by all means, learn to Love and give to others before loving only, and giving only, to yourself. Then and only then, does one fully learn to Love their own Life, and only then does the joy of all Life has to offer become much greater. And only then, does one truly learn how to Love Life. If one is living only for their own joy and fulfillment in Life, that one, then, doesn't fully understand what I mean when I say, Love Life. And to really reap all the benefits of a Love Life attitude, we must get beyond but loving and giving to only our family and a few chosen friends. Give without expecting anything in return and your return will blow your mind.

Jared Forgave

I really do LOVE LIFE with all my heart my friends. Joy is an inside job and I am totally responsible for my own joy in life… no one else. I met a young man, Jared, in Best Buy one day who attempted suicide at 13 because of a stupid and cruel thing a teacher said to him. He totally loves his life now. He has found such peace with his love life attitude that he said to me when I grimaced at his telling of the idiotic teacher's statement, "Oh, I forgave her a long time ago and got on with my life." Jared discovered that the ignorant teacher is not responsible for his joy… he is. So he forgave her, got that out of his way and pursued happiness. Jared is really cool.

She Missed Her Friend

6/27/13. In the morning first thing, Frehley, of Mount Vernon, Indiana, was standing next to her car awaiting my approach. She said she worked the third shift and had been searching for me since she got off work. She told me that one of her very best friends killed himself when they were 18 and that she still very much feels the heartache. She had a copy of his obituary with a picture of the very handsome young man. He had been gone four years now. She said he was very popular in school, as was my son, and so many others I've become aware of. She told how she had felt guilty for the first few years and had now come to terms with the guilt realizing there was nothing she could have done for her friend. But most of all she said, she just plain old missed him! A suicide is the hardest form of death for friends, I feel. It leaves them totally bewildered as to why. Not to mention the guilt it creates. At my son's funeral I looked at a building full of fine young ladies and gentleman bidding farewell to their charming, witty, and oh so handsome 26 year-old friend. I saw shock and bewilderment on their precious faces. Bless you Frehley, I know exactly where you're coming from sweetheart. What a friend is Frehley, to still care so much that she hunted me down to talk about him. But a few minutes after Frehley and I parted company, she came back again and had a bag of ice she had purchased for me and promptly dropped it on the road to loosen it, picked it up and emptied it in my cooler. She gave me another hug for my growing hug collection and was gone.

Rick Knight of Grayville, Illinois came up to me and said he had to share the story of his 21 month old grandson who had just been released from the hospital to his 20 year-old mother after 499 days in there! Little Jonah Goodman has Marfan Syndrome, a disease that attacks nearly every part of the body, the palate, the lungs, the joints, the connective tissues, and the little angel's heart. Rick said Jonah was sent home because there was nothing else the doctors could do for that oh so precious baby boy. Rick said to me, "Steve, I know you have a huge following, can you please ask your Facebook followers to send prayers and thoughts for my grandbaby and make more people aware of this horrible disease, Marfan syndrome." And I did.

Page, also from Grayville, walked up to me and handed me a twenty and a black ribbon with Velcro to be worn as an armband. It was embroidered with "Medic 12". Page explained that her EMT partner for years was Robbie Phillips from Albion. That he was Medic 12 and she was Medic 13. Robbie, Medic 12 took his own life two years ago when he was 38. You could see in her eyes the deep pain over losing her friend and other half of her team.

How to get on the Today Show

7/4/13. In the Vandalia, Illinois, Mickey D's, ordering breakfast, the lady waiting on me had seen me pull up with my cart and asked if I was famous. I said no but that one could look me up on the internet and I handed her a card. She asked several questions including, had I ever been featured in a major newspaper. I told her that I had been in USA Today before. She asked for two more cards for her friends. As I was receiving my order, she handed a card to a friend and said pretty loud, "Hey, this guy's been on The Today Show!" I quickly said, "No, I have never been on The Today Show, you misunderstood me, I said USA Today newspaper." The lady said okay but the one she told was now somewhere else in the restaurant. While I was eating I heard twice, "Yeah, he was on The Today Show!" One young lady came up and asked me how long ago I was on The Today Show and did I get to meet Al Roker. I explained to her I had never been on that program. As I was getting up to leave, two men about my age came up and asked for a card and one of them said, "Wow, you were on The Today Show huh?" Geez.

Later, walking past a house on Vandalia Lake where a huge party was going on, a man with a huge beer belly and a huge smile on his friendly face, walked across the road toward me with a can of Pepsi in one hand and a monstrous turkey leg in the other. "Here," he said, "I seen ya coming down the road and figured you could use something to eat man. My names "Rat" Gates." I thanked Mr. "Rat" Gates and went on down the road just a lovin' life.

Friendliness in Royal Lake, Illinois

Just outside a little community called Royal Lake, Illinois, Beth, of Chesterfield, Illinois, and her little boy Ty, stopped their car and walked up to where I was taking a break. Bev was so very excited about meeting me. She said she had been looking for me and said that she followed me on Facebook. She asked me to walk back to her car with them because she had a lot of stuff for me. And she did! She brought me bags of ice, a whole rotisserie baked chicken, a fruit bar, an ice cream bar, 2 bananas, and a candy bar. I thanked her over and over, I just couldn't believe she went to all that trouble. Bev explained to me that just a few weeks ago, at the same time a friend of hers introduced her to me on Facebook, her family was being told by doctors that her father was not going to make it through the rare heart problem he was hospitalized for. She said that my story gave her a strength to hold on, Love Life, and stay positive. Bev's father beat the odds and is still with us!

Four more people stopped to hand me water. One farmer walked down his driveway to hand me an ice cold Pepsi. He said that he had just passed me on the big tractor taking up most of the road. I thanked him and he said he was on his way to plant more soy beans. I said, "Enjoy." He said, "Oh I do enjoy it, I enjoy it very much. I like watching come up from the earth what I've put lots of work into." He went on to say, "And soy beans are a good crop, benefits a lot of people. I like your sign." This is why I keep walking with that sign over my head and telling my story.

The Landing Restaurant, Kampsville, Illinois

In The Landing Restaurant at the village of Kampsville, Illinois where there is a free ferry crossing of the Illinois River. I was four miles from where I woke up in my tent to a pouring rain. My first 45 minutes in Kampsville, IL, I spent on the porch of the old American Legion building dodging the downpour. When the rain let up I headed out to find a c-store or something to get something to eat as cheap as possible cause funds were low. I was walking past the ferry, a barge and a tugboat (could watch them for hours), and a pretty young lady pulled up and asked, "Just what the heck are you doin'?" I told her, and she told me where The Landing was and handed me a ten saying she wanted to buy my breakfast. Cool, eggs over easy and sausage instead of Little Debbie powdered donuts! As I was unhooking my cart in front of The Landing Restaurant, a lady walked out on the porch and asked what I was doing. She said she and her group had seen me out the window and just wanted to make sure I was okay. She asked if I was okay financially and I said yes I was. She said, "This is a very giving community and we want to make certain you don't need anything." I told her I could certainly vouch for it being a giving community and showed her the ten dollar bill still in my hand. I told her the young lady gave it to me for breakfast. She said, "We were going to get your breakfast." Upon entering the restaurant, the lady was already at a table of three bib overall wearing farmers, telling my story. After the waitress brought my coffee, the lady came to my table and handed me three fives and said, "Here, I'll have more soon." She then seated herself with her group of about eight ladies and I could hear excerpts of my story being told again. At one point, I heard her say, "Hey, he's encouraging people to love life, that's awesome." About 15 minutes later she came over and handed me another $36.00 and said, "It is such a good thing you're doing, thank you for letting us help." I went over to the tables and thanked everyone for their generosity.

Lost my House!

I had done about 17 miles and came to a place called Mozier, IL, right on the Mississippi. The restaurant, (the only thing there) I was going to eat at was closed. Well, I sat down on a bench in front of the place to at least take a little break. As I sat there I looked at my cart and I couldn't believe what I was seeing, my tent wasn't where it was supposed to be. My house was gone! Damn, that's just wasn't a good thing at all. I immediately headed for a house I had just passed and went up and knocked on the door. A guy came to the door, Kevin. I handed him my card and told him my situation and offered to pay him for gas if he would drive me the six miles back where I thought I had forgot to strap my tent back down. Kevin explained that he was watching his three little ones ages 2, 4, and 6 and couldn't possibly leave until his wife got home. I thanked him and boogied full steam ahead doing something I literally hate to do, go backwards. I went four and a half miles to the home of Bernie, who I had met earlier in the day when he joined me on my break enjoying the luxury of a guard rail to sit on. Well, Bernie wasn't home. So, off I chugged trying to get to the spot where I figured my tent to be, hoping to get there before dark and planning to just camp there for the night. I went about a half mile more and an old van pulled up beside me and it was Kevin! He said, "Hey man, my wife got home early and I figured you could use some help." Then he said, "Damn man, you flew to get this far!" I said, "It's my house man…. gotta have my house." We loaded up my gear and went to the place I thought it was and there it laid in the tall grass. I had eaten a melting candy bar on my break and had washed my hands and forgotten to strap my tent back down atop the container I had to open for the hand soap. Kevin took me back to his house where I pitched my tent and charged all my stuff and his lovely wife brought me a meal fit for a king. The next morning Kevin brought me a huge cup of coffee. I walked the eighth of a mile (all I lost) to the little restaurant, had a good breakfast and continued on my way. I figure I must have needed the extra exercise. Love Life and for God's sake, enjoy who you are, you're special just like me.

Skylar the little Gentleman

A young man, no more than 12 or 13 years-old came up to me just as I was walking into Payson, Illinois and said, "Sir, would you please explain to me exactly what you are doing sir." I immediately said, "Absolutely!" And began explaining and then answering his questions. Listen folks, a kid that age addresses me in that manner I will give them my undivided attention for as long as they want! A car pulled up behind us and Skylar Ditto told me that was his mom and grandmother in the car. I said to Skylar's mom, Shawna, "This in one fine lad you have here ma'am." A smiling mama said with great pride, "I know!" I gave them all cards and made my way down to the local c-store to eat and charge up stuff. The store attendant gave me a free ice cream! While I was eating my ice cream, in walks Skylar's mom, Shawna, and asked would I mind stepping outside and letting their family each be photographed with me. There were seven of them and I had my picture taken with each one of them individually and they all seemed just as thrilled over it as I was. I love it.

Subject of a Sermon

I did 20 miles one day and was about 8 miles south of Warsaw, Illinois. Two people stopped and offered me rides, four stopped and gave me water, and there were four happy life loving bikers that stopped me as I was walking by them. A young lady pulled up beside me just long enough to say, "I'm on my way to work man but I just had to tell you, you were the subject of our preacher's sermon yesterday morning! Wow I can't believe I'm seeing you, this is so cool! Our preacher said, "If a man can make the effort it takes to walk all over the United States telling all to love life, surely, the rest of us can make the effort to love it!"

Not Always Easy to Love Life!

A car pulled in front of me and stopped just before the bridge into Missouri. As I approached the car, a young lady, late 20's to early 30's, got out, and walked up to me without saying a word turned and faced the same direction I was. She was nearly touching me she stood so close. I had no idea what was going on. She was very plain looking but pretty. She quietly said, "What are you doing?" I told her and she asked several questions very straight faced and with no emotion. She asked, was I ever bothered by animals, where did I sleep, how did I eat, and questions like that. She said, "I've never camped before." Finally, I looked at her and said, "Okay, what's up with you? You seem in great despair." She said her little boy had severe autism and other very serious problems. She said her 5 year-old little girl, who was waiting for her in the car, recently had a stroke! She was blind for a while but now has her vision back. One of her arms is locked in position and she cannot use it. She looked straight ahead and said, "My husband left me and took off. And I just gave my little boy up for adoption and it's killing me. I'm trying hard and I just can't get out of this despair. "Then you're not trying hard enough." I told her. I told her of losing both my babies and then I nodded toward her car and said,

"Do you want to lose your little girl too?" "No, no." she answered. I told her that she has to let go of everything that has happened up to now and look at nothing but the happiness and wellbeing of her little girl. And that her little girl's happiness is not going to happen unless she herself gets her own joy back. I said, "You and your little girl have life Patty, and that is a precious gift to be thankful for and appreciate to the fullest. You've never camped before you said, that would be a perfect way for you to get your mind off everything except regaining your joy for you and your baby girl." I told her to do some research and find some trails in her area and get out there on them with her little one. To buy a cheap tent or borrow one maybe, and find a place to go camping. I told her, whatever it takes, you've got to fight hard against the negative thoughts and maintain your happiness for you and your precious baby girl. I told her how useless being negative is, that it accomplishes nothing. I told her that things would go much smoother for her and things will look much clearer to her when she concentrates on being happy and positive. I told her that I loved her and I am very concerned for her. She smiled at that. We talked quite a while and then her baby started fussing and she said she had to go. She told me she was going to try very hard and thanked me for talking to her and that she was glad she had stopped. We have to Love others!

Shelby's Dad

Shelby, from Nevada, MO. Said she didn't think she could tell the story of why she related so to my LOVE LIFE sign without crying. I said, "So? Cry, I do it all the time." Shelby sobbed as she told of her and her 53-year-old father driving home from her high school graduation a little more than 2 years before. She said her dad had been a single parent since she was a baby. Her father started having a heart attack and just minutes from the hospital her car broke down! Her phone wasn't charged and no one would stop. She finally found her dad's phone and called 911. When she got off the phone, her father was gone. Shelby said she fought guilt for so very long because she didn't think to keep her phone charged, and because, she felt if she hadn't panicked, she would have remembered where her dad kept his phone. She told me she made herself Love Life like her father would have wanted. She pursued a nursing career. More perspective fuel for the rest of us. Love Life, it is certainly not difficult to do.

Praise God, not a Dry County!

Around noon, near Kahoka, Missouri, it started raining a very light rain. It felt good and was a great contrast to the intense heat of the past few days. A Clark County Missouri Sheriff's Deputy stopped and offered me a ride out of the rain. He said he could at least take me to the county line a couple miles away. I thanked him and told him I was in fact enjoying it very much. I explained to him that I had already put my phone and wallet each in Zip-Loc bags and all my other gear was secure and dry in dry-sacks. He said I could call if I changed my mind and a deputy would come and get me. It rained lightly on me the rest of the day and there was almost no traffic, which made it very nice because there is no paved shoulder, so I didn't have to keep getting off the highway when a car came.

While I was checking in the motel in Memphis, Missouri, the sky really opened up and it started pouring. I got soaked running to the store across the street to get something to eat and a beer. I didn't see the beer cooler in the c-store and I asked the clerk, "Please don't tell me y'all are a dry county or don't serve alcohol on Sunday." "Heavens no!" she said, "We have a big old beer cave right behind you there." "Praise God!" I said. She giggled at that. You know, I just didn't mind getting soaked at all knowing I had a nice dry motel room to run back across the street to.

Arch and Laurel's Farm

I was looking desperately for a place to pitch a tent. A couple pulled up and asked did I want a ride into Centerville. I told them no and asked did they know of an area where I might be able to pitch my tent for the night. They said no and left. Ten minutes later they came back and the driver said he had gone to the farm just in front of me and asked would they mind if I camped on their property. I couldn't believe it, was that cool or what! I tented on the farm of Arch and Laurel Marshal. Laurel offered me dinner but I had just ate. She served me lemonade and the three of us sat out on their porch and talked until dark. I exited my tent about 5:45 the next morning and was met by Arch Marshall, who handed me a cup of coffee and an invite to breakfast. We had slab bacon and fresh eggs straight from the Marshall's chickens and lots more coffee. Fertile eggs by the way, I know this, because I wanted to kill that fuckin' rooster way early that morning.

The Appanoose County Sheriff

The Sheriff of Appanoose County, Iowa, Gary Anderson, pulled up in front of me in the afternoon. He said they had received a call from a driver saying I was walking in the middle of the road. I said simply, "That sir is a lie. I've been doing this for 13 years and I am well aware that walking in the middle of the road is the quickest and surest way to get that run down feeling." The Sheriff and I talked about how difficult it was for me to walk on that particular stretch of road without any shoulders. He was very understanding about my situation. So much so, he tried to talk me into letting him drive me the remaining five miles into Centerville. I turned down the ride. After I told Sheriff Anderson that I would have over 32,000 miles of walking America when I reached Centerville, he excused himself, saying he would be back in a minute. He came back from his vehicle with a really cool medallion and handed to me. It was a medallion with Appanoose County Sheriff Gary Anderson's name and the Iowa County served engraved on it. It is beautiful and I am very proud of it. Sheriff Gary Anderson is a fine man. He would not leave until he was certain I was okay and that he had filled me in on the locations of motels, stores, restaurants, and anything else I had asked about. Sheriff Anderson gave me his card and told me to call if I had any problems at all.

Cowboy Up!

I was going to try for 25 miles into Leon, Iowa but only made it 12 miles into Corydon. As I was walking past the Nodyroc (Corydon spelled backwards) Motel Sharon Anderson came up to me and said, "I knew you were coming, some friends in Promise City told me a man with "LOVE LIFE" over his head was walking my way and I made up my mind right then to give you a room." And then she hugged me. A free motel stay… I'll do 25 miles another day.

At the motel, rodeo cowboy John Steenhoek, owner of Heartland Rodeo Company came up to me and laughingly said, "Hey, I'm the guy that was sitting at the table across from you in that store in Downing, Missouri the other day when you were trying to figure out how to eat that monstrous double cheeseburger in front of you." Then I recognized him, he had been the only other customer there. I remembered him laughing then too. Probably because I kept saying, "How in the hell do you eat this thing?" I told John I'd like to get a picture of him with my sign and as I was pulling my cart into a good position for the picture, I heard him yell out, "Hey, cowboy up! I need my cowboys out here!" All of a sudden there were all kinds of people in front of me! Some were part of John's Heartland Rodeo Company of Downing, Missouri, putting on the rodeo at the Wayne County Fair, and the others were members of the Muessigmann Band from Sioux City, Iowa who were appearing at the fair. They were all just a great bunch of people and every single one of them asked me for my card and each told me they thought what I was doing was great.

Found out what RAGBRAI is

As I was leaving Corydon, IA, in the morning, a man out for his morning bike ride rode up to me and asked was I the guy he heard on NPR a few years back. He said my story had touched his heart and had inspired him. A great start for my day! An Iowa State

Trooper stopped by just to see if I was okay and see what I was doing. He was very nice. An old man in bibbed overalls pulled his pickup alongside me, handed me two ears of sweet corn and said, "Here, just picked these. I'm on my way to church, you have a great day sir." I ate them right on the spot, they were delicious! Karen, stopped on her bike to talk and share some energy bars. She was on her way home from having ridden in the 41st gathering of RAGBRAI. She explained to me that RAGBRAI is an acronym for Register's Annual Great Bicycle Ride Across Iowa. It was started in 1973 by the Des Moines Register, and is the world's largest bike touring event. She said they had over 10,000 participants that year! Karen said she loved riding the stretch of Iowa Route 2, we were on, because of all the hills. It was indeed the most hills in a 25 mile stretch I've seen since I started this walk.

No Cardboard Pizza

7/29/13. Near Kellerton, Iowa, a truck stopped with Carl and his 16 year-old son, Michael. Carl asked where I was going. I told him I heard there was a bar in Kellerton that served sandwiches and Carl said, "Well not exactly, they actually only serve cardboard pizza and potato chips. If you're looking for a place to crash tonight out of the rain, you can come to our place and spend the night there." Y'all know what I said. Carl fed me some kind of really good linguini dish with oysters and I took a shower and did my laundry. I told Carl what I commonly tell those who have opened their homes to me, "Anyone instrumental in my obtaining a shower has a friend for life."

Carl asked, "So, what's your philosophy?" I said, "Concentrate on realizing what a precious gift life is until you fall in love with the act of breathing, until you can get past any obstacle, knowing that nothing is as important as having life. To Love Life no matter what. Loving life is just something we as individuals determine to do. We simply make our mind up to Love Life and take the energy we've spent blaming it and put it toward loving it. Life is never our enemy; our attitude toward Life is our enemy, or our friend. Treat Life as a person you see in your room when you awake, reach over and grab them and make them to do exactly what you want to do that day. Repeat this daily until Life automatically does exactly what you want every day. You will eventually discover it was but your own reflection in the mirror, you'll recognize the smile.

I Need to Pay Back

It was nearly 8:00 PM before I reached Leon, Iowa one night. Just as I entered town, a man, Steve, pulled up in his truck and offered me a place to stay for the night. He had obviously been drinking. I thanked him and turned down his offer. He kept insisting I let him help me. I kept thanking him and saying no. When I finally had climbed all the hills to reach the motel, there was Steve's truck in front of the motel office. I didn't know what I was going to have to deal with when I went in to pay for a room. Well, Steve was standing there and the clerk was handing his credit card back to him, he had just purchased a room for me. I told him that I had money to pay for the room he did not have to do that. Steve, looked at me and then at the young lady tending the desk and said, "I've done a lot of bad things in my life, I need to start paying back." I said, "Thank you very much for the room Steve." Outside, he offered to drive me to the store. I thanked him but declined saying that I did not want to ride with him because he had been drinking. He looked down at the ground and said, "Well, thanks for letting me help ya anyway." His phone rang, he got back in his truck and was on his phone as I walked on to the store.

Strongest Power in Universe

Love is the strongest and yet, gentlest power in the Universe. Loves power is manifested through gentleness and patience. Those we Love, we can more easily be gentle and patient with. Gentleness and patience are obviously instruments of Love. Let's use them then on every fellow human being we have opportunity to display them to, and not only to our closest loved ones. We need not run up to every individual and shout, "I Love you!" We need only to practice gentleness and patience to display Love, to change, each, our little portion of the world. If we all were each gentle and patient with all, the condition of human kind would start to change immediately. The power of Love would take over and change the world. It all starts with a Love Life attitude. Let's Love Life and start watching our own little portion of the world begin to change.

Glenn Miller's Birthplace

8/1/13. I did 15 miles and had settled in a motel room in Clarinda, Iowa, birthplace of the famous composer and band leader, Glenn Miller. I busted my butt that day and took advantage of the terrain being a little flatter than it had been the previous few days. I was hoping to get a motel room at a somewhat reasonable price. As soon as I walked into town I saw a Super 8 Motel. They are usually reasonably priced and there were the restaurants and stores within walking distance that I look for when choosing a motel. But, even as tired as I was, I decided to see if I could find another motel. No more than two blocks away was the Celebrity Inn. I walked in, told the lady at the desk, Peggy, that I was walking the United States and why, and told her I would appreciate any discount she could give me. Peggy said, "I'll give you the room." Blow me away! I couldn't help it folks, it just caught me so off guard, I started crying. Peggy reached out and patted my hand and said, "It's okay, I think you're going to make me cry too." I thanked her over and over. I saw Peggy's husband Roger later working on his 1987 Chevy pickup that looked brand new. As I walked up to him he said, "So, you must be the guy that's walking." I shook his hand and expressed my sincere appreciation for the gift of the room for a night. And Roger said, "You probably work every day walking and get pretty tired out there, I'll bet you could use a day off, if you want the room for one more day just to goof off, it's yours." I choked up, I managed to get in, "thank you so very much," and then I turned and headed for the store across the street. I cried again. After I bought my groceries, I went to Roger and accepted the room for the next day as well. I told Roger and Peggy that I would be willing to help them in any way around the motel. They both said no, that they just wanted me to rest. So, I took the next day off too!

See why I'm learning to shrug off the negative things and believe the positive is on its way? When something negative happens to us, we give it the utmost attention. We pay little attention though to the many good things that happen to us. We just take all the good things for granted and then scream our heads off if something negative happens. In my life, I've learned to pay more attention to the good things and almost no attention to the bad things. I hardly ever have bad things happen anymore. Or, maybe I just don't notice them anymore. Love Life my friends.

Fremont County, Iowa

Right after taking a break two Fremont County, Iowa, Sheriff's Deputies pulled up in two different cars and asked what I was doing. I gave them each a card, proudly showed them my Sunshine State driver's license, and told them why I walked. One of them told me that someone had called in and said that I had been sitting in a roadside ditch. I told them that I had indeed taken a 10 minute break sitting on the bank of a ditch. "Is that illegal in Iowa?" I asked. They both chuckled and said no. We discussed how in a small rural area like I was in, people can get a little nervous about strangers and things out of the ordinary. They asked lots of questions, including, "How many pair of shoes have you gone through? I told them it was now about 50 pair. They even offered to take me to the county line if I wanted a ride.

See, I meet the coolest people ever. It's because I try always to Love Life, which reveals my inner joy. Sometimes, out here on the road all alone, I just start dancing and shouting for no other reason than the sheer joy of being alive to fulfill my part in this wonderful life… being me! Being satisfied with who we are brings joy and if we have joy within we have strength.

"Timber Jack"

Figure 18. Timber Jack

8/6/13. Out in the middle of nowhere one morning between Nebraska City, and Auburn, Nebraska, from behind me I heard, "Wahoooo!!" I turned to see a guy on a totally loaded down bike. I had the pleasure of meeting Jack Smith who calls himself "Timber Jack" Smith because he was in the timber business in Michigan before he retired. "Timber Jack" is from Battle Creek, Michigan, he's 71 years old and he left Oregon on June 1 to bike all of the Lewis and Clark Trail. He most definitely was loving life! Jack told me that after his retirement he was sitting watching TV one day, as he had been doing nearly every day since his retirement a few months earlier, and he said this happened to him, "I realized I was getting fat and wasting my life away. I took that damn TV and threw it in the dumpster out back. I went right straight to the bike store and bought this bike and all the gear and made up my mind to change my life right then and there!" He said he had done a couple other long distance road trips on his bike, as well. He said, "Hell, I even got rid of the sorry-assed girlfriend I had too. The one I got now is thru-hiking the Appalachian Trail right now. I'm thinking I'll probably do that myself next year." He said he was happier than he had been in years! He really didn't have to tell me that, it was quite obvious "Timber Jack" was a Lover of Life.

Candidate for Governor of Kansas

8/9/13. As I was leaving Sabetha, Kansas in the morning, a gentleman walked out from some kind of manufacturing facility I was passing and said he just had to know what I was doing. Of course I told him. He handed me a twenty and said he would love to help. Three different people stopped by to offer water and I got lots of waving and horn honking. Ken Cannon, stopped by to talk. When I told of my little boy's suicide, Ken looked down at the ground and said, I can relate." I immediately said, "I am so very sorry for your loss!" Ken started telling his story. He is a former high school and college basketball coach, a former college dean among other accomplishments. In 2010 Ken decided to run for Governor of Kansas. On January 2nd, 2010, he announced his intentions and made it official. On January 8, 2010, Ken's handsome 27 year-old son, Kirk, was found dead in Sunset Park, Salina, Kansas. Ken said the police ruled it a suicide. Ken is not sure it was a suicide. After sharing the circumstances with me, if I were him, I would be doubtful too. But, at any rate, Ken Cannon's little boy is gone! He told me that in order to keep from going insane, he fought against the urge to just quit everything and basically, just lay down and die. He decided to stay in the governor's race and fought hard. I know personally what courage it took for Ken not to give up. After he lost his bid for Governor of Kansas he stayed busy doing good things. He has written a book, "Bummy and the Coach, 100 Years." He has started a leadership retreat for young people called Dream Weavers, which focuses on leadership characteristics. Of course, Ken and I related to each other having experienced the same pain. Before Ken left, he said, "I used to believe in coincidences, I don't any longer. I'm really glad I met you." And I said, "No one meets me by accident. I call what I do Trail Therapy. Love Life with all your heart and in the process you will develop a love for everyone else's life as well. Love and respect for our fellow human being will solve all problems. Nothing is as powerful as love.

Derry and Dog, Beefy

Figure 19. Derry with dog Beefy.

8/11/13. In Marysville, Kansas, on a Sunday, I was sitting outside the Verizon store which was in an old gas station outside of town, and waiting for them to open at noon, I heard someone whistling. I looked across the road and there was a young man with a dog behind him and he was using a one gallon jug of water as weights, pumping it with each arm at least 8 to ten times before changing hands. And it was really hot out, I couldn't believe it. I yelled at him and he happily came over and introduced himself as Derry, from Chico, California. We talked about how good Sierra Nevada Torpedo IPA beer is, it's made in Chico. He introduced me to Beefy, his mixed German Shepard and pit bull dog. Derry said he was glad Beefy looked like his father, the Shepard. I could see the pit in his shoulders and his waist. Derry said they just got off a freight train at Marysville and were walking to Wally World He said he would try to hop another train tonight or very early next morning. Derry said that his rule of life is to always treat everyone nice and with respect. The young man was very at ease and comfortable with the way he was living. I was very impressed with him. I gave him some money. People give me money. As he walked off toward Wally World he started working out with that water jug again.

When the Verizon store opened I was glad that the young lady, the only person in the store, was a delight to work with. Some Verizon stores I've gone into are akin to jumping into a huge aquarium stocked mostly with piranha. But Haley was a sweetheart. She is seven month's pregnant with her second child. She told me she very recently lost her father at only 60 years-old. She was the youngest child she said and so was most definitely daddy's girl. Even though one could readily see the pain in her eyes, she spoke very positive about her father's death. She said he had a heart attack and died instantly. Then she said, "I miss him terribly but, hey, he always said he didn't want to live to be real old and he always said he wanted to die fast and not have a slow death." I told Haley I was terribly sorry for her loss but that I admired her very much for not wallowing in self-pity and instead being positive. She said, "That's what my dad would want."

The Sun made me New Again

8/12/13. The farmer's field I camped in overnight, about 3 miles from Blue Rapids, Kansas, was not high enough. I was aware that it was raining all night but was not concerned because my Eastern Mountain Sports "Sugar Shack" tent has more than proven itself in fierce thunderstorms like that night's. However, when I sat up to survey the weather outside about 4:00 AM, it caused the tent's bathtub floor to be lower than the 8 inches of accumulated water on the ground outside and so, the bathtub floor became just that, a bathtub. So there I sat in the water for nearly two hours being thankful that it is August and the wonderful sun would take care of my little problem. When it got light enough, I charged outside to wade around and get my soaking wet gear together. Thankfully, I use lots of plastic bags and so the only thing really soaked was me, my clothes, and my sleeping bag. I walked on into Blue Rapids, Kansas and waited for the sun to make me new again!

It was nearly 3:00 before I got everything dried out and reorganized. I only did 8 miles because just out of Blue Rapids, Joe Sauer and Helen Stucky-Risdon stopped and Helen invited me into her home 4 miles down the road in Waterville. She is founder and director of Wellness Weavers, an organization aimed at helping communities learn more about healthy living. After my shower I told Helen and Joe, "Anyone instrumental in my obtaining a shower has a friend for life!" And she served real roast beef! With potatoes and carrots, and onions and stuff. So much better than Mickey D's and convenience store fare. Helen is an awesome cook. See, I told y'all, anytime something bad happens to me something good comes right behind it. I am loving life and enjoying meeting new and interesting people in my adventures. Love Life until you only see the good in people.

Over the Rainbow

8/13/13. While sitting on a guardrail taking my first ten minute break of the day near Randolph, Kansas,, a young lady pulled up, got out of her car and walked up to me and said, "I saw your sign and turned around and came back, I'm Betsy, I want to help you." She pulled from her pocket 4 crumpled up one dollar bills, straightened out every one of them before handing them to me. Then went to her car and came back with two bottles of Gatorade and a new bottle of aspirin. She then plopped herself down right beside me on the guardrail. She said she was on her way to work and couldn't stay long. She told me she had a difficult time staying happy in life because she has a hard time coping with some things. I told her that I had lost both my children and that I am still able to love life with all my heart. She said she could sit and talk all day but she had to go or she would be late for her first student. She teaches Saxophone and clarinet she told me. As she raised up she turned to me and said, "Will you pray for me to be able to cope better?" I said, "I now have you in my heart for prayers and positive thoughts." She drove down the road a piece where she could turn around and as she was passing by me again, she slowed down and said, "I'm terribly sorry for your loss." There was such a simple sweetness about Betsy.

Later, about 6:30 pm, I was in a little store in Randolph, Kansas just finishing my sandwich and I looked up and there in front of me was Betsy! She said she had come looking for me. We sat outside the store and talked. She told me her mother was going to have cancer surgery the next day. It was easy to see she was very frightened. She said to me, "I have a million questions for you but they're all running around in my head and I just can't bring them to my mouth." Betsy converses really well, but, there is a childlike side to her. She asked if I ever got upset about politics. I said no, that I never followed politics at all, ever. She asked why and I said, "Because, I'm not a follower." She giggled a lot at that. They closed the store and so we had to leave the premises. Betsy hugged me several times and told me several times that she loved me. I told her I loved her too, each time. We said goodbye and I hit the road looking for a tent site. About a football field away, I heard the horn playing. I turned around to see Betsy sitting in the trunk of her old Buick playing "Over the Rainbow" on her sax for me. She played it beautifully. I stood there applauding… and crying. I went back to where she was and thanked her. She grinned real big and said, "Hey, you're walking in Kansas, I gave you the perfect background music to walk in the land of Dorothy." I said, "Betsy, you may be the sweetest person in the world." What a smile that got! She said to me, "I'm going to try real hard to love life like you said but I've had a lot of bad luck." I said, "Has your bad luck been worse than mine Betsy?" She said instantly, "No! I will try real hard."

Later, Betsy called me and said, "Thank you for being the messenger who was sent to tell me how to love life. Christians talk to me sometimes, but they're just a pain in the ass." I said, "How's your mother?" She said her mom was doing well. She said that she loved me and asked could she call me often. And of course I said, yes. Love Life my friends. See what love does. Just love, don't expect anything in return, just love.

The Beauty of Life

Push on and love the gift of Life we've been so wonderfully blessed with. When we awake and feel that sweet, sweet air on our upper lip, we have indeed been gifted another day! Realize the miracle of that moment first and foremost, and grab onto it and hold onto the beauty of our precious gift of Life. Give that moment precedence over all other thoughts that are attempting to cause us to put the realization of the beauty of our being alive yet one more day, in second place. Absolutely nothing is more sacred than our gift of Life. Hold onto the moment as long as it takes for the realization of the beauty of Life to supersede and conquer all negative thoughts and simply, Love Life.

I did an Insane Thing

8/15/13. I did 20 miles and one mile of it was helped by 60 MPH gusts at my back! I swear to you, at one point, I had to hold onto a sign post to keep from being blown into the traffic. My sign makes a great sail. And of course I got soaked. I made it into a nearby I-70 truck stop just out of Junction City, Kansas, where the nice people let me hold up out of the storm. However, the manager, a young lady, came up to me and with a pretty stern face, said, "Look, you can stay here for a little while, but what in God's name would possess you to do such an insane thing as walking in such severe weather?" I told her of the loss of both my children and that I wanted to make sure I shared the message of loving Life with as many as possible. She said, "Stay as long as you like sir, the coffee is on me." The storm didn't let up until 10:00 PM and so I had to pitch my tent on a soggy grass strip at the rear of the truck stops truck parking. Pretty noisy all night but at least I was out of the rain.

Beauty from the Heart

8/16/13. Near Herrington, Kansas, I followed a game trail from the road into very high grass and found a spot where deer had bedded down. Deer pick pretty flat spots to bed on. So I pitched my tent there, perfect. Walking into Herrington in the morning, I was balancing my budget (looking in my wallet) figuring out what things I could purchase of what I needed, with the small amount of money I had, when a stunningly beautiful young Mexican lady walked up to me and said in a very thick accent, "Beautiful! Beautiful!" She handed me $30.00 and said again, "Beautiful!" I thanked her and tried to ask information about the location of stores I needed to visit in Herrington and she didn't know enough English to understand me. As the gorgeous young woman was walking toward her vehicle, she said one more time, "Beautiful." I mean, the young lady could have easily been a model or movie star. Her beauty obviously began at her heart.

Liquor Stores Are Good

8/18/13. A tanker truck hauling gasoline stopped and Gene asked what I was doing. I told him and after I finished the same basic story that I tell everyone, he said, "Pray for my wife will you please. Her name is Melina." I said, "Sure." Dave walked back across the street, climbed back up in his semi and was gone. I never said one thing to that man that, in my mind, that would have inspired him to ask prayer from me??

About 6:00 that evening I went into Superior Wine and liquor Store in Marion, Kansas (the only thing on the highway besides Pizza Hut) to buy ice and get me a single beer. There was a young lady there talking with the owner, Dave Yates. The young lady, Chelsea, said she had seen me on the road earlier and started asking me lots of questions. Soon, me, Chelsea and Dave were laughing and having a great time. Chelsea made a run to the grocery store for me and while she was gone Dave and I talked about life. About how life is about giving and paying forward. Dave would not let me pay for my purchases and suggested I tent behind his building. He said that on his way home he was going to stop at the police station and let them know I was behind his shop so they could check on me. Later in the evening Chelsea came up to my tent to check on me. We ended up in a long conversation about some serious things going on in her life. She put her arms around my neck and said that I had helped her a lot. Good, I hope so. She was very sweet. I pitched my tent on a perfectly flat and freshly mowed spot behind his Liquor Store as Dave had told me to.

Lollygagging, Great Word!

8/19/13. Only did about 12 miles because I was lollygagging, killing time and goofing off so that I would reach McPherson, Kansas (only place with motels for a while) on Wednesday morning because I would have money for a motel, yes! While walking the two miles out of my way to go into Marion for breakfast a lady pulled up beside me in her pickup and asked what I was doing. I told her and she said to go to the c-store around the corner and wait for her. So, I did. She wasn't there. I decided to go the Mom & Dads Café for breakfast. Then the lady pulls up and now she has a man with her. The man was Adam Stewart, reporter for the local paper, the Marion County Record. He steps out of the truck, his hair is soaking wet and he doesn't seem to be in a real good mood. He has a pad and pen in hand so, from experience, I know this guy's a reporter type person. I said, "And how are you sir?" He said, "I was doing just fine until just a few moments ago while I was enjoying my morning shower, she (he nods toward the pickup driver lady) bangs on my door screaming for me to hurry up and get dressed!" I smiled real big and said, "Well I thank you so very much and I will make it worth your while." And then I said, "A morning shower huh, wow, I bet that felt great huh? I haven't had one of those in a few days... can y'all tell?" During the interview Adam mellowed right out. I love small town newspapers. I Love Life too and all the interesting people in that life. I started loving people more as I discovered that I alone am responsible for my happiness in my walk in life and never anyone else. That caused me to stop blaming others. And in not blaming others, it became much easier to love others. Now ain't that just really easy to figger out!

A Hundred Bucks

9/5/13. Near Hugoton, Kansas. Nathan, passed me in his truck and then turned around to find out what I was about. We sat in his truck and spoke awhile and then he said, "As soon as I saw your sign I decided to give you a hundred bucks. I have a wonderful wife and three children, I really love life. I've been very blessed in my life, I'm a farmer and I've done well, I pay back every chance I get. Are you hungry?" I said yes and we went to a Chinese restaurant. Nathan then drove me to all three of the town's motels until I found one with a vacancy. I did 16 miles and I Love Life.

Love Life, God Bless

9/6/13. Just out of Hugoton, a man pulled his 18 wheeler over in front of me and when I got beside his passenger window he reached down a ten to me and said in a heavy Mexican accent, "Thank you! Love life, God Bless." I was fighting a fierce wind in 99 degree heat about 3:30 PM when a young Mexican couple with two children pulled over. The pretty lady, who spoke no English, walked up to me and handed me a 32 oz. blue Slurpee and a twenty dollar bill. I thanked her several times, and she just smiled a most beautiful smile, turned and walked back to her car. I did 19 miles today and I'm in my tent behind oil storage tanks and I Love Life.

Keyes, Oklahoma

9/9/13. A man named Winston stopped on his way to take 2 bales of hay to his new filly, he said. While he was looking at my rig, I noticed that I had evidently not fastened the strap tight enough and the plastic lid to my storage box on the cart had blown off!

Winton said, "Well, jump in my truck here and we'll just go find it!" It was about 2 miles back down the road where I had taken my last break. It was at the side of the road and had not been touched. I couldn't believe we actually found it. I thanked him over and over. He also insisted on giving me twenty bucks. And that is how I came to be in a motel room for the night.

In the morning in the Keyes Country Store, in Keyes, Oklahoma, while I was eating my breakfast, a tall thin cowboy came in the door, looked at me, touched the brim of his hat, and said, "Howdy." He filled up his own coffee cup, paid Tracey Perez the owner, and on his way out he stopped at my table and slid a folded twenty dollar bill under my plate and said, "Have a nice day sir." And when I went to pay for breakfast, Tracey would not accept it. I thanked her but insisted on tipping her precious little girl, 12 year-old Patricia, who had brought out my biscuits and gravy, with a smile from heaven. They are out there, out there when needed, the giving hearts.

Mississippi Strong Man

Started raining early in the morning and I stayed soaked all day. Coming into Dalhart, Texas, a very big man wearing a cowboy hat, Gene from Cleveland, Mississippi, stopped. He said he was there in Texas to shoot prairie dogs, but the rain had pretty much stopped that for the day. He asked was there anything he could do for me. I told him not really, I was just going to try and find a reasonable motel and get out of the rain. He suggested we load my cart up into his pickup and he take me around town to the several motels to find a room. I looked at his truck loaded down with coolers and tool boxes and said, thanks, but I don't think it will fit. He said that sure it would and told me to keep the light end steady and just watch. That 65 year-old man picked up that one hundred pound plus cart with ease and set it on top of all his gear! In the parking lot of the first motel we came to, He told me he would like to pay the difference if the room was more than the $60.00 I wanted to spend. I told him thanks but I thought I could talk them down. While I was trying to talk the clerk down from $72.00, Gene walked in and started telling the clerk what I was doing and why he should give me the room at a lower price. To no avail. Gene asked could he please pay the $12.00 difference. I got the room with his help. You just have to Love Life and all living it with us.

"To Love Life is a way of Life, not an expression occasionally used to express joy for the moment. To Love Life is to adopt an attitude that one's Life is a gift and to be appreciated to the point that our conscious bothers us when we even slightly stop seeing it as such. Then, we are powerful. Powerful because we have established pure Love in our life." ~ Steve Fugate

XIT Ranch in Texas

9/12/13. Well, I just had the best darn time on this day! I woke up to pouring rain and the local weather said it would be like that all day. So, I had to check my account and balance my budget, basically, I just looked in my wallet, and BINGO, I was able to get a room one more day in Dalhart in the Texas Panhandle. The local station was wrong though, it stopped raining by 10:00 and I went sightseeing. On my way to the XIT Ranch Museum I saw a 1961 Ford Econoline pickup truck in excellent condition. I love old cars. A gentleman was walking out of the building the fine ride was parked in front of and I yelled out, "Hey, good morning sir, how are you? You wouldn't happen to be the owner of this sweetheart would you?" And that's how I met 67 year-old John Watkins a lifetime resident of Dalhart and an absolute history buff. John said that a local hardware store owner, Davis Thompson, bought it brand new and only used it to go from his house to the hardware store, and then the beer store, and then back home, daily. He said he also drove it in the XIT Ranch Days Parade every year. It was in the parades when he was just coming into his teens, John told me, that he just fell in love with the little odd looking truck. He said he vowed to own it one day. Well, twenty five years ago he was able to buy it. It is the only vehicle he owns and drives it daily. John also shared a lot of the history of the cattle industry in the area. He was quite entertaining.

I enjoyed myself thoroughly visiting the XIT Ranch Museum, in Dalhart, Texas. The XIT Ranch was once the world's largest ranch, 3,000,000 acres. The 3,000,000 acres was given by the Texas government in 1881 to a New York Company that agreed to build a $3,000,000 red granite capital building in exchange for the land. To this day, it is the largest state capital building in the United States. Only the U. S. capital is larger. But the Texas capital's dome is seven feet higher. See how much fun I had! See how much fun one can have when you commit to Love every single bit of Life presented to you every day! I am making my children so very happy by being so very happy with every part of Life presented to me. I am also making my children very proud of their daddy. Please Love your Life no matter what, concentrating on all the good in life, dismissing the bad immediately.

As I was leaving Dalhart, Texas, a very pretty blonde lady came out of a business across the street from me and yelled for me to wait. She crossed the highway, told me she loved my sign and handed me $30.00! Just as I was leaving the tiny town, Texline, Texas, a man pulled his pickup next to me and asked where I was leaving from and where I was going to. I told him and he handed me a fifty dollar bill and told me he got fifty dollars' worth of pleasure from seeing my sign! And I said to him, "Thank you sir, you just got me a motel room when I reach Clayton." In Clayton, I went into the first motel I came to, knowing I would have to pay at least $65.00. A very pretty young lady was at the desk and she let out the cutest giggle when I told her I had walked over 32,000 miles and had crossed America six times, and said, "That is like the neatest thing I ever heard!" I told her the rest of my story and told her I would appreciate any break she could give me. She said I could have the room for fifty dollars even. I handed her the fifty and told her about the guy giving it to me earlier. She smiled big. I love my life so very much because I see so much love coming my way. I make certain of course that I'm sending much love the way of others.

Hail Hurts!

9/18/13. I finally knocked out the 84 miles between Clayton and Springer, New Mexico. Actually, it was 86 miles from my motel in Clayton. Sunday, I had to quit early after but 10 miles because a huge storm was coming in. I scooted into my tent just as the rain started pounding it. It rained hard all night. Monday I did 23 miles and a lot of hills. Tuesday I did 26 miles and stopped at the Gladstone Mercantile. It wasn't much for resupplying but I had a great rib dinner there. I didn't get to meet Thelma the owner, but I had great conversation with her daughter, Shelly. She gave me two bags of ice. The wind was fierce after I left the store and the climbs kept getting harder as I got closer to the Sangre de Cristo Mountains, of course. About 7:15 I was searching for a tent site because it was getting dark, when two guys got out of their car with a big professional looking camera and asked could they film me and get my story. I told them to film away and ask all the questions they wanted but to not get in my way pitching my tent. They were from Canada. The wind got bad again. About 2:15, a hail storm with very strong winds pounded me for several minutes. The hail was dime sized. Thank goodness I added the little porch over my head back in Dodge City. I simply grabbed each side of it and pulled it down as far as I could to cover me. The hail stung like heck hitting my knuckles though. And as soon as the sun came out some, I dried right out and was good as new and good to go!

I had an absolutely lovely Wednesday. I did 27 miles and settled in a motel room in Springer for 2 nights to rest and get some business taken care of. Love Life my friends and if you ever get caught in a hail storm, think of me. I find myself just overjoyed to be in a motel room and appreciating that I am alive. I have learned, storm clouds always pass. Something that always stuck with me from Psych 101, is that something like 95% of the stuff we worry about never actually occurs. So, I figure, why bother? When we do not worry so much we are much more likely to be aware of our fellow human beings needs and then get to enjoy one of the greatest gifts one can enjoy in this life, giving love to our fellow human beings. There is absolutely nothing more powerful than Love, the healer. Let us all try to keep our eyes off ourselves and stay more aware of others, you may just have the honor and privilege of healing a broken heart while it is yet beating. Love Life my friends and *never* give up.

Trail Maintenance

9/19/13. I sat in my motel room watching it rain. I had all my chores done. I washed all my filthy clothes in the bathtub and hung them on just about everything in the room to dry. I dried out my tent, lubricated the ends of my tent frame poles so they'll continue to snap together easily. First, I use emery cloth on each joint. I aired out my sleeping bags and I reinforced all the patch jobs on my cart. I also had to start taking a toothbrush to all the zippers in my tent to keep the sand from chewing them up while in the arid territories. It got really bad in Arizona, Nevada, and Eastern California. I learned that trick from Bo Hilleberg, designer and founder of Hilleberg the Tent Company, after I told his daughter, Petra, at their Colorado offices, that their zippers sucked. He called me from Sweden, and, he sent me a new tent too! Before settling in to my motel room I also went to the post office and I bought supplies and food for the 26 mile walk to Cimarron, New Mexico. I'm excited about Life.

Don't Worry be Happy

9/21/13. In Russell's Truck Stop just outside Springer, New Mexico, restaurant manager Jennifer, inquired about my walk. As soon as I told her of my son's suicide, she sat down across from me and told of losing her nephew to suicide and the difficulty her family was having dealing with it. We talked quite a while, mostly about the healing that occurs when we discipline ourselves to concentrate on how great it is to have the gift of life, and to love that life. To Love Life right past any and all hardships. Like in all things, practice makes perfect. Jennifer insisted on picking up my bill for breakfast.

The Word Love

Love is not just a word, Love is the term used to describe the most powerful force in the universe. Love is a term not to be used lightly. It may leave the lips a thousand times a day to fall straight to the floor if it doesn't first pass through a heart unblocked by the dividing forces of anger, blame, and hatred. The power of Love exhibited depends on the purity of that Love, on how diluted and polluted it has become, by anger, blame, and hatred. Love never separates, Love never divides its participants. Where there is division there is no Love. We cannot realize and use the real power of Love until we understand the purity of Love.

Fremont Ranch

On a Sunday, while having breakfast at the historic St James Hotel, the waitress bent down and whispered, "That family over there has paid for your breakfast." It was a family of five from Texas I had spoken to briefly out in the hallway looking at all the pictures and expressing our disbelief that 23 people had been killed in or outside the hotel in the late 1800's. I was able to thank the father before they left. The whole family just smiled. Outside the hotel, after just taking the picture of cowboys Ernie, and grandson Orion, Ernie shook my hand, wished me luck, and slipped a twenty into my hand. Just as I started to walk to my cart and prepare to leave, a young lady with her 6 week-old infant strapped into the backseat, stopped and handed me a Ziploc full of dry treats, nuts, crackers, Gatorade mix, etc. We spoke of the importance of introducing our children at a very early age to the outdoors. She said that was no problem for her as both she and her husband worked on the nearby 137,000 acre Fremont Boy Scout Ranch.

I tented that night on Fremont Scout Ranch land. There were signs everywhere warning not to trespass, but it started to pour the rain and so I found a well-hidden spot to tent. I normally obey those signs to a T, but, I had nowhere else to go. It rained all night. Hey, I was a Boy Scout once. The next day, the biggest, fattest, and healthiest looking black bear I ever saw, crossed the road no more than 50 feet in front of me! How cool is that. I saw a lady with Maine tags on her car, stopped and obviously looking for something in her car. She glanced up at me and I said to her that she too, was from a very beautiful state. She said she had lost her cell phone and was trying one more search to find it. She said she was fairly certain it had fallen from her pocket during an earlier short stroll into the woods. She said she was really worried about it, that she had much more important things on her mind. She said she was on her way to help take care of her 52 year-old son who has Lou Gehrig's disease. She burst into tears. We spoke a while, I patted her hand and said I would keep her son in my heart for thoughts and prayers.

Laughing Sam Gamble

9/25/13. Walking on U.S. 64 without any shoulders, twisting and winding through the mountains between Eagle Nest and Taos is not the easiest route I've ever taken. But, it is certainly one of the most beautiful! As I was at the edge of Taos, I saw a sign I just could not believe. "Road Narrows," you gotta' be kidding! And then, my taxi service arrived. He was cowboy Sam Gamble from Texas who has one of the greatest and loudest laughs I ever heard. He said he would gladly take me around to check out the numerous motels in Taos. We loaded up my cart, and I climbed into Sam's truck with his five miniature pincher dogs. Sam drove me to several motels in Taos, waiting patiently for me while I checked prices. At my chosen motel, he drove me over to my room and helped unload my cart. Sam said to me while laughing that great laugh of his, "I just like to help people." An understatement I assure you all. Now, can anyone give me a legitimate reason why I should not Love Life, every minute of it?

Most Hated Man in Taos

9/27/13. While walking back to my Taos, New Mexico motel room in the dark, from eating dinner, I saw a guy taking down a portable sign. Obviously handmade. On the sign, "Robbed at Gunpoint – Call Amos" and then a phone number. I asked him what it meant. He said that locals would understand it, it was ridicule of the current mayor of Taos and his administration. He had a huge chain in his hands and showed me where it had been cut with bolt cutters. He said, "They're cutting the chains and stealing my signs because I'm a pain in their asses and I won't go away! My signs are legal and they're stealin' 'em! So, I just take 'em down at night now." I was quite amused at the little guy's enthusiasm. He gave me his card:

"JEFF NORTHRUP "The Most Hated Man in Taos," his address, phone number, and Email address. Jack Wrap-it, Box Jockey Emeritus. Preacher (really), Ne'er Do-Well, Public Nuisance. Bon Vivant, Sore Loser, Busybody"

And so I gave him my card and as soon as I told him I was from Vero Beach, Florida, he said, "No kidding! I've got a great friend down there running for city council!" He pulled out his phone, dialed, and said, "Hey Buzz, I got a guy in front of me here in Taos that's from Vero Beach... here talk to 'im," hands me the phone and walks off hauling all his stuff to his car. Though we did not know each other, Buzz and I knew a lot of the same people. He remembered my business being on U.S. Highway 1 at one time, he said. You just never know who you'll meet and you never will unless you go meet them. That's what I do, I go meet people.

Special Treat in Taos

9/28/13. Walking through downtown Taos, New Mexico, continuing my walk after a two day motel stay in the beautiful city, someone shouted my name, and getting out of a rental car was my good friend Roger Bell, from my hometown of Vero Beach, Florida! He and his girlfriend had just flown in from Florida and were riding around exploring New Mexico. How cool is that! What a treat! And cooler yet, he got me a room for one more night in Taos! Yes, that 6 Degrees of separation is alive and well in my life.

Stop Giving, you Give Up

9/26/13. It was really nice not having a frozen tent over me that particular morning. *That* would happen again many times before I was done with this walk though, occupational hazard. Tuesday, a really cool guy, Ed Brady, from Eagle Nest, stopped, freaking out over my beautiful "LOVE LIFE" sign. He said he was a self-improvement coach. That he helped people to have a more positive outlook on life. Ed said his spiritual name is All Faa Raa. He laughed constantly. While Ed and I were talking, Andrew J. Gonzales of Angel Fire, New Mexico, stopped. They knew each other. After Ed left, Andrew told me he was the father of five boys and that he was out of work and going through hard times. He said he was a family man and that his family was everything. He told me he thought my sign to be beautiful and wrapped his arms around my neck and just started crying. So we just stood there on U.S. 64 hugging and patting each other on the back. *Everyone* needs love. He insisted on giving me $5.00 and I insisted that he should not. Andrew said, "If we stop giving then we have really given up. Life is about giving. You have given to me with your sign." Later, he found me and tried to give me some small propane canisters for a cook stove and can goods. I explained that I did not cook out on the road and that the cans were too heavy.

Very Humbling

9/29/13. Walking across the Rio Grande Gorge Bridge just outside Taos I met two ladies who just had to know why I walked with "LOVE LIFE" over my head. After my story, they both gave me some money. One of the ladies with tear filled eyes, told me her mother had committed suicide many years before when the broken hearted lady was in her teens. She told of how it still haunted her, as we stood in the middle of a bridge where many have done what her mother and my little boy did. We spoke for a long time. She thanked me many times for spreading the Love Life message and for caring about the victims left behind after the suicide of a loved one. Later, at the end of the bridge, the same lady walking by me, saw that my shoe was untied and to my embarrassment she insisted on tying my shoe so I would not have to unstrap from my cart. As she was stooped down in front of me, she looked up at me and said, "If I could, I would wash your feet for what you're doing." I couldn't help it, I started crying. An extremely humbling moment.

Handmade Apache Scarf

A beautiful young Apache lady stopped to see me on her way back from classes in Farmington, New Mexico. She gave me a delicious chicken sandwich and listened to my story. After she returned to Dulce, she shared with her mother, Verta, my telling of how cold it was in my tent the night before. Her mother promptly went to work making me a most beautiful neck scarf! Becky said she was dead set on finding me to give me my precious gift and just as I was entering Bloomfield, she found me. Money cannot buy that scarf! I was so very touched. And as if that were not enough, Becky gave me some money toward a room. See why I Love Life? And that means I love all the people in that life. And if you Love all the people in that life, they will feel it and love you right back. It works for everyone, not just me. Sitting looking at the beautiful neck scarf made for me by an Apache woman I've never met. It was presented to me by her beautiful daughter. Truly, a gift from the heart. It touched her heart deeply after being told I had been cold while crossing her tribal lands. She had the ability to do something about it and she did. It left me thinking about giving, and how very important it is to give. Nothing is more important than love. Giving is a means of transportation for love. When another's distress touches your heart, perhaps you have the ability to do something about it. The giving of the scarf warmed my heart much more than the gift scarf will ever warm my neck. Touch the heart of another by the giving of your available abilities. This is how we spread love and how we change the world. And, when we touch the heart of another, our mind is then taken off our own little problems so that we then may concentrate on making ourselves Love Life no matter what.

Blue Mushy

10/13/13. Early in the morning as I was approaching the small convenience store in Beclabito, New Mexico for my coffee, a 10 year-old Navajo boy gave me a Styrofoam cup and said, "Here sir, some blue mushy for you." I told the store clerk about it and she said it was a hot cereal made from fresh ground blue corn meal. She said the little guy sells it outside their store every morning while waiting for his school bus. It certainly touched my heart, and it was very good. Went up to Four Corners with the intention of stepping into Utah and Colorado and got there just as the Navajo manager of the Four Corners Monument, Louise, was closing the gate at its 6:00 pm closing time. She allowed me to spend the night locked up in the Four Corners Monument Park! It was so cool! I took all my pictures and then made my bed inside of a closed in vendor's space, snug and out of the wind. Two guys working late on the new restrooms gave me a cold pop and some snacks before they went home at dark. The next morning, a Navajo couple stopped and gave me a hot cup of coffee. The same couple gave me coffee again on my way to

Red Mesa the next morning! Numerous people have stopped to give me water and food. I Love Life because there is so much to love about this most wonderful of gifts we have all received. The best part of it for me: the wonderful and precious human beings sharing it with me!! Love Life my friends.

"Love Walker"

10/25/13. As I was leaving Kayenta, Arizona a young Navajo man ran alongside me, handed me a huge breakfast burrito and said that it was compliments of the Blue Kettle Restaurant. A few minutes later, a couple stopped and gave me PowerAde and a big banana muffin. I only did 10 miles Monday and stopped at the Canyon Café and Anasazi Inn at Tseg. While eating in the café, a very well dressed and distinguished looking Navajo gentleman with a long gray braid, approached me and asked was that my rig outside. I acknowledged yes, and he said, "So you are "Love Walker?" I love our first people, and that made me feel so good. About 5:00 AM the next morning, in the same café, the young Navajo waiter told me his full Navajo name and his clan. We spoke of changes he and his people have had to make and he said, "Evolving is painful." After paying my bill and turning toward the door, he said something to me in Navajo and then translated it, "Be well grandfather." The sincerity in his young handsome face is what made it such a wonderful compliment. You want to see pure childlike curiosity and hear some basic wisdom of life, hang around some of our Native Peoples.

My Friend David

10/27/13. A Navajo lady gave me a bag with McNuggets, a candy bar, and a Coke. A couple stopped and gave me twenty bucks. Another Navajo man brought me a sandwich and water. My friend David Bateman met up with me near Cameron, AZ the same night. We stayed at the Cameron Trading Post. The room was great as was our meal and both were certainly reasonably priced. It was great spending time with my friend. We laughed a lot! We toasted our good time with a nice Bourbon my friend brought me. I knew I would continue on toward Flagstaff with a Love Life attitude appreciating my most wonderful gift of life filled with the greatest friends ever and the most exciting adventure of meeting new and interesting individuals every day! I know that facing every day with a Love Life attitude is not always easy. I also know though, that the effort is always worth it. Please, Love Life today my friends and do not forget to do so tomorrow as well.

Annie Keithline!

The highlight of my walk through Oak Creek Canyon, was having 24 year-old Annie Keithline run up to me all excited telling me she used my story and advice to orchestrate her own walk of America. She said she has always had to prove things for herself and she just got tired of seeing people living in fear, afraid of each other. Annie said she set out to see if all the fear is really justified, she says with an absolute conviction that it is not justified. A man at a little place way out in the boonies early into New Mexico told me about Annie, she had come to his store pushing all her belongings on a jogging stroller. It was an absolute pleasure to meet this little dynamo of LOVE LIFE energy! She said she has met nothing but wonderful people and never been harmed or threatened during her walk of the South or of the West. She is doing America in sections. She is now doing the West and has decided not to continue through Flagstaff because of the weather. She instead is having her boyfriend, Samuel Perkins, drop her off in Phoenix before he heads back to Lafayette, LA, where the two met, and she will walk from there to Los Angeles. Sam came out to see Annie on his vacation. On their way to Las Vegas, they stopped again and Annie handed me this glass of some kind of green natural vegetable concoction and insisted I drink it, she insisted it was good for me. Like everything else good for me, it looked like snot and tasted terrible. She was so sweet and wonderful, I drank every drop. What a woman. Annie, is a shining example of a Love Life attitude and letting go of fears. Love Life like me and Annie do.

Susanna Sophia Hart

11/5/13. In Cottonwood, Arizona, I had just strapped on my harness in preparation to walk out of the parking lot of my motel in the morning and Dwayne, maybe in his fifties, hollered from across the street that he wanted to hear my story. He listened and then told me he had lost his 17 year-old son only 8 years before. He didn't say how, it doesn't matter, his little boy is gone. He talked about how the pain never goes away and that he cries nearly every day. I know, and he knew that I know and that gave him some comfort. And so, because we both spoke out we were both comforted. As I was walking out of Sedona, who should pull up beside me, my new and wonderful friend, Susanna Sophia Hart, whom I had met when I walked into Sedona. She was sincerely concerned about my condition, a mild cold. She insisted on getting me a motel room. She had messaged me Sunday asking if I wanted her to bring by some chicken noodle soup or anything. I unfortunately was sleeping and never got her message. She is a very special person. I seem to meet a lot very special people don't I? It is because I am in love with the act of breathing, I LOVE LIFE and it shows. Just like it does in all human beings who sincerely appreciate and love their gift of life.

Aguila, Arizona

11/13/13. In Aguila, Arizona, near the Harquihala Mountain Wilderness, I waited outside in the shade while my phone charged inside the only store in town. Also in the shade with me were seven young Mexican men laughing and having a grand time playing scratch-off tickets. Occasionally one would jump up, obviously with a winner and go into the store and come back with more scratch-offs. Another Mexican man, Juan, probably in his late sixties, who spoke very little English approached me and was attempting to find out what I was up to. Remarkably, we were able to communicate. As soon as I told of the death of my children, he grimaced. He then told me he had been married five times and had eight children. Laughing, he said he had an ex-wife in Sonora, Mexico, one in Albuquerque, New Mexico, one in San Antonio, Texas, one in Tucson, and one in Phoenix. Then, beaming with pride, he showed me a picture of his 19 year-old son in an army uniform stationed in Texas who had been to Afghanistan. I wish Juan had let me take his picture, he would not. He was very flamboyant looking with his thick gray/white hair worn long with thick sideburns. He wore his shirt open halfway to reveal the big gold chain around his neck. He laughed a lot and everyone seemed to like him. A few minutes later I heard him explaining to the ones playing the scratch-offs about me walking there from Florida and why. Sometime later, one of the young gamblers walked up to me and handed me ten one dollar bills and with a sweeping motion of his hand indicated that they had all chipped in. I walked up to each shaking their hand and thanking them. They were beaming! In the pictures I took of them, there are only six young men. That's because the seventh who was wearing a big floppy straw hat and was astraddle a bicycle, starting yelling, "No, no!" when I aimed my phone at him. While trying to pull his hat down over his face and back up on the bicycle at the same time, he nearly fell over. Both I and the others broke into laughter. That man did not want his picture taken and I'm thinking there may be more to it than just crossing the border illegally. Had I spoke the language, I still would not have asked why. Some things are just better left alone.

In Hope

11/16/13. Sitting at a picnic table in the little spot called Hope, Arizona, an RV Park and a Shell station, I was approached by a beautiful young woman, Silver, who began excitedly telling me she and her boyfriend had looked me up on-line after seeing me walk through the Wilhoit, Arizona, area. She sat right down with me, going on about how great she thought what I was doing was. Then she told me that she had made the decision to take her own life not too long ago. She said she was stuck in a factory job in Portland, Oregon making very little money and some other things going on that made her think she would be in the spot she was in for the rest of her life. Silver looked at me and said, "Steve, I was getting ready to do it and I suddenly thought of what it would do to my father." And with a most precious look on her pretty face, she continued, "and my dog, I thought about how my dog totally depends on me." I couldn't help it, I reached out and grabbed her precious little hand in both my hands and said, "Thank God you did not do it! Thank God you chose life! How wonderful that you thought of someone else other than yourself and you are still alive!" She said, "And in retrospect, I can now see, I didn't try anything, I didn't even try to get out of my mess, I just gave up. I didn't see all the options I now see." She said she had inherited some land in Wilhoit, and she and her boyfriend were going to build an earth-ship type house on it. Then she laughingly told me, "There was no way I could do the things I wanted to do on less than $500 a week so I now dance in a Portland, Oregon club where I can make $500 bucks a night! And I really enjoy it." I said, "Makes sense to me." I don't give a damn what she does, she's alive! I asked 22 year-old Silver if I could tell her story, and she said for me to absolutely tell it because it may help someone else and show them not to give up so quickly, that there is always an answer. She gave me a most wonderful hug and explained that she was heading to Portland and that her boyfriend stayed in Wilhoit taking care of their animals. I just loved her! And she definitely has her head on straight now. Somewhere in Portland, Oregon in a topless club there is an angel dancing and celebrating being alive! LOVE LIFE my friends and hang in there with it, it is definitely worth sticking it out.

As I was leaving Hope, a sign said, "You're now beyond Hope." How can I not Love Life!

My Personal Caterer

Sunday, 11/17/13. Between Hope and Bouse, Arizona, over 30 miles of nothing, a lady pulled up in her SUV and asked could I use some extra food. As I started to unstrap from my rig, she said, "No need for that, just come up here to the rear of my truck." I did and she simply pulled the lid off my cooler, then reached in her own cooler and got a package of smoked ham, some string cheese, and a large Orange Crush and dropped them into my cooler. She then lifted from her cooler a huge lump of ice and dropped that in my 5 gallon cooler as well. She then said, "Have a good day and be careful." Then she was gone. That would be great if I could have stations like that along the way :). I just Love Life so very much because I know that my attitude spreads joy to others and inspires them to keep going and to never give up! Guess what? Your Love Life attitude does the same thing. Please join me in making a huge change in the world. Only love can change the world.

Played Poker with Wyatt Earp

Had to go into California last night and out of the town of Parker, Arizona to find a tent spot. As I arrived on the California side of the bridge over the Colorado which was elevated over an RV resort, a man, Larry, yelled up from his RV asking what I was doing. As soon as I told him he left his chair to meet me at the base of the bridge. He pulled out his wallet and handed me a twenty and said, "You can't do something like this without money, welcome to California sir." He went on to tell me that I was now in Earp, California, where Wyatt Earp grew up. Larry said when his mother was a young girl, she helped take care of an old man that used to play poker with Wyatt Earp. So, the very first person in the very first house I passed upon my entry into California, helped me out!

No Open Fires

11/25/13. Walking in the 51 miles of nothing through the Colorado River Indian Reservation on the Arizona side, a pickup with an ATV in the bed and pulling a pop-up camper stopped, and the young man driving said he had just come down out of the mountains after a few days. I asked if he had had a good time. With a huge smile, he said, "It was just too much fun!" He gave me a cold Coke and then said he had something left over he would love to give me. He reached in his cooler and pulled out a huge sirloin! It was in a Ziploc bag marinating in teriyaki and some other stuff he said. So, that night I found the most remote place I could find so my fire wouldn't be seen from the road and waited until dark before I started so the smoke wouldn't be seen. The fire conditions are extreme on most of the reservation. I had even seen signs in a couple areas stating, "No Open Fires." I gathered up some mesquite, lit my fire and stuck my big fat sirloin on a sharp stick and held it right in the fire. The rarer the better with me so it took little time to cook. I quickly smothered the fire with sand and poured water on it as well. That was the first steak I'd had since I left Florida and I'm here to tell y'all that thing was absolutely awesome! God, it tasted so good. That steak was probably my Thanksgiving meal because when I left there in the morning I had about 90 miles of desolate country in front of me before I would get to Brawley, CA. So, I would probably only get Vienna sausages instead of turkey on Thanksgiving. Always be very thankful for your turkey and your family and friends you enjoy it with.

If I Can Love Life...

November 27, 2013, Blythe, California, in the Palo Verde Valley of the Lower Colorado River Valley region, an agricultural area and part of the Colorado Desert along the Colorado. My morning: I walked 2 blocks in the cold morning air for coffee at the Shell station where the Kenny Logins Caddyshack song, "I'm Alright," was blaring out, "I'm alright. Nobody worry 'bout me. Why you got to gimme a fight? Can't you just let it be? I'm alright....." I looked into the open doors at the two young Mexican ladies behind the counter, with a huge smile while snapping my fingers, and said, "Well that'll certainly start one's morning on an upbeat, now won't it!" They both just stared at me without comment. "Here, let me give y'all my card," I said, "no politics, nothing religious, just about my walk. I've now walked nearly 34,000 miles and crossed these here United States seven times!" They took the cards but remained stone faced. I got my coffee and went to pay the stoic clerks. I handed over my money and said, "I walk with "LOVE LIFE" over my head because I lost my handsome only son to suicide and then I lost my beautiful only baby girl to an accidental drug overdose, because she just couldn't get over the loss of her little brother." Now, they're listening. Then I said, "If I can love life, just about anybody can by God! And do I ever love it! And, with all my heart!" They were both nodding in agreement and both wished me the best with broad smiles. One had moist eyes.

I Stepped outside and a Hopi man was unloading the stores Pepsi delivery. "How are you this fine morning?" I said. "Cold," he said with a smile. "I'm from Florida," I countered. He said, "Oh shit!" I gave him my card and told him why I walked and said, "I run into people fairly often whose tragedies make mine pale. So, I really don't want to hear about ones three flat tires in one week. Life is about using perspective. About looking at the good things and not the bad shit on the nightly news." He agreed wholeheartedly and said real loud as I was walking back toward my motel, "Thank you sir!" Love Life and spread it my friends, we can change the world!

Thanksgiving, Vienna Sausages, NOT!

November 28, Thanksgiving Day, 2013 and Yippee!! While in the store in Palo Verde, California, (last store for 55 miles) having coffee, a lady, Cathy, invited me to pitch my tent free in the trailer/RV park across the road. At 4:00 they were having their annual community Thanksgiving dinner and I was invited she said. So, I had turkey and NOT Vienna sausages for dinner! I did have two cans for breakfast though. It was a potluck dinner courtesy of residents of the trailer park. I don't have to tell you how good it was, we all know how each cook tries to outdo the other with their fine traditional recipe.

Ernie Andros!!

Figure 20. Ernie Andros's car.

12/13/13. In the very cold Santa Rosa Mountains, near Borrego Mountain, and quite far away from anything, I look up and was totally astonished to see an old man in jogging shorts and a tie-dyed tee shirt running toward me! He said, "Where you heading?" I said, "Where you heading?" 90 year-old WW II veteran Ernie Andros said he was running coast to coast to raise money for the LST 325 Memorial. Ernie was on an LST as a U.S. Navy Corpsman to the U.S. Marines. He explained to me that they had to cancel the planned voyage of LST 325 to Normandy and Omaha Beach where it was 70 years ago on D-Day, because of a lack of funds. This didn't sit well with Ernie and the 90 year-old dynamo is doing something about it and going to raise the money to take it there another D-Day celebration!

When I met Ernie on the road, I took several pictures of both him and his car. To my utter dismay that evening, I realized that every picture I'd taken as far back as Sedona had disappeared! I was so upset over it because I so wanted to share what this 90 year-old national treasure is doing. Well, yesterday, 6 miles out of Julian and starting the steep climb up the mountain, who should pull up, Ernie Andros! I couldn't believe I would get another chance to take his picture again. He said that he got to thinking about how much I could help him work out his route and he would buy my lunch when I reached the top of the mountain and Julian. It was 11:15 then and so I put it in gear and pulled that 100 pound plus cart up the mountain in a cold wind to meet Ernie at Granny's Kitchen at 2:10. Amazing what the offer of free food does to motivate me. The owner and staff of the wonderful little restaurant and friend, Irishman, Patrick, a most colorful gentleman, were waiting for me along with Ernie applauding me as I arrived. Talk about a treat waiting inside! Granny's Kitchen is wonderful! The food is a great match for the atmosphere in this place! People just hang out in there because it's just a great place to be! I loved it! Please do yourself a favor and stop there when you're in Julian, CA. They called Fox News 5 in Sacramento and the news crew interviewed me and Ernie there in Granny's kitchen. He proudly told during our interview, referring to being a Navy Corpsman during the war, "I never lost a patient!" That's quite a feat and add to that, the enemy always tries to kill the medics when possible and puts bounties on their heads.

Like Me, Lost All

12/28/13. At the Stagecoach Inn in Aguanga, California, several people came up to me expressing interest in my walk and praise of my "LOVE LIFE" sign. As I was leaving the establishment, a gentleman with snow white hair and snow white beard came up to me and said, "My name is CJ, I don't know for sure why you are walking and carrying that sign, but I just feel I need to help you in some way." And he handed me a ten. I told him my story and he said, "Well, sadly, we have something in common, I lost my son and my daughter." "I am so very sorry for you loss sir!" I said. "I am sorry for your loss." He said. He continued, "I guess we just didn't realize how bad my son's heart problem was because he just always stayed so active, we lost him at 39." He hesitated for a moment and then continued, "I lost my daughter three years later. I really do not want to go into it. I'm just going to call it, we lost her because of her being Bi-polar." You can call it any damn thing you want sir, you lost all your babies!! He stood silent a moment, then wished me well and abruptly left. Love Life folks and be so very thankful for the way your life is going because you have the power within you to change it if it starts veering away from the way you want it to be. Do not bitch, just change it.

"I don't do regrets I do adjustments" ~ Steve Fugate

Profiled!

1/9/14. I am determined to be happy because that goes with my gift of LIFE. I decided to try a motel downtown Lancaster, California, because it was on my direct route. Though such located motels can be pretty shabby, this one looked very nice. As I was about to enter the lobby, a gentleman looked at me and my cart with a scowl. I entered and asked the lady at the desk if she had a vacancy even though the sign said "VACANCY." She said yes. As I handed her my card and was telling her I was walking, the scowling gentleman opened a door behind her and whispered something I was unable to hear. The lady then turned to me and said she was very sorry but all the rooms were taken. Now, I had to walk backwards and off my route over a mile and a half to where most of the motels were. Just as I neared the one I had chosen, I called just to make sure they had availability even though I had just confirmed it online. The lady was very pleasant and asked smoking or non-smoking, I chose the latter. She asked how many days and I told her at the price of $55.00 I might get it for one more night but wasn't sure yet. She said that wasn't a problem, just let her know. As we were talking I saw the motel sign. I unhitched my cart and walked in smiling big and handed her my card. She said, "You're walking?!" I told her yes, and why I walked. She said she wasn't sure they even had a room and if so, it would be $75.00 plus tax and it would have to be a smoking room. I reminded her that only minutes ago it was she told me a totally different story and was much more pleasant. She looked out the window at my cart and said, "That thing is all full of trash and stuff!" I explained that was my luggage containing my clothes, sleeping bag, and tent. I was very tired and needed a room and so I kept repeating what she had said to me on the phone. She finally said that I could stay but for only one night and in a smoking room. I took the room.

Now, I could get all mad at a business located in Los Angeles County accustomed to dealing with lots of bad situations and cause myself to be miserable, or, I could look past it and be happy I could forget all about running into John Moran on his bike earlier in the day who kept me from continuing the wrong way. And forget about Ra Cienfuegos stopping and giving me a bag of assorted fresh fruit and forget about Larry, who sells jerky for a living stopping and giving me a huge bag of fresh Honey Turkey Jerky. And I could bitch and moan and forget all about the times I've been given free rooms by motel owners. Well, I'm not going to forget those positive things and trade them for the negative. I cannot change those motel owners I can only change me. And by God, no one is going to steal my happiness!

Love more than Judge

1/13/14. In a motel room in Gorman, California. Now, as y'all remember, my last motel experience in Lancaster, 1/9/14, was not the best one may wish for. Well. Tonight when I approached the front desk at the Econo Lodge, I was greeted by Ben, an Indian, as was the one who denied me a room in Lancaster. And the one who very reluctantly rented me in a room, also in Lancaster. Ben excitedly said, "You, you one with "LOVE LIFE" sign, good! Room usually $54.00 plus tax, I give you room for $49.00 plus tax, how that?" Then he insisted I show him all about my cart and explain what all I was toting on it. Later, in the lobby, a very old Indian man, probably Ben's father, said, "You man walking world?" I explained I was walking America, not the world. He said, "Let me feel leg?" I lifted my right leg and he squeezed my calf and said, "Yes, feel strong, is good to know you sir!" Later, the owner brought me a couple packages of microwave popcorn.

Life is about balance, we have perspective as a tool to help us stay in balance. That way, we can Love more than judge.

"Moved"

1/19/14. On Friday, a lady walked up to me and I said, "Hi, how are you today?" and she said, "Moved." She had in her hand a copy of an article her husband, Patric Hedlund, had written up on me from our morning interview for The Mountain Enterprise in Frazier Park, California. She said they were going to print my story on February 1st and feature my story for their Valentine's Day special edition. She said she had a young friend who lost her grandmother to suicide and has a hard time dealing with it. The young friend is going to attempt a thru-hike of the Appalachian Trail in March and she felt it would be perfect for the young lady to talk to me. I agreed and asked her to please hook me up with her. She offered to take me to a nearby town and have a machine shop work on my cart. I thanked her but declined. Just after that, a lady who doesn't want her name revealed, came out of a convenience store as I walked up and while wrapping her arms around my neck, said, "I've been waiting for you, they told me you were coming I said, "Great! I collect hugs!" She told me she had a terminal disease. She said that she loved life with all her heart and was staying positive in hopes she would beat the disease. While we were hugging again, her friend pulled up, got out of her car and said, "Hey, I want in on all this hugging!" So we had a group hug. Later that evening at Pine Mountain Club, a guy named Bob stopped and insisted we go to his house and let him work on my cart. I did and in an hour I was repaired and back on the road. Saturday, I spent the day walking on Mil Protrero Highway and Hudson Ranch Road which is some of the most beautiful scenery I've walked in California. I was having a grand time walking and loving life because the great things in life so outweigh the little inconveniences.

Want to Trade Places?

1/26/14. In a truck stop charging up all my stuff and celebrating being clean. $8 bucks for a shower, a bargain indeed. My clothes now sparkling clean and my belly full. I slept great in my luxurious tent the previous night and was well rested. I was loving Life and thankful that all my needs were met. I introduced myself to the two very pretty young Mexican ladies managing the truck stop, explaining to them about my cart outside and what I was doing. I wanted them to know I was not loitering and was indeed using and paying for services provided. They had both seen me walking the day before and commenced asking me several questions after telling them my story. One young lady asked, "Are you really happy?" I assured her I was indeed very happy and loved life."

She said, "I'm not happy and I should be at least as happy as you are." She shared some problems she was having and we spoke on them some.

I left the young ladies with this story: "I met a man on the beach and shared my story, telling of the loss of my two beautiful babies. He commenced to telling me about his 33 year-old son being a drug addict and how he had spent thousands putting him in rehab over and over again. He said he was at his wits end as to what to do. So, I asked him, "You want to trade places with me?" No way! Absolutely not!" he said. After a moment he said, "Thank you sir." Both young ladies shook their heads in understanding and agreement. The one said, "Thank you sir." Love Life, Life is well deserving of our Love.

Abdul

1/27/14. I was in my tent at Five Corners, California where CA 269 ends and intersects with CA 145, on the southeast corner across the road from the Five Corners Liquor Store. I went in the store to see if they knew who owned the property across from them so I could ask permission to tent there. The store owner was Abdul, who spoke very little English. I began by telling him how many miles I'd walked, how many times I'd crossed America and so on. For the most part, all he did was stare at me. And I'm thinking, this is going nowhere. Then, all of a sudden, he started explaining that the property belonged to some huge corporation somewhere. He walked outside and looked at my cart and then walked back in and started asking me all kinds of questions, struggling with his English, but getting his point made. I figured out that he was saying he didn't think the big company would mind. I thanked him and ordered some fried chicken from his deli. He would not let me pay and told me to get a drink as well. I fetched a small size drink and he said, "No, put back, get big one." He also told me he opened at 5:00 in the morning and for me to come in for coffee. And as promised, Abdul gave me a morning greeting with coffee, and, two fried chicken leg quarters for the road. We just never know what is inside another, the reason we have to leave all judging at the door. Love Life and all who share it with us.

Rusty and Nancy

1/28/14. Minutes after leaving Abdul, Rusty, husband of Nancy Gragnani who I had met earlier, pulled up and handed me a bag of oranges from his grove. He had driven about 20 miles looking for me. He left me his card, "Don Gragnani Farms" and said to call if I needed anything. Later in the day, a lens fell out of my glasses and I could not find it on the road. I had an extra pair that needed a lens secured back into place and there was no way I could see that little screw to repair them. I can barely see without my glasses. I called Rusty for help and he drove several miles and repaired them for me. As it was so late, Rusty suggested I tent across the street at his friend's ranch. I pitched my tent in Garland's yard, he is employed by the ranch. He kept checking on me and he gave me an ice cold beer to help make my tent prettier.

Rusty & Nancy came out later and brought friends to meet me, Tony Marchini, Patricia, Christiana, Connie, and Andrianna Amach. Christianna interviewed me for her school paper. Nancy brought me two Big Macs and a huge bag of trail mix. A gentleman from another home on the property, Robert, came over to investigate the noise we were making. Rusty explained what was going on and he left. He returned minutes later though, with bananas, apples, soda pop, and two fat tuna sandwiches! Garland brought me coffee in the morning, then Robert's wife, Shelly, had me over for another cup at her place. We talked a long time. She has had much tragedy in her life.

Last night, Nancy treated me to dinner at Reno's Bar & Grill (awesome food!) and several of her friends were there wanting to meet me. I believe that everyone in the bar came up to meet me. They had all seen my interview on the local Fresno ABC Channel 30 news. At one point, a waitress told me there were two youngsters outside with their parents who wanted to meet me. I'm guessing both, a young lady and young gentleman, were about 12. They wanted their pictures taken with me. I loved it. Before I left, a waitress handed me $120 dollars which had been collected at the bar for me. While we were standing there, a man walked up and handed me a $100 dollar bill!

Joey and Patricia

1/30/14. It was very difficult to leave Kerman, California. So many people were stopping to greet me, give me food, give me money, and have their pictures taken with me, that it took me nearly six hours to cover less than two miles! Tony, and another great guy, Chris, kept coming by and checking on me. I finally gave up trying to make any miles and tented in the yard of a friend of Chris. The friend and his neighbor kept checking on me asking if I needed anything. It took me nearly six hours to cover a mile and a half!

The next morning, a young man, Rosendo, told me he was on his way to a business meeting in Mendota and would ask Joey Amadores, owner of the Los Amadores Motel if he would give me a room there. As it turned out, Tony Marchini, of JS Chevrolet in Tranquility, California, had already asked him as well. Joey Amadores called me telling me he would be honored to provide me with a room! During the 17 mile walk into Rosendo, I was stopped many times for pictures and greetings. Two Mexican men stopped and expressed to me how very much they appreciated my endeavors. One handed me a folded up bill which I put straight into my pocket. Moments later when I stopped to place the bill in my wallet, I saw Ben Franklin's face! And I'm fairly certain Ben winked at me. Mike stopped his truck and gave me two big and delicious chicken sandwiches. Bill Percy walked the very long lane from his home to invite me in for a meal. I declined as I was anxious to get to my motel room.

About a mile out of town, Joey and Patricia Amadores were waiting for me and put their car's emergency flashers on and escorted me into Rosendo! It is a very good thing Joey and Patricia are patient people because I was stopped repeatedly for pictures, and to be given food and cash. Midway during running the gauntlet of kindness, Patricia had to take the huge amount of food and put it in their car. Yes, I cry a lot out here. I stayed in the motel owned by Joey and Patricia free of charge.

We Give You Home

2/9/14. In Fresno County, somewhere between Firebaugh, and Merced, a Vietnamese couple, Thai and Diamond Dang, stopped to talk. They said they had seen my story on a Fresno TV station. They were super excited about meeting me. They said that after seeing the TV program they decided they wanted to help someone spreading such a message of Love.

Thai and Diamond, were part of the huge exodus of Vietnamese who fled Viet Nam after the collapse of South Viet Nam. They are called Boat People. Approximately one third of them did not make it to safety. There are now 1.6 million Boat People spread out over the world. These precious individuals have experienced horrors most of us Americans cannot even imagine. Thai & Diamond use the fruits of their success in America to help former American POW'S and disabled veterans of the Viet Nam War.

On Valentine's Day,. I received a phone call from Thai Dang, telling me he and Diamond had booked me a room in Oakdale, California. In a very heavy accent he said, "Sometime, when love life, life love back. This you time. I tell motel lady you story and to treat you good. It Valentine Day, you tell people about love, you need love, me and Diamond, we give you love." At my really nice room, the head housekeeper, Altair Miranda, brought me a coupon for a free complete breakfast at the restaurant next door, compliments of the motel management he said. He also brought me rolls of plastic bags and some other things. He was totally fascinated with my walks. A guy got out of his car and handed me a box of chocolates! John, from there in Oakdale, said his good friend, Thai Dang called him and asked him to take me some chocolates for Valentine's Day! We hit it right off and talked long.

Thai and Diamond, paid for several motel rooms for me after driving many miles to meet me in Fresno County and then again at South Lake Tahoe. As they were driving me to find a motel room in Lake Tahoe, Diamond, asked, "Steve, you have home in Florida?" To which I said no and explained that I lived in my van and was quite happy living in it. Diamond then said, "Oh, we give you home!" Thai, then reached over and patted his wife's leg and said, "Good idea Diamond! Yes, we give you home." I have never seen any two people as hooked at the heart as are Diamond and Thai Dang! They gave me a brand new Jayco 25 foot Jayflight Travel Trailer. I cry every time I think about it.

Devastated Hearts

2/12/14. In a motel room in Turlock, California. The day before, walking through the San Luis National Wildlife Reserve, being really cautious due to a very thick fog, a man, maybe in his mid-thirties, pulled over to talk. I was surprised that anyone would risk pulling over on such a narrow shoulder in that fog. He told me he had seen me on the news out of Fresno. He told me over and over how wonderful he thought my walk was. After he had crossed the road back to his truck, he turned around and just looked at me without saying anything. Then, after opening his mouth several times with nothing coming out, he blurted out, "My brother killed himself!" He started crying. Through his tears, he said, "Thank you for what you're doing." He then quickly jumped into his truck. Later in the day, walking into Stevinson, another man stopped and handed me sixty dollars while expressing the gratitude he felt after seeing me on the Fresno news. Then he started telling of five friends who lost their children to suicide over his 70 years. As he said, "I knew every one of those youngsters personally," he started crying. Then he said, "Here, here's some more." And he handed me another forty dollars. Let's make sure we are listening closely to others. Let's make sure others are feeling our love. Let's keep ourselves as happy as possible, our fellow human beings need to feel our joy over our love affair with life! Love Life my friends.

Lodge Closed… No Problem

3/17/14. It was getting near tent pitching time and because the weather report said the low 20's for the area, I was hoping I could get a room at the lodge at Calpine, California. When I got to the lodge it was obvious that it was now closed. Disappointing to say the least. There was a man sitting on the ground next to the lodge working on putting new brake shoes on a car. I said, "Excuse me sir is this the only lodge in the area?" he looked up and said, "Hey Steve!" I hadn't recognized him at first, it was Kenneth, I had met earlier in the day as he was working on the highway, an employee of Caltrans. He said he was also the caretaker for the closed lodge and that there was no electric or water in the rooms, but I was welcome to stay in one and at least sleep in a bed and not have to pitch my tent. He also let me do my laundry and take a shower in his apartment also located in the lodge. A friend of his came by and invited us to a cook out at his friend's house. The friend was a very sweet young lady in her late 30's who had once been both a police officer and a firefighter in New York City and retired early from a California police department. She was able to do that because she had taught herself the skill of buying and reselling homes. I thoroughly enjoyed being around her. She gave me three big bags of dried mixed fruit and offered me more stuff that I turned down because of weight. We spoke a lot about the beauty of life. The next day I received a text from her telling me she sincerely appreciated what I was doing. She explained that at 15 she swallowed a bottle of sleeping pills and it was a miracle doctors were able to save her! How blessed her family, her friends, and the rest of us are that such a fine high quality human being is still with us. I am so very thankful for all the precious human beings I encounter in life.

Wow!

Near Stockton, California, a young man named Devon, 22 years old, stopped and offered me a ride. After saying no thank you he said, "So what's your story man?" After telling of my son's suicide his eyes welled up with tears and he said, "I tried to do that just recently, because my heart was broken." I went right in on him about how we do not have the right to take our own life because it does not belong to us alone, it also belongs to those who love us. And about how it is usually the very sensitive individuals who do so, the very ones society so sorely needs. And that they get in so much pain they become blinded and cannot see that they are being self-centered, looking only at their own pain and not the horrible pain they're about to inflict on their loved ones. After I finished my lecture to him he said, "Thank you. I appreciate your heartfelt concern and I can't hear too many times why I shouldn't do it. But let me tell you why I didn't do it." He told me he was sitting at his desk with a full bottle of prescription sleeping pills in front of him and that his intentions were to swallow all the contents and go to sleep to never wake up. Devon said that just as he was getting ready to take the pills, he saw a very real vision in his mind. He said he saw himself falling from a cliff. He said he kept waiting for this very vivid picture in his mind to stop he said, but instead, he just kept falling! Then, he told me, he all of a sudden yelled out to himself, "Wait a minute here! If I'm falling for so long, I must've been at pretty damn high place to fall from!" He said he then realized he had everything to live for and was not about to let an emotional upset allow him to forget who he was or his aspirations in life. He then looked at me and said, "Yes, I love life!" Heed the words of Devon, "Love Life!"

God, I Love What I Do!

4/13/14. I am loving life and enjoying the beauty of life. A lady stopped and gave me an eggplant wrap from Trader Joes. It was pretty good. But the real delight was her excitement over my "LOVE LIFE" sign! As she was leaving, a guy stopped to thank me for my walks. He had seen me on The Weather Channel and said he really appreciated my endeavors because he had once been suicidal. I grabbed his arm and told him how very wonderful it was that he was still with us! I said, "Don't you ever think about that again!" He said, "Never, I love life and am way past that now." I love hearing those stories. He was a fine young man and most definitely now has his act together. He gave me his business card and told me to look him up in Bend, Oregon, if I needed anything.

Yesterday, a man stopped his rented truck and stood beside it snapping pictures of me as I walked toward him. He said, "I'm Peter, and I'm from Alaska. I've decided to drive all over the country taking pictures of animals instead of hunting them as I once did. I saw that "LOVE LIFE" sign and I just had to find out what you're about." I told him and he said, "You're the messenger for the rest of us to remind us what's really important in life." He asked if I took donations. After I said yes, he pulled a brand new one hundred dollar from his wallet and handed it to me. I said, "Sir, that's a lot of money, I thank you." Peter, from Alaska said, "I believe in what you're doing sir, I'm a recovering alcoholic and drug addict. Thank you for the reminder. I would have probably spent that on something much less important than what you're doing."

"Live Like Luke"

Figure 21

Early on a Sunday in late March of 2014, walking over Lee Summit in the Plumas National Forest, Doug Sheehy stopped. After answering his question of why I walked, he shared his story. Only nine months before, on June 10, 2013, his son Luke had been killed. Luke was a Redding, California, Smoke Jumper, and died while fighting the Saddle Back Fire, in the Warner Mountains, within the South Warner Wilderness, in far north eastern California. We both cried at times as we spoke of the fresh horror my new friend was facing and of ways I had learned to handle my own horror, with much more time to deal with it. Doug showed me a sticker on the window of his SUV, "Live Like Luke" explaining that Luke's approach to Life was to always Love it! He said Luke was always happy and full of joy. He told me that right before Luke jumped into the Warner Mountains, what would be his last jump, he texted to all, "Fuck yeah! Jumping into the Warner's!" His father and all his friends knew Luke, had always expressed a desire to one day, jump into the beautiful Warner Mountains. Doug, an accomplished musician, in honor of his brave son, composed a song, "Fuck yeah!" Upon parting, we agreed to stay in touch.

Figure 22.

About mid-May, 2014, Doug called me while I was walking in southeastern Washington State, somewhere around Walla-Walla. He told me that he and his wife, Lynn, were travelling to Boise, Idaho for Family Day at the Wildland Firefighter Foundation, May 19, 2014. It's a day for those who have lost loved ones to share and support one another. He told me they would be honored to have me as their guest at the annual event.

Doug asked that I go out of my way a few miles to Grangeville, Idaho, in the Idaho Panhandle' where smokejumper, Sarah Doering, the Grangeville Smoke Jumping Base, would meet up with me and relay me to the Smoke Jumping Base at McCall, Idaho. At the McCall Smoke Jumping Base, I was able to meet many of the brave men and women who make up the ranks of smokejumpers. They cheerfully showed me the base and explained all functions and procedures. There, I met Smokejumper Kyle Esparza, a longtime and dear friend of Luke Sheehy. Kyle, a USFS Smokejumper, based in Boise, was there in McCall, as the second part of the relay team to get me to Boise to attend the annual remembrance of the brave men and women lost in the line of duty putting their lives on the line. After asking individually, both Sarah and Kyle why they did it, they each, with ear to ear grins, said, "It's fun."

In Boise, I met Brendan Mcdonough, the only survivor of the elite Granite Mountain Hot Shot Crew out of Prescott, Arizona. Brendan was on lookout position when 19 of his courageous fellow Hot Shots perished at the Yarnell Hills Fire, Yarnell, Arizona, on June 30, 2013. Brandon, was asked to speak to all of us in attendance at the annual gathering. Soon after the fine young man rose to speak, he started sobbing. He said nothing else… it spoke volumes! Later, Doug Sheehy was asked to perform. He said to the audience, "I hope none of you have a problem with the word "fuck." No one said anything, he then commenced to perform the song honoring his precious son, "Fuck Yeah!" Everyone understood. The words "fuck yeah" were quite beautiful to us all. I also met and became friends with Tom Ashcraft, the grieving father of Andrew Ashcraft, one of the 19 Granite Mountain Hot Shots killed.

Helen Keller, Role Model

4/25/14. A lady named Rachelle stopped Wednesday to tell me how very beautiful she thought my "LOVE LIFE" sign was. She just kept hugging me! She explained to me that both her daughter and son, both in their twenties, suffered from an extremely rare genetic condition, they were both going blind! She said, the three of them had embraced life with a Love Life attitude and faced every day with complete joy. She told me that her children were doing all they could to embrace life to the fullest. They had both travelled the world extensively. Rachelle said that Helen Keller was a real role model for them and that they loved to read her description of colors. She tried, but without success, to reach her son on the phone so I could tell him what was over my head, "LOVE LIFE." Rachelle really was joyful about life despite what had been dealt to her and her precious children. Her joy certainly gave me a boost of energy.

Why They're Called Random Acts of Kindness

As I was walking into Kooskia, Idaho to do some last minute shopping for the 100 miles of nothing I was facing as I headed for the Montana state line, John Swan walked up to me and asked why I was walking. We had a most interesting conversation on my favorite subject, Life. And though I had no plans of getting a motel room, I had one the night before and I had done only seven miles, John said, "See that motel down there just past that bar sign? Well, I'm going to drive down there and get you a room sir." I just cannot turn down a shower and clean sheets. I have found Love, just around so very many corners.

Large Abundance of Good People!

5/9/14. In the home of Ray and Gloria, between Pomeroy and Clarkston, Washington. They live on 8 acres in the Blue Mountains. There is no electricity, 2 dogs, 2 ducks, lots of chickens, and lots of love. Ray and Gloria lost their beautiful 41 year-old, youngest daughter, July 25, 2013 in a house fire. She was the loving mother of five. Ray started following me on Facebook after seeing my story on Yahoo News. He decided to try and find me today after seeing I was in his area. Well, when he pulled up, not far out of Clarkston, Idaho, I was concerned that one of the wheels on my cart, would collapse completely before I made it to a bike shop in Lewiston, Idaho. Four spokes had blown out of the small 16 inch wheel. Ray drove me into Lewiston and the owner of Covey's Bike & Board, Justin, put new spokes in and only charged ten bucks. Be a Ray, or a Gloria, every chance you get so we can keep Love traveling from place to place.

You May Want to Move to Montana?

Vananda, Montana, I had my tent pitched and was in for the night when a pickup pulled up with its lights right on me. I peeked my head out and said to the cowboy, "Am I on your property sir?" He said, "Yup, and my wife, Anna, will be real disappointed if you don't come up to the house and let her feed you." I thanked Russell, very much, but explained that I was in for the night. He said, "Alright, I'll be back then with a plate of food." He brought me a great home cooked chicken dinner, a couple sandwiches for the next day and a cold beer. I Love Life, I love Montana!

Tenderfoot Motel White Sulfur Springs, Montana

6/6/14. Wednesday, a fine young man, Tyrell Jacobs, stopped with a sandwich, jerky, and bottles of water. He had no idea what I was doing, he just loved my sign. Being an avid backpacker himself, he asked me, "You got any trash you want me to take for you?" Only a backpacker knows to ask that question because they know trash is extra weight and bother, but also know how conscious we are of keeping our beautiful land clean. After I told him of my relay ride to the Wild Land Firefighters Foundation Annual Memorial Ceremony from Grangeville, Idaho to Boise, Idaho by Idaho Smokejumpers, he smiled big and proud as he told me he is a Montana Wild Land Firefighter. Tyrell suggested to me that I check out the Tenderfoot Motel when I reached White Sulfur Springs, Montana. He said it was a really cool place with private cabins. He was right, that place is great!

As soon as I walked into the lobby of The Tenderfoot Motel, Dean Anderson, owner, said, "We've been waiting for you, Tyrell Jacobs and his parents called and told me about you. Your room is free. We had a suicide in town last night. Everyone knew him and it is just a shame. I just do not believe it is an accident you're here. I've called the local newspaper for interview with you tomorrow. I would like for you to speak to as many here as you can. You may stay here as long as you need." He told me there was also a 16 year-old high school senior who had killed herself less than a year ago. I told Dean I would talk to anyone at any time day or night and for as long as they wish! Love Life is contagious and I'm going to spread it everywhere and whenever I can, using the power of Love that comes with a Love Life attitude.

Life Spoils Me Rotten

Life spoils me rotten. Because I love it so very much and trust it to treat me fairly as I treat it fairly, by not complaining and whining about it, nor about the other beautiful individuals sharing it with me. I try to not complain about life, I just Love Life. I try and never complain about my fellow human beings, I just love them. I do not tell them what they should do or how they should do it, I just love them. And most of all, I do not judge them for choosing to live their life differently from the way I've chosen to live mine, I just love them. If I am judging them, blaming them, and complaining about them, I cannot love them. I am maturing past the ignorance of blame and judgment, so that I may love you no matter who you are or how you've chosen to live your Life. My goal in Life is to have a heart governed mind.

Go Ahead and Cry Man

6/13/14. In a motel in Harlowton, Montana and it was storming outside. I just made it into town in time. I had phone service for the first time in 55 miles, since the past Tuesday. Tuesday, a young man, Chuck, a Forestry Service Ranger, pulled up across from me and jumped out his truck super excited! He said, "Man, you were in Plumas National Forest on route 70 down in California a few months ago, right?" "Yup, that was me." I said. He went on to tell me he just got transferred back to this area of Montana, where he is from. Then he started getting all choked up and the tears started streaming down his cheeks as he said, "Man, I was going through a very rough time when I first saw you with that sign. It really helped man, it really did help me pull through." I reached for his hand, and said, "It's okay man, go ahead and cry, that's what I'm out here for." Chuck said, "It is so great I saw you again, it's reassurance man. Thank you for what you do." He asked was there anything he could do for me and I explained to him that having stopped and telling me what happened back in California was the best thing he could ever do for me! Love Life and Love, Love, Love our fellow human being.

Cupcakes and Cold Beer

6/25/14. I was in a Forsythe, Montana motel room after a 100 miles of nothing more than c-stores and a little café here and there. Yes, the shower felt awesome. Yes, I had an ice cold IPA! Bought one of those lemon pepper rotisserie chickens with the intentions of snacking on it throughout the evening. I ate the whole damn thing as soon as I opened it.

Sunday morning, a lady stopped and gave me a couple bottles of water and a cupcake. Later in the day a young man stopped and handed me a Styrofoam container holding a big fat cheeseburger and still hot fries and said, "I passed you a few days ago and was unable to stop. I told myself, if I see that guy again, I'm going to get him a hot meal!" My location at the time meant he had to drive a very long way to find a place to buy food for me. I enjoyed the burger, but the effort he went to in order to get it to me is just incredible kindness to a stranger. Monday afternoon, a weathered Montana cowboy pulling a trailer with his saddled horse, pulled alongside me, got out and walked to his truck bed, reached in a cooler and said, "I got some cold water for ya. I got cold beer too if you want one." What kinda' beer ya got?" I asked. He said, "I got Bud Light and a Fat Tire Amber Ale." As he handed me the Fat Tire Amber Ale, he said, "My wife told me I better stop and give you something to drink if I saw you. My wife was the pretty lady that stopped and gave you water and a cupcake." I hope none of you out there have any doubts about why I Love Life.

Big Earth Movers

6/28/14. Yes Life is good! Even when it looks like it's getting worse. The climbs ended after about four miles but a guy stopped and warned me there had been a washout on a railroad track a half mile in front of me and they were having four big earth movers bringing in dirt from about five miles up the road. He said they were moving really fast in order to get the job done before nightfall. It was pretty scary, I had to go into the ditch when they passed each other. All but one was very careful of me and he would even stop to let me get out of the way. That driver stopped and gave me a can of tomato juice, a great sandwich made from an omelet, and a twenty dollar bill! He said to me, "I spent a lot a time on the road back in the day. People were always kind to me. Just payin' back. You be safe sir." A young man, Chris, stopped in his '89 Toyota truck he started with a pair of needle nosed pliers and hauled me around Miles City to find a motel. I wished I had got a picture of him, he had a beautiful smile and was just full of life. I am so blessed to have had opportunity to be the recipient of so many heart-warming smiles!

Should Have Taken His Offer

7/2/14. I was in a motel room in Baker, Montana, courtesy of some dear friends. I got there pretty fast because of strong winds at my back all day Saturday and Sunday, making a sail out of my beautiful "LOVE LIFE" sign. I just had to make sure my feet moved fast enough to keep up. I love it when that happens. I do prefer when there's no rain with it though. About 12 miles west of Baker, I had just pitched my tent when a cowboy who had to be in his late eighties, pulled his truck up beside my tent which was pitched near the gate to his pasture. He said, "I'm going in here to check on my cows, I'll be back in about ten minutes, you can go stay up at the house if you want." Are people cool or what. I thanked him but declined because I was in for the night. A decision I regretted when I woke up at 11:30 pm in the fiercest wind, lightning, and rain I've faced so far on this walk. I held onto my tent poles for about 25 minutes to be sure my tent didn't blow apart. I was so glad that I had all lines staked out. I've learned to always do that no matter what the weather looks like when I stop for the night and no matter the forecast. The storm stopped, I slept like a baby, I woke up loving life with all my heart and so very thankful for all the wonderful friends I have. I really do Love Life. I do hope that I am able to convey my Love Life message enough to influence others to love their gift of life no matter what, to fall in love with the act of breathing, and to discover that their life will then improve one hundred percent!

Don't Spill the Beer!

7/8/14. Somewhere between Newell, South Dakota and Faith, North Dakota, I walked against a mild headwind that helped keep me cool and keep the swarms of gnats away. Being as the wind was a friend, I hadn't really noticed just how strong it really was. Well, stopping for the night and pretty exhausted, after pitching my inner tent (no see-um screen and aluminum frame,) instead of continuing on and immediately staking down the outer tent over it, I remembered the treat I had on ice, a bottle of Angry Bastard IPA! So, I turned to my cooler and opened up the ice cold Angry Bastard. As I gulped down my first drink with the intention to set it down and continue the construction of my portable home, I turned to face my tent and my tent was gone! I mean, flat ass gone! I looked back to the west, the direction the wind was blowing, but, no tent! See, I'm in the beautiful rolling prairies of North Dakota and the tent was in a little valley when I looked in that direction and… no tent! Then, suddenly, it popped into view! And I gave chase! Chasing after the dome shaped tent rolling rapidly away from me hell bent on escape! I first tried a gentle jog (I had already walked 20 miles) but *that* was not going to get it. The tent was gaining ground on me and so I had to accelerate into a full blown run! The direction the wind was taking my tent ran parallel with the highway, only about 150 feet away. Now remember, I am an old man chasing a 5' x 7' object across the prairie, and, I have a bottle of beer in my hand! At least two cars tooted their horns in encouragement. I didn't dare look their way and take my eyes off the tent, but, I'm betting they were laughing their butts off! I heard a couple people yell out stuff. One sounded like, "Don't spill the beer!" I found it nearly a quarter mile away. The tent had broken but I was able to repair it. I had purposely stopped an hour early to rest. This whole episode took an hour and 15 minutes. I sat down, drank my now, not so cold IPA, finished building my house and went to bed loving Life. It truly is my friends, a most wonderful privilege to enjoy being alive. Make the best of it by loving it, Love Life.

Memory Rose

7/22/14. A very pretty young Lakota lady, stopped to see if I was okay. The precious little darling told me she had lost her own precious little darling in January past. After a full term pregnancy, her daughter, Memory Rose, was stillborn. We spoke of the Life lessons little Memory Rose came to teach her. Love Life with all your heart my friends, there are so very many out there in pain who need to feel our joy. It translates as Love for them. There are so very many who need their broken hearts mended by the Love we can share.

A Very Wonderful Love Filled Day

8/3/14, Most of you are unable to be as blessed as I, and walk in and experience daily, the beauty of Life, to experience the daily display of human kindness. So, I'll share my blessing with y'all. In just one week: An SUV pulled alongside me and the Lakota man said, "We met you back on the Cheyenne River Rez, my son insisted I stop, he wants to share with you." And a little guy no more than 8 years-old jumped out grinning big, and handed me the other half of his beef jerky. *That* will touch anyone's heart! A man brought me 2 ham sandwiches, chips and cold drink after he and fellow employees saw me walk past their workplace. A lady pulled up and handed me a sack full of sandwiches and fresh fruit and said, "This is a bribe, I want to hear your story." A man pulled a big rig over on the narrow road to give a cold water and an apple. He said, "Thanks man, I love your sign." A man on a BMW Motorcycle from Napa, CA on his way to Minneapolis for a BMW rally, stopped the week before on his way and again on his way back. He gave me a $20 and said, "I know you're doing something important, may I hear your story please." Stopping on his return trip, he sat down in his folding chair and asked of my expertise on gear he should purchase for his next venture. A middle-aged couple from Minnesota, on their way to Sturgis, stopped their bikes, because, as he said, "My girlfriend said we had to stop because she had to have her picture taken with you." She told me, "Your sign made me realize how blessed we are. He lost his wife to cancer two years ago. I went through a terrible divorce at the same time. We just met a few months ago and are in love and helping each other daily. Thank you!" and gave me a big hug! At least 20 people stopped and handed me bottles of water or sodas. Now that I've shared, y'all have no excuse, you now have to LOVE LIFE too!

Double Barrel Steak House

8/5/14. I'm going tell you how cool people in this part of South Dakota really are. The day before, a Codington County Deputy Sheriff stopped to offer me a ride and just check on me. After thankfully turning down his offer, he told me about a really good restaurant about 11 miles up the road in Henry. So I pushed myself really hard to try and make it before dark. I made it by 8:00 pm but the recommended place was closed on Mondays. Two ladies were coming out of a bar next to the closed eatery and I asked did the bar serve food. They said no, but said there was a place down the street that did. I hustled to it. Well, the place is what *all* Bar & Grills should be. As I walked up to the Double Barrel Steak House, I saw a swarm of people on the front deck, all laughing and loving life. A chorus of voices asked where I was walking too, how far, from where, etc. I started answering all questions and handing out cards. I asked if I could pitch my tent near the establishment after I had eaten there. Well, two of the owners were there and they each gave me a twenty, and some others also handed me some money ($130.) Red Wookey, one of the owners said, "Heck man, you can stay in the lodge and have a bed and a hot shower if you want. Guess what I said. I went inside and was served by Red and Kathy Wookey's lovely daughter, Bridgett. I had an awesome rib eye steak, one of the best ever. Corney Waldner, another owner came in while I was eating, paid for my meal and gave me another $20. After eating and answering some of the best questions ever, nearly everyone there helped load my cart on Red's truck and escorted me a couple blocks over to the hunting lodge, Pepper Slough Lodge. As luck would have it, it was not scheduled to be used again until the next day. I had the whole lodge to myself. How cool is that! Ya don't need money when ya got cool friends! Red and Nancy, and Rob Fuller (an employee who says he has the best boss in the world,) and Dean Paulson, showed me where everything was in the lodge. After a fantastic night of having a whole rustic hunting lodge to myself, Rob Fuller and Dean Paulson came and got me and took me to Dean's house where Dean, and Rob's wife Cheri, served up fresh from the farm eggs, with thick and delicious slab bacon and pancakes. Now that's what I'm talking about! Later in the day, a part owner with Red in the Pepper Slough Lodge, and hunting guide, Marty Maciel, stopped and said, "Hey what did you think about our lodge?" I loved it! If y'all ever get to Henry, South Dakota, for God's sake, check out the Double Barrel Steak House and the Pepper Slough Lodge! Tell them the LOVE LIFE guy sent ya!

An Honorable Story

8/9/14. Near Watertown, South Dakota, Bob stopped to ask if he might take my picture. He told me he was a freelance photo journalist. His New Mexico license plate said Disabled Veteran. The plates frame said Viet Nam Veteran. Bob told me he was very involved in helping Vets deal with PTSD. He told me a very moving story. In 1990 he was part of a group made up of disabled veterans from both Viet Nam and America, given permission to visit the Soviet Union to help Russian soldiers suffering from PTSD after their war with Afghanistan. He said that upon arrival, a Russian soldier came up to him and asked could he please get a message back to America for him. The Russian soldier told him that he had been in a battle in Afghanistan where a U.S. Marine, a member of Marine Recon, there as an advisor to the Afghans, was killed. He said that he and his fellow soldiers admired the American Marine's bravery and they recognized the special unit he was with and gave him a burial with full honors. He gave Bob the U.S. Marine's name and asked could he please locate his parents in the States and tell where he was buried, of his bravery, and that he was buried with honors. Bob was able to locate the parents and the parents then expressed the importance for him to carry back their sincere appreciation to the Russian soldier for letting them know. He was able to get the message back to the compassionate Russian soldier. Wow! Love Life, there is a lot to Love, there are beautiful hearts everywhere. The beauty of Life.

It's the Thought…

8/13/14. Montevideo, Minnesota, only minutes after checking into the Viking Motel the manager knocked on my door and said, "I just checked you out online and I cannot accept this money," and handed me back the cash I had paid her. Her husband came up to me with paper and pen and said, "Please write down some way we may help you in your endeavors." I wrote, "LOVE LIFE." And we talked a very long time. Two hours later, he showed up at my door with a new tent, a new sleeping bag, and various other items he thought I might use, all from Wal-Mart… bless his heart!! I, as graciously as possible, turned down all except toiletry items and handkerchiefs. He was able to return the items and get his money back. Just the proper tent and sleeping bag alone, to fit my requirements, is about $1200.00. Again, bless his heart. Ask me again why I Love Life.

Love Life, Leave the Bullshit at Home

8/22/14. Rained all night and everything got wet cause of being too lazy to get up and secure everything. So, not the best scenario to wake up to. Soon as I hit the road, a precious lady gets out of her car and while sobbing wraps her arms around my neck and firmly plants her lips on my cheek! "I love you for what you're doing!" she said. A second lady, Amy, runs from her car, gives me money and a huge hug. They then take pictures of each other with me. The first lady plants another kiss on my cheek before they leave. A little later, a lady stops and while crying gives me a long emotion-filled hug and tells me she lost someone very precious to her, to suicide, Rick, her brother-in-law, and best friend. Later, a lady stopped, she too was crying, and said she was Rick's mom. She gave me some money as well. She said her friend needed to talk to me and so she called her. Her friend had lost her son, Jonathan, to suicide. We talked for a while via phone. The next morning, a very pretty young lady stopped and told me she had seen me online and my story had inspired her to think differently about her life. Later that morning, Janice Pierce stopped and while sobbing, wrapped her precious little arms around my neck and told me of losing her handsome 20 year-old son, Joe Pierce, to suicide July 9, 2013. She gave me his picture to carry with me, and some money. We talked a very long time.

While Janice and I were talking, a man came up and asked me if Jesus Christ was my personal savior. I told him I believed in the teachings of Jesus the Christ. That appeased him and he left. I then continued giving my full attention to the broken hearted sweetheart in front of me grieving for her beautiful baby boy. On the way to eat dinner in St. Cloud, MN, a man dressed in a robe, an Ethiopian, I believe, came up to me and said, "One God, there is only one God!" I said, "Okay." He continued, "Allah is the one God. Jesus was prophet, but just a man. Mohammed was the only real prophet of Allah and Mohammed was the last prophet!" And I said, "Okay." I do not want the words from what you've read and been told, I want to feel the Love created within your heart from what you've learned. Love Life, open your heart to others, and leave the bullshit at home.

His Wife Loves His Heart

10/9/2014. In Evart, Michigan, coming out of a convenience store where I had purchased some Nyquil to deal with the sniffles I'd had for a few days, Russell, approached me to find out my story. After telling my story, he said, "You need anything?" I said no, and then he asked, "You need some money?" To which I also said no. He then said, "Are you sure sir, because I would really like to help." I said, "Okay, I do accept donations sir." He smiled big, reached in his pocket and pulled out folded bills in a clip, extracted a hundred dollar bill and said, "I have a very successful paint & body shop, I pay back whenever I can sir. You have really inspired me. Go get a motel room and take care of that cold so it don't get worse." The next morning, Russell came to my room and gave me another hundred dollar bill. He pulled out his phone and showed me where his wife had sent him my Facebook posting just about an hour before, of his giving me the money, and she said to him, "The reason I've always loved you so very much!" His eyes were filled with tears as he wished me well and headed off to work. Good people are everywhere, Love Life because of it!

Life is the Most Important

10/15/2014. Near Sheridan, Michigan, I saw a guy on the opposite side of the road walking toward me and picking up aluminum cans. We waved and smiled as we passed. An hour or so later I saw a guy on a golf cart retrieving his mail. It became obvious he was waiting for me to approach. "Where you goin' and where you been?" He asked. I told him, and all my story. His name was Charlie and he was a retired pharmacist. He had a heart attack during the year and an infection in his foot that turned into MRSA. He was hospitalized and nearly didn't make it! Charlie told me he had recently had two panic attacks. I asked if breathing problems caused them. He looked down at the ground and explained that his neighbor had come to him about their property boundary lines and was claiming several feet into Charlie's property. I said, "You have been given back your beautiful gift of life and you give a damn about a few feet of property? You are breathing in the greatest gift you will ever receive, your life! No matter how your neighbor's claim works out, you are alive my friend! From now on, think about nothing but your precious gift of Life when those negative thoughts, brought on by fear of losing a few feet of property, begin attacking you." I told him that it takes a lot of practice every single day to keep negative thoughts from controlling our Life. He said to me after we had talked long, "Steve, you are awesome. I wish my wife could have heard you." It is the Love I felt in my heart for Charlie that is awesome!

While we were talking, the guy picking up cans walked up to us. Charlie knew him. I shook his hand and introduced myself. I could barely understand him, he had a very apparent speech impediment. He seemed to be pretty much in his own little world. You could tell by the gentle way Charlie spoke to him, that he had a special place in his heart for the man. I said my goodbyes and left while Charlie continued speaking to the man.

About half hour later, a young man in his early twenties, and his mother stopped to find out what I was doing. The young man was a successful musician and had a fantastic outlook toward Life. He had a lot of wisdom for his years. I saw in his proud mother's face, where much of the influence to seek such wisdom came from. She asked me was I sure there wasn't anything I needed. While they were both telling me how much they admired my endeavors, the sweet gentleman picking up cans walked in the ditch next to us to retrieve a can he had spotted. I reached out my hand as he walked by, we shook hands and he continued on his pursuit of earning money a very hard way. I Love Life because there is just so very much to Love and appreciate. My desire is to fully embrace Life and all its precious inhabitants, with all my heart.

A few days later, a car pulled up in front of me and stopped on the very narrow road with no shoulders. Though the passenger was close to a deep ditch and lots of high weeds when she opened up her door, she said loudly, "I am determined to give you a hug!" And she very slowly and carefully made her way to me, wrapped her precious arms around my neck and said, "Thank you, Thank you so very much for causing my husband to look at what's really important!" It was of course, Charlie's wife.

She Loved Her Man

11/28/2014. The front desk of my motel called and announced a couple wanting to see me. She had seen my story in the Meadville Tribune, Meadville, Pennsylvania. I invited them into my room. She had made me sandwiches for the road the next day. The gentleman had scruffy looking long hair and beard and was definitely rough around the edges. Some call them "rednecks," I prefer, "good ole boys." He asked mostly questions about the specifics of the walk. Questions about the Appalachian Trail and my hike of it, what kind of gear, and so on. After he had told of his short hikes on the Appalachian and Alleghany Trails, she asked me to tell exactly why I walked. After I told of the deaths of my precious babies and the pain it caused, he shuffled his feet some, cleared his throat a couple times, all while looking down at the floor. It was obvious he was trying to say something. We both waited patiently for his words. When he looked up, his eyes were moist, and he said this, "My very best friend came up missing when we were 21. I went looking for him. There was a place we always went deep in the woods where we would just talk about everything. I went there and found his body. He killed himself. I helped carry his body out. I actually tried to kill myself once. I had the gun barrel in my mouth. After watching the pure hell that my buddy's death caused his parents and family, I swore I would never even think about it again."

I hugged him and told him I was very sorry for his loss and that I was delighted he was still with us. LOVE LIFE with all your heart, defeating all negatives so that Love will flow from you thus relaxing those around you, possibly freeing them enough to speak up! She, turned back toward the door as I let them out and very quietly said, "Thank you sir."

A woman who loved her man so very much she had alternative motives (good) behind searching me out, bringing her man with her. She knew his darkness and her Love wanted him free! Gentlemen, thank the Living God for that maternal instinct in a good woman who uses it also for the wellbeing of her man. If you have one of those women in your Life, don't you dare ever take her for granted!

Called the Law on Me, Good!

2/7/2015. In Otego, New York, as it was rapidly getting dark, and colder, I went behind a church building to pitch my tent against a wall out of the wind and on blacktop instead of the wet ground. An advantage to a freestanding tent. Just after I had fallen asleep, about 10:30 PM, someone said, "Hey, you okay in there?" It was a New York State Trooper who said someone had called on me being there. The trooper was way cool. He stooped down to the tent so I wouldn't have to come out of my sleeping bag. He told me it was 11 degrees and dropping. I handed him my card for identification and he said, "Wow, this is really great, can I keep this card?" He told me if it got too cold for me, to just dial 911 and they would come and get me to take me somewhere warm. He also told me he would check on me periodically during the night. About 30 minutes later, two young men walked up to my tent and one said, "Hey man, we're sorry we called the law on you. We're just not used to seeing a tent in the church parking lot." I laughed and told them it was fine. Then one said, you think you could forgive us if we let you sleep inside that warm building tonight and gave you some of my dad's famous split pea and ham soup while it's still hot?" And I immediately said, "You are hereby forgiven!" And the three of us headed for the door. I slept on the floor of an office and the hot soup was wonderful! I just have to appreciate my fellow human beings.

Another Needed Coincidence

2/27/2015. Took off from the motel on E. Water Street in Elmira, NY, heading east, I thought, hoping to get a few miles in for the day when I spotted a street sign that said, W. Water Street... huh?? Crap, I had gone the wrong way! I had gone over a mile! I turned around and as I was telling myself what a dumbass I was, an older lady in a really old and rough looking car pulled alongside me. She said, "Do you need anything, are you okay?" I thanked her and told her I was fine and needed nothing. I also answered no when she asked if I needed any money. I told her why I walked after she asked. She then reached in her purse and drew out a twenty and handed it to me. Then she said, "Here, that's not enough." and handed me another twenty. While I was thanking her, she repeated, "Here, that's not enough." and handed me yet, another twenty! I asked was she sure she wanted to give me that much money. She said yes and then asked if I needed more! I assured her I didn't need more, and she said, "Well, I guess you're the reason I went the wrong way." She laughed and told me she would never have been in that part of Elmira, but a friend had called her and said she had a plumbing problem and wasn't sure she would have enough money to pay for it. She said, "So, I drew out some money for her and when I got there, the repair wasn't as expensive as she thought it would be. So, I've got this money on me, you sure you don't need more?" I again told her no. She said, "Look, I'll get this back, I always get back what I give and then some. I've always given." She finally accepted that I wouldn't take any more. She smiled sweetly and said, "You stay safe and you stay happy, okay?" I said okay and she pulled away. Am I spoiled rotten or what! I'm spoiled because of the wonderful and special people I meet. That lady had a Love Life attitude. I've got a Love Life attitude. Just have a Love Life attitude and you too will meet others with a Love Life attitude. Life is simple.

Pissed Off "Fat Chap"

In 2011, Near Warren, New Hampshire, on a Sunday morning, a really big guy stopped and asked if I would like to go to the hostel he was caretaker of, just off the Appalachian Trail. His name was "Fat Chap" and I had heard of him in the "AT" community. I had heard of his kindness to fellow hikers. He told me that "Baltimore Jack" was at the hostel for a few days. "Baltimore Jack" was an absolute legend on the "AT;" he hiked the trail eight times and was noted for the bottle of Jim Beam Bourbon he kept with him. I have run into "Baltimore Jack" a few times over the years and we've shared our Kentucky Bourbon's. I'm sure I would have enjoyed the talk of old times. I was all set to go on with "Fat Chap" for free food and lodging for the night and then all of a sudden I just didn't feel good about going. I apologized and asked him to say hi to "Baltimore Jack" for me. He was upset with me and told me he wouldn't say hi for me; that I should do it myself. At any rate, he dropped me off at Annie's Restaurant there in Warren, New Hampshire.

I was sitting in Annie's having breakfast and thinking how stupid I had been for turning down free food and lodging when a lady came in and sat down at the counter next to me. We started up a conversation and as soon as I told her why I was walking, she commenced to explain about her thirty year old son. He was depressed and suicidal. Every day she said she lived in fear that he would do it. We talked for over two hours. She insisted that I had helped her and that our conversation had been a breath of fresh air for her and she said she had renewed hope. She insisted on paying for my breakfast and went out the door with a bounce in her step. She just needed to talk to someone, someone who could relate.

I was glad with the choice I made. And, I remembered that "Baltimore Jack" usually drank a bit more on Sundays, liked his privacy and could even get a bit cantankerous. He was a damn nice guy though, helped me out at Hot Springs, North Carolina when my young hiking partner lost his tent. Both "Fat Chap" and "Baltimore Jack" are part of the charm of the Appalachian Trail community.

Now, fast forward to February 13, 2015, in Candia, New Hampshire: It was seriously cold and I was having much difficulty pulling my cart through the snow piles at the side of the road. A gentleman stopped and invited me to stay for the night where he would be playing music with others at, Henderson's Pickin' Parlor. I jumped at the chance and got the key from the lady who ran the C-store next to the music store, as per instructions. It got damn cold outside but was toasty warm inside the Pickin' Parlor. It was made even warmer listening to all the talented pickers who kept showing up to jam. A lady came in, sit down, took her guitar from its case, looked over at me and said, "I know you. I met you at Annie's Restaurant in Warren. You changed my Life, you helped me to deal with my son's problems. My son is doing so much better now." She said her name was Darlene and I then remembered her. I told her of my rejecting Fat Chap's offer that Sunday morning and not really knowing why. She asked if I remembered what the last thing she said to me was, I did not. She had told me, "We will see each other again." She thanked me over and over and said, "For years I've thought you were an angel sent to me."

NOTE: "Baltimore Jack" may you rest in peace. He passed May 2, 2016. A true legacy and contributor to the awesome Beauty of Life, which can be so easily found on that most beautiful footpath, the Appalachian Trail. Proud to have known you "Baltimore Jack"

Love Life Pay Forward Man

Near Portsmouth, NH, and it was bitterly cold. The morning was warmed up considerably though when a man jumped out of his car holding a large coffee and a Danish and said, "I drove by you and thought, bet that man sure would like a cup of hot coffee! So, I went back and got you one. Here's a Danish and in this bag is a bunch of creams and sugar for you too." Wow! Friday morning, a young black man in a really nice car pulled alongside me and said, "I've been very successful in life, I'm truly blessed, and I have to pay forward man. May I donate this to you?" He handed me a fifty. Wow! Friday night, as I walked from the grocery store in the bitter cold back to a motel room paid for by someone else, a young man stood on the corner with a sign "Homeless veteran looking for work." I handed him a twenty. He asked "Sure you want to give me that much sir?" I said "Yes, people give to me, I have to pay forward man." He said, "Wow!" Love Life pay forward man.

Stony Point, New York

Figure 23. Vincent "Vinny" Forzono.

In 2005 as I was walking by The Cove Deli, in Stony Point, New York, a man came out and yelled, "Hey, come over here and get something to eat!" It was the then owner, Anthony Brigandi. His friendliness was special. Though I'm nearly always treated kindly by most, the kindness of some just cannot be called anything other than special. He fixed a wonderful sandwich and one for the road as well. We had great conversation, as he was delighted over my Love Life message. And he thought it quite humorous playing a recording of Johnny Cash's "I've Been Everywhere Man," while I was eating my sandwich. Anthony and I became lasting friends. Whenever I would be walking anywhere in New York, he would come and see me. In 2015 I went to Stony Point, again, and was welcomed by Anthony and his many friends. I found out why Anthony's kindness was so special. He grew up in a community of special kindness. I stayed in the home of his boyhood friend, Dominic Posillipo. I met many of his friends and all possessed that special kindness and friendliness. I met 10 year-old Vincent Forzono, who suffers from hydrocephalus. Never have I met a braver young man! The community of Stony Point embraces him and encourages him. I met Donna Jean, and Kimberly, and many others. The Love is everywhere in Stony Point, on the Hudson.

Pills, Pills, Pills!

Walking past a Dunkin' Donuts shop in Delaware, a handsome young man came running out and told me he had just found out about me on the internet and had been waiting for me so he could buy me a coffee. He said he became suicidal when he lost the Love of his Life to suicide a few months before. While explaining that he had sought professional help, he pulled out his phone and started scrolling through his pictures. He showed me a picture of nine bottles of prescription medicine. "This is what they prescribed for me and told me to come back in six months." He went on to explain what the contents of each bottle was supposed to do for him. He said, "I just stared at the bottles for days without taking even one pill. All I could think was that I would become dependent upon them." He told how he knew deep down, he was capable of pulling through without all those chemicals in his body. Then he looked me right in the eyes and said, "You know all that I wanted Steve, I just wanted somebody to tell me, "Hey, it's gonna be okay buddy!" They didn't have to smother me with kisses, I just wanted to feel some concern, some caring." I said, "Love is caring, you just needed to feel some Love. Love heals." He said that he was doing much better and that finding out about my walk through such horrendous weather to remind others to, "LOVE LIFE" was a great boost for him. We talked a long time. Such a fine young man. I am so delighted he was able to stay with us! We all have this kind of concern for our fellow human being, but we have to stop long enough to quit thinking about ourselves and let that concern rise to the top where others can experience it. When someone is expressing their heart to you, make sure you're not looking for the opportunity to tell about your own woes while they're talking. I can personally guarantee you, being there for another will heal your own personal problems.

Stuff I've Learned Along the Way

What irony; it is the tender hearted and so very sensitive individuals who can so easily allow life to get them down, that our world so sorely needs. The rest of us in the world need their perspective and the wisdom learned from having been there. Concentrate on who you are, not who anyone else is, and allow yourself to be who you were created to be. It is inside you, it is inside us all. It is up to you to get your mind off the actions of others and stop allowing these actions of others to distract you from being an intelligent and capable human being perfectly equipped to handle your own life. Be silent and calm, think long and hard on every problem life presents to you. Let all your decisions be made without anger, without blame, resist self-pity, thus not allowing anyone else's actions or reactions to keep you from being you. To convert self-pity to self-reliance, love your gift of life with every fiber of your being and convert self-pity to what it is supposed to be; hard earned wisdom and compassion for others. Love Life.

Someone doing a story about my walks once asked that I put together a list of the discomforts and hardships I face in taking on such an endeavor. I spent about two days thinking of the adversities I encountered during my many miles of walking and the list was getting pretty long. I was even thinking that it would be nice knowing others finally knew what "I" went through on these walks. And while "poor me" was adding another woe to my list, all of a sudden, I started sobbing. What came into my mind was: In all my miles and all the discomforts faced, not one time were any of them so severe I became so broken-hearted and so frightened of life that I felt the only way out was to end my life. I felt truly ashamed. I tore up the list.

I met a 35 year-old young lady in Waco, Texas, a few years back. She was absolutely one of the coolest individuals I ever met. Her wisdom of life and her attitude toward that life was incredibly positive. She did indeed Love Life. After finding out she had been abandoned as a toddler by her mother, raised up in foster homes, been physically and mentally abused, sexually molested, raped as a young woman, and fought with depression and suicidal thoughts into her twenties, (who wouldn't have?) I just had to ask, "And you are not at all bitter toward those responsible for those horrible things done to you?" She looked me straight in the eye and very sweetly replied, "What, and be upset at those who've helped form me into who I am now? Those are things done to me by people I would never want to be like. I'm much better than that and so I must never allow myself to stoop to that level by giving them even the slightest control over my emotions, I'm in charge of me and my emotions, not anyone else." She also said, "If I dwelled on the bad things done to me by bad people, I would then stay in a bad state of mind which would then keep me from meeting and enjoying the really beautiful people of this world." And I'll never forget her saying this, "I am way too strong to hang around with those that negative, even in my thoughts. I do not allow them to hang around in my mind either."

Whoa! Twenty five years my junior and she taught me great wisdom in mere moments. She absolutely proves we can change our lives. She, like me and numerous others, found our inner strength and rose above the adversities. Love your gift of life just as it comes to you and you can turn it into the life you so desire. Anger and bitterness serve no good whatsoever and are such a waste of our precious time here in this magnificent universe. Be the beautiful individual you were created to be and never allow any actions by anyone to control your thoughts. Our thoughts are who we are and I believe we will reap positive from the positive thoughts we sow.

"We all, to reach contentment, must make our stand with the courage of our convictions and establish who we are. This marks our place in the universe. This establishes how we will be seen and treated by others, and how we will be judged in Life. This, is our respect." ~ Steve Fugate

There is only one person in this life we can change, and that is ourselves. Worrying about what anyone else does is a total waste of time because we cannot change them. But you can change yourself; you can change yourself into someone confident and strong enough to allow no one else's attitude or actions to deter you from being you. All the things we go through in life are but sculpting tools used to shape us into a better person. We all have the ability to handle all our own problems. The bad things we've had to face in our life become tools for making us a better person by converting them into lessons on how to better understand ourselves. Understanding ourselves and looking at our own faults to correct, instead of the faults of another which we cannot correct, make us much less judging and much more understanding of those others. We become a better person when we stop the self-pity, the blame, and let go the anger and move forward, forward toward maturity! I never started maturing until I saw these truths. So, I was 54 years old when I started maturing.

One of the most common questions asked of me is if doing what I've done, walking the United States over 40,000 miles with the words "LOVE LIFE" in big red block letters over my head, changed me. I usually jokingly reply, "Those two words melted off the sign and dripped right down through the top of my head and lodged firmly in my brain."

Actually, it was the learning to use perspective which changed me and lodged the love of life so firmly in my heart and then to my brain. Many individuals stopped because of my sign, and upon hearing of my personal tragedies, would open up their hearts and share things which had crushed their hearts. Yes, the loss of both my children is horrific, but you just would not believe the things that have been shared with me. Perspective is the light needed to better see down Life's path to becoming a better person.

And something else just as hard for me to believe, the incredible number of random acts of kindness bestowed upon me. And the magnitude of those random acts of kindness I received is truly incredible as well. Many times those acts of kindness were offered to me even before hearing of my personal tragedy. Yes, there are that many wonderfully kind people out there. Again, perspective.

I firmly believe that because each and every one of us is so truly unique one from the other, that each of us is equipped from within with our own answers in Life. If one can but push past the tears and the ache in their precious heart, there is a place of rest within. A sanctuary within which allows us to deal with the pain in our own special and unique way. A unique way hard-wired into our very being already there waiting for a great act of faith to be shouted out into the wide open ears of the universe: "*I Love Life!*" You are then telling the universe how much you do truly love and appreciate your gift of life and that you are then trusting that everything will be okay. And it most assuredly will become okay. Anything short of love and appreciation for our beautiful gift of life is a negative and negative never accomplishes anything and never has in the existence of human kind, it serves absolutely no good purpose. We are all created equal in our rights to the universal laws, those laws of life. Love Life my friends and use the perspective I present to you; if I can Love Life most anyone can. Be determined to Love Life.

In my mind, Love Life means just that, to love the life you have right now, the life which is in front of us right now and not one we wish it to be. To love life is to love the fact we are alive, that we have air to breathe. That we realize before anything else is presented to us after we awake, that we have indeed first been granted the gift of life. I call it falling in love with the act of breathing. My key to a love life attitude is to look not for perfection outside me, but to find the perfection of who I really am inside me, the one I was created to be the "I am". Who we really are is a calm and gentle soul. A soul that judges not, hates not, and angers not, a soul that only knows Love.

Push on and love the gift of life we've been so wonderfully blessed with my friends. When we awake and feel that sweet, sweet air on our upper lip we have indeed been gifted another day. Realize the miracle of that moment first and foremost and grab onto it and hold onto the beauty of our precious gift of Life. Give that moment precedence over all other thoughts that are attempting to cause us to put the realization of the beauty of our being alive yet one more day in second place. Absolutely nothing is more sacred than our gift of life. Hold onto the moment as long as it takes for the realization of the beauty of life to supersede and conquer all negative thoughts and simply Love Life.

I believe when one focuses on the Love of their gift of Life, no matter what is going on around us, we are exercising faith. We are defeating the fears which generate anger, blame, complaining, worry and doubt. We then are able to start finding our own strength within: our own special individuality, uniquely different from everyone else in the world. We then do not succumb to the fear which causes us to stay in the herd, and can then better hear the different drummer, the beating of our own heart. Our strength is not in numbers, but is instead in finding who we truly are within, discovering and then relying on our own unique individuality, our own intuitiveness, and then following our own heart. After all, no one can better know you nor what is best for you than you.

Had I allowed self-pity to persist in my life after the deaths of both my children, I would either no longer be on this earth or I would have gone completely insane. The single hardest thing I've ever had to do in my life other than bury my babies was to convert my heart wrenching pain into a positive energy directed at others and away from myself. The world is changed each time one of us gets our eyes off ourselves and allows our real purpose in life, love and concern for our fellow human being, to come forward. Self-pity is self-centered. Someone once stated very simply, "If you want to be happy in this life forget about yourself." Yes, it works. Go and love your gift of life and watch that focus to do so in every circumstance change your life forever.

"Believe in yourself and you'll have no reason ever to be disappointed in another." ~ Steve Fugate

Life became my mentor in my solitude following the death of my beautiful son, Stephen (Stevie) Lee Fugate and my beautiful daughter, Michelle (Shelly) Lynn Fugate

Morgan. Life can teach us all we need to know to survive our particular environment, our particular circumstances, if we allow life to do so. As Kahlil Gibran said, *"Pain is an unseen and powerful hand that breaks the skin of the stone in order to extract the pulp. Your pain is the breaking of the shell that encloses your understanding."* I am ever learning to Love Life.

Printed in Poland
by Amazon Fulfillment
Poland Sp. z o.o., Wrocław

20710260R00172